For Lew Mudge—
An old pot keeps
cooking!
Thanks for many things.

Ted
12-21-83

THE BIBLICAL ARCHAEOLOGIST READER

VOLUME IV

THE BIBLICAL ARCHAEOLOGIST READER IV

Edited by

EDWARD F. CAMPBELL, JR.

DAVID NOEL FREEDMAN

Published in association with
The American Schools of Oriental Research
by
THE ALMOND PRESS
SHEFFIELD
1983

THE BIBLICAL ARCHAEOLOGIST READER, VOLUME IV

THE ALMOND PRESS
in association with
THE AMERICAN SCHOOLS OF ORIENTAL RESEARCH

British Library Cataloguing in Publication Data:

The Biblical archaeologist reader. Vol. 4
1. Bible—Antiquities
I. Campbell, Edward F.   II. Freedman, David Noel
220.9'3   BS621

ISBN 0-907459-34-X
ISBN 0-907459-35-8 Pbk

Published by
The Almond Press
P.O. Box 208
Sheffield S10 5DW
England

Printed in Great Britain by
Dotesios (Printers) Ltd
Bradford-on-Avon, Wiltshire
1983

PREFACE

With this volume we come to the end of the current series of BA Readers and complete our selection of articles from the original *Biblical Archaeologist*, which was begun by G. Ernest Wright in 1938 and carried on through 1975 by Wright and his successors, E. F. Campbell, Jr. and H. Darrell Lance. Since then the journal has been changed in format and style, and a judgment about the quality and permanent value of its contents can be postponed to a later date.

About the quality and value of the original BA there has never been any doubt. From the beginning it served a basic purpose and filled an important gap in the communication network linking archaeologists and biblical scholars with the reading public, including especially members of the clergy and students of the Bible. It is a testimony to the high standard consistently maintained by authors and editors alike that the 152 issues of the BA through those years yielded enough material to fill four substantial volumes. The problem for the editors of the books has not been what to include in the anthology but what could be dropped without serious loss. In the end it might have been easier simply to reproduce the entire series and spare ourselves the agony of having to make choices.

The current selection has been made from the BA since the appearance of BA Reader III, and it reflects the variety of articles published between 1969 and 1975, a period of accelerating archaeological work in the lands of the Bible. This was the time when the great debate over the "New Archaeology" began, a debate which has continued ever since and is likely to go on in various forms and adaptations for some time to come.

The articles are classified under four headings: Biblical Archaeology and the New Archaeology; Archaeology and the Common

Life; Archaeology and the Religious Life; and Archaeology and the New Testament Backgrounds. Many different scholars from America, Europe, and the Near East have contributed to the volume. They represent a broad spectrum of approaches, methods, and special interests.

It is with pride that we present this latest collection of articles from the BA and bring down the curtain on one of the great eras of archaeology in the Near East.

D. N. Freedman
University of Michigan

CONTENTS

III. ARCHAEOLOGY AND THE RELIGIOUS LIFE

LIST OF ILLUSTRATIONS

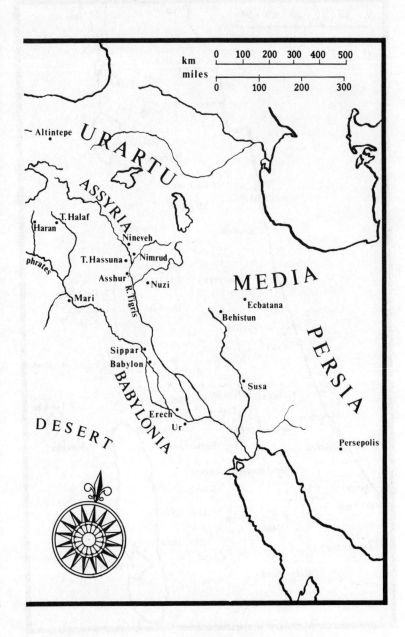

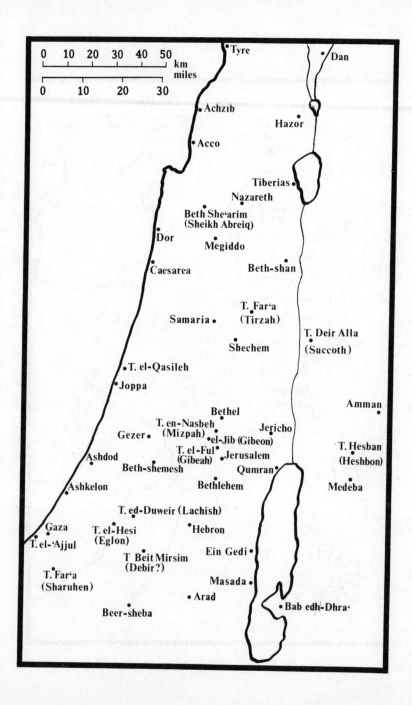

Part I

BIBLICAL ARCHAEOLOGY AND THE NEW ARCHAEOLOGY

W. F. ALBRIGHT'S VIEW OF BIBLICAL ARCHAEOLOGY AND ITS METHODOLOGY

F. M. CROSS

Recently there have been suggestions made that the term biblical archaeology be dropped. In this view it smells of theology, of biblical literalism, of amateurism, apologetics, and many like evils. Rather, so goes the claim, we should speak of Palestinian or Syro-Palestinian archaeology. It should be manned by full-time specialists in field archaeology.

My purpose here is to speak of William Foxwell Albright's understanding of biblical archaeology, its scope and methodology. Since Albright long used the term in a special sense and developed its use, it may be prudent to listen to his definition of the term and the methodology which it denoted.

Albright defines the geographical and temporal scope of biblical archaeology as follows: "all Biblical lands, from India to Spain and from southern Russia to South Arabia, and to the whole history of those lands from about 10,000 B.C. or even earlier, to the present time."[1]

If this seems expansive, it must be remembered that Albright was a humanist and a generalist. He was concerned with the evolution of human religion from the Stone Age to the emergence of Christianity and Judaism in the Graeco-Roman world, the evolution of higher culture from the Ice Age to the Greek intellectual revolution of the 6th-5th century, and the convergence of the religious and philosophical traditions in the Hellenistic synthesis. I am not sure that his grand designs are his greatest contribution to human learning. But to understand his approach these grand designs must be perceived.

In dealing with more narrowly Near Eastern archaeology and history, Albright remained a generalist with a specialist's precision in designated areas. On the one hand, his expertise in the ceramic chronology of Palestine was unmatched in his day. He was the father of scientific ceramic typology. At the same time, he was baffled by highly skilled field archaeologists, perfectionistic stratigraphers, who completely confused the history of a site because they read the text of the Bible uncritically, knew little history and no Semitic language, not even Hebrew. He held that both archaeological studies and historical studies must be held together, if not in the same scholar, at least in scholarly discourse. Biblical archaeology could never narrow to "dirt archaeology" of Palestine.

Biblical archaeology included papyri from Egypt, the onomasticon of the Amorites, a cylinder seal from Greece, Phoenician ivories from Spain, an ostracon from Edom, a painted Athenian pot, a skull from Carmel. In short, the whole ancient world, its literature, history, material culture belonged to the subject matter of biblical archaeology.

Perhaps William Albright is the last of the general Orientalists, biblical archaeologists in his sense. Yet I should plead that the separation of fields has gone too far in our own pursuit of specialization. For example, Assyriology has separated from Northwest Semitic and biblical studies. Perhaps it had to do this to gain autonomy. But I think it is time for communication between the East and West Semitic worlds to be restored, and for biblical scholars to be trained regularly in Akkadian. The separation of Palestinian archaeology from historical studies and linguistic studies I find grotesque. Similarly, I suggest that the retirement of biblical scholars exclusively into biblical theology is dangerous. They become pendants of the systematic theologian, scholars without a discipline. In any case, William Albright was a generalist with its advantages and dangers. And biblical archaeology was a term designating synthetic efforts drawing on all the crucial disciplines of the humanist.

Albright's approach stemmed from essentially a "history of religions" approach to biblical lore. He shared Herder's passion to place the history and religion of Israel in its context, in its contemporary world, to treat biblical history as part of and continuous with ancient Near Eastern history. Early in his career he belonged to the Pan-Babylonian school, was trained in it, embraced it. His increasingly critical stance over against this tradition never caused him to cease his restless search for the continuities between cultures of the Near Eastern world and Israel's culture, especially biblical religion. To the surprise of his students, sometimes, he admired such scholars as Engnell and Eissfeldt more than a von Rad or a Noth. He was wary of form-critical analyses of biblical literature which did not take Canaanite and ancient Near Eastern forms sufficiently into account. He was wary of all syntheses constructed on the basis of internal biblical data alone. One manuscript, one papyrus, he regarded as worth a thousand theories. And finding a new bit of archaeological evidence immediately altered his own theories. He was suspicious of scholars who did not change when new evidence appeared. In effect, every new bit of data properly altered the totality of his synthetic view.

My third and last point is this: the central methodology exploited and developed by William Foxwell Albright was the typological method. Here he introduced systematic precision into the fields of ceramic forms and into the history of poetic canons and style, into the typology of linguistic change, and into the ono-mastic and palaeographical typologies. Further, he constructed an approach to historical and archaeological method based on the postulates of typological method. In historical process there is irreversible change; historical process is marked by continuity between the old and the new. A typological sequence involving the emergence of new patterns or styles may go slowly or quickly. Often the novel "bursts" on the scene, but the continuities are not broken. Typological sequences are intelligible in retrospect; at the same time, they are unpredictable in the future.

Again, the more ordinary a typological series, the more re-liable the results of typological judgments. The typology of reli-gious ideas or art forms is far more difficult to establish than typo-logical sequences of scripts or pots. In brief, he was a master typo-logist, and reflected upon the significance of such sciences for his-torical method. Few of his successors seem to be as fully aware of their methodological presuppositions.

William Foxwell Albright regarded Palestinian archaeology or Syro-Palestinian archaeology as a small, if important, section of biblical archaeology. One finds it ironical that recent students suppose them interchangeable terms.

NOTE

[1]*Archaeology, Historical Analogy, and Early Biblical Tradition* (1966), p. 13; cf. also Albright, *New Horizons in Biblical Research* (1966), p. 1.

2

FROM THE PATRIARCHS TO MOSES.
I. FROM ABRAHAM TO JOSEPH

W. F. ALBRIGHT

(Among the unpublished manuscripts left by the late Prof. Albright was a long paper summarizing his current thinking—never for Albright his "definitive" position!—on the period from the patriarchs to Moses. When Prof. D. N. Freedman, Albright's literary executor, offered the manuscript to us for publication, we accepted it gladly, both for its intrinsic interest and as a final tribute to perhaps the greatest giant that the field of biblical archaeology has ever known. Because of its length, we have divided it into two parts which we shall publish in consecutive issues. The manuscript came to us without footnotes; and since Albright's manner of footnoting is inimitable, we have not attempted to fill the lack apart from some obvious references. The illustrations and captions as well as the appended suggestions for further reading are also editorial additions.—Eds.)

Some two or three centuries before Abraham, the wandering Semites of North Arabia began to harass their settled neighbors as never before in recorded history. The "Asiatic nomads," as they were called by the Egyptians, and the "Westerners" (*Amurru*) or "Dedanites," as the Babylonians named them, finally overran Palestine and parts of Syria so completely that almost all fortified towns were destroyed. In fact, we find scarcely any pottery in Palestine or Eastern Syria from the 21st century B.C. Stone burial cairns were heaped up all over the ancient burial grounds at Bab edh-Dhra[c] overlooking the Dead Sea from the east. In the sepulchral cavities of these burial cairns little or no pottery is found, since the nomads of the time seldom used any.

Nomad raids into Egypt and Babylonia became so destructive that both countries began building fortifications to keep them

See illus. 20

out. Interestingly enough, the walls were completed almost simultaneously. The Egyptian "Wall of the Prince (Built) to Keep the Asiatics Away" was finished by Amenemmes I, the first king of the great Egyptian Twelfth Dynasty, between 1991 and 1960 B.C. In the 9th year of Shusin, the fourth king of Ur III, "The Wall Which Keeps the Dedanites Away" was finished (about 1967 B.C.), after it had been started by his grandfather, Shulgi (about 2031-1984 B.C.). The length of the Babylonian wall is given in contemporary documents as about 175 miles. The Egyptian wall naturally extended from the neighborhood of Suez to somewhere southwest of Port Said, and the line of the wall may have stretched some distance along the sea, both on the north and the south, in order to impede outflanking attempts. This wall was, therefore, about 100 miles long. When we compare both walls with the 1500 miles of the Great Wall of China (completed in the 3rd century B.C.), it is easy to see that their construction was perfectly within the capacity of the Egyptians and Babylonians at that time—even when we recall the vastly greater population and national resources of China under the Ch'in Dynasty, over 1700 years later. It is virtually impossible to suppose that the walls received names with almost identical meanings unless there was influence from one direction or the other. It would, however, be rash to guess which power was originally responsible for the name. The fact that the names did coincide illustrates once again how close were the overland links between Babylonia and Egypt even in this troubled period.

In the name of the Babylonian wall, the Beduin are called "Dedanites" (written *Didnu, Didanu* or *Dadnu*, later *Dadanu*). In Genesis 25:3 we are told that Dedan was the younger brother of Sheba, the name of the famous people which established the Sabaean trading empire in what is now Yemen. Three groups are said to have descended from Dedan, all with meaningful names: "Caravaneers, Metalworkers, and Nomads." In other words, the Dedanite nomads of the Patriarchal Age later specialized as traders and caravaneers, as miners and metal-workers, and as nomad hunters and herdsmen. As in the case of so many originally nomadic tribes of Southwestern Asia, the names of the tribes and clans eventually became attached to settlements called after their founders, whether tribes or families. So the name Dedan became attached to the site now called el-ᶜUla, south of Midian proper and north of Medina in western Arabia; it was still called Dedan in the third century B.C.

We learn from the Sumerian Martu Epic (probably composed before 2300 B.C.) that the Western nomads then lived in tents, ate their food raw, did not bury their dead, raised no grain and depended on small cattle for subsistence. We need not, however, take all of these statements literally. In a Sumerian letter composed in the reign of Shulgi of Ur, about 2000 B.C., we learn about a nomadic or semi-nomadic group of tribes without a general ethnic name who were called *Sagaz* in Sumerian and ᶜ*Apiru* (later ᶜ*Abiru*) in Semitic. Of them it is said:

> . . .As for their men and their women—
> Their men go where they please.
> Their women carry spindle and spinning bowl,
> Their encampments are wherever they pitch them,
> Their decrees of Shulgi, my king, they do not obey.

From about 2300 B.C. on, the ᶜApiru had a bad reputation as robbers in Babylonia. Raiding was undoubtedly one of their chief side-occupations, but their main characteristic was that they did a great deal of traveling on foot. As a result they were nicknamed the "dusty ones" (ᶜApiru) like other ancient grooms and medieval peddlers who spent much of their time walking in the dust behind their animals, just as nearly three centuries later (in the Mari Letters), the ᶜApiru women manufactured textiles for sale. From their name comes the word "Hebrew" (applied to Abraham in Genesis 14:13).

The ᶜApiru were not, however, content to stay in Northern Mesopotamia. About 1830 B.C., they occupied Babylon and founded the First Dynasty of Babylon, to which Hammurapi belonged. Colonies of their two most important tribes, included among the ancestors of the dynasty in question, the Awnanu and Yaᶜurru, were settled in (trading) colonies near the frontier city of Sippar on the Euphrates north of Babylon.

Their sister towns of Sippar were Euphrates "port authorities" (*karu*) and were each administered by a "college of judges" headed by the "overseer of the merchants." In other words, the two ᶜApiru tribes in question then controlled the trade of the Euphrates Valley with Babylonia. This was quite a change from the situation in the 22nd-20th centuries, when Sumerian literature credits the ᶜApiru with ambushing caravans, smuggling and open rebellion against their Babylonian overlord! Other colonies of the Awnanu were settled near the important South-Babylonian city of Erech (Genesis 10:10), also on the Euphrates. Here an Awnanu dynasty was established by Sin-kashid about the beginning of the 18th century B.C. Erech was only forty miles up the Euphrates from Abraham's traditional home at Ur.

A few years ago evidence turned up in cuneiform tablets of the Hammurapi dynasty which showed that there was a close treaty relationship between the Awnanu and Yaᶜurru tribes, on the one hand, and the kings of Babylon on the other. Then came the even more striking discovery that among the immediate ancestors of the kings of the First Dynasty of Babylon were the same Awnanu and Yaᶜurru, at that time the two most important subtribes of the Banu-Yamin. The latter name, meaning "Sons of the Right" (south just as in the Arabic name *Yemen*) is preserved in Biblical "Benjamin." North of them lived other ᶜApiru, called "Sons of the Left" (*Manu-Sim³al*) (north), just as in the Arabic name *Sham* (Syria). We shall return to this later. Both these names, Awnanu and Yaᶜurru, survive in Genesis 38 as already extinct clans of Judah.

In other words, just as in recent Arab times, there was a constant integration of different tribes into a single one, accompanied by disintegration of one tribe into separate groups. In modern Arab times we find famous medieval tribal names scattered all over Arabia and adjacent lands, including northern Africa. This, of course, has always made the problem of fixing early genealogical trees and tribal affiliations very difficult for both Israelites and Arabs; it explains why we have so many conflicting traditions of the relationship among Hebrew and early Arab tribes. In such cases there is no simple solution. The problem is far too complex, and the only way we can get any kind of historical impression is by having different traditions and genealogical reconstructions preserved from ancient times, both (or all) reflecting factual tradition.

Systematic long-range caravan trade may be traced back in the ancient Near East for many thousands of years. The first clear-cut proof of such trade between Egypt and Asia is found just before and just after the foundation of the so-called First Dynasty in Egypt about 2900 B.C., when we find Asiatic pottery in Egyptian tombs and Egyptian pottery in Palestinian sites—especially at the recently excavated site of Biblical Arad. In Southwestern Asia we have our first detailed account of caravan trade between countries as far apart as Babylonia and the central Turkish plateau (later Cappadocia) in the time of the great kings of Accad (Genesis 10:10) about 2300-2150 B.C. Before and after 2000 B.C. trade and commerce developed rapidly between Mesopotamia and Asia Minor, but until the 19th century B.C. we lack documents to give us much detail.

Between 2300 and 1800 B.C. donkey caravans linking Egypt and Sudan were very common and are described in some detail. However, it would appear that the old trade routes between Palestine and Egypt were no longer much used between 2200 and 1900; when a small caravan of Asiatic nomads appeared in central Egypt in 1892 B.C. with manganese eye-paint from Midian for sale, the event was so striking that it was depicted on the walls of the tomb of a district governor at Beni-Hasan in Middle Egypt. Here we have a wall painting showing Asiatic men and women on foot, together with a donkey loaded with young children and another carrying, among other things, bellows used in metal-working. The men are dressed in embroidered kilts and the women in gaily decorated tunics. The men carry composite bows as well as darts and throw-sticks. Two game animals are also led to the presence of the Egyptian recorder. The Asiatics are said to have been 37 in number and are called "Beduin of Shut" (probably northern Transjordan, including Moab). One man holding a lyre presumably entertained the party with traditional chants and songs about the deeds of their forefathers. The donkeys are of the usual small Mediterranean type (burros).

It is to be noted that the date of this scene falls shortly before the period of intense caravan activity in Mesopotamia, which is documented in the north by thousands of Old-Assyrian cuneiform documents from Cappadocia, mostly dating between about 1850 and 1775 B.C. In southern Palestine and north-central Sinai it is established by the discovery of a great many caravan stations with pottery from the 19th century B.C., for which see our description below. At Serabit el-Khadem in southwestern Sinai during the same age there are many inscriptions which mention donkey caravans. Characteristic of them are lists giving the exact number of men of different classes, as well as of the donkeys which made up each caravan. The total number of donkeys listed in several caravans under Amenemmes III (1842-1797 B.C.) varied from 200 to 600, but a caravan of 1000 between Egypt and Sudan is recorded earlier (1927 B.C.). Donkeys could not live off the land like camels, so they either had to have water and grain taken along on other donkeys or to utilize caravan stations in which just enough grain, fodder, and water could be produced to supply them.

In the north, between Asshur on the Middle Tigris and Cappadocia in Asia Minor, donkey caravans were elaborately planned, as we know from the Old-Assyrian tablets of the same period. Here they used large black donkeys (the Damascus donkeys of Assyrian and modern times) which were probably bred by crossing wild asses (onagers) with ordinary Mediterranean burros. In the documents we often find regular demand for such black donkeys. Each of these could carry as much as double the load possible for an ordinary burro. They were also valued much higher; 20 shekels was the average price of the black donkey, or almost as much as for a slave laborer. The average number of donkeys included by any one of the many merchants who provided goods and donkeys for the caravan was generally not over ten, but when a large number of merchants arranged with a caravan master (generally mentioned by name), the total number of donkeys might average between 200 and 250 (according to the excavators of the trading center at Kanesh in Cappadocia). Of course, there were also much larger donkey caravans, like the 3000 donkeys sent in a single convoy mentioned in the Mari letters. The 20 donkeys sent by Jacob to Egypt on two separate occasions were presumably attached to a much larger convoy, just as often attested in the Cappadocian tablets. The ordinary caravaneer who fed and watered the donkeys and did all the menial tasks and who was trained to fight in defense of the caravan against robbers is always nameless, as is clear from both the Old-Assyrian caravan records and the accounts of caravans between Egypt and Sinai. These humble people were the "dusty ones"; they were strictly anonymous, but they also had special marshals or leaders who presumably looked after the general organization of the caravans. Both the lowest class of caravaneers and the middle group were hired for the occasion, as a rule. Above all was the caravan leader or chief caravaneer who would correspond to the wagon-master in our 19th-century West.

The narratives of Genesis dealing with Abram (Abraham) may now be integrated into the life and history of the time in such surprisingly consistent ways that there can be little doubt about their substantial historicity. A striking feature about these narratives is that they appear in different recensions, first handed down orally and later in writing. Where these recensions differ from one another they give us a better insight into what really happened. It is only when we have traditions which survive in different lands or different circles independently of one another that we can really control our source material. In other words, we cannot see ancient happenings in perspective unless we have diverging and often contrasting traditions about them. But contrasting accounts are not necessarily contradictory.

Among the ancient Hebrews, before there was a nation called Israel, these narratives were handed down in either prose or verse, or in both forms combined. For several centuries the Hebrew tribes lived separately in Egypt and Palestine, and during some periods they may even have been cut off from one another. Most of the time there must have been frequent communication between them, since Palestine and Egypt generally formed part of the same empire between about 1600 and 1175 B.C. Some of the traditions were genealogies and narratives explaining the relationship between different Hebrew and related Northwest-Semitic groups (tribes and clans). Others were stories about the Patriarchs themselves and were put into substantially their present form in different periods.

As we have already noted, the relationship between Hebrew tribes and clans was complex and shifting, just as is true of comparable Arab genealogical lists and efforts to relate different tribes and families to one another. Sometimes tribes were split up into a number of clans and sometimes families grew into tribes. At other times a group would split in such a way that it was later attached to different ancestral backgrounds in different parts of such books as Genesis and Chronicles. Even if we compare the Greek translation of Genesis, made in the early third century B.C., with the Hebrew text as we now have it, we find numerous divergences in details of tribal relationship. For instance, in Genesis 25:3 the Greek text includes three names which have been accidentally dropped from the extant Hebrew text. Two of them, Reuel and Teman, appear in different passages both as clans of Edom and as clans with nomad Arab affiliation.

One of our most valuable sources for understanding the complexities of early Hebrew tribal history is Genesis 49, the so-called Testament of Jacob, in which Jacob blesses and curses his tribal offspring with remarkable objectivity. From this chapter we gain extremely valuable historical clues with regard to the background of the tribes in Israel. As we shall see below, we have a most important—though fragmentary—account of Joseph which clarifies numerous points otherwise not clear in the narrative about him (Genesis 37-48). But whereas the Joseph story in these chapters is a prose masterpiece describing events of great dramatic impact, the accounts of Abram do not conform to any special literary type, but are in fact quite heterogeneous in content. Yet, though often misunderstood for thousands of years, they bear the imprint of their basic authenticity in the events and situations which they describe.

A very important point, which has in the past been commonly overlooked, is the problem of Abram's chief occupation. To treat him as a mere wandering shepherd, as Joseph's brethren describe themselves in Genesis 47:3f., will not do at all. In any case, it was not factually true of Jacob but is a typical example of the self-depreciation which we find in letters of the second millennium B.C. written by inferiors to superiors.

All the ancient versions of Genesis, from the Greek translation of the third century B.C. on, render the Hebrew consonantal stem *SHR* (Genesis 23:16; 34:10, 21; 37:28; 42:34) as "to trade (in), trader," etc. The late E. A. Speiser, in his valuable Anchor commentary on Genesis (1964), challenged this rendering (except for Hebrew *soḥer* "merchant"), preferring the translation "to move about freely (in)." I have opposed this interpretation because of its intrinsic improbability and more recently because of the cognate Old-Assyrian words from the same verbal stem, meaning in the caravan texts clearly "to trade, barter," and "goods for barter" (divided equally between goods for men and goods for women). The latter word has a close Hebrew cognate with the same meaning.—As I write these lines, I learn of an article by the foremost Assyriologist of our generation, Benno Landsberger, which takes the same position as mine.[1] So we may continue to accept the time-honored English translations, which make far better sense in their context!

Abram is described as setting out from Ur in southern Babylonia, and going on to Haran in northwestern Mesopotamia, then to Damascus and from there traveling on down by way of Shechem and Bethel to the south country and Egypt. Most important is the fact that in Genesis 20:1 we read ". . .from there [from Mamre near Hebron] Abram journeyed toward the south country [Negeb], and he spent his time between Kadesh and Shur, while he was a foreign resident in Gerar."

Between Kadesh and the southern end of Shur (the Wall of the Prince, described above), B. Rothenberg and Y. Aharoni discovered in 1956-57 an ancient caravan route from the oasis of Kadesh to the southern end of the Wall of Egypt (see above).[2] Like the minor caravan routes previously discovered by Nelson Glueck in the Negeb between Kadesh and the Patriarchal towns of Gerar and Beer-sheba, it dates from the 19th century B.C. In a more recent expedition Glueck has confirmed and extended the evidence for intensive caravan activity at this time.[3] In their expeditions Glueck and Rothenberg found scores of settlements, marked only by stone foundations of igloo-shaped stone huts as well as small storage basins for water and occasional remains of hillside terraces. Many potsherds were also found strewn over these sites, on most of which—including all the sites along clear-cut caravan routes—there were *no* sherds from any period except Middle Bronze I (20th and 19th centuries B.C.). Since the desert of central Sinai is an arid plateau covered with broken flint, it would be quite impracticable for laden camels, whose soft, spreading pads would be cut to pieces, whereas loaded camels get along very nicely in sandy regions.

A similar picture is provided by Genesis 13:1ff., where we are told that Abram went up out of Egypt and that he was very rich in cattle, silver and gold, after which the text reads "and his caravan journeyed by stages from the south [Negeb] to Bethel." It is noteworthy that in these texts we have words which have specific reference to caravaneering and related occupations.

When Abraham is said to have been a foreign resident in Gerar, the meaning of the verb used (*yagur*) is derived from the participle *ger*, which means "resident alien" everywhere in the Hebrew Bible. The true site of Gerar was discovered at Tell Abu Hareira by an Israeli settler after the end of the war of 1948-9. In 1953 I examined the ruins and discovered a rich deposit of 19th-18th century pottery. The site is very large and ideally located as a base for caravans bound for Egypt.

Another informative passage is Genesis 15:2, where Abraham says to the Lord, ". . . the heir of my house is the son of Mesheq, Eliezer." The name *Mesheq* is glossed "Damascus," so its seems that we have in this passage a reference to the widespread north-Mesopotamian practice attested in the cuneiform documents of Nuzi in the 15th century B.C.; a "banker" who outfits and advances money to a man has himself adopted formally as the latter's son. The original purpose of this legal fiction was to make it possible for houses or lands to be used as collateral for a loan, since they were otherwise legally inalienable and it was therefore difficult to get commercial loans. A great many such *tuppi maruti* tablets were excavated by the University of Pennsylvania between the World Wars. This Eliezer ben Mesheq was, to judge from the gloss, a native of Damascus which was in antiquity and the Middle Ages one of the most important places for outfitting caravans in the whole of Palestine and Syria. In the first place it enjoys almost unlimited supplies of water, cattle, and grain. It was famous in Assyrian times for its donkeys from which it received its Assyrian name "the City of Asses." As already noted, these are the famous black (i.e., dark brown) donkeys of the contemporary Old-Assyrian business documents from Cappadocia, and they are still called "Damascus donkeys" today. They are much bigger and stronger than ordinary donkeys of the Mediterranean world.

Even more important than the preceding passages is the famous chapter on the invasion of Palestine by the kings of the East and

Abram's part in their defeat (Genesis 14). In 14:14 Abram is called specifically "Abram the Hebrew," that is, Abram the ᶜApiru. In the next verse we are told that Abram had 318 *HNKM* born in his house. In other words, they were his personal retainers, with whom he attacked the Easterners by night, defeating them and recovering the captured property. The term *hanaku* (as the word is spelled in a cuneiform letter from 15th-century Palestine) means specifically "retainer(s)" and was originally an Egyptian word for "retainer" borrowed by the ancient inhabitants of Palestine. In the Egyptian Execration Texts dating from between about 1925 and 1825 B.C., the word *hnkw* is used in the sense of "retainers (of a local Palestinian or Syrian chieftain)."

Genesis 14 teems with archaic matter, and is quite impossible to explain unless its nucleus, at least, goes back to early Hebrew tradition. Elsewhere I have dealt with other points in this intriguing chapter, especially with the names and historical places of the Eastern kings.[4] But neither this chapter nor Genesis 23 is intelligible unless we recognize that Abraham was a wealthy caravaneer and merchant whose relations with the native princes and communities were fixed by contracts and treaties (covenants).

When did Abraham live? We have hitherto not had consistent information about the date of Abraham, since no two traditional reconstructions of the chronology agree. The Greek Bible, for instance, translated from Hebrew in the 3rd century B.C., gives higher dates for the Patriarchs than the Hebrew Bible. In Genesis 15 we have two apparently contradictory estimates. First comes an estimate of 400 years (Genesis 15:13) for the Oppression, and three verses below there is a statement that they will come back to Palestine in the fourth "generation," apparently after the death of Abraham. Since Abraham died well before the settlement in Egypt, these two dates would seem to collide rather sharply. But the difference is actually small. The Hebrew word used is *dor*, which is usually translated "generation," but which means in the cognate Syriac and Arabic words "lifetime," among related senses. Furthermore, the same word in its older form *darum* is used specifically for "lifetime" in an inscription of Shamshi-Adad I, king of Assyria in the second half of the 18th century B.C. Seven *daru* are said to have elapsed between the reign of a king of the great Semitic dynasty of Accad about 2300 and 1750 B.C., roughly 550 years, yielding an average of about 75-80 years to a *darum*. This happens to be just the time which is sometimes assigned to *dara* in Syriac. We must remember that many peoples, among them early Greeks and Etruscans, computed time by a succession of lifetimes and not by generations. Later on, just as happened with the Greek word *genea*, which also meant "lifetime" in the early poets, it came to mean "generation." Accordingly, it is clear that the two successive estimates, four lifetimes and four centuries, reflect essentially the same original tradition, and that after the settlement of Israel in Canaan the Israelites looked back on a period of roughly four centuries or more between Abraham and Moses. Such vague dates naturally do not walk on all fours, and we are safe in following the archaeological evidence and in dating Abraham somewhere about 1800 B.C.

We have a very good archaeological clue to the date of Abraham in the pottery of Middle Bronze I as pointed out first by Nelson Glueck (see above). No pottery has been found along the southern desert routes (in the Negeb proper) from before the 20th century B.C. or after the 19th. Approximate dates are fixed by the duration of the Middle Bronze I, which began after the end of the Early Bronze IV about 2000 B.C., and came to an end just as—or shortly after—Middle Bronze II began at Byblos (Biblical Gebal). The beginning is fixed by the tombs of the first autonomous princes, contemporary with the very end of the Twelfth Dynasty and extending down past the reign of Yantin. The latter was contemporary with Neferhotep of Egypt and Zimri-lim of Mari (whose slightly younger contemporary was Hammurapi of Babylon). The first Hyksos period began about a generation after Yantin's death, and ushered in the archaeological phase known as Middle Bronze IIB. about 1700 B.C.

In short, our synchronisms between historical and archaeological data fix the end of Middle Bronze I about the last quarter of the 19th century B.C., and the beginning of the Middle Bronze IIA (which was a short phase, for which Miss Kenyon allows only half-a-century) about a century later. Whether Abraham himself lived well into the 18th century B.C. we do not know, but I suspect that he did.

An interesting sidelight on Abraham's age and early Hebrew relations to the settled states between which they traveled and in which they lived is found in a well-preserved monument of King Yahdun-Lim, inscribed about 1750 B.C., discovered by André Parrot at Mari.[5] Unexpectedly, it throws light on the role of Melchizedek in the life of Abraham. The reference to him has always been a puzzle, and in late antiquity both Jewish and Christian writers vied with one another in setting up strange hypotheses about him. While the text of Genesis 14:18 was probably shortened by accidental scribal error during the many centuries of Israelite history, Salem has nearly always been identified by tradition with Jerusalem. However, Jerusalem is written in full both in the Egyptian lists of potential foes (Execration Texts), drawn up during the late 20th and the 19th centuries B.C., and the Amarna Tablets. Except once in late Hebrew poetry it is not written in this short form anywhere in the Old Testament. On the other hand we have, in the Yahdun-Lim inscription, a list of kings reigning in the Euphrates Valley or near it; each of these has allies from a different semi-nomadic tribe. The list runs as follows: La'um king of Samanum and the land of the Ubrapu; Bahlukulim king of Tuttul and the land of the Awnanum; Ayalum king of Abattum and the land of the Rabbu. Here is a case which seems to be essentially like that of Melchizedek, since we have four kings of important city-states on or near the Euphrates associated intimately with different tribes of ᶜApiru. They are listed in geographical order from south to north. Farthest north beyond the bend of the Euphrates south of Carchemish is the tribe of the Rabbu or the Rabbayu, as they are variously called. In this period obviously the activities of the ᶜApiru were associated with different cities along the Euphrates route just as Abraham was allied to Melchizedek of Jerusalem which is located directly on the watershed ridge road south of Shechem and Bethel and north of Hebron and Beer-sheba. There could scarcely be a more striking parallel to this datum of Genesis 14. As we have already indicated, there are a number of other remarkable parallels to Genesis 14, which we shall not discuss here since they involve too many technicalities.

The inscription of Yahdun-lim is especially significant for another reason: here we have the tribe of Rabbayu/Rabbu (literally, "archers") at the extreme north of the Euphrates route near Aleppo, whose king is explicitly stated to have been allied to the confederated rebels against Mari. In 1964 André Finet showed that the ᶜApiru who are mentioned in different Mari letters as living in the territory of Aleppo and crossing the northern bend of the Euphrates in the general vicinity of Carchemish are also called in these letters *Banu-Sim⁾al*, "Children of the Left," that is, "Northerners."[6] It follows inescapably that the southern tribes, including the Ubrapu, the Awnanu, and the Yahruru or Yahurum (later Assyrian Yauri) were *Banu- Yamin*, "Children of the Right," or Southerners.

In a Mari letter from the Assyrian king Shamshi-Adad to his son, the viceroy of Mari, he instructs the latter how to avoid possible bad effects of the announcement that a census is to be taken of the Banu-Yamin and their "brethren," the Rabbayu who are on the other side of the Euphrates in the land of Aleppo. This proves that the Rabbayu considered themselves as bound by tribal ties to the Banu-Yamin. In other words, the principal tribe—possibly the only one—of the "Children of the Left" was the Rabbayu or Rabbau (shortened in Akkadian to Rabbu). The Rabbayu, like the Banu-Sim⁾al, are also described as living in the extreme northwest of Mesopotamia, in the region north of Haran and Nahor. In any case they occupied the regions contiguous to the Euphrates, above Carchemish and Haran, just as the sister tribe, the Yahruru or Yahurru, is described in the Mari letters as living along the Tigris River.

The tribe of Rabbayu, which lived on both sides of the Upper Euphrates, is actually mentioned in the archaic Testament of Jacob (Genesis 49:23). The Blessing of Jacob is of great historical importance, since it is an independent, though very brief, witness to the historical figure whom we meet as the hero of the story of Joseph (see below).

The Age of Isaac and Jacob

The stories about Isaac and Jacob are quite different in their literary form from the narratives about Abraham, as well as from the story of Joseph which follows them. Isaac plays an integral role in the Patriarchal tradition and cannot be ignored by any serious historian. And yet it is difficult to find any point at which to tie him down to contemporary history. That they belong in a direct line of succession is clear from the traditional order of genealogy which omitted many names as in most such traditional genealogies all over the world but usually gave the first names and the most recent names in correct sequence. Contrary to frequent past suggestions, the names are definitely names of persons. The name *Ya^cqub*, "May (such-and-such a god) protect," is common in the Patriarchal Age, being found both in cuneiform and hieroglyphic texts as names of Northwestern Semites. The name Isaac (*Yiṣḥaq*) is not found outside the Bible, but the Ugaritic epics contain the word, used of a god, quite frequently, so we may safely translate it "May (such-and-such a god) smile (favorably)." It is extremely interesting to note that the narratives about Isaac and Jacob are chiefly devoted to matters of intimate personal history which can seldom be verified or disproved by inscriptions.

However, there are two areas where we can illustrate these traditions vividly from external records. The first is in the details of the family law and practice which are preserved in them, where we often have striking departures from later Israelite and Jewish customary law, but where E. A. Speiser and others have established close similarlity to the family law of the mixed population of northern Mesopotamia, which we now know chiefly from the rich business and legal archives of 15th-century Nuzi, east of the Tigris River.

The second point of contact in external sources is in the numerous references in the Mari tablets from the late 18th century B.C. to the relatives of the Palestinian Hebrews who remained in Mesopotamia. It is no accident that the two Mesopotamian cities which are mentioned most frequently in this phase of Patriarchal history are Haran and Nahor, now known from both the Mari and the slightly earlier Old-Assyrian tablets from the 19th and 18th centuries B.C. Both bear the same names as in the Bible, then pronounced Kharran and Nakhur. Haran is situated on the upper Balikh River and is now inside the borders of Turkey, whereas Nahor lies some distance to the east in the western part of the Khabur basin.

Some prominent scholars reject the demonstration given by Speiser and his students of the virtual identity of much Patriarchal customary law and that of Nuzi, chiefly on the dubious ground that the Patriarchal narratives are presumably not authentic and that the Nuzi texts are too early or too late anyway. This attitude will not hold at all. In the first place, the ᶜApiru are known from cuneiform texts of Nuzi as well as from Biblical references to have been a very mixed group ethnically; they spread very widely and intermarried or adopted a great many non-Semites as members of their groups so that they are often considered to be a class rather than an ethnic entity. To a certain extent this is true, but both points of view are in part correct. They were indeed a separate group without the original unity that characterized many of the Northwest-Semitic peoples; on the other hand they were already actively forming elaborate patrilocal groupings from which patriarchal tribes and clans emerged. Under the circumstances, this would give rise to great confusion in tribal groupings, especially when one bears in mind the entire Biblical tradition. Many of the ᶜApiru mentioned in cuneiform inscriptions bear non-Hebrew and even non-Semitic names. The very non-Semitic name Arphaxad is included in Genesis 10 as an ancestor of Abram, and there are non-Semitic ancestors of the two ᶜApiru tribes of the Banu-Yamin listed in the genealogical tree of the forebears of the First Dynasty of Babylon, recently published by J. J. Finkelstein.[7] Furthermore, the mixture of Hurrians and Northwestern Semites is very evident in the Mari texts. In addition to this, one of the tribal aggregations associated closely with the ᶜApiru in the Mari documents, the Khana people, were almost certainly of Gutian origin from the mountains east of the Tigris. When we think of the ᶜApiru and other Northwestern Semites in northwest Mesopotamia, we must remember that they were separated by a considerable stretch of desert from Babylonia proper with trade routes running down the Euphrates and Tigris to connect them. For some time after the reign of Hammurapi, the Babylonian kings retained control of much of northern Mesopotamia. Meanwhile the Northwestern Semites continued to stream into Babylonia, and by the reign of ᶜAmmisaduqa (1668-1648), the country was no longer officially considered as partly Sumerian and partly Accadian, as it still was in the great Code of Hammurapi, but as partly Accadian (Semitic Babylonian) and partly Amorite (Northwest Semitic).

In judging the date when originally mythological narratives of Genesis 1-10 became current among the Hebrews, we must remember two things: The periods spanned by the lifetimes of Isaac and Jacob may have extended from the 18th century B.C. to the 16th. During the 16th century there were many irruptions of foreign peoples into the Fertile Crescent, accompanied by movements of already established peoples from Mesopotamia into Palestine and Syria, fleeing before the hordes from the north and east. The reign of the Babylonian kings ᶜAmmiditana and ᶜAmmisaduqa in the first half of the 16th century probably formed the climax of the expansion and acculturation of the ᶜApiru and their congeners. It was also the culmination of Old-Babylonian culture.

From the time of ᶜAmmisaduqa, for example, we have some of our most important Babylonian astronomical tablets, as well as elaborate specimens of examination papers on clay tablets, requiring a knowledge on the part of the student of that day which would in some respects exceed that of a graduate scholar of Greek or Roman times or even of the Middle Ages. In Babylonia a graduate scribe had to prove by examination that he knew both Sumerian and Accadian grammar. Since these languages were as far apart as Hungarian and English, this was naturally no light requisite. Furthermore, any graduate of a scribal school had to prove that he was fully competent in whatever area of specialization had been picked out for him.

Patriarchal Literature—the Atrahasis Epic

One of the most extraordinary documents which has yet come from Babylonia was published (with English translation) by W. G. Lambert in 1969.[8] The three now published Old-Babylonian tablets (which largely supersede the much later Neo-Assyrian fragments) represent our only cuneiform literary text written in a mixture of literary Babylonian and vernacular "Amorite" (Northwest Semitic). This has already been recognized by leading Assyriologists, basing themselves on "Amorite" words, solecisms, and grammatical peculiarities not known in the contemporary "hymnal-epic" style of Old-Babylonian poetry which was an inheritance from the great age of Sargon of Accad and his successors (24th-23rd centuries B.C.).

Though the tablets are dated in the reign of ᶜAmmisaduqa, the epic had probably been composed some generations previously and handed down orally without having been thoroughly revised by a trained Babylonian scribe. It is thus the best yet known example of the mixed Northwest Semitic-Accadian higher culture of Patriarchal times. In view of the increasingly clear Sumero-Accadian origin of the demythologized cosmogonic narratives of Genesis 1-11, it is very important to have a mythological epic which circulated in a transitional form among the relatives of the Patriarchs in Mesopotamia.

The epic in question is easily the most sophisticated of all known ancient Near-Eastern mythological epics—Sumerian, Accadian, Egyptian, Canaanite (Ugaritic), Horite (Hurrian) and Hittite. The first lines tell us that the seven great gods were forcing the lesser gods to do the heavy work in heaven and earth under the orders of Anu (=El, god of heaven), Ellil (=Bel, Canaanite Baal), and Ninurta, lord of combat. The lesser gods became increasingly bitter at the hardships which were their lot. They revolted, setting fire to their tools and declaring open war against the high gods. Finally they besieged the temple of Ellil and tried to storm it. The high god was then aroused from sleep and an impromptu council of the great gods was held. Ellil was greatly distressed by the disaffection of the lesser gods who were, as another god tells him, his own sons:

> My lord, the lads are your own creation;
> They are your own sons,   What is it that you fear?

Finally Ellil is induced to bring Anu, king of heaven, and the king of the subterranean fresh-water ocean, Ea (Enki), to a council. A god was sent out to interview the lesser gods and an assembly of all the gods was called. The complaint of the lesser gods was that they were completely exhausted by their labors and were therefore revolting against Ellil and the other high gods.

When Ellil heard this speech he began to weep and addressed Anu, god of heaven: "While the great gods are seated before thee, call a god and have them throw him into the sea"—obviously to obtain a confession by ordeal. Here we have a unique account of the debate which ensued. Ellil suggests that they determine the identity of the ringleaders by the ordeal, and Anu protests. Finally the craftsman-god Ea intervenes and suggests that the divine midwife Mami, lady of the gods, be asked to make a new creature named "man" (*lullu*), in order to take over from the lower gods the labor of sustaining all the gods.

Mami accepts the commission, and it was decided that a god should be slaughtered so that all the gods might be purified by the vicarious sacrifice. Then Ea goes on to say, "With his flesh and blood let Nintu mix clay; let the divine and human be mixed together with the clay. Until the last days let us hear the heart-beat of the (human) spirit which comes into being from the divine flesh of the gods. Let it be the living sign that the spirit exists, so that this be not forgotten."

This was agreed on by the assembly, which said unanimously, *anna* ("Yes"). Then all together they slaughtered Iluwe, the god who had been chosen as victim. In due course the birth-goddess announces that her task is finished; she says to the lower divinities, "I have removed your heavy load, I have imposed your toil on man." So then she proceeded to bring fourteen assistant midwives together and to nip off fourteen pieces of clay, seven on the right, seven on the left; between them the birth brick was placed. Seven lumps of clay were formed into males, seven into females.

This summary description will give an idea of the structure and content. The account of the creation of mankind is followed by the goddess Mami's instructions as to future human weddings and pregnancies. Then we are told about the labors of man to sustain the gods—higher and lower. But 1200 years from creation the irrigated lands had become so extensive and the population so increased that "it was bellowing like a bull," and Ellil again suffered from insomnia. So he decreed that man should be decimated by pestilence.

Now "the Man," Atrahasis, appears for the first time in the published remains of the epic and appeals to Ea for help in stopping the pestilence. Ea responds by advising Atrahasis to call a general strike of mankind against divine worship and at the same time tells him to have special honor paid to Namtar, god of destiny. This advice proved successful in warding off the pestilence.

After another 1200 years there was again a population explosion, and the land was again "bellowing like a bull." This time Ellil did not wait for a divine council but decreed a tremendous

drought which lasted for years. Again Atrahasis turned up and
interceded with Ea who persuades Ellil—just how is quite
uncertain—to change his mind and let man continue to exist.
Unfortunately the text is badly damaged in these columns, and it is
difficult to follow the complicated maneuvering on the part of gods
involved on both sides of the dispute over man's fate.

We may probably assume that the next catastrophe, the great
flood, followed the second crisis again after 1200 years. The total
length of the antediluvian age would then be 3600 years. This
length of time is quite comparable to the chronology of the Greek
Bible (2242 years) and the Hebrew Bible (1656 years). It is far
shorter than any of the Sumero-Accadian figures which vary from
some 240,000 to 432,000 years. It is interesting to note that the 3600
years correspond to a single Babylonian round number, the *shar*
(Greek *saros*). It would seem to follow that the Hebrew numbers
preserved in Genesis 5 go back in principle to the Patriarchal Age!

Again Atrahasis intervened for the third time to save at least a
fraction of mankind from the Great Flood. The account of the
Flood in the Atrahasis epic, which continued to be copied by
cuneiform scribes down into Assyrian times, is in some respects
more like the biblical account than the other known cuneiform
myths. But unfortunately this part of the narrative is too ill-
preserved to give us much information. A fragment of this part of
the Atrahasis epic has recently been discovered at Ugarit; it is
written in a somewhat barbaric Middle Babylonian, no later than
the 13th century B.C. No trace of the deluge story has been found in
any original Canaanite source, whether of late or of early date. This
tablet, like many others at Ugarit, was copied for scribal purposes
or for literary interest, from Mesopotamian cuneiform originals
and does not throw any light at all on a possible Canaanite story.

It is interesting to note that both the god Iluwe, whose death
made man's creation possible, and Atrahasis, the favorite of Ea,
"who lived in his temple" and intervened three times to save man
from destruction, are figures which have definite West-Semitic
affinities. *Iluwe* is probably the same name as *Iluwer*, name of one
of the chief gods of the Northwest Mesopotamians, whose name
appears variously as *Mer, Ilumer*, and *Iluwer*. The name is
shortened here to *Iluwe*, just as we have in the Amarna tablets the
West-Semitic name *Balume²ir*, also spelled *Balumme*. *Kothar wa-*

Hasis, also simply *Kothar* or *Hasis*, was an appellation of the great craftsman god of the Canaanites who was identified with Ea in the Ugaritic vocabularies. In other words, the figure of Hasis or Atrahasis, which meant "very intelligent," was actually a god identified with Enki or Ea by the people of Syria. It is interesting to note that *kothar*, Hebrew *koshar*, also meant "very skillful."

One of the most unexpected features of the Atrahasis epic is the end of Tablet III which describes the steps taken by the gods to assure themselves against a recurrence of the situation that brought about three near-destructions of mankind: "Henceforth there shall come into being only a third of the people—among the people (there shall be) the woman who bears and the woman who does not bear. Let the *pashittu*-demon come into being among the people; let her snatch the infant from the knees of the woman who bears." The divine warning then adds women who are prevented by ritual celibacy or deliberate mutilation from bearing children.

No other cuneiform mythological text or, for that matter, any other mythological narrative from the ancient Orient, is so astonishingly modern in some respects. Throughout the text there appears full awareness of the menace of over-population as well as of methods used to control it. It is almost post-Malthusian in its sophistication with regard to the menace of over-population and possible means of keeping it down. Closely related was the menace of swelling slave populations or barbarian hordes. There were numerous methods of keeping them down by exposing infants at birth and by saving, in general, only male infants. Our next-oldest reference to such population control is in the life of Moses when the Egyptians planned to reduce the number of Israelites by systematically cutting off all *male* children, in order to prevent a slave revolt. The decimation of an enemy either by slaughter of all but young females or by killing a certain fraction of male warriors was common among ancient peoples. David resorted to executing two-thirds of the captured Moabite warriors when he conquered Moab. This is a case of extremely harsh methods in order to keep down semi-nomadic raiders. Something similar is reported by an Assyrian king of the 13th century B.C. But here the gods slaughtered their human slaves systematically in order to prevent them from multiplying and endangering the peace of the world—described succinctly as the sleep of the warrior god Ellil.

It is remarkable how many parallels we find in the Atrahasis epic to Northwest-Semitic language and custom, especially among the Hebrews and "Amorites." It is easy to see that this particular elaboration of the original flood story was unacceptable to Mosaic cosmogony which owes so much to Mesopotamian accounts of creation and early human experience. That the story of Atrahasis was not also adapted to Mosaic religious purposes is presumably due to its blatant polytheism. Yet its very existence at such a remote date proves that we need not date the original Hebrew recensions of the narratives in Genesis 1-11 any later in general than the Patriarchal Age. In this particular case we have echoes of "the man Atrahasis" in late Old Testament times and even later, as I first pointed out in 1920. The nearly complete epic text published by Lambert brings us closer to the higher culture of early Patriarchal days than perhaps any other discovery of modern times.

Joseph

The story of Joseph is one of the finest prose compositions in Biblical Hebrew. Beautifully written in the classical tongue of the early Monarchy, it holds the listener's attention by its dramatic presentation. On the other hand, it was clearly adapted to the literary taste and moral needs of the Iron age. This need not cause doubt as to its basic historicity, especially since we have an independent witness, hitherto completely misunderstood, in the Testament of Jacob (Genesis 49).

First we may recall what was said above about the evidence for the tribe of Rabbayu or Rabbu (literally "archers") in both the Yahdun-Lim text and the slightly later Mari letters. They lived on both sides of the upper Euphrates in northern Syria and northwestern Mesopotamia and formed the only known tribe of the Banu-Sim³al ("Sons of the Left," Northerners). In Genesis 49:23ff. we have a very archaic saying or perhaps two sayings on Joseph. The Testament of Jacob contains astonishingly objective blessings and curses, mostly dating from before the time of Joshua at latest.

Like the Song of Miriam in Exodus 15 which dates as we shall see from the early 13th century B.C., the Testament of Jacob was remembered with astonishing accuracy, in spite of the archaism of language and style that characterizes both—or perhaps partly because of it. Since early alphabetic texts from Syria and Palestine were usually written without word-dividers, the same situation was true of biblical texts. A natural consequence was that obscure early words and grammatical prefixes or suffixes were often wrongly divided, and the sense of an entire verse might be forgotten. Revision of the text of the Testament of Jacob follows the same principles that we shall see in the Song of Miriam (Exodus 15). Because of the exceptional significance of both poems for the national consciousness of ancient Israel, consonants and vowels were remembered; and archaic features of early Hebrew grammar also survived. But remembered words and grammatical forms had often changed their meaning long before the Greek translation of the third century B.C., so we must draw on our rich new material found in ancient—often contemporary—inscriptions.

We can now translate the first line of the Blessing of Joseph:

Son of Euphrates is Joseph,
   Son of Euphrates, lofty of source.

The second word in each half-line, which has been translated every possible way except the correct one during the past 2200 years, has now been found twice with the first vowel spelled out (*PORT*) in different scrolls from the great Qumran find. The Hebrew name was *Porat*, as stated by the Jewish historian Josephus; it survived in the Christian Syriac translation used in Palestine. In the Mari texts several tribes of the ᶜApiru are located specifically on the Euphrates (see above) or the Tigris, and so it is not at all surprising to find the most northwesterly tribe called "Sons of the Euphrates." Since both branches of the upper Euphrates emerge from the mountains of southwestern Armenia, the phrase "lofty of source" is very appropriate.

The next line refers to an attack on the Wall, that is, the Wall of Egypt built at the beginning of the second millennium (see above); and in the following lines we may read "(from their nomad camps) the Rabbau drove him," with no change in consonants. The meaning of the words *nawôt*, "nomad camps," and *mārer*, "to drive (out, away)," is established by the Mari, Amarna, and Ugaritic tablets of the 18th-14th centuries B.C.

The next half-line has also been misunderstood for over 2200 years. Render: "The masters of divination were unfavorable to him." The Hebrew expression translated "masters of divination" has been rendered in the past "lords of arrows." Now, however, thanks to the work of Samuel Iwry and subsequent finds, we know that the phrase in question is the normal plural of the appellation of the Canaanite god Resheph, patron of divination and good (or ill) luck in general in early and late Canaanite, that is, in Ugaritic and Phoenician. The following line is again separated from its original context, but can make good sense as it stands:

> His bow remained steady
> And the arms of his archers were firm.

Here we obviously have a quite independent and very instructive form of the Joseph tradition. In the tradition found in the Testament of Jacob, Joseph came from the northern Euphrates Valley and thus represented the Hebrew Banu-Sim³al, the "Sons of the North." He was a member of the now well-known Rabbau (archer) tribe and was driven out by them, apparently before they launched an attack on the Wall which he and the archers under his command were defending. He had suffered serious misfortunes, as is implied in the statement that the omens of the diviners were unfavorable to him.

The Egyptian "Story of the Two Brothers" (known from a Ramesside copy) has often been compared with the Joseph story, but actually there is nothing in common except the attempted seduction of the hero by the wife of his superior—his older brother in the Egyptian tale, his master in the Hebrew story. The cuneiform biography of Idrimi, excavated by Sir Leonard Woolley at Alalakh in northern Syria, offers many striking similarities, though not enough to show any factual dependence. Idrimi was the youngest son of a king of Alalakh in the early 15th century B.C. There was some sort of palace revolt, and Idrimi and his older brothers fled to Emar on the Euphrates. His older brothers were not sympathetic to their younger brother's plans and hopes, so the latter had to flee, taking with him his horse, his chariot, and his groom. He first fled to the land of the Bedouin (Sutu) and from there he turned westward to the land of Canaan. A little later he spent seven years among the ᶜApiru. While he was among the ᶜApiru he claims to have been releasing birds to observe their flight and to have looked into the entrails of lambs until after seven years the storm-god (Baal) had become favorable to him. Then he built ships and landed his men north of Ugarit, the people of the land which his family had ruled accepted him as king, and his older brothers came hurriedly to meet him. When they were reconciled to him, Idrimi confirmed their princely status. Note that we have not only one parallel but a whole series of close parallels to the Joseph story—forced separation from his family after a quarrel with his older brothers; a long sojourn in a foreign land; a series of oracles, in the case of Joseph through dreams, in the case of Idrimi through ornithomancy and extispicy (or hepatoscopy); exaltation of the hero; and final reconciliation with his older brothers.

In spite of these resemblances there can scarcely be any direct borrowing in either direction. It seems likely that a number of common elements in both narratives were shared by story-tellers among the Northwestern Semites in the middle centuries of the second millennium B.C. The fact that the North-Syrian Hebrews appear in both narratives is probably more or less accidental, though it is not impossible that some common elements would be especially familiar to the Hebrews. Of course, it cannot be denied that the presence of a number of common features may have attracted other features often found with them into the complex of a given set of traditions.

In any event it is clear that the poetic narrative in Genesis 49:23ff. is very ancient, since the first two half-lines are arranged in typical late Canaanite order, ABC:ABD, in which each of the letters indicate a single poetic "foot." The first two "feet" are identical in the two parts of the verse line while the third is different. This is a very archaic stylistic device in Canaanite poetry, one which is extremely common in Ugaritic and early Hebrew verse of approximately the same age. It appears also in contemporary Egyptian translations from Canaanite magical texts. *Ben Porat Yosef* was presumably vocalized according to the Late Bronze tradition which we find in the 13th-century Balaam Oracles, *Bilᶜam benō Beᶜor*, "Balaam son of Beor," which would yield a normal three-foot half-line.

The name "Joseph" in itself is an obvious abbreviation of some such name as Joseph-El, which means "May God Give Increase."

So far we do not find the name "Joseph" in the Mari or other early documents containing Northwest-Semitic names, but it must be very ancient like nearly all the other known Hebrew tribal and clan names in the Pentateuch. Since the name Rabbau, "Archers," refers to their chief vocation, we may safely suppose that Joseph gave his name to one of its subdivisions which traced its genealogy back to the famous ancestral figure. While the saying about Joseph in Genesis 49 does not specify details, it is clear that it refers to his being a member of the Egyptian archer troops which helped defend the Wall against attacking Semites shortly before the conquest of Egypt by the Semitic Hyksos about 1700 B.C.

John Van Seters has recently shown that the famous Ipuwer prophecies must have been composed just before the Hyksos invasion instead of several centuries earlier, as had been thought by many Egyptologists.[9] We learn from Ipuwer that Semitic archers were fighting both for Egypt and against Egypt; the Semitic mercenaries are blamed for espionage, informing their kinsmen outside Egypt of the weakness of the country and suggesting that it could easily be conquered. While we cannot date the conquest of Egypt by the early Semitic Hyksos exactly, it took place about 1700 B.C. These early Semitic kings of Egypt ruled roughly for half a century, and they seem to have belonged in part to a tribe of the Banu-Yamin, judging from the name Yam^{c}ay in letters of the Semitic alphabet on Hyksos scarabs. This is a shortened form of the name of the Yam^{c}i^{c}ammu tribe of the Banu-Yamin mentioned in the Mari texts and has parallels in the lists of Palestinian chieftains in the Egyptian Execration texts from about 1900 B.C. The second of this group of Hyksos kings was named Ya^{c}qub-^{c}eli. Just what these similarities in name mean we cannot, of course, be sure, but it does seem highly probable that Hebrew tribes and groups formed a substantial part of the Northwest-Semitic movement which established the first phase of Hyksos rule in Egypt, before it was attacked by the non-Semitic invaders from Syria who set up the Fifteenth Dynasty about 1650 B.C.

The date of the story of Joseph as we have it in Genesis 37ff. is more difficult to determine. That the traditions go back to the Hyksos period is probable, but the Egyptian personal names are not Middle Egyptian, in contrast to the early date of the Semitic personal names in the Patriarchal narratives. In 1959 J. Vergote published an important book on Joseph in Egypt and concluded that the career of Joseph is to be dated in the New Kingdom and that the tradition underlying the extant Biblical narrative was handed down from Ramesside times.[10] I have always preferred a date in the tenth century B.C. to which belong most of the early prose narrative in Genesis-Numbers, though different recensions of it were edited in approximately their present form about the seventh century B.C. The Egyptian proper names in the Joseph story are seldom earlier in their extant form than about the tenth century, and they were revised again by the Greek translators who lived in Egypt during the third century B.C. in order to conform to Egyptian onomastics of that time. That the biblical story of Joseph is substantially identical with the story as known in Moses' time I do not doubt, and a considerably earlier date is quite possible.

There are now a number of striking examples of early date. In Genesis 37:3 we hear of Jacob's favoritism toward Joseph; Jacob loved Joseph more than his other sons, and had "a coat of many colors" (King James) made for him, or, as rendered by RSV, "a long robe with sleeves." Unfortunately, the only otherwise attested meaning for the word *passim* in Northwest Semitic is that of tablet-shaped objects. This can apply only to the rectangular panels of colored cloth sewn together into a wide strip and wound around the body like a *sari*. It is seldom that we can pinpoint a garment fashionable at one time but not used in other periods so closely as we can in this case. At Mari it was in use at the end of the 18th century B.C.; it occurs in a mural fresco of the palace of Zimri-Lim. It may well be that the style continued in use for some time, but this is as close a synchronism as we can reach in dealing with archaeological typology and changes of ancient fashions. Incidentally, the next fashionable men's garment style was a sari-like robe edged with fur (16th-15th centuries B.C.) well known from Syria and Palestine.

In the Joseph story we also find references to two towns of Canaan which were both occupied during this general period, as we know from the excavations of G. Ernest Wright and his staff at Shechem and of Joseph Free at Dothan.[11] Both of these fortified towns were later in the tribe of Manasseh though Shechem is sometimes supposed to have been in Ephraim. In any case Manasseh and Ephraim were the only recorded sons of Joseph, and thus both were involved in the tradition of early occupation which we find in ancient sources. For example, the early occupation of this area by the Joseph tribes is attested in Genesis, in Chronicles (about 400 B.C.), and later in the book of Jubilees and the Testaments of the Twelve Patriarchs, both of which were composed about 200 B.C. or a little later. In them we find shorter and longer accounts of the attack of the Canaanites on Jacob and his family, and the capture by Jacob and his sons of towns in north-central Palestine. There is no reason to doubt that these traditions, however deformed they may have become in the long history of transmission and translation through Greek, Ethiopic, and Armenian, do contain some authentic details handed down from much earlier times. They do not contradict the Hebrew tradition, which does not describe the conquest of any part of this area in the time of Joshua or later—though the defeat of several "kings" of towns in the area is listed schematically in Joshua 12. We find a very similar situation in regard to the tribe of Judah, which was already settled in the territory later occupied by Judah, according to Genesis 38. That Shechem had already become Hebrew before the time of Joshua is reasonably certain from the fact that no trace of a destruction in the period of the Conquest (second half of the 13th century B.C.) has been found there during Wright's excavations.

Suggestions for Further Reading

See especially Albright's *Yahweh and the Gods of Canaan* (1968) where most of the documentation for the present article can be found by checking the volume's indices and the footnotes of Chap. 2. Among more recent studies which pertain to this period, see e.g. William G. Dever, "The 'Middle Bronze I' Period in Syria and Palestine," and Paul W. Lapp, "Palestine in the Early Bronze Age," both in J. A. Sanders, ed., *Near Eastern Archaeology in the Twentieth Century: Essays in Honor of Nelson Glueck* (1970); Dever, "The Peoples of Palestine in the Middle Bronze I Period," *Harvard Theological Review* 64 (1971), 197-226; Nelson Glueck, *Rivers in the Desert* (2nd ed.; 1968); Lapp, *The Dhahr Mirzabaneh Tombs* (1966); A. Malamat, "Mari," *BA* 34 (1971), 2-22; A. Parrot, *Abraham and His Times* (1968); G. Posener, J. Bottéro, and K. Kenyon, "Syria and Palestine, *c.* 2160-1780," *Cambridge Ancient History* (3rd ed.; 1971), Chap. XXI; R. de Vaux, *Histoire Ancienne d'Israel des Origines à l'Installation en Canaan* (Paris, 1971).

Notes

[1] *Vetus Testamentum Supplement* 16 (1967), 176-90. (Reference provided by Prof. Robt. D. Biggs.—*Eds.*)

[2] Beno Rothenberg, *God's Wilderness: Discoveries in Sinai* (1961).

[3] *BASOR* 179 (1965), 6-29.

[4] *BASOR* 163 (1961), 49-54.

[5] J. B. Pritchard, ed. *Ancient Near Eastern Texts* (3rd ed., 1969) p. 556.

[6] *Syria* 41 (1964), 117-42.

[7] *Journal of Cuneiform Studies* 20 (1966), 95-118.

[8] W. G. Lambert and A. R. Millard, *Atra-ḫasis: The Babylonian Story of the Flood* (1969).

[9] J. Van Seters, *The Hyksos: A New Investigation* (1966), pp. 103-20.

[10] J. Vergote, *Joseph en Égypte*.

[11] G. E. Wright, *Shechem: Biography of a Biblical City* (1965); J. P. Free, *BA* 19 (1956), 43-48.

3

FROM THE PATRIARCHS TO MOSES.
II. MOSES OUT OF EGYPT

W. F. ALBRIGHT

Among the Hebrew groups first settled in Palestine, whose migration from Mesopotamia probably goes back to the late Patriarchal Age, presumably well after 1700 B.C., were several extinct clans of Judah and Benjamin. In the case of Judah (Genesis 30:4 ff.) one of the two most important tribes of the Banu-Yamin of the Mari texts appears as *Onan* (Greek *Aunan*) which reflects the cuneiform transcription Awnanum or Awnan, the ᶜApiru tribe which played the largest role in the time of the Hammurapi dynasty. Of even greater importance was the extinct clan of Er which is almost certainly a shortened form of the very rarely mentioned name of the Judahite clan of Yaᶜor (I Chronicles 20:5; cf. 4:21). This name is obviously identical with that of the tribe of Yahrurum or Yahurrum so often mentioned in the cuneiform texts with Awnanum; it appears as Yauri in Assyrian royal inscriptions. (It should be explained that there was no such sound as ᶜ*ayin* in Mesopotamian cuneiform; the spellings *Yahurru* and *Yauru* compel a transcription *Ya*ᶜ*ur* =Hebrew *Ya*ᶜ*or*; ᶜ*Er* is a shorter form of the latter name.) There it figures as an important nomadic group in northern Mesopotamia against which the Assyrians had to fight in the 14th century B.C. Curiously enough, we have another extinct clan of Benjamin named *Rapha* (Greek *Raphe*) which is a typical shortening of the name of the third most important tribe of the Banu-Yamin, namely the Ubrapu. In other words, there were quite a number of close ties between tribal names of Hebrew settlers in central Palestine with tribes of the Banu-Yamin in the earlier Patriarchal Age. The name of Benjaminite Jericho, not found outside the Bible until very late times, may, after all, be derived from the tribe of Yarihu, a minor subdivision of the Banu-

Yamin. If we turn to the lists of ancestors of tribes and clans in the Old Testament, we find a great many similar phenomena, as pointed out in the first part of this article.

Once settled in Palestine and Egypt, the pre-Mosaic Hebrews often gave up their primary vocation as donkey caravaneers. Though remaining shepherds and agricultural workers, they also took up—or resumed—other occupations, such as mercenaries, bandits, and vintagers, illustrated both in Genesis 49 and in archaeological sources. For example, in 49:11 we read, with reference to Judah:

> Tethering his young donkey to a vine,
>> And the foal of his she-ass to a grape-vine,
> He washes his garment in wine,
>> And his robe in the blood of grapes.

Since wine was one of the chief exports from Palestine to Egypt, and since the ᶜApiru appear as vintagers in Egypt during the 15th century B.C., tending vineyards was a natural occupation for Hebrews. The archaism of the text is illustrated by the fact that the description of the donkey sacrifice solemnized at Haran (Abraham's second home) between the Banu-Yamin and the "kings" of the region in the Mari tablets repeats the very same words for "young donkey" and "foal of a she-ass" that we have in the Blessing of Judah cited above! In both cases the allusion to donkey caravaneering is unmistakable.

In the Blessing of Issachar (Genesis 49:14f.) we should read (with the aid of a vital suggestion by Francis Andersen):[1]

> Issachar is an alien donkey driver
>> Who camped between the hearths;
> He saw how good was a resting-place,
>> And how pleasant was the land,
> He bent his shoulder to carry burdens
>> And became a forced laborer.

The usual translation "Issachar is a strong ass . . ." simply will not do, since a donkey does *not* "bend his shoulder" but merely stands there waiting for the load to be placed on his back. Andersen's reading *ḥammor*, "donkey driver," instead of *ḥamor*, "donkey," is obviously correct.

Similarly we must follow the early Greek translation in Genesis 34:2 and render "Shechem, son of Hammor the Horite," instead of "Shechem, son of Hamor the Hivite." This naturally derives from a tradition that Shechem was founded by a Horite donkey-driver and was afterwards conquered by the Hebrews. Cuneiform tablets from Shechem and Amarna, belonging to the 15th-14th centuries B.C., prove both traditions. In the former century a prince of Shechem bears the Indo-Aryan (= Horite) name *Birassena*, but by the Amarna period Shechem was ruled by an ᶜApiru chieftain with the good early Hebrew name *Labᵓayu*, "the Lion Man" (cf. the name of David's friend, *Barzillai*, "the Iron Man"). It is interesting to note that Labᵓayu's scribe knew very little Babylonian and wrote his letters in almost pure early Hebrew. Labᵓayu himself was bitterly denounced by his Canaanite neighbors as a brigand and rebel, but in writing to Pharaoh he poses as his most loyal subject.

From the Amarna correspondence about Labᵓayu we can understand the force of the Curse of Simeon and Levi (the tribes which sacked Shechem according to Genesis 34). We should render Genesis 49:5ff.:

Simeon and Levi are brothers,
   Goods got by rapine are their wares.
Into their council let me not enter,
   In their company let me not be seen
Truly in their anger they killed men,
   And in their fury they houghed oxen.
Cursed be their wrath—how fierce!
   And their rage—how cruel!
I will scatter them in Jacob
   And disperse them in Israel!

It would be very difficult to describe the activities of the ᶜApiru as seen by their sedentary neighbors more precisely than in this remarkable curse. The ᶜApiru are traditionally traders, but banditry has become their chief occupation.

Three others of the sayings of Jacob in this chapter illustrate the situation among the ᶜApiru in Palestine during the late Patriarchal Age; it is said of Benjamin, the splinter group which inherited the name of the Banu-Yamin of Mesopotamia:

> Benjamin is a wolf after prey . . .
> In the morning he eats to . . .
> In the evening he divides the spoil.

Of Judah it is said, among other things:

> A young lion is Judah,
> On prey, O my son, wast thou nurtured.
> Crouching on all fours like a lion,
> Like a lioness, who will attack him?

In contrast to these rather sanguinary descriptions of the early tribes in Palestine, we have a simple statement about Naphtali, which has been almost universally misunderstood:

> Naphtali is a racing stag
> Which bellows with trumpet notes.

The male of the red deer, which formerly spread all over western Asia and Europe, has branching antlers, and when in heat is fond of racing at full speed over rough terrain, shrieking with high trumpet tones or bellowing with deep organ notes. Incidentally, many years ago I published a large potsherd containing a deeply incised representation of a stag which had been discovered by a friend on the site of the ancient Kinnereth in the heart of Naphtali. The sherd came from the side of an incense stand of about the 12th or 11th century B.C. While this saying does not illustrate the tendency of the ᶜApiru toward robbery and mercenary activity, it does suggest the qualities which a tribe was supposed to possess in order to be respected among the early Hebrews.

There is a very important reference to the historical movements which ushered in the Fifteenth Egyptian Dynasty. In Numbers 13:22 we are told that "Hebron was built seven years before Tanis in Egypt." This almost certainly refers to the construction of a great fortress at Avaris in the eastern Delta by the founder of the Hyksos Empire, Salitis, first king of the Fifteenth Dynasty. Some years ago I proposed the identification of Salitis with Zayaluti who was the head of the Indo-Iranian Manda warriors in Syria about 1650 B.C. This identification has been rejected by some scholars, but the spelling and sound changes involved have excellent parallels, and there are several good Indo-Aryan etymologies for the name. This would then be the first known reference to the Indo-Aryan aristocracy of Southwestern Asia who were largely merged with the mass of Hurrians and are therefore called Hivites (Hebrew text) or Horites (Greek text) in Genesis.

It has long since been demonstrated that the site later occupied by Tanis was identical with the city of Avaris, mentioned by Manetho, as well as with the city of Raamses or Rameses, probably founded by Sethos I and certainly finished by Ramesses II who called it "House of Ramesses" and made it his residence. While there have been other proposed sites in the neighborhood, this remains by far the most likely. In Biblical tradition the area occupied by Israelites is called variously "Land of Goshen," "Land of Ramesses," and "Plain of Tanis" ("field of Zoan" in the AV of Psalm 78:12). The first name is Semitic and cannot possibly be Egyptian in origin; it probably refers to some kind of soil. The second name is anachronistic for the time of Jacob but carries us back to the beginnings of Israel as a nation under Ramesses II. The third designation has often been supposed to be very late, but Otto Eissfeldt has shown that this Psalm cannot be later than the tenth century B.C. in its present form.[2] The argument about the location of Avaris continues and cannot easily be settled until much more elaborate excavations have been carried out at the site of San el-Hagar with the aid of caissons or other means of digging under water since the water level in this part of the Delta generally submerges all levels to about the Roman period.

In the preceding verse (Numbers 13:21) we are told that Hebron was then occupied by Ahiman, Sheshai, and Talmai. Since the names are not Hebrew in any case, but Ahiman is Mesopotamian Semitic and Talmai is Hurrian while Sheshai is in any event not Semitic, we are most certainly dealing in the verse with persons or clans going back to this period of non-Semitic irruption into Palestine and Egypt about the middle of the 17th century B.C.

The ethnic background of the remaining kings of the Fifteenth Dynasty is still uncertain, though the names suggest mixed origins. It is certain that men bearing Semitic names still played an important role during this period; it is also certain that about 1600 B.C. the Hyksos established an empire of considerable extent whose monuments have turned up in the most unexpected places—in Minoan Crete, the Hittite capital east of Ankara, and northern Babylonia, for instance. During this period it seems reasonably certain that there was no particular hostility to the Hebrews who may indeed have played an important role in affairs of state. But then about the middle of the 16th century Amosis, the first king of the Eighteenth Dynasty, rebelled and by about 1530 had completely regained Egyptian independence and had driven the Hyksos out of Egypt. Since the Hyksos rulers needed all the support they could get from minority groups in order to keep the Egyptian majority under control, it is highly probable that Amosis was the "king who knew not Joseph" of Exodus 1:8.

We have good evidence that Semites who had been settled in Egypt for generations became state slaves after the liberation of Egypt from its foreign rulers. This evidence comes from the Proto-Sinaitic inscriptions, discovered by Sir Flinders Petrie and others since 1905. From the temple of the goddess Hathor, identified by the Egyptians with Canaanite Baalat, "the Lady," and from the areas of neighboring turquoise mines, have come numerous short inscriptions in an alphabetic script. Without insisting on the necessary correctness of details in my own decipherment of 1966,[3] based on the partial decipherment by Sir Alan Gardiner in 1915, it may be said that my date for them between about 1525 and 1450 B.C. is almost certainly right and that most of them probably date from the early 15th century. As deciphered, the script is earlier than that of inscriptions dated by their archaeological context in the 14th and 13th centuries and later than that of a few short inscriptions from Palestine which date from the 18th-17th centuries B.C. My own decipherment has the advantage of closely following the development patterns of cognate dialects—South Canaanite, North Canaanite (Ugaritic), early Hebrew, etc. Accordingly, it has been accepted in principle by some of the best scholars; but, of course, it must be regarded with caution until more inscriptions have been found, enabling us to check it. Nearly all the inscriptions are mortuary in character as might be expected from the fact that they were mostly found in or near a field of burial cairns. Such cairns were the normal memorials to the deceased in desert regions. Other inscriptions are votive, including the first inscription partially deciphered by Gardiner. The forms of letters are modeled roughly on Egyptian, but the phonetic values attached to them are based on acrophony, that is, their pronunciation depends on the first consonant of the Canaanite word which they represent. For instance, water is *m* (Hebrew *mayim*, Phoenician *mem*), house is *b* (Hebrew *bayit*, Canaanite *bet*), a human head is *r* (Hebrew *rosh*, Canaanite *roshu*, Ugaritic *reʾshu*, Aramaic *resh*), a fish is *d* (Hebrew, Phoenician, and Ugaritic *dag*), etc.

Representations of divinities and objects among the Proto-Sinaitic monuments, both in the round and in outline, are invariably Egyptian or Egyptianizing in character. In no case can we identify a Canaanite divinity among the gods and goddesses who are invoked in the inscriptions. Among the Egyptian gods who appear are Ptah, who was later identified by the Canaanites with Semitic El; Hathor, later identified with Baalat; probably Osiris and Anubis, as well as a few other divinities. These identifications are based both on representations and the inscriptions. If the decipherment is correct, the personal names are mostly Semitic with a few common Egyptian names interspersed.

Moses

When we come to the period of Moses, we find ourselves in the full light of history in the sense of having extensive documentation for the events and activities of the age. The idea that Israel was at that time an ignorant nomadic people is nonsense—though there were undoubtedly some nomadic and semi-nomadic elements in it. That the Israel of the Exodus is contemptuously called by two derogatory terms, *ʾasafsuf* and *ʿerebrab*, in Numbers 11:4 and Exodus 12:38 merely suggests that it was a mob or rabble of mixed origins.

It is no accident that Moses himself bore an Egyptian name, since Hebrew *Moshe* cannot be separated from the short Egyptian name *Mase* (which became *Mose*). It is a common abbreviated form of longer names beginning with the name of an Egyptian god and ending with the verbal form "is born." For instance, among the many names of this type we find *Remose*, "the son-god is born," *Ahmose*, "the moon-god is born," *Thutmose*, "the (ibis-headed) god Thoth is born," etc. The change of sibilants is a later development in Hebrew, like *Pelishtim*, "Philistines," for Egyptian *Pelest*. There are also several other Egyptian names among the immediate relatives of Moses. Hur, who took Moses' place (with Aaron) on two recorded occasions (Exodus 17:10-12, 24:14) bore a very common Egyptian name of that period (which was then pronounced *Har* but which became *Hur* in Hebrew just as Egyptian Kash became Kush [Cush] in Hebrew). According to later Jewish tradition (Josephus) Hur was Miriam's husband. Phinehas was a very common Egyptian name in that period, meaning "the Negro" or "the Nubian," presumably given to a man because of mixed blood or swarthy complexion. There are a number of other good Egyptian names among the descendants of Aaron, such as Merari and Pashhur.

There can be no doubt that the concentration of Egyptian names among the close relatives of Moses is significant. It does indicate that Moses' background was strongly Egyptianizing. This of course agrees with the old Jewish traditions reported by Josephus. It is not necessary to accept the highly romanticized account of Moses' early life given by Josephus to recognize that he must have had not only some Egyptian education but also extraordinary native qualities in order to accomplish what he did.

Living in northern Egypt, probably in the vicinity of Memphis and Heliopolis (Egyptian and Hebrew On), young Moses must have become familiar with the extremely mixed civilization of the eastern Delta where people of every ethnic origin lived and worked together. In those days cuneiform was the official script of Egypt in communicating with foreign rulers and Asiatic vassals, and the Ramesside capital at Tanis was soon to become the center of Egyptian contacts with all countries of southwestern Asia and the Aegean. The gods of the Canaanites were accepted in Egypt as well as in Palestine and Syria, especially Baal, Resheph, Hauron, and the three closely related female divinities—Asherah, "the Holiness," consort of El, Astarte, and Anath, sisters and consorts of

Baal. In fact, Northwest-Semitic culture was in the process of being absorbed into Egyptian life. In those days cuneiform and Canaanite epics, magical and divination texts, etc. were being copied, translated, and adapted for Egyptian use. An Egyptian scribe wrote the letters of the prince of Tyre about the middle of the 14th century, and Pharaoh's commands to his Asiatic vassals were written by Egyptian scribes in Babylonian cuneiform as indicated by the obviously Egyptian mistakes they made in spelling and idiom. In short, it was an area and a period of quite extraordinary mixture of cultures.

While Moses was still young, he was forced, like Sinuhe nearly 700 years earlier, to flee from Egypt and take refuge among the semi-nomads of northwestern Arabia. In Moses' time they were the Midianites who had established a kind of protectorate over the Edomites, Kenites, Moabites, and other tribes of southern Transjordan, as we know from Biblical texts recently studied by Otto Eissfeldt.[4] Much later in the lifetime of Moses war is said to have broken out between the followers of Moses and the Midianites, in which the latter were defeated (Numbers 31). From this narrative we learn that early tradition (not late tradition as usually supposed) considered the Midianites as donkey nomads. The Israelites are said to have taken from them a booty of 61,000 donkeys as well as large and small cattle; there is no mention of any camels. (In Palestine and Syria donkey caravans appear in the Amarna tablets shortly before the time of Moses; they are also explicitly mentioned in the Song of Deborah not long before the Midianite irruption.) Not much over a century later the Midianites and nomad allies are said, in the account of the exploits of Gideon (Judges 6-8), to have sent hordes of camel-riding warriors to raid Palestine. This explains why there is no reference to camels in the account of the life of Moses, except once at the end of a list of all domestic animals; the camel also appears among unclean animals. Otherwise we hear only of large and small cattle and donkeys.

Since 1969 Beno Rothenberg and Yohanan Aharoni have excavated an Egyptian sanctuary at the important copper-mining site of Mene^ciyeh (Timna) in the Arabah between the southern end of the Dead Sea and the northern end of the Gulf of Aqaba.[5] Here were found numerous Egyptian objects together with pottery characteristic of the time; some of the Egyptian objects bear inscriptions mentioning Sethos I (about 1315-1304 B.C.), his son Ramesses II, the latter's son Merneptah, Sethos II, Ramesses III, IV, and V. In other words, Egyptian activities extended from about 1310 B.C. to about 1150 B.C., with an interruption under Ramesses II. The unexpected discovery that the area south and southeast of the Dead Sea was under Midianite suzerainty under much of the Mosaic period clarifies features of the Biblical tradition which had been very obscure. For instance, it explains why the list of kings of Edom in Genesis 36 does not start until well after the Israelite conquest of Palestine; it helps to explain why the Midianite clan of Reuel (Greek Raguel) was also an Edomite clan; it explains why the early name of Petra is said in all our available sources, including Josephus and recently discovered Nabataean inscriptions, to have been Rekem which is the name of a Midianite clan in Numbers.

These and other newly discovered facts, in agreement with Biblical tradition, show that the Midianites were much more important than we have hitherto assumed and make it certain that for some time they controlled the caravan routes of western Arabia between Palestine and Egypt on the one hand and Dedan and Sheba on the other. The Egyptians had been sending naval expeditions periodically to Somaliland for myrrh and frankincense, and now the Midianites were in competition with them by sending overland caravans of especially-bred desert donkeys. It must be remembered that the difference between a desert-bred donkey and an ordinary donkey from agricultural territory was just as great in Arabia as in Armenia and northern Mesopotamia (see above in Part I). It was also at that time, probably after the date of the Proto-Sinaitic inscriptions but before the time of Moses, that the Midianites or other caravaneers carried our ancestral alphabet from the north down into South Arabia where forms of letters closely resembling North-Semitic forms of the 14th-13th centuries B.C. have been found by A. Jamme and others.[6] In short, the Midianites were far from being as primitive a people as usually supposed, and Moses may have been very much more influenced by them than I, for one, thought possible a few years ago.

Recent analysis of the Biblical passages bearing on Moses' relationship to the Kenites and Midianites, with the aid of the Greek version, shows clearly that his father-in-law, Jethro, was an ethnic Midianite and a metal-worker ("Kenite") by profession—as well as a priest on the side. *Reuel* (*Raguel*) was his clan-name and *Hobab* was Moses' son-in-law. (In pre-exilic Hebrew "father-in-law" and "son-in-law" were both spelled *HTN*.) Jethro is portrayed as a wise old man, but Hobab is described as an energetic young man, familiar with remote desert routes. At that time the Midianites controlled the caravan routes of West Arabia, as we have seen. Their homeland was the region east of the Gulf of Aqaba which contains many small oases where deflector dams could provide water for irrigation.

In estimating the contribution of Moses we must, accordingly, beware of rating his own education and early experience of life at the now customary low level. In view of the extraordinary tenacity of Jewish legal and scriptural tradition, as illustrated by early rabbinic works such as Sifre which collected material extending back in some cases to pre-exilic times, it is decidedly unsafe to down-grade the antiquity of the Mosaic tradition. It is impossible to understand the contribution of Moses adequately unless one takes the traditions about his career very seriously indeed. We shall see that Moses was trying to restore the faith of the Hebrew fathers; his purpose was to reform, not to innovate. Nearly all great religious innovators in history have considered themselves as reformers; they were not trying to invent a new religion but to renew an old one. We shall return to this question below.

Most instructive for the background of the historical tradition of the Exodus and desert wanderings is the list of the first stations on the route from the Egyptian capital to eastern Palestine which we find in Numbers 33:7ff. with parallels and occasional additions in Exodus 12-14. The variants in the different Hebrew texts dealing with the route from Rameses to Shur (the line of the Wall of Egypt) have been attributed to different alleged sources by different literary critics, one of the most recent of whom employs such designations as J_2, J_3, E_2 and P (besides "minor" ones). No two of the leading critical "authorities" attribute all variants to the same sources; two or even three sources are suggested for single verses. If one takes the Greek translation of the third century B.C. with its own recensional variants and the different Hebrew parallel texts and their variants and then compares them, it becomes obvious that what we have here are several different recensions of the same original list which was handed down in written form from no later than the tenth century B.C. Nor is there any reason to doubt that the list is substantially correct as it may be reconstructed from the different recensional variants. In Exodus 14:3 we have in the middle of the condensed narrative a good poetic line with two half-lines,

> Trapped are they in the land (Egypt),
> The desert has barred them in.

This poetic quotation is obviously early and it guarantees the use of oral sources by the editor of our master list of stations in Numbers. While it is quite probable that the Egyptian section of the list was remembered more exactly than some of the desert wanderings, there is no reason to doubt the antiquity of the latter list. This does not, of course, mean that all caravan stops are mentioned, but it does guarantee the general order of the list and the antiquity of the names. If there were any doubt, it should be removed by the verse quotations from the original poetic form of a similar list preserved in Numbers 21.

Today it is no longer considered as heresy by "critical" scholars to recognize that the different documents which can—within limits—be recognized in the first four books of Moses are recensions of an original J document, based on both verse and prose traditions, which was composed in the tenth century B.C. Following the work of the late Ezekiel Kaufmann of the Hebrew University in Jerusalem, it would appear that the so-called Priestly Code ("P") goes back to the early or middle seventh century B.C. and that the Priestly Code has included much "J" material. "E" was a recension of "J" prepared especially for the Northern Kingdom about the ninth century B.C., and the combination of both recensions of "J" as "JE" probably dates from the late eighth or early seventh century B.C. "P," the Priestly Code, utilizes much material from "J" and "JE" besides including much cultic and narrative material which was not preserved in "J" but which was very ancient. We may, therefore, follow the Mosaic traditions preserved in Exodus and Numbers with confidence, remembering that "discrepancies" often enable us to see obscure matters in clearer perspective.

Probably the best-preserved early poem of any length in the Bible is Exodus 15:1-18. The idea sometimes expressed that verse 21 is the only relatively early part of the poem, which is otherwise post-Solomonic or even post-Exilic, is nonsense. It is the title of the entire hymn with a slight textual variant at the beginning. Such titles were in the form of initial lines or stanzas of an original poem, just as in cuneiform lists of poetic compositions. Examples are found in Psalm 68 which has preserved a considerable number of such titles for liturgical purposes.

Because of its outstanding importance for Israel's national consciousness, Exodus 15 has been preserved with extraordinary accuracy in detail. There are only two or three places where something has happened to the text and some archaism has disappeared. Cf. verse 14 where "Philistia" is anachronistic and presumably replaced an older general term such as *Khuru* or *Khatti*. In this poem archaic words and phrases are heaped up, and very early grammatical forms are preserved even with the correct original vowels. In the Song of Miriam we have at least three, perhaps four, instances of repetitive parallelism after the model ABC:ABD in which each letter represents a separate beat (or foot). The first two feet of each half-line are identical, following a characteristic feature of Canaanite style in the Late Bronze Age, now well-known from the epics of Ugarit. There are even direct quotations from the Baal Epic or a hymn to Baal. In verses 17f. note especially the mention of "the mountain of thine inheritance, O Yahweh," where the Baal Epic says "the mountain of thine inheritance, O Baal." In Canaanite poetry this referred to Jebel Aqra, the Mountain of the North (Zaphon), where Baal-zephon was worshiped and where the gods were supposed to assemble as on Mount Olympus according to early Greek epic cosmography. This does not mean for a moment that the Baal Epic was consciously imitated, but simply that the phraseology was familiar and applied perfectly well to the mountains of Canaan from which part of Israel had gone to Egypt and to which it was returning to dwell with its kinsfolk who remained in Canaan. There is not the slightest basis for identifying this mountain with Zion in the original poem, though it is certainly true that after the building of the Temple it was so identified.

The description of the catastrophe which overwhelmed the Egyptian army that pursued the followers of Moses clarifies the prose traditions which we find in chapter 14:21 and 22. In verse 21 we read that "The Lord drove the sea back by a strong east wind all night and made the sea dry land, and the waters were divided." The following verse says "And the people of Israel went into the midst of the sea on dry ground, the waters being a wall to them on the right hand and on the left." As has happened in a number of clear cases in early Hebrew tradition, the poetic form explains later prose accounts. In 15:8 the poem reads:

> At the breath of thy nostrils the waters were heaped up;
>> They were raised like the dikes of irrigators;
>>> The deeps were curdled in the midst of the sea.

Here the prose tradition helps to illuminate the poetic form, but the poem clarifies certain aspects of prose tradition. Apparently a southeast wind had driven back the shallow waters of the Sea of Reeds (the Egyptian designation of a shallow lake east of Rameses). After this came a north wind which blew the water back over it just as the Egyptians were crossing in pursuit. The reference to "the dikes of irrigators" refers to the fact that in both the Delta and Babylonia the alluvial terrain constantly rises, forcing the construction of higher and higher dikes. These dikes often look like low mountain ranges or giant billows when seen from a distance across the plain. In other words, the verse and prose must all be taken together, and the inconcinnities which remain must be explained in the light of the original metaphors and some misunderstanding of them in later transmission. In the poem nothing is said about two walls of water between which the Israelites were supposed to have walked as though on dry land and which melted when the Egyptians passed through, drowning them. The word rendered "curdled" in our translation above is also translated (**RSV**) as "congealed." It explicitly refers in Exodus 15:8 to the subterranean waters (*tehomot*) "in the heart of the sea." The poetic original contains no less a miracle than the prose though it is not quite so startling.

The date of the Exodus was probably in the early 13th century B.C., as may be inferred from a number of lines of evidence. The city of Rameses had already been founded and was the administrative center of the followers of Moses in the eastern Delta. The Exodus is said in I Kings 6:1 to have taken place 480 years before the foundation of the Temple in the fourth year of Solomon which can be dated by Tyrian and Egyptian synchronisms about 965 B.C. From other Biblical texts as well as from Phoenician tradition we know that forty years was generally a round number for a generation. There were thus twelve generations between the Exodus and the building of the Temple. If we allow the usually 25-30 years for such generations we arrive at a date somewhere about the beginning of the 13th century B.C. Moses himself is said to have lived for three periods of 40 years which would make a total of three generations or presumably 80 years (or more, since tradition emphasizes his long life and the excellent state of his health when he died). If we assume that he died not long before the critical period of the Israelite conquest of the low hill-country of Judah (the Shephelah), we arrive at a date not far from the middle of the 13th century for his decease. Moses and his followers lived on the Asiatic frontier of Egypt and because of their varied activities and their numerous ties with neighboring lands and different ethnic groups, might be expected to follow international political movements very closely. The frequently expressed view that they were ignorant shepherds or slaves without any societal organization and without any real knowledge of what was going on outside Egypt is incredible in the light of our growing knowledge of the cosmopolitan world of the Late Bronze Age. By far the most suitable date is the seventh or eighth year of the reign of Ramesses II, about 1297 B.C. This date, published in 1968,[7] is a little earlier than my previous one which was based on a too low chronology for the reign of Ramesses the Great. Now, however, astronomical calculations on the basis of lunar events have apparently fixed his accession in 1304 B.C. In the fifth year of his reign the young Egyptian king was roundly defeated by the Hittites and narrowly escaped with his life from the battlefield at Kadesh on the Orontes. This defeat was followed by a general revolt in southern Syria and Palestine which broke out in his sixth or seventh regnal year and was not finally put down until the ninth year. The rebellion extended at least as far south as Ascalon in southern Canaan (later occupied by the Philistines) and the Egyptians hastily moved their administrative capital south from Memphis to Thebes. We may accordingly consider a date about 1297 B.C. as by far the most probable, though it cannot be said to be established beyond doubt since even expert astronomers are sometimes misled by obscure words or phrases in the inscriptions.

At that time the peninsula of Sinai was far from being the complete desert that most of it is today. In the first place the amount of tree cover, reinforced by scrub vegetation of many kinds, was incomparably greater than it is today. During the past 3000-odd years the stand of tamarisks has suffered particularly because of the presence of domesticated goats and camels as well as th activity of charcoal-burners. When I was in Sinai over 20 years ag , strings of desert donkeys carrying charcoal for sale in the big cities of northeastern Egypt were a common sight, and the situation must have been very similar in antiquity, especially in the days when there was a good deal of copper available for easy mining and smelting in Sinai. The amount of game was also far greater. In those days there were not only a great many more small animals, but there were also wild cattle, wild goats (ibexes), and gazelles—not to mention ostriches and other large and small birds which have virtually disappeared from Sinai today. This short list does not exhaust the possibilites but merely gives some idea of the animals we know to have been common in Sinai at that time. In much earlier times bird life had been still more abundant as illustrated by our finding (1958) of quantities of small flint crescents which were used by fowlers to top their reed arrows. There were also a great many more migratory birds than there are today. We have an interesting reference to the unexpected windfall of quail from which the Israelites benefited at a particularly difficult period in the early part of their trek (Exodus 16:13).

But the most valuable single means of subsistence available to Israel in Sinai was manna. It is now known, thanks to the work of F. S. Bodenheimer,[8] that manna was produced by the excretions of two closely related species of scale insects (just as honey is excreted by bees), one of which produced it in the mountains of Sinai and the other in the lowlands of Sinai. Naturally the amount of manna was partly determined by the relative amount of tamarisk sap available to these insects. An exceptionally favorable season might provide a great deal of the sweet, highly nutritive substance, and a bad season might yield very little. It is scarcely surprising that the Israelites did not know that they were to become the beneficiaries of an unusually good season for manna production when they first emerged into the desert. Later on they would be able to feed themselves by hunting game animals and to subsist on all sorts of plant growth which did not at first seem attractive but improved with practice in preparation. It must be remembered that Moses was an old hand at desert travel and was doubtless familiar with every possible mode of subsistence and that there doubtless were others among his followers who were familiar with the desert. Later, according to traditions, there was his son-in-law, the Midianite Hobab, who guided them. In view of the extraordinary wealth of Egypt in fruit and vegetables of different kinds, it is not surprising that the Israelites regretted the food of Egypt.

Most of the caravan stations mentioned in the list in Numbers cannot be identified with certainty, but the general picture is clear enough. The first thrust apparently took them to south-central Sinai and then up the old caravan routes of the Middle Bronze Age to the double oasis of Kadesh-barnea from which they are said to have made their first attempt to invade Palestine proper. Since "forty years" evidently included Moses' latter years in eastern Palestine as well as the travel in the desert before they reached a base of operations east of Jordan, the desert wanderings proper need not have lasted for more than a comparatively brief period. There is no way of estimating the number of Moses' followers at that time. It may have been only a few thousand; it may have amounted to some tens of thousands in which case there is no need to assume that they all traveled together since they would have had to scatter out in order to find sufficient food—even manna.

At this point we may ask ourselves about the make-up of "Israel" which now emerges as a distinct people. In our available sources it appears for the first time in the famous Israel stele of Merneptah, son and successor of Ramesses II, where we read;

> Israel is laid waste, his seed is not,
> Huru has become a widow for Egypt.

As we know from an ostracon found at Lachish in the destruction level of the last Canaanite occupation, the burning of the town by the Israelites cannot have taken place before the fourth year of Merneptah and probably took place in the very year of the stele in question, the fifth year, about 1234 B.C. Several other Canaanite walled towns of the low hill-country north and south of Lachish were destroyed about the same time, so this may be taken as the probable date of the campaign of Israel against the low hill-country of Judah (Joshua 10:16ff.). The name has been found in the tablets of Ugarit where it is applied to an individual, indicating that it was still in use as a personal name, but no present conclusion can be drawn from this fact. We have no evidence at all that it was applied in earlier times to the Hebrews in Canaan, but this gap in our knowledge is again inconclusive. At present all we know is that the Hebrews in the northeastern Delta were called "Israel" before the time of Moses and may have brought this name with them to Egypt from Asia.

The Work of Moses

A common attitude to Moses held by modern scholars follows the German Romantic view of history that reached its apex in the work of German literary and historical critics of the school founded by Julius Wellhausen in the late nineteenth century. According to this view, Moses was only a wandering nomad. Wellhausen was a specialist in late pre-Islamic Arabic verse composed orally by nomad poets and written down in the seventh or eighth century A.D. This poetry describes the life of camel nomads in Arabia between the fifth and the seventh centuries A.D. Wellhausen's ideas have been adopted by many other scholars who are not strict Wellhausenists. For instance, the late Ezekiel Kaufmann of the Hebrew University maintained that Moses, Aaron, and Miriam were members of a family of primitive diviners like the Arab *kahin* of pre-Islamic times.

It has already been shown above that Moses had been exposed to strong Egyptian influence in his formative years and that several members of his immediate family bore Egyptian names. We have also pointed out that the Midianites among whom he later spent a number of years were at that time a highly developed and very powerful tribal confederation which controlled the caravaneering and much of the mining activity of north-western Arabia in the thirteenth century B.C.

We shall now see that Moses (or somebody in his circle) was also at home in the late Patriarchal traditions of Israel. The influence of ancient Sumero-Babylonian religious epics on the early chapters of Genesis is well known; it includes the accounts of Creation in Genesis 1-2, the primordial garden at the Source of the Rivers in the west, the number and high longevity of the antediluvian patriarchs, the account of the Flood, the Tower of Babel, the list of post-diluvian patriarchs with reduced longevity, and various features of style and allusion. As long as there was no direct evidence anywhere for an intermediate stage between Sumero-Babylonian and Hebrew texts, it was possible to minimize the significance of the comparisons. Yet Mesopotamian origin remained the most plausible hypothesis because of the almost complete absence of any remotely similar myth among the North Canaanites of Ugarit whose mythological epics and shorter religious texts have come to light in great quantity since 1930, or in the South-Canaanite mythology as described by Eusebius, bishop of Caesarea, on the basis of earlier pagan Phoenician sources. But now we have the Atrahasis Epic (see Part I, above), our first cosmogonic text from a mixed West-Semitic ("Amorite") and Sumero-Babylonian milieu, which dates from no later than the early sixteenth century B.C. and may well be a century or two earlier. As already pointed out, this text is amazingly sophisticated for such an early composition. It also demonstrates the high level of culture attained by the relatives of the Patriarchs.

In Genesis 1-11 other ancient myths have been carefully sifted and thoroughly demythologized. It is hard to believe that this process of adaption began after the Israelite conquest of Palestine when they were far more exposed to Canaanite influences than they were to Mesopotamian. It therefore becomes almost certain, in my opinion, that the original cosmogony preserved in Genesis 1-9 and 11 was derived from the Hebrew Patriarchal tradition, itself originating in the mixed culture of Mesopotamia. In other words, I see no reason to doubt that most of this material was approved in Mosaic circles and subjected to still more editing and demythologizing in subsequent centuries. The account of Creation in the first chapter of Genesis is partly Sumero-Babylonian in structure and partly Northwest Semitic. The late Umberto Cassuto, who became professor at the Hebrew University in Jerusalem after he was exiled from Italy by the Mussolini government, pointed out that the *tanninim* "great sea monsters" (RSV)—the great whales of the KJV (Gen. 1:21)—are explicitly said to be created by God, whereas in the Semitic Babylonian tradition the great female sea-monster Tiamat (=Heb. *tehom*, literally "the Great Deep") comes into being before the gods. In Canaanite literature there are stray references to *tannin* as a great cosmogonic sea-monster. This is an obvious—and no doubt very early—example of demythologizing. In the same sense the *tehom* which one would expect to turn up a second time as the primordial sea-monster conquered by Yahweh in Genesis 1:2 has disappeared from the context. Some years ago I pointed out that there are a number of linguistic archaisms in the first chapter of Genesis which would be hard to explain after the Israelites were settled in Palestine but which were still normal in the time of Moses.

The situation with regard to the Babylonian origin of the case-law in the Book of the Covenant (Exodus 21-23) is very similar. Here, however, we are not dealing with either Canaanite law or early Patriarchal customary law, identified by the late E. A. Speiser with the mixed Hurro-Accadian legal practices and customs described in the Nuzi tablets of the fifteenth century B.C. (see Part I above). So when we compare the fragments of a case-law code in Exodus, occasionally supplemented by similar material later in the Pentateuch, our closest parallels are found in the two now-known Semitic Babylonian codes of laws from Eshnunna in eastern Babylonia (from the middle decades of the eighteenth century B.C.) and the famous Code of Hammurapi inscribed about 1690 B.C. Not only is the structure of the laws the same—going back to an older Sumerian formulation with the key words "If . . . provided that . . . then . . ."—but a number of laws are identical in content. The complete identity of certain laws was not realized by scholars until very recently, when the text was compared systematically with the Greek translation of the third century B.C. as well as with the more recently discovered Code of Eshnunna. While we may now point to several laws identical in wording as well as to general similarities, there are also even more significant differences. The Babylonian codes reflect a feudal society with sharp contrasts between masters, lower classes of "half-free" persons, and slaves with a sliding scale of penalties, depending on the social status of the two parties involved in litigation. The sliding scale of penalities is almost totally absent in the Mosaic code, though of course we do find quite independent parallels to cuneiform law much later in the ancestral Germanic "Salic" laws. The Codes of Eshnunna and Hammurapi were both products of a mixed Northwest-Semitic and Sumero-Accadian civilization; they also preserve common features which have not been found in older Sumerian codes or in later Hittite and Assyrian codes, though the latter all share the same general structure and often contain details similar to those of the Babylonian code. It is only in the Code of Hammurapi, however, that we have explicit references to the principle of an eye for an eye, which means, of course, equal justice for all, regardless of station and in complete opposition to the vendetta. It is interesting to note that the Code of Hammurapi is considerably more humane than either of the two later cuneiform codes. The Hittite code is stricter in its differentiation of classes than the Babylonian code, and the Assyrian code is draconic in the severity of its penalties which far exceeded anything in the other law codes, presumably in reaction against a period of anarchy. The Hebrew code is much milder and treats Israelites and resident aliens on an equal basis; it also provides for much more humane treatment of slaves who are protected against cruelty on the part of their masters and have a chance to earn their freedom. The fact that many words and grammatical constructions in the Book of the Covenant were completely misunderstood in later Jewish tradition is alone a strong argument for the very early date of the Hebrew Book of the Covenant. I have therefore no hesitation in dating it to Moses or his immediate followers. Whether it was received by Mosaic circles as a fragmentary survival of Hebrew tribal law we cannot say. (Note that in the two very ancient poetic passages in Genesis 49:10 [Testament of Jacob] and Judges 5:14 [Song of Deborah], the term *mehoqeq*, "law-giver," is used of leaders of two different tribes of Israel.) It is even possible that it had been preserved in archaic written form since the ancestral Hebrew alphabet is known to have been used by the Semites in Egypt no later than the seventeenth century B.C. and was in common use at the turquoise mines of Sinai no later than about 1450 B.C.

Turning from demythologized cosmogony and case-law to the religious heritage of the Hebrews utilized by Moses and his followers, we may first deal with stray words and formulas. I have no doubt that here again Moses' intention was to reform, not to innovate. In the first place, the new faith of Israel accepted as designations of the one God the principal appellations of high gods in Patriarchal tradition. It is stated explicitly that this is so in the well-known passages in Exodus where Moses is commanded by God to use the name *Yahweh* instead of the more familiar *Shaddai* of Patriarchal times. This Shaddai is labeled as the personal name of the God of Abraham, Isaac, and Jacob. We now know that the word is itself authentically Northwest Semitic with close Accadian parallels meaning "the Mountain (god)" or "the One of the Mountains," the "Mountaineer." The original form was, of course, *shaddayu*, "one of the mountains, mountaineer," and the formation is the same as that of *rabbayu*, later *rabbay*, properly "archer" but also the name of the archer tribe belonging to the "Sons of the North," *Banu-Sim³al* (see above). The Babylonian equivalent, *il abi*, literally "god of the father," was identified with *El³eb*, the divine patron of the shades or ghosts in the underworld, also "ancestral deity," otherwise called *Eb* and *Ub* (Hebrew *ob*, "ghost"). The two expressions must not, however be confused, since the god of the father was the god specially worshiped by caravaneers and traders such as the early Assyrians who organized caravans between Assyria and Cappadocia, and the later Nabataeans and other caravaneering tribes of North Arabia in early post-Christian times. The same term was used for both—the "paternal deity" in Greek translation. It is reasonably clear why traveling merchants or caravaneers would prefer to stake their success on the favor of a single divinity rather than on a whole pantheon since a portable shrine or symbol of a single divinity could be carried anywhere.

Other appellations of high gods which go back to early times but which are used in Biblical passages exclusively as alternative names of Yahweh are *El*, "God," which was also the name of the head of the Canaanite pantheon but now becomes an appellation of Yahweh, and *Elohim*. *Elohim* is the Hebrew plural of *Eloah* (early *Ilah*); its equivalent is already used repeatedly in the Amarna tablets in the sense of the totality of manifestations of Godhead (which might include Pharoah). Still other appelations were ᶜ*Elyon*, "the Most High," ᶜ*Eli*, "the Exalted One," and *Zur*, "the Mountain."

There is now some evidence strongly favoring an earlier date for the name *Yahweh* than the time of Moses, but it is not yet clear whether it was a personal name or the first word of a liturgical formula which served as the proper name of a divinity (as so often in the ancient East). In any event, it is clear that the name originated in a pre-Mosaic liturgical expression meaning "It is He who creates what comes into being." This has often been supposed to be far too abstract for the period of Moses or even earlier. Actually this is not true at all since we have the same formula used of the head of the Egyptian pantheon long before (and after) the time of Moses: "He creates what comes into existence," or "It is He who causes to be what is." (Two quite different formulas with the same meaning are used.) In Babylonia, too, we have the causative "to bring into existence" again and again used of a high god in liturgies and personal names. The notion that causative ideas were too abstract for the ancient Near East is absurd, especially since the Semitic dialects as well as the related Egyptian language all had simple causative forms built into their verbal systems, just as we have an adjectival form (e.g. "loving") built into our verbal system.

It has recently been pointed out that in the Northwest-Semitic dialects of the Patriarchal Age (down to Moses) we often find a change (common in both the Mari and Amarna tablets) of the sound *ya* to *e* (pronounced like *ay* in English *hay*). This change would automatically turn the old verbal form *yahwey*, which underlies the divine name, into an *ehweh*, which would become *ehyeh* in Biblical Hebrew, meaning "I shall become" (Latin and English "I am," in Exodus 3:14). This simple phonetic explanation does away with reams of abstruse exegesis.

Since Moses had probably reached his early manhood within the generation after Akhenaten's death, there is no good reason to deny that he was influenced by the monotheism of Amarna. For instance, we find the emphatic statement that the Aten (solar disk which was used as a name in order to eliminate the cruder forms of solar religion) is "the only god, beside whom there is no other." It is true that practical monotheism (or "henotheism") was by no means unknown in the ancient East, but it was still rare in comparison with the vast religious literature mentioning hosts of gods and goddesses or praising a single divinity in highly mythological language under a multitude of different appellations. It would be only natural for Moses, given his outstanding qualities to see that ethical monotheism was the only answer to the problems raised by the tragic situation of the Hebrew people in his day.

In recent years it has been discovered, thanks to new Aramaic, cuneiform, and hieroglyphic inscriptions and documents, as well as to the Dead Sea Scrolls and other Biblical texts, that the Hebrew words hitherto rendered "testimony" (i.e., "witness") have been completely misunderstood. Hebrew *ᶜedah* and *ᶜeduth*, etc., are actually synonyms of *berith*, "covenant." Their original meaning was "oath(s), covenant, treaty," and they designate the tablets of stone containing the words of the Sinai covenant, as well as the ark and the tabernacle as "tablets of the covenant," "ark of the covenant," etc. The number of passages referring to the covenant of Moses' time are nearly doubled, and it becomes clear that the "covenant" was not merely an informal agreement, but a formal treaty between God as suzerain and his people as vassal. This was the official position of the so-called "Priestly Code" which took care to avoid using the much more general term *berith*, "covenant."

Some years earlier G. E. Mendenhall had demonstrated that the covenant of Joshua 24 follows the model set by suzerainty treaties drawn up by Hittite kings between 1500 and 1200 B.C.[9] In these treaties vassal kings pledged allegiance to the great king, and minor agreements were made. Treaties of this type begin with a historical preamble just as in Joshua; in later suzerainty treaties from southwestern Asia the historical introductions were omitted. We now see that the Sinai covenant was regarded in subsequent periods as binding on the people of Israel. It becomes idle to speculate on whether it existed at all or not.

An extremely interesting aspect of Israelite religion was its continued official hostility toward divination except in some very restricted forms such as use of the *urim* and *tummin* (whatever they were) and divination by use of the ephod, as well as, of course, divination by dreams. Other forms of divination do appear frequently in our sources, but they do not seem to have been approved by normative tradition. In view of the proliferation of elaborate systems of divination among people who were under strong Babylonian influence, this condemnation of diviners as well as of magicians of all kinds is characteristically Israelite, and the exceptions only illustrate the general rule. Divination by dreams which was so common in the time of Joseph and is often mentioned in the contemporary Mari tablets scarcely appears at all in Israel from Moses to the Exile. A very clear illustration of the situation is found in Numbers 12:6-8 which quotes three stanzas of an important early poem about Moses. These stanzas contain two very close parallels to the slightly earlier Canaanite literature discovered at Ugarit since 1930, and there is thus no doubt about the high antiquity of the poem. The extract preserved may be translated as follows:

"If there be a prophet among you
   In a vision I will make myself known to him,
      In a dream I will speak with him.
Not so is my servant Moses:
   Of all my household he is most faithful.
Mouth to mouth will I speak to him;
   (Not!) in a vision and not in riddles,
      But the glory of Yahweh shall he see."

It is clear from these verses that the tradition of Moses' own time recognized that he communed directly with God but emphatically not in dreams or trances. Another very good illustration of the early attitude of Israelite monotheism to divination in all its pagan forms is found in the remarkable account of the activity of Balaam (Numbers 22-24). Balaam came from the North-Syrian town of Pethor in the land of Amaw (RSV), from "the primeval mountains," an expression describing the mountainous region of greater Armenia.

The Oracles of Balaam in Numbers 23-24 are extremely archaic in style and vocabulary. The spelling of the text in the Hebrew recensions betrays an early date for its written form—no later than the tenth century B.C. The prose text is later as Otto Eissfeldt has now proved, but it is not as late as sometimes supposed, and there is, in fact, very good general agreement between the prose narrative and the poetry. For instance, the frequent mention of the elders of Midian as enjoying political status above the Moabite king can be explained only by recognizing the fact that Moab as well as Edom was then a vassal state in a loosely organized Midianite "empire" (see above).

It was long ago pointed out that various features of Balaam's activity point to the profession of a Babylonian *barum*. In the Mari texts, dating perhaps about 450 years before the time of Balaam, the *barum* appears principally in connection with armies. He was an official diviner who advised the king with regard to military actions to be taken. The activity of other diviners in the Mari texts has mostly to do either with formal oracles or with dreams as explicitly stated by the use of the Babylonian word for "dream." In general, the Mari tablets mention oracles obtained by professional diviners (who bore the name *apilum* or *muhhum*). The former was an official giver of oracles; the latter was an ecstatic prophet who received his oracles while in a state of trance. There were also dreams which came to everyday human beings without any oracular prerogatives at all but which, for some reason, impressed themselves on intermediaries who passed them on to the royal officials of Mari. In this respect Balaam fits the Mari pattern of *apilum* very well since it is explicitly stated in the prose text that the oracles came to him at night and he reported on them the next morning. In the poetic text, however, it is clearly said that he delivered the oracles while in a state of trance or quasi-trance. Both of these activities were expressly denied to Moses in the verses quoted above. The Balaam oracles themselves further suggest the futility of divination and magic by saying:

> "For there is no omen against Jacob
> And no spell can work against Israel."

One of the most striking features of the Mosaic movement is its negative attitude toward practices and beliefs connected with the afterlife. It has often—probably quite correctly—been supposed that the evident Mosaic hostility toward the mortuary cult was due to revulsion against Egyptian beliefs about the "resurrection" of the mummy which were inseparably bound together with elaborate magical practices. There was also a very real everyday problem connected with the cult of the dead in Egypt—it was incredibly expensive. It is true that the use of a large part of the total economic resources of Egypt for the construction of super-pyramids during the Memphite dynasties was later abandoned, but even after the pyramids had ceased to be built or had dwindled to minuscule size, the amount of wealth involved in furnishing a single tomb like that of Snefru (who also had two gigantic pyramids) or Tut-ankh-amun (who had no pyramid) was fabulous. Middle-class people and even some of the poor spent a great deal more than they could afford. Nor should we forget that a good part of the capital amassed by successive generations went to the maintenance of costly endowments in the vain hope that funeral rites would be contined indefinitely. In Egypt there was in most periods extremely little connection between virtuous behavior on earth and a happy hereafter in the Osirian field which had to be doubly assured by all kinds of magical devices. It is true that there was in theory a court of divine judges set up in the "West"—Amente, which became in Christian Coptic the ordinary word for "hell" (!). It is also true that the famous Negative Confession, attested from about 1500 B.C. on, may be compared in some ways to the so-called apodictic law of Moses. In practice, however, we may be sure that a great many deceased persons depended more on spending money for magical protection than on past good behavior to get into the happy land of Osiris.

In Palestine and Syria the Northwestern Semites also had a great many practices in common with their non-Semitic neighbors of the eastern Mediterranean basin which were abhorrent to early Israelite monotheism. In north Arabia and Palestine in those days the dead were usually buried inside a pile of stones over a stone base surrounded by more carefully prepared stones. At the turquoise mines of Sinai dead miners were buried in a small cavity under the cairn. Sometimes a mortuary stele was erected over the cairn. In Palestine the word for "cairn," *bamah* (usually rendered "high place"), was often also applied to a mortuary stele, with or without an inscription. The famous Mesha Stone which contains an autobiographical sketch of King Mesha's activities as king of Moab in the ninth century B.C. is called explicitly a *bamah*, and in the Greek Bible the word is regularly translated as "stele." One type of sanctuary is called the *beth-bamoth*, or "house of steles." A number of such mortuary chapels have been found in explorations or excavations at such sites as Ader and Bab-edh-Dhra^c in Moab, and in Gezer, Hazor, Byblos, and elsewhere. In the Mari texts such a mortuary chapel is called *bit kimti*, "house of the family." This term for a family is also found in later Hittite and Assyrian cuneiform texts. We now know, thanks to the discoveries at Ugarit and Byblos in Syria, that deceased kings of those cities between about 1500 and 900 B.C. were believed to become gods after their death. In Hittite tablets "to become a god," said of a king, means simply "to die." We also have tablets published within the past few years which list the ancestors of the kings of the First Dynasty of Babylon and the contemporary Assyrian kings as honored "shades" (royal ghosts) who participated in the funeral ceremonies after the death of King Ammisaduqa of Babylon in the 16th century B.C. It is interesting to note that in a recently published Etruscan funerary inscription of a king of Caere (modern Cerveteri) north of Rome about 500 B.C. the raising of the king to the rank of divinity after his death is mentioned, and the same word *bmt* appears as a burial monument of some sort. Memorials of important heads of state or tribal leaders received special veneration, much like popular saints or Moslem *weli*s, revered by the masses.

It is thus increasingly clear that the Northwestern Semites also paid far too much attention to the dead and that local cults sprang up around cemeteries of the more important people. There were Northwest-Semitic divinities who were originally human beings. Among the best-known today are Itur-Mer, the tutelary god of the Mari Dynasty in the 18th century B.C., and the later Ikrub-Adad, to say nothing of North-Arabic heroes.

The cult of semi-divine heroes was widespread over the eastern Mediterranean basin and is particularly well known from Greek lands where there were whole armies of heroes who received divine honors after their death. They are generally grouped with demigods in Greek tradition. It is only reasonable, therefore, to suppose that Moses who took such pains to turn early Israel away from pagan practices would make a special effort to prevent his own grave from becoming a source of a paganizing hero-cult. All that was necessary was to persuade some of his closest followers to swear a solemn oath to keep the place of his burial secret. The tradition in Deut. 34:6 thus makes extremely good sense, because Moses' sepulcher might otherwise have become a famous goal of pilgrims and a possible invitation to idolatrous cult. So even in death Moses remained true to his faith.

We have seen that ancestor worship played a much greater role in the pagan religion of the Semitic neighbors of Israel than recent scholarship has believed. In other words, some earlier scholars, though almost completely without the material we now possess, were essentially correct in emphasizing the mortuary aspects of early Semitic religion. This, of course, might lead—and did lead in the famous case of the calling up of Samuel's ghost by the female medium of Endor—to practices closely resembling modern spiritism.

Because of the fundamental difference between orthodox Israelite faith and the notions of the pagans, it is difficult to say categorically just what the prevailing beliefs of the Israelite masses were. In Israelite graves there is certainly a great deal less grave furniture than is found in corresponding pagan tombs in the vicinity; a good illustration comes from recent Israeli excavations at Achzib north of Acre where we have a striking difference between graves of late Monarchic and Persian date in an Israelite cemetery and roughly contemporary tombs in a neighboring Canaanite cemetery. Both Israelites and pagans certainly believed in the immortality of the spirit, and we have allusions to the Rephaim (probably "judges") of Sheol (including some recently deceased personages in the spirit-world) as well as the ordinary rank and file of the deceased *oboth*. The words used are substantially the same as we find in Ugaritic inscriptions and even more ancient Northwest-Semitic sources for "spirits of the dead." Just as the Atrahasis epic (quoted in Part I above) emphasizes repeatedly, the divinely given life of man continues to exist in spirit-form to the end of time. There is no reason whatsoever to doubt that this Patriarchal belief was still dominant in early Israel. At the same time there were two opposing tendencies. The 5th century (?) writer Ecclesiastes, no doubt in common with other intellectuals—Jewish and pagan—of his time, was skeptical about any survival of the spirit after death. On the other hand, in passages as early as the Psalter and Job, dating probably from before the Exile, we find clear belief in a resurrection of the buried corpse at some more or less indefinite time, perhaps carrying on Egyptian and some early Phoenician and Israelite ideas of resurrection. So we are not forced to suppose that the Mosaic reaction against the abuse of mortuary cults was the only trend in Israel. The present writer holds that it was not exclusive, though undoubtedly orthodox in Israelite times, saving Israel from many spiritual missteps along the way. Both Jews and Christians are still divided within their own ranks by eschatological beliefs which vary in both along similar lines.

Suggestions for Further Reading

The footnotes of Chap. 4 of Albright, *Yahweh and the Gods of Canaan* hold much of the documentation for the second part of this article. In addition see his more recent article, "Midianite Donkey Caravaneers," in H.T. Frank and W. L Reed, eds., *Translating and Understanding the Old Testament* (1970). For recent general surveys of the period, see the appropriate sections of John Bright, *A History of Israel* (second ed., 1972) and Roland de Vaux, *Histoire Ancienne d'Israel des Origines à l'Installation en Canaan* (1971). Special studies of interest include Dewey M. Beegle, *Moses: The Servant of Yahweh* (1972); Frank M. Cross, *Canaanite Myth and Hebrew Epic* (1973); Cross, "The Origin and Early Evolution of the Alphabet," *Eretz-Israel*, 8 (1967), 8*-24*; Delbert R. Hillers, *Covenant: The History of a Biblical Idea* (1969); Herbert B. Huffmon, "Prophecy in the Mari Letters," *BA* 31 (1968), 101-21; and D. J. McCarthy, *Old Testament Covenant: A Survey of Current Opinions* (1972).

Notes

[1] Apparently in a personal communication; see W. F. Albright, *Yahweh and the Gods of Canaan* (1968), p. 265c.—Eds.

[2] O. Eissfeldt, *Das Lied Moses Deuteronomium 32, 1-43 und das Lehrgedicht Asaphs Psalm 78 samt einer Analyse der Umgebung des Mose-Liedes* (1958).

[3] *The Proto-Sinaitic Inscriptions and their Decipherment* ("Harvard Theological Studies," Vol. 22; 1966).

[4] *Journal of Biblical Literature* 87 (1968), 383-93.

[5] *Palestine Exploration Quarterly* 101 (1969), 57-59.

[6] Frank M. Cross, *BASOR* 134 (1954), 22.

[7] W. F. Albright, *Yahweh and the Gods of Canaan* (1968), p. 159.

[8] *BA* 10 (1947), 2-6.

[9] *BA* 17 (1954), 26-46; 50-76.

4

WHAT ARCHAEOLOGY CAN AND CANNOT DO

G. ERNEST WRIGHT

For a majority in the Biblical world Albright's work has established the basic chronology for the events related in Joshua (a 13th century date of the conquest) and the historical support for the background of the narrative. Yet a carefully defined statement of what archaeology is and is not, does and does not, has been hard to articulate. Such a statement must follow the experiments of reconstruction, and first attempts may need future modification when the polemical period which is always created when general assumptions are badly shaken, is past.[1]

While the term "archaeology" was first used by classical authors simply to mean "ancient history," its revival in modern times has meant a narrowing of its meaning to the ruins of past civilizations and cultures, especially their excavation. For Albright and his students archaeology has included both epigraphic and non-epigraphic discoveries, even though the investigation of the two must develop each its own set of disciplines. Yet in the antiquarian field generally, philologists and archaeologists are usually separate, the former studying documents and the latter the methodologies of conducting an excavation and the study and presentation of what is found. The field has suffered from too much compartmentalization at this point.

Furthermore, archaeologists themselves have suffered from too great a separation from one another in their various fields, and usually too great a separation from humanistic disciplines on the one hand and from the natural sciences on the other. Anthropological archaeology, for example, starting from its primary point of reference, primitive man, has developed methodology and cooperation with natural sciences more quickly than other fields, because the very nature of most of the deposits dealt with required them to do so in order to extract a maximum of information from a minimum of deposit. On the other hand, the humanistic aspects of the subject have often been short-changed and the results impoverished by over-zealous attempts to remain non-historical and "scientific" when actually they are simply trying to reconstruct all they can about human beings for whom "science" has only a partial application.

Classical and most of early Near Eastern archaeology has been dominated by a museum mentality which requires objects for display to a contributing public primarily interested in art and art history. Archaeologists from this background have been slowest of all to develop an interest in ever more precision and control in methodology. They have to their glory maintained their full humanistic interest, but separation from the natural sciences with exceptions has been most notable in the information derived from the queries put to their material.

Excavation of the great Near Eastern tells has brought such wealth of architecture and objects that there seemed no need to ask further questions than those of the historian regarding chronology, interconnections and typological history.

The conceptual framework and methodology of excavation has been most highly developed and refined in the historical period by a few exceptional persons whose primary training has been in other countries, but who for one reason or another began excavations in Palestine: Petrie and Kenyon from England, Reisner and Albright from the United States. That small corridor between continents has few natural resources, and thus was and is very poor as compared with the centers of world power in antiquity. To gain any positive result from work in the country requires one's turning his attention from an expectation of rich stores of anything, and certainly not great palaces and a wealth of inscriptions, the latter forming the primary guide to where in time one is located while digging. Pottery chronology and the stratigraphy of the deposits of earth have to be the primary concentration. It was Petrie who in 1890 left Egypt for a short period of work at Tell el-Ḥesī in the southern coastal plain. There he proved that ceramics could be a primary chronological tool by demonstrating the differences in pottery between levels cut into the steep cliff of the tell eroded by a winter stream. It was Reisner who left Egypt in 1909 and 1910 for two seasons of work at Samaria and encountered an intricate jumble on the tell which required an entirely different strategy from anything he had used in Egypt.

It was Albright, beginning in 1920, who developed the pottery tool into an instrument of some precision by taking it out of the mists of oral tradition, articulated its use in writing, and provided a critical assessment of the whole discipline in the light of his knowledge of the entire Near East. Following his work one could begin to write archaeological histories of the country—something impossible before the discipline had been subjected to his critical work and his ceramic sequences.

Reisner's methodological principles were generally not followed, except for the new care with which recording and find spots were handled and the ideal evolved of being able to reproduce on paper a tell's stratigraphy in which the exact location of all artifacts could be spotted. It was with Kenyon's re-introduction of Reisner's principles independently, as they had been developed in the archaeology of England, that the new revolution in precision and field control was now put in practice for all to see in East Mediterranean archaeology. The key to this control lay in digging and distinguishing the soil layers as a geologist would do, rather than focusing primarily on building or wall sequences, following the lead of the chief interests of the expedition's architect.

Palestine west of the Jordan is the most intensively dug and explored area of its size in the world. Its very poverty has been a major factor in the development of precision in archaeological field work to a level seldom reached in the historical periods anywhere else in the classical and Near Eastern worlds. Consequently, it cannot be overstressed that the proper use of archaeology as a "scientific" tool in Biblical study was impossible before the work of Albright, while the period of the 1960s is the time of a revolution in controlled archaeology, following the period 1952-1958 of the Kenyon expedition to Jericho.[2]

Even these new methodologies fail to extract a maximum of information from the occupational debris of antiquity. Beginning in Palestine in 1970, certain American explorations were able to staff their expeditions with a more or less full complement of natural scientists. Such cross-disciplinary approaches were a "first" in the Near East's historical period. They were modeled after the great pioneering prehistoric enterprises of Robert J. Braidwood in the 1950s, which have refocused our knowledge of human prehistory with regard to what happened before, during, and after *the Neolithic revolution* when the first villages were established in the Near East. Hence it can be predicted that the 1970s will see far more controlled information made available to the Biblical student than the archaeologist has hitherto been able to provide.

With regard to Biblical events, however, it cannot be overstressed that archaeological data are mute. Fragmentary ruins, preserving only a tiny fraction of the full picture of ancient life, cannot speak without someone asking questions of them. And the kind of questions asked are part and parcel of the answers "heard" because of predispositions on the part of the questioner. Archaeology can *prove* very little about anything without minds stored with a wide-ranging variety of information which carefully begin to ask questions of the mute remains in order to discover what they mean. It is all too easy for lack of information and imagination to gain less than the remains can supply, or for fertile imaginations to suppose that the ancient trash heaps tell us more than a more controlled mind can believe they do. It is small wonder, then, that disagreement and debate arise. A destruction layer in the ruins does not tell us the identity of the people involved. Indeed, we know that certain black soot and charcoal layers do not necessarily mean destruction. An accidental fire in one part of the town or city, certain industrial pursuits, or even an earthquake may be the answer.

Yet the mute nature of the remains does not mean that archaeology is useless. It simply means that ancient cultural and political horizons and sequences can only be reconstructed by hypothesis from every kind of critically sifted evidence available. At some points more data are available than at others. Hence the historical reconstructions have only varying degrees of probability. Yet in antiquity it is most important to recall that models and hypotheses are the primary means by which reconstruction is possible after the basic critical work is done. And, furthermore, it takes a great deal of humility to say frankly what the physical sciences have had also to say; predisposition of minds at any one period frame the type of questions asked of the material and become a part of the "answers" we suppose we have obtained from our investigations. Final *proof* of anything ancient must be confined to such questions as how pottery was made, what rock was used, what food and fauna were present, etc. Certainly that proof does not extend to the validity of the religious claims the Bible would place upon us, and we must remember that the Bible is not a mine for scientifically grounded certainties about anything. It is instead a literature that places before us one of history's major religious options.

What archaeology can do for Biblical study is to provide a physical context in time and place which was the environment of the people who produced the Bible or are mentioned in it. Inscriptional evidence is of exceptional importance for Biblical backgrounds and even for occasional mention of Biblical people and places. For the rest, archaeology provides evidence to be critically sifted. It then is used along with other critically assessed data, where it exists, in order to form *hypotheses* about the how, why, what and when of cultural, socio-political and economic affairs in thirteenth century Palestine, for example. These hypotheses will stand or be altered as new information makes change necessary. Final and absolutely proven answers are impossible to provide. One generation's questions may not be another's, and in every case the questions asked are integral to the answers. Thus one generation's research differs from another's.

Furthermore, Martin Noth's predisposition, for example, has led him to a negative view of the historical background of the confessional events surveyed in the Books of Exodus and Joshua, along with many of his predecessors and contemporaries. To this writer, such a negative assessment, deriving from the last century's criticism, is not only a defensible, but an indispensible tool in historical *methodology*. But when the tool becomes the dominant item of the conclusion, it then is most often a bias or predisposition of the author. There is no reason whatever that the opposite predisposition should not be held, namely one toward a positive view of the evidence, even though the actual course of events may have been far more complex than tradition has remembered. Whether optimism or pessimism is the predisposition, the fact is that in Exodus and Joshua we have dominant and central confessional and literary themes presented both in the book and in confessional liturgical statements. This requires explanation. A necessity is upon us to explain their presence in the earliest literature (e.g., Exod. 15) as well as in the latest. Something formative to Israel's worldview happened in her earliest historical experience. Can a hypothesis be suggested which explains without claiming too much or too little? By definition such a hypothesis is devised to explain most completely what we *now* know, *not* what it may be necessary or possible for another generation to say.

The situation with regard to Joshua, ranging from extreme negative assessment to positive, has numerous parallels in other fields where scholars try to assess literary tradition, philological analysis, tradition-history, form, language, text, archaeology and historical background—and then try to come up with a story of what *really* happened! Faulty analysis or overemphasis at the wrong place can throw the resulting hypothesis "out of gear" entirely. Yet one must forge ahead, under the critical light of his peers, in the knowledge that the work has to be as carefully done in this time as possible, and then restudied a generation later, if not sooner!

Father Roland de Vaux has reviewed the evidence for the Trojan War and that for the Phoenician colonization of the Mediterranean, and finds precisely the same problems being struggled with in the same way, with the same radically different conclusions.[3]

With regard to the Phoenicians ancient authors assert that Cadiz and Utica, for example, were founded as early as 1100 B.C., while Carthage was founded in 814 B.C. and became the Phoenician power of the west *par excellence* for centuries. Yet Rhys Carpenter in 1958, basing his results on purely archaeological evidence, disregards the literary tradition completely and says the cities in question were not founded much before *ca.* 700 B.C., and only gradually during the next two centuries spread to Sicily, Sardinia, Cadiz, Spain and the Balearic islands. Now with 10th and 9th century inscriptions existing on Cyprus and Spain, which Carpenter had no training to handle critically, and 8th century specimens in Sicily, Sardinia, and Malta, the skeptics can only defend themselves by challenging the archaeologist's methods, especially the discipline of paleography, etc. Nevertheless, the basic point has been made by the archaeologists in general agreement with the ancient authors: Phoenician colonization preceded the arrival of the Greeks.

What can be said about the tradition made immortal by Homer in the *Iliad* and the *Odyssey*? Schliemann evidently found the ruined tell of Troy, but then came the debate as to which stratum was destroyed and by what agency at the site. Carl Blegen, the last excavator, accepts the city's identification, and claims the city destroyed in Homer's traditions must be identified with Stratum VIIa, in which Mycenean pottery still occurs in abundance. Thus Homer's story of the expedition against Troy must have a historical basis. Archaeology for Blegen thus "proves" that there must have been some kind of coalition of Achaeans or Myceneans who fought Troy and its allies and defeated them.

Yet a more "judicial" answer has been that Troy VIIa was destroyed by human violence, but the excavations have provided not one scrap of evidence of a Greek coalition or any identification whatever to answer the question of "Who did it?" Perhaps it was destroyed by the Sea Peoples. The best procedure of all, in this viewpoint, is to dissociate the whole archaeological discovery from myth and poetry, and even from the legend of Troy itself.

Yet in both instances still other scholars raise basic questions with regard to both viewpoints as to whether the two extremes are really in methodological tune with the use of archaeology as "proof" or as evidence. The skeptic always has the advantage because archaeology speaks only in response to our questions and one can call any tradition not provable. Thus since no proof can be attained anywhere, one extreme simply asks that archaeological data be presented and the attempt to prove anything in literary tradition cease forthwith.

Both sides of the controversy use the term "proof" in ways inadmissible, even absurd, with regard to any past cultural, political, socio-economic history.

Whether it is Trojan history, Phoenician history, or what history remains in the book of Joshua, we must begin with the fact that we have *actual texts*. These must be interpreted by all the means of literary analysis available to us. Then we must reconstruct the archaeological and ecological context as best we can both in the given area and in the widest possible context. Only then can we examine the question as to whether the one illumines the other, or whether a reasonable hypothesis can be reconstructed which best explains what we know at this time. The dictum of de

Vaux is axiomatic: "Archaeology does not confirm the text, which is what it is, it can only confirm the interpretation which we give it."[4] Conversely, archaeology, dealing with the wreckage of antiquity, proves nothing in itself. It must be analyzed in a variety of ways, and then with all other data available, not in a pure vacuum mistakenly called by some "science." Its meaning in the overall picture of a cultural continuum is expressed by interpretation. Here again, it is the interpretation that is usable, and that is the product of a human brain with the use of the tools available to it. A person is not more infallible than his sources and predecessors. Instead, the brain belongs to a limited person, living and working in a given time and space. Ambiguity and relativity enter every sphere of human activity. Some minds rise above others as masters of their peers, but the solid *proofs*, which so many assume possible at the end of either scientific or historical work, cannot be attained by finite beings. We are historical organisms by intrinsic nature, and ambiguity is always a central component of history, whether of the humanities, of social science, or of natural science.

Notes

[1] For outstanding attempts at such statement, see especially Roland de Vaux, O.P., "On Right and Wrong Uses of Archaeology," *Near Eastern Archaeology in the Twentieth Century*, pp. 64-80. For a treatment of the same subject from the standpoint of a classicist, see M. I. Finley, "Archaeology and History," *Daedalus* (Winter, 1971), pp. 168-186.

[2] Cf. Kenyon, *Beginning in Archaeology* (1952); *Digging up Jericho* (1957); and G. Ernest Wright, "Archaeological Method in Palestine—An American Interpretation," *Eretz Israel* IX (1969), pp. 120-133.

[3] See R. de Vaux, *loc. cit.* (n. 1).

[4] R. de Vaux, *op. cit.*, p. 78.

5

THE "NEW" ARCHAEOLOGY

G. ERNEST WRIGHT

Wherever one looks today, there seems to be a searching for foundations, for identification, for new definition of what we are, no matter the cultural subsystems to which we belong. The various "worlds" of academia are nearly all cluttered with chaotic discussion, no matter whether they be the philosophy of science, scientific method, the borderline half-sciences which call themselves "social science," or the humanities. To the physical scientists there seems to be nothing more humorous than those practitioners of the social sciences who are expending so much energy in trying to impart to their disciplines the same rigorous methodology as characterize the hard sciences, to whom they look up with the only respect they will accord to anyone. Not being nuclear physicists or chemists or the world's greatest experts on DNA or on the behavior of an obscure mollusk on Pango Pango, a sizable number of social scientists throughout the better part of this century, have been trying hard to gain the respect of the hard scientists, though with indifferent results. The discipline of psychology turned itself into a biology of the nervous system, only to discover that as practitioners of that "science" they lost out to medicine and chemotherapy, on the one hand, and to the psychotherapists, the descendants of Freud and Jung, on the other. Physical anthropology has succeeded in becoming closely related to medical osteology, but the rest of anthropology and sociology, no matter how hard they try, remain classified in the minds of the hard scientists as little more than pseudosciences.

Consequently, according to my physician, who ministers his medical art to a large number of the Harvard faculty, an extraordinary phenomenon is occurring. The majority of the faculty in the social sciences, as well as in the humanities is undergoing constant treatment for nervous and cardiovascular diseases, though their colleagues in the natural sciences have far less of such trouble! What ails the humanists who have no desire to be scientists? It appears that, like the social scientists, they maintain their century-old "rigamarole," but have lost all their certainties as to what they are doing and for what reason. And to complicate the picture, even the sciences are not as popular among students as they once were. Enrollments have declined to the point where the Harvard deans two years ago felt compelled to put out a lengthy document as to why every student should have some exposure to science.

Thus we come to archaeology! Where does it fall in the academic hierarchy? Is it a hard science, a social science, or a humanistic discipline? Here chaos is king! Archaeologists ally themselves with each of these three groups, and there are even some who wish to straddle the fence as "humanistic scientists"—which is probably where I belong. Yet, for myself, I remain highly amused by the whole business and refuse to take myself so seriously as to put my whole heart and soul into the inner games and quarrels of academia, or to take them very seriously. I think it vastly more important to see myself as simply an ordinary, very ordinary, human being, always trying to learn what it means to be a human being among my students and colleagues. The radically serious side of academic game-playing is not for me! It's just not worth it. All too soon I'll be dead and gone, and while some people may miss me as a human being, their number will be few in academia where human and humorous self-criticism is a rare commodity indeed, and one's death is not mourned, only perhaps noted, as at Harvard by a black bordered card sent around by the President.

I

I would now like to turn to a bit of autobiography as an archaeologist. My field experience and home-based training were received from the late William Foxwell Albright of Johns Hopkins University, who really created Palestinian archaeology as an objective discipline set solidly within the framework of the whole Eastern Mediterranean archaeological picture. Thus it has come about that the Egyptian and Mesopotamian fixed chronologies, with help from C-14 determinations in the early periods, are closely tied to Palestinian archaeological strata and typology of artifacts from the Neolithic through the Byzantine periods. By now, the archaeological chronology of that small area is more closely controlled for a longer period than is the case for any other country of the world. Two expeditions, one in Israel and one in Jordan, under the sponsorship of the American Schools of Oriental Research, are now pushing that range further, from the Byzantine era down through the Middle Ages. My own specialty, under Albright's initial inspiration, has been the study of the evolutionary processes of artifacts, especially ceramics, and my initial concentration was upon prehistory.

During 1940 and 1941, it was my privilege to have been a contributing member of the Henri Frankfort prehistoric seminar in the archaeology of the Near East and the Aegean at the Oriental Institute, University of Chicago.

I emerged from that seminar with certain fixed convictions. Two especially I should like to emphasize. First was the feeling that far too much money was being spent for far too little information gained from digging. There simply had to be a revolution in digging method in the field so that we could at least gain some precision and control over the data extracted from the ground. When, for example, the Hallstatt and the Beaker Cultures of the Danube and Central Europe could be tied into the Aegean and thus to the Near East only by the most fuzzy of educated guesses, something was surely rotten in Denmark. When a very expensive German expedition "dug" at practically every surviving synagogue of importance in Galilee, but still could not date them or relate them to any ecological system, then one was led to despair over a so-called archaeology that was little more than a treasure hunt. When a technologist tried to use Hallstatt as the synchronic clue to the introduction of iron into common use in the Near East within the pages of the *American Journal of Archaeology*, despite the fact that the only definite stratigraphy for control was in Palestine, I was ready for complete despair over the whole so-called discipline, which was anything but a serious academic enterprise.

The first member of our Frankfort seminar group to take the field after World War II was Robert J. Braidwood of the University of Chicago. His area-wide expeditions in Iraqi Kurdistan, followed by those in the hilly flanks on the Iranian side of the Iraqi border, and currently on the Turkish southeastern frontier zone, had and have one major objective: a focus on the Neolithic revolution, that phenomenon which James Henry Breasted some thirty years earlier at the foundation of the Oriental Institute had called the transition from a food-gathering to a food-producing economy, the revolution that made possible within some 3,000 years or so the development of the city and the rapid urbanization of human culture.

With this as his central aim, Braidwood simply could not narrow his sights to those that had been traditional among field archaeologists, even those whom Breasted had trained in the Oriental Institute. Braidwood's avowed aim was to recreate the "New Past," but his professional archaeologists were few in number and it was difficult to achieve his purpose. What made his expeditions a landmark in modern archaeological method and scope was his academic acumen, his vision that a human cultural epoch could never properly be reconstructed without involving virtually all of the chief disciplines which compose the modern university. Being himself *the* anthropologist of the Oriental Institute's community of scholars, he went outside that community to the natural scientists, primarily geology, paleobiology, both faunal and floral, ceramic technology which involves both geology and chemistry, in addition to specialists in the various dating mechanisms. Furthermore, there was a wide regional rather than a specific site orientation of limited regional perspective, into which specific sites fit together as a unit of cultural interinvolvement.

Behind Braidwood's initial objectives was a theorem, not proved or provable, but which spurred him on to seek explanations which he could use to turn the theorem from a hypothesis into a "natural law." The theorem was that the Neolithic revolution involved the domestication of animals and the growing and harvesting of food that would feed both man and his dependents, human and animal. Once this had been achieved, village conglomerates could come into being, ever larger human groupings with the development of increasingly complex social structures, until about 3000 B.C. the city and urbanization could emerge. All of this was carefully distinguished from the smaller clan groupings which could subsist under a hunting economy. Braidwood logically reasoned that the dramatic shift should have occurred on the hilly flanks of the Fertile Crescent where both the animals and cereals, later to be domesticated, grew in their wild state, so that just "one small step for mankind" need be taken in the domestication of what already was present in the environment, and could be easily adapted.

Some two decades later it must be said that Braidwood's theorem, though to some already law, has not been proven. Like all mutations in the evolutionary process, the initial stages are most difficult and often impossible to discover. If he is correct, all we can say is that the revolution moved so quickly to oases and river valleys that only the smallest hints of origin in the hilly flanks remain.

Nevertheless, Braidwood's vision has transformed the field of anthropology for a large number of anthropologists. Regardless of what is happening in New World and European archaeology, anthropologists in the Near East have suddenly become historians of Pleistocene Man, down through the Neolithic Revolution to the borders of urbanism and civilization. And I myself, with specialization beginning with the Neolithic and carrying through the first great epoch of man's civilization, the Pax Romana, have found myself in constant conversation with anthropologists. Not that they welcome it, least of all with Palestinologists, but because of the simple necessity of overlapping interests and controls.

I think that Braidwood would be the first to express, as he has to me, certain doubts about whether he would use again some of the excavation methods that he initially employed at Jarmo in Iraq. Today, when one refers to digging methodology, one generally finds the references to Sir Mortimer Wheeler's *Archaeology from the Earth*, or perhaps to his greatest pupil in method, Kathleen Kenyon and to her *Beginning in Archaeology*. After all, the interest in archaeology within the modern history of the British Isles has been intense and all British archaeological students have the possibility of field training in a discipline that has become, in England, very sophisticated.

Yet there are structural difficulties which I see in the Institute of Archaeology of the University of London, and in the publication of Kenyon's fieldwork in Palestine. They pose insuperable problems for me, so that I cannot recommend them to my graduate students as models to follow, nor to the new excavation projects constantly under formation with the encouragement of, and financial and staffing advice given by the American Schools of Oriental Research.

One of these difficulties is the fact that in London the Institute of Archaeology stands alone, archaeology as a discipline having little connection with other disciplines of the University. Thus a student can be trained there without knowing anything about the social sciences or the historical disciplines. A person with that background, when asked to write for the *Cambridge Ancient History*, for example, simply produces a very inferior and traditional set of archaeological facts, while the larger explanations and generalizations based upon those facts are glaringly deficient because of the extreme limitations placed on curiosity and overall vision of the discipline.

A second problem is the failure to develop a specialized, highly trained staff which will stay with a project through its publication. Few, if any, social or natural scientists work constantly with a British dig; anything accomplished by them is done usually after the project is completed. The result tends to become largely a one-man or woman show. Typically, five-meter-square plots are spread over the site, the square supervisors often without adequate previous training, being on their own most of the time, knowing little of what is going on in other squares, while the Director visits once or twice a day. What is finally published tends to be mainly what can be absorbed by one mind, that of the Director. Today, with the necessity of interdisciplinary work, an integrated team approach is no longer a simple luxury; it is a requirement of responsible expeditions.

The greatest genius in archaeological methodology and the pioneer, before the British, was the American George Andrew Reisner. The methodology he developed and described in Egyptian archaeology between 1899 and 1942, as Director of the Harvard-Boston Museum of Fine Arts Expedition, came to a climax in his excavation of the tomb of the Fourth Dynasty Queen Hetep-Heres. For tell-archaeology, the most succinct and clear methodology, based upon the geological model of layer removal, with analysis of the factors which caused layer disturbance, is articulated in the introduction to Vol. I of Reisner's *Harvard Excavations of Samaria*. These factors must be understood, and any disturbances removed, before layer excavation can continue. Every object and every piece of pottery must be labeled with the locus number within the layer. And no object should ever be separated from the number of the pottery basket or bucket being filled from the same locus where the object is discovered. This ensures that it will never be separated from the context which dates it. And it cannot be emphasized sufficiently that a good excavator is never one to whom the process comes naturally. It can only be learned by instruction and experience. A good supervisor for one five-meter square, for example, needs at least two, better three, seasons of experience before she or he takes over the full direction of the digging in addition to the daily diary, top plans, balk cutting and drawing, etc. A field supervisor over a given digging sector, with oversight of a given number of area supervisors, may or may not need a longer training period, depending entirely upon aptitude. There is simply no short-cut for such rigorous method. The disgrace of archaeology is still the number of people who are simply turned loose with no training at all. There is only one result; there can be only one result: Far more evidence is forever lost than is recovered.

Much more needs to be said about the methodology of an expedition in the field. Theorize all one wants, tightly controlled field method in extracting data from the ground is worth more than all the pre-dig or post-dig theorizing put together. What can be done with information after it has been extracted from the ground depends entirely upon how it was extracted and how dependable the context which the "dirt" archaeologist has preserved for it. The key to everything archaeological is the dirt work. Without sound control at this point, the theorists to whom we now turn, who aspire to far too exalted a station to say anything about such trivial subjects as dirt methodology, are simply blowing hot air.

II

Current excavators, except the oldtimers, have what they consider to be possession of the "new" archaeology. At the extreme left wing are those "new" archaeologists who have been influenced

by the writings of Lewis R. Binford, and, in Great Britain, of Dr. D.
L. Clark. Take this Binford dictum, for instance:

> We assume that the past is knowable; that with enough
> methodological ingenuity, propositions about the past are testable;
> and that there are valid scientific criteria for judging the probability
> of a statement about the past. . . .[1]

Note the use here of "testable propositions" and "valid
scientific criteria" for testing statements about the past, all possible
if we have enough "ingenuity." That these words mean that
archaeology should be a pure science using only "scientific
criteria" is made clear by the following Binford quotation:

> Explanation begins for the archaeologist when observations
> made on the archaeological record are linked through laws of
> cultural or behavioral functioning to past conditions or events.
> Successful explanation and the understanding of process are
> synonymous, and both proceed dialectically—by the formulation of
> hypotheses (potential laws on the relationships between two or more
> variables) and the testing of their validity against empirical data.
> Hypotheses about cause and effect must be explicitly formulated
> and then tested.[2]

Three anthropologists who base themselves directly on
Binford's work but attempt to bring it to an even more precise
scientific point are Watson, LeBlanc, and Redman in their
Explanation in Archaeology: An Explicitly Scientific Approach
(1971). With all the enthusiastic missionary concern of youth to set
the whole discipline of archaeology and all their elders on the
straight and narrow course which leads to the Elysian fields of
perfection found only in purely scientific archaeology, they begin:

> One distinctive feature of scientific archaeology is a self-
> conscious concern with the formulation and testing of hypothetical
> general laws. General laws in archaeology that concern cultural
> processes can be used to describe, explain, and predict cultural
> differences and similarities represented in the archaeological record,
> and thus to further the ultimate goal of anthropology, which is the
> description, explanation, and prediction of cultural differences and
> similarities primarily in the present. . . . Emphasis on formulation

and testing of general laws means that archaeology is conceived as a formal scientific discipline with the same logical structure as all other scientific disciplines.[3]

Hence the first chapter of the book, on "The Logic of Science," is largely abstracted from two works of a philosopher of science, Carl G. Hempel. His writings, the authors say, are frequently referred to by scientifically oriented archaeologists and are their primary source. The crucial issues of knowing are as follows:

1. "Knowing of the World," which is an "empirically observable behavior of the entities which make up this real world." They are "orderly and can be predicted and explained when adequate observation, hypothesis formulation and hypothesis testing leading to the confirmation of general laws have been accomplished."

2. There is the matter of "truth." Absolute certainty is impossible. Yet "just what constitutes 'confirmation' and 'appropriate testing' must be mutually agreed upon within each particular scientific discipline . . . which we will not go into further here." Unfortunately the authors appear to forget this point as "inconvenient" during the remainder of the book.

3. There are Explanation and General Laws.

Explanation in the logic of science means "Subsumption of a phenomenon under a general law directly connecting observable characteristics. . . ." A scientist explains a particular event by subsuming its description under the appropriate confirmed general law, that is, by finding a general law that covers the particular event by describing the general circumstances, objects and behavior of which the particular case is an example.[4]

The book then goes on to the "explanatory frameworks of archaeology" which are Systems Theory and the Ecological Approach (pp. 59-107), and concludes in the third part with observations on how the logic of science can be incorporated into archaeological method (pp. 111-172).

One thing about the Binford group is very clear: They are not in conversation with natural scientists. Recently, I have spoken about the position here described to a number of these scientists and I have yet to find a single one who thinks the position is tenable. If they do not laugh, they mutter "no way," or "impossible," or "no understanding of what science is." Pure science deals with not more than one or two variables; and, they insist, whenever the human being and the human brain are concerned, there are so many variables that it is impossible to control them in such a way as to formulate a scientific law. No wonder that the literature of these so-called "anthropological scientific archaeologists" is so vague when one searches for illustrations of what these laws are. The nearest that Watson, LeBlanc, and Redman come to such an illustration is in a study of the Broken K Pueblo in Arizona. By a study of the distribution of artifacts in the different rooms, they conclude that one group is for males, one for females, and one for ceremonial occasions. To this innocent observer, that conclusion seems most odd, because males and females customarily spend a good deal of time together, else the race would not be renewed by youth. An important argument for the female rooms, which seem to have had few artifacts in them, is the presence of potters' instruments. How does one know that Broken K potters were all female? To be sure, they are today on Cyprus, though in the whole Islamic world they are male. One guesses that the reason for the assumption is that modern Pueblo women make the pots. But this is an argument by analogy, which is by no means proof. Because modern women make the pots, can it be assumed that the women of any given antiquity were also potters?

I talked recently to a mathematician about human beings and scientific laws. He said the law idea only made sense when the mass of all data about something could be translated into mathematical statistics. This would include insurance actuarial tables, the various number of telephone calls made in the U.S. at each hour of a given day, the use of water in large cities during TV breaks when a large and predictable number of toilets were flushed, etc. But such mass statistics ignore the individual entirely. The individual includes not only the single human being but each and every one of the artifacts he makes. I cannot conceive of any general law that governs a given set of artifacts. It has been my experience that each artifact has its own evolutionary process and that it is impossible to predict how or in what direction that process will go. Sequence dating will work with individual artifacts when one end of its evolving process is pinned down, as was the case with the "wavy" ledge handles Petrie placed in rough order in Egypt over 75 years ago. Vestigial examples occurred only in 1st Dynasty tombs at Sequence Date *ca.* 65-70. The best examples on foreign imported pots were artificially put at s.d. 40, and everything else was distributed in between. The difficulty into which Einar Gjerstad put all of us who work in the Eastern Mediterranean littoral was that his elaborate Cypriot pottery analysis was based chiefly on external decoration. The typology that he developed had a very large artificial element in it; and, since he did not believe that stratigraphy had anything to do with typological considerations, he could take groups apart with perfect ease with no synchronic or diachronic data to impede his dogmatic assignment of types.

Another problem which the scientific archaeologists have not faced is the view of man implicit in their work. B. F. Skinner, in his *Walden II*, and recently in his *Beyond Freedom and Dignity*, spells out in detail the complete social determination and the complete power of manipulation to which he believes man is subject. This has caused one reviewer to remark: "Professor Skinner knows nothing about people. His considerable knowledge is confined to rats, with which he has worked throughout his life, formulated his laws, and then transferred them to human beings. Unfortunately, this kind of argumentation from analogy has its obvious weak spots!"

Finally, the charge today made generally against all social sciences is that made, for example, by A. R. Louch in *Explanation and Human Action* (1966). He studies the social sciences in order to examine their claims about laws. He concludes that these laws have no basis in reality or else they are trite truisms. The philosophers of action during the last 20 years believe just as passionately as do Binford, *et al.*, about their so-called archaeological science, that the whole claim of the social sciences has been annihilated, that the laws of chemistry and physics, etc., cannot be transferred to human beings.

Here the humanists join forces with the natural scientists against such social scientists in archaeology and their pretensions to scientific knowledge about the human past. Furthermore, the extensive verbalization of abstract theories and the almost complete disinterest in the improvement of control in dirt

archaeology lead one to wonder whether the methodology is as
deficient in the dirt as it is in theoretical models of human
determinism.

III

What I have said so far is nothing particularly new to most
people, nor do I expect it to do anything but infuriate the
confessional advocates of the "new scientific" archaeology. I have
not left myself time for more than an outline of my own views on
the subject of archaeology. Perhaps I have spent too much time on
what the classicist M. I. Finley of Cambridge University has called
"the familiar polemic of the social scientist against history,"[5]
carried back into prehistory, though the understanding presented
of history and of historical method shows at least as poor training
in that subject as in the humanities generally. Try as they may, by
whatever circumlocutions, the anthropologists cannot get away
from cultural, social, and political history—at least not after the
work of V. Gordon Childe and Robert J. Braidwood. In the Near
East, for example, anthropology is accepting responsibility for
cultural history in pre- and proto-history before writing, literature,
and civilization begin.

So much for the extreme left wing of modern archeology. At
the extreme right wing I would place much of classical Graeco-
Roman archaeology together with an embarrassing number of large
excavations in the Near East, especially of French, Italian, or
Japanese origin. Such a generalization is by no means fair to many
individuals who are exceptions. Yet classical archaeology was
begun, and until this day is nourished far too much, by wealthy
patrons of the fine arts. Objects and important public buildings
and monuments have been the chief interest. Thus the development
of field method has not been thought necessary. Objects, artifacts,
and inscriptions will provide the chronological data—or so it is
assumed. Note the marvelous analysis of 6th-5th century Greek
vase painting as primarily an art form. But can one condone the
failure of the classical archaeologist to develop a tight ceramic
chronology in other periods when most digs throw away the
common wares and look only at those which are painted?

The Near East, with its riches of vast tells in the historical era, furnishes another disgraceful example which is carried right into our own day. Unfortunately, some excavators of famous sites in Lebanon, Syria, and Cyprus, as well as farther east in Iran, can hardly be considered as more than troglodytes, or as australopithecines who have never made it into the modern world. Jean Perrot, in five years at Susa, has accomplished more for our understanding of the cultural history of the site than a half-century of his predecessors. Glorified treasure-hunting is a shocking term to have to apply to major modern expeditions, but only the new generation of young people is beginning to change that image.

As for me, I would place myself and my students in the middle, with a bias more toward the sciences than toward fine arts. The reason for the bias is that fine arts has yet to develop a discipline with sufficient precision to deal with artistic cultural meaning and process. However, my students can be divided into two groups. First come those who too long hold on to chronology, historical cross-references, and stratigraphy as the central and almost sole aims of excavation. That they still remain in that category is on the one hand, my fault because I failed to clarify my own ideals and to recommend more involvement with fine arts, and on the other, their reaction to the variety of personal infighting now typical of the field of anthropology.

The second group of my students are those who are greatly influenced by, a few even converted to, the "new science" of anthropological archaeology. Anyone who has read their descriptions of aims and procedures in the yearly proposals of the Idalion, Cyprus Expedition will immediately recognize the jargon. Yet that is agreeable to me, because we must explore these frontiers to their maximum.

Idalion, Cyprus is my most ambitious undertaking in archaeology. It is completely interdisciplinary. I like variety of background and training within the staff so that no one becomes a "yes-man"; and, through the interchange of people from a variety of backgrounds, no one will become fixed on too narrow a base.

For myself I remain unabashedly a humanist. I was trained in the humanities, and only humanists in the true sense can in the end make any sense out of the seeming chaos of human cultural systems, synchronically or diachronically. I believe archaeology is far too restricted when treated as a discipline in and of itself, whether by those who presume to be pure scientists, or by those who belong to other wings of anthropology or fine arts. In my opinion, archaeology must use all of the science that it can, but in the final analysis it is dealing with human beings, and therefore it can never be anything other than one among the several branches of cultural and humanistic history.

Notes

[1] Lewis R. Binford in Sally R. and Lewis R. Binford, eds., *New Perspectives in Archaeology* (1968), p. 26.

[2] Lewis R. Binford, *Southwestern Journal of Anthropology* 24 (1968), 270.

[3] P. J. Watson, S. A. LeBlanc, and C. L. Redman, *Explanation in Archaeology: An Explicitly Scientific Approach* (1971), p. 3.

[4] *Ibid.*, pp. 4-5.

[5] *Daedalus* 100 (1971), 172.

Part II

ARCHAEOLOGY AND
THE COMMON LIFE

6

SECONDARY BURIALS IN PALESTINE

ERIC M. MEYERS

One of the most prevalent and yet least understood of ancient Palestinian burial customs is that of ossilegium, or secondary burial. Such a practice is characterized by the collection of skeletonized remains at some point after the flesh had wasted away and by their deposition in a new place of repose. This type of burial contrasts with the more familiar primary inhumation which transpires shortly after death and remains undisturbed.

By and large the frequency with which secondary burials appear in the long history of Palestinian tombs has been overlooked. Perhaps this oversight derives from the traditional view which held such a practice alien to the spirit of Semitic peoples, for whom disturbing the repose of the dead was thought to be so repugnant. Such an attitude is reflected in the biblical statement of Numbers 19:15: "Whoever in the open fields touches one who is slain with a sword, or a dead body, or a bone of a man, or a grave, shall be unclean seven days (RSV 19:16)." Thus it is striking to note the repeated occurrence of second burials which could only be effected by human transfer. This apparent contradiction no doubt explains why so many elaborate theories have arisen to interpret this custom, which seemed to indicate a disrespectful treatment accorded to the dead. However, because of the scholarly focus on bone containers themselves, ossuary burials have often escaped such theorization.

Palestinian archaeologists have usually regarded secondary burial as callous and primitive despite the often elaborate tombs in which these burials are found. By way of explanation they relate them to nomadic peoples whose wanderings would have required two burials: at the time of death and then a later transfer to the family or tribal burial ground. Building on the researches of classical scholars, others have maintained that once the corpse was

Illus. 1-7

devoid of flesh it was not longer in need of care, the "soul" being no longer sentient.

This study will offer a new perspective which will allow for an understanding of all forms of secondary burials; the weaknesses in the above theories will hopefully become apparent. We shall also attempt to relate the practices of ossilegium to notions of afterlife in ancient Palestine. This is a somewhat hazardous task because of the absence of written documents in the earlier periods. However, the biblical evidence is extremely helpful in explaining a good deal of the material in somewhat later times and may well provide insights into the meaning of the earlier practices.

Secondary Burials from Earliest to Biblical Times

It is not impossible that the Neolithic plastered skulls of Jericho represent one of the earliest stages in the development of secondary burial practices. The choice of the skull as an object of veneration is quite understandable: The ancients must have already concluded that the intellectual powers of man resided in the head. In wanting to retain and preserve the skull, they hoped to keep nearby their ancestor's wisdom. This would indicate the existence of a belief in the intimate connection between the corpse with flesh and the corpse without flesh. Why else the preservation or treatment of skeletal remains?

In attempting to understand the Jericho skulls and other tomb materials from high antiquity we turn to the evidence from Çatal Hüyük, the largest Neolithic site in the Near East. This site covers the millennium from *ca.* 6500 to 5600 B.C. and provides some most startling discoveries. What is most impressive is the fact that secondary burials are entirely normative for that community.[1] Moreover, the marvelous wall paintings found in homes and in sacred shrines offer a fruitful avenue of interpretation since they portray various phases of a burial procedure which is quite obviously of singular importance to the community.

The techniques of ossilegium found at Çatal Hüyük are not unlike those attested in Palestine in various periods. Disarticulated burials were found beneath the floors and sleeping platforms, though care was taken to preserve the skeleton in its anatomical position. Such burials were also found in the so-called vulture shrines over a period of a century and a half. In House E IV, 2, three skulls were found in a shallow grave beneath the floor and piles of disarticulated bones were found beneath the platforms. This suggests a strong sense of kinship with the dead such as is found at pre-pottery Jericho.

The presence of ochre-burials perhaps can be compared with the plastered skulls of Jericho. Aside from ochre being applied to the bare skull, as for example was the case in House E VI, 8, the bones of the trunk and arms were also coated. In some cases green and blue paint was applied. This type of procedure, however, proved to be the rare exception. Some of the skulls were preserved in cloth bags while other bone piles were preserved in their original parcels of cloth or skins.

The wall paintings from the two vulture shrines indicate that the dead bodies were taken away from the village where they were cleaned of their flesh in a process of excarnation carried out by birds of prey. Afterwards the bones were collected and reburied. Mellaart believes that this took place during a spring festival when funeral rites were held. Another painting in Shrine VI. B. 1, shows the objects familiar from the excavations under the sleeping platforms, namely human skulls with gaping mouths and empty eye-sockets. The excavator conjectures that this painting resembles metamorphosis for emergence from the grave. Also pictured are gabled houses which probably represent the house of excarnation.

Whatever conception of afterlife may lie behind such practices, we may emphasize the very real sense of continuity that was felt between the realm of the living and the realm of the dead. In requiring excarnation as a preliminary to final interment, the inhabitants of Çatal Hüyük preshadow the much later practice of the Persians and the Parsees who after excarnation preserved the bones of the dead in *astodans* or ossuaries. In being brought back to the houses of the living the deceased as it were continued to partake of the experiences of the living, while the living could enjoy the nearness of the dead.

In turning to Palestine, the evidence for secondary burials in the Chalcolithic period is considerable and is known usually because of the domiform ossuaries found in the coastal region in such places at Ḥederah, Benei Beraq, Givatayim, Azor, Ben Shemen, and Tel Aviv. While many of these ossuaries are house-shaped, others are in the shape of animals. Although the bones were collected into individual ossuaries, in several instances some bones were merely laid in bundles or were laid out in piles alongside the ossuaries. That these cases are contemporary demonstrates a relationship among these several variations in the technique of ossilegium. Thus it is unlikely that those buried outside the actual ossuary were to share any lesser future than those buried inside the ossuaries.

Because no such individual ossuaries have been found in the south some scholars have believed that the custom of bone-gathering was restricted to the coastal plain. It is just as important to note, however, that secondary burials without ossuaries do occur as far south as Beersheba. This suggests that there is no real discontinuity between the northern and southern cultures as has often been thought. Most recently the possibility has been raised that the coastal cemeteries may well have served the so-called Negeb culture as well because of the presence of secondary burials in the south.

With the demise of the Chalcolithic culture and the beginning of the Early Bronze Age or Proto-Urban period, communal burials were established alongside the nomadic encampments which dotted Palestine at strategic locations. Not surprisingly many of the collective burials made in artificial caves are secondary. Tomb A 94 at Jericho is a case in point. Though all but the skulls were subsequently cremated, the bones in the tomb had been collected and brought to the communal burial place. It is intriguing to speculate that secondary burials were directly related to a semi-nomadic way of life, but the attestation of such a custom in settled periods as well shows the need for caution in such speculation.

One of the characteristics of these early secondary burials is the frequent absence of long bones. In Jericho tombs A 94 and K 2, they have been cremated or discarded to make room for careful preservation of the skulls[2]. At EB I Gezer jars not nearly large enough to hold all of the disarticulated bones were utilized for the secondary burial of human skeletonized remains.[3] These examples need not astonish, since the preservation of only part of a skeleton is a regular feature of secondary burials in Palestine. It is apparent that all the skeletal remains of a deceased person did not require preservation in order for future life to be achieved. When we take into account the nature of mythopoeic thought, which provides a very good framework for understanding the practices of high antiquity and where the differentiation between death and life was not accentuated, it is not strange at all to find only part of a body standing for all of a man.

The recent excavated cemetery at Bâb edh-Dhrâᶜ has brought to light further evidence for disarticulated burials in the period between the great nomadic intrusions. These burials provide one of the most exciting archaeological discoveries in recent years. Secondary burials are found in all but the final phase of the cemetery, which extends roughly from 3200-2200 B.C. The earliest or shaft burial phases of Bâb edh-Dhrâᶜ have close affinities to burials of the Proto-Urban period at Jericho. The sight of the neat little piles of skeletonized remains with the skulls separated from the long bones is most impressive. One is no less impressed with the great care that was lavished on the tomb and with the quality of the tomb furnishings themselves. Collected remains were placed on a mat or platform rather than left on the floor. Several figurines have been found in some of the bone piles, an occurrence which makes the existence of a belief in a life beyond the grave all the more probable.[4]

The charnel houses date to the third phase of the cemetery, which corresponds to EB II-III. These funerary buildings are rectangular mudbrick structures and contained huge quantities of disarticulated remains and pottery. Some of the pottery contained bones. Most likely the great cemetery served as a burial ground for the Cities of the Plain. It seems unlikely, however, that before transfer to the cemetery these groups of deceased were decarnated by boiling as the excavator suggests. Perhaps at this time excarnation was still practiced. This could account for the delicate bones of the skull being well preserved as they were at Çatal Hüyük. The fact that the biblical writers so strongly threaten excarnation by birds of prey and or beasts as a severe punishment for sin suggests that excarnation was still known in biblical times (Deut. 28:26; Jer. 7:33, 16:4, 19:7, 34:20; Ps. 79:2).

The final phase of the cemetery at Bâb edh-Dhrâᶜ is marked by the appearance of cairns and by the absence of secondary burials. The cairn burials are presently attributed to the post-urban phase or to the destroyers of the fortified town in the 23rd century.

The collective secondary burials of the Middle Bronze I period have long been recognized and interpreted as representing a semi-nomadic culture. Indeed at a first glance it seems quite compelling to explain such a phenomenon in terms of the tribal burial area associated with such a group. However, one of the weaknesses of this theory, which certainly does not apply to the Bâb edh-Dhrâ[c] material or to the settled culture of the Chalcolithic period, is that it cannot be applied to the Dagger Tombs or articulated burial groups at Jericho which are contemporary with the disarticulated groups of Jericho.

Secondary burials of varying sorts are now well attested in a variety of locations in MB I Palestine: [c]Ain es-Sâmiyeh (Mirzbâneh), Jericho, Lachish, Megiddo, Tell el-[c]Ajjul, el-Jib, Khirbet Kûfîn, Hablet el-[c]Amûd, and most recently Tiberias and el-Fûl.[5] Though the excavations at el-Fûl (Jebel Qa-ʾaqir) reiterate what has long been known about such burial customs, they do provide some additional information. Unusual features in a number of the tombs at this site are the body-recess, lamp niche, and panels with graffiti on them. The last of these suggests a rather vivid conception of afterlife and provides important new data. The beautifully preserved tombs probably were cut by professional grave diggers, and it is amazing to find a single disarticulated burial in such an elaborate setting.

At Mirzbâneh, too, the carefully hewn tomb chambers in most cases contained only the remains of a single adult. One of the curious characteristics of this cemetery is that no group of bones or particular bone such as the skull was required in the secondary deposition of the remains. Another common feature is that a layer of soft lime was built up under the bone piles. Some of the bone piles seem merely to have been dumped from a container to the floor. In Jericho Tomb J 21 one of these textile containers was partially preserved. In contrast to this is the example of secondary articulation of bones in Mirzbâneh Tomb B6 where the skull was laid topmost over a pair of femurs. This parallels very closely the later Jewish custom of laying out neat little bone piles with the skull topmost. In still other tombs at Mirzbâneh a mat replaced the bedding of lime, a practice which is also attested in late Hellenistic bone chambers. Paul Lapp, the excavator of the Mirzbâneh tombs, notes that such practices continue among some local Arab groups even today. Similar customs have also been observed by P. Bar-Adon among contemporary Palestinian Beduin.[6]

Given the widespread provenance of secondary burials in this period and the existence of a native tradition of ossilegium, we find it difficult to accept the argument for the particular origins of Lapp's Intermediate Bronze Age people on the basis of similar secondary burial customs elsewhere. Moreover it is really not surprising to find secondary burials also in the MB II period in Palestine. Several examples will suffice.

In the MB II cemetery at Munḥata in the upper Jordan Valley there are collective secondary pit burials in all the tombs. This is quite unlike the usual MB II B custom of reusing MB I shaft tombs. Most of the human skeletal remains are skulls with a disproportionately small number of long bones. The pottery was mostly whole or smashed *in situ*, indicating deposition at the time of collective secondary burial.[7] The closest parallel to Munḥata material comes from Jericho Tomb A I where there are preserved eight or nine crania but only a small number of long bones. Perhaps slightly earlier than this tomb group are the MB II A tombs at Ras el-ᶜAin, where rectangular stone-lined pits are covered with slabs. In the walls of the tombs are recesses which evidently served as ossuaries.[8] These burials thus represent yet another type of tomb in which secondary inhumation occurs.

Secondary Burials from Biblical To Hellenistic Times

With such a lengthy tradition of bone gathering in Palestine it is not strange to find this practice continuing into the Iron Age. Certain typological features of Iron Age tombs have long been a puzzle to archaeologists and only recently have there been attempts to understand them in terms of the custom of ossilegium. L. Y. Rahmani of the Israel Department of Antiquities has greatly enhanced our understanding of a number of these features.[9] Perhaps the most outstanding characteristic of Iron Age tombs to be viewed in light of secondary burial practices is the communal ossuary or repository which was adopted to insure the safekeeping of the bones of former burials.

Unlike secondary burials in the earlier periods, primary and secondary interments often occur in the same tomb chamber in the Iron Age. When a corpse became decarnate the bones were simply swept into the communal ossuary or removed to a repository. Also, Jewish law enjoined a speedy burial, usually on the day of death. It is virtually impossible, however, to determine the place of initial burial even when the tomb is undisturbed. The deceased who died far away from the family tomb had to have a temporary tomb at the location of death until decomposition was complete. Only then were his bones gathered and transported to the family tomb. One of the most interesting examples of such a case is found in the story of the reburial by David of the bones of Saul (and his sons) and of Jonathan (II Sam. 21:13; cf. I Chron. 10:12 and another source in I Sam. 31:11-13) and the vigil of Rizpeh over their remains. The II Samuel account is the only case in the Bible where the period of decomposition is noted. From 22:10ff. it may be deduced that this period took approximately eight months, from May until December, after which the bones of Saul and Jonathan were interred in the family tomb of Kish in Benjamin. The excarnation motif, so prominent in a positive way at Çatal Hüyük, also clearly underlies the statement in Jeremiah 7:33: "And the dead bodies of this people will be food for the birds of the air, and for the beasts of the earth; and none will frighten them away." Without someone like Rizpeh to ward off the flesh-eating birds and animals it would become virtually impossible to effect a proper secondary burial by Israelite standards.

The non-Palestinian tomb group of Hadhramaut in southwest Arabia has typological affinities to numerous Palestinian tombs and also to the Transjordanian cemeteries of Sahab B and ^cAmman. We discuss this tomb group out of chronological sequence since it offers strong albeit indirect evidence that many Iron Age tombs contain secondary burials, the bones of which had been brought from afar.

Tomb A5 at Hadhramaut is a single chamber, horseshoe in shape, with a solitary bench cut into the eastern side. The entrance fill and interior deposits were undisturbed at the time of excavation. The skeletal remains were incomplete, yet neatly piled up with the crania lying on their bases separated from their skeletons. The burials were apparently brought in at intervals in their disarticulated states. Tomb A6, although disturbed, presents some noteworthy features which may shed some light on similar Palestinian tombs. The characteristic feature here is the recess, six of which are cut into the northern and western arcs of the horseshoe-shaped chamber. The presence of disarticulated bone piles again leads to the conclusion that this chamber was intended for secondary burials only and that the recesses were used as bone depositories as they were, for example, in Gezer Tombs 58 and 59. Though these tombs date to the late Iron Age, they at least raise the possibility that many Palestinian tomb features represent the second burials of those who died elsewhere rather than of those whose first and second burials were in the same tomb.[10]

In turning to the Palestinian evidence from the Iron Age we may observe a number of tomb features which become fairly standard by Iron II and continue into the later periods. The rectangular tombs of the Sea Peoples (900 Cemetery) and of the Philistines (500 Cemetery) at Tell Fara^c (south) exhibit several of these features, namely, the bone chamber, the pit repository, and the central depression;[11] these are best understood in the context of secondary burials. Aside from their rectangularity, only recently observed as being influenced by the Aegean world, these features are also associated with secondary burials in Aegean tomb groups. This coincidence raises the question of the circumstances of their introduction into Palestine.

The elaborate LB II tomb at Ras Shamra ascribed to the wealthy Aegean element of the population may well provide a clue in what appears to be a cultural borrowing at Tell Fara^c.[12] That at Ugarit there are secondary burials into a family tomb is not to be dismissed too lightly since economics did not dictate the propensity for bone gathering. In Mycenean tombs similar to the Ras Shamra ones, numerous larnakes or bone chests have been found.[13] Only recently some larnakes have been excavated at Arkhanes in Crete in which only the skulls were reburied.[14] In some instances larnakes occur alongside the simpler type of secondary burial into bone piles, offering a parallel which supports our interpretation of the Chalcolithic materials where both simple secondary burials and secondary burials into house-urns were attested side by side.

The 900 Cemetery at Tell Fara^c contained no Philistine pottery but included wares very close to those in the 500 Cemetery dated to the end of LB II. Tomb 934, the largest of this complex, gives some evidence that its central depression was used as a sort of communal ossuary. Off the central depression what appear to be two repositories are cut into the side. Though the rest of the tomb group shows no clear indication of secondary burial but only the moving aside of earlier interments, it is quite easy to understand how separate compartments, a characteristic feature of this tomb group, came to be used in secondary burials. Tomb 542 of the 500 Cemetery in fact has a compartment that is later used as a bone chamber.

Still more evidence for the custom of bone collecting comes from the 200 Cemetery at Tell Fara^c, which also dates to Iron I and is attributed to the influence of the Sea Peoples. The type of grave here is the cist grave of the much earlier type known from the micro-dolmenic cist cemetery of Ghassul. In Tomb 201, the largest of this group, 126 skeletons were recovered; in Tomb 239 twenty-six skulls were uncovered. These burials then are best understood as secondary. Also at Tell Zeror secondary burials into cist graves are found where it appears that other Sea Peoples (possibly Tjekker warriors) were buried.[15]

In short, it is a distinct possibility that many of the innovative features associated with secondary burials in Iron Age Palestine may well be derived from Aegean prototypes already known in the Levant by LB II-Iron I. The strong Israelite attachment to the family tomb and the well-established custom of secondary burial doubtlessly facilitated the process by which such architectural features were adapted; the bone gathering practices of the Aegean peoples could only have reinforced the corresponding Israelite customs.

There are a number of other tombs which also seem best understood in terms of the tradition of ossilegium. Tomb 58 at Gezer offers convincing proof that Iron Age recesses were used for storing collected remains. The sunken rectangular recesses most closely resemble those in Tomb A6 at Hadhramaut. Tomb 58 is a single-chambered bench tomb dated to Iron I. Macalister correctly identifies the circular cells as ossuaries for bone piles. Moreover, both tombs contained Philistine ware. Tomb 59 was probably used for secondary interments. Many human bones were collected into vessels, some into large sherds, small jugs, bowls, and flat saucers.

This is precisely the type of veneration for human remains one would expect in a secondary burial.

Tomb 96 from Gezer dates somewhat later, to *ca.* 975 B.C., and is typologically closer to Tomb 58. Unlike the benches in Tomb 58 and 59, which were roughly rectangular, the benches in Tomb 96 follow the natural contours of the chamber. At the south end are two small recesses below the floor level. They were probably intended to be used as ossuaries, for they contained over 200 burials. This type of recess may well be the typological link between the earlier material and the later 10th century repository.[16]

Tomb 54 at Tell en-Nasbeh with its discoid recess at the east end is also probably related to these innovative features. Though disturbed, fifty-four jawbones were discovered, strongly suggesting that this recess also may have been used as an ossuary for human remains. Similarly, Tomb 5 gives some indication of being used for secondary burials. The ledges apparently were used for the primary burials and the chamber at the rear for collection of skeletal remains.[17] This arrangement, which is highly reminiscent of the Aegean tomb models at Mycene and Tell Fara^c, foreshadows the later Palestinian bone chamber.

The more standard Iron II repositories such as are found in Tombs 120, 218, 219, and 223 at Lachish or in Beth Shemesh Tombs 2, 3, 4, 7, and 8 clearly were designed to provide a compartment for storing earlier burials, though it is difficult to ascertain with certainty the place of primary burial. As more and more family members came to be interred with their fathers, their remains were gathered into the communal ossuary. The pushing aside of former burials indicates that primary burial did occur in the same tomb but it need not be interpreted as harsh treatment of the dead, as has often been suggested, since the emphasis is on joining one's fathers in the very same grave.

The Relation of Secondary Burials to Israelite Conceptions of Man and of Sheol

Viewed against the background of secondary burials in Palestine, the biblical idiom "to be gathered (*n^{3}sp*) to one's fathers" takes on new meaning. In this expression may be discerned the echoes of a time when secondary burial was practiced in pastoral

Palestine. Surely this is one of the most striking of all idioms for
death in the Bible: "The Lord said to Moses, 'Go up into this
mountain of Ab^{c}arim, and see that land which I have given to the
people of Israel. And when you have seen it, you also shall be
gathered to your people, as your brother Aaron was gathered'"
(Num. 27:12-13). Of all the patriarchs only Moses and Aaron are
buried outside of Palestine, but it may be assumed that neither was
denied entry into Sheol. Moses' denial of entry into the promised
land is taken by P to be the result of his own sin of pride (Num.
20:10-14), while the Deuteronomic account explains this punishment as a consequence of the sinfulness of the people (Deut. 1:37;
3:26; 4:21). Whatever the reason for not reaching Palestine, it may
be stressed that the punishment was not to be carried over in death.
Moses and Aaron are gathered to their people in a larger sense and
the justification for using the "gathered" idiom with reference to
them is thus telling.

Because of ancient Israel's hesitancy about physical contact
with the defiling dead, her preoccupation with ossilegium must
necessarily reflect a distinct theology of afterlife which made care
of the bones take precedence over the reluctance for touching
them. The Israelite view of the individual as *nephesh* must
constitute the basis for such a theology. According to that view
man is seen as a solitary unit even in death, when the bones of a
man possess at least a shadow of their strength in life. The body in
the Israelite conception is merely the soul in its outward form while
the bones of a dead man represent a manifestation of that soul in a
weakened state. After all, the dead still mutter as shades (Isa. 8:19;
29:4) and feel the worms gnawing at them (Job 14:22; Isa. 66:24).
Hence the soul retains a very intimate connection with whatever
may constitute the physical remains of the dead. Even in death, the
unitary quality of the individual is not destroyed. The suggestion
that the bones once devoid of their flesh are no longer in need of
care, therefore, must be rejected. Death merely indicated a
diminution rather than a cessation of the power to exist.

Such a unitary conception of the individual and preoccupation with the remains of men only reinforce our understanding of
the thought patterns of the ancients. One of the most peculiar
aspects of ancient thought is the notion that a part can stand for a
whole, *pars pro toto*.[18] It is precisely this notion which gave rise to

the proverbial expression: "The memory of the righteous is a blessing" (Proverbs 10:7), the most common of all Jewish epitaphs. Indeed the force of a name in ancient society was very great. There is a coalescence between the symbol and what it stands for. Hence, the most important thing of all was that the names of the dead be recalled by the living. Even today when memorial services for the dead are held in synagogues, the names of the dead are read aloud, emphasizing their continued presence among the living. The same applies to the bones of the dead. However incomplete they may be, they represent the full significance of that man and it is hard to imagine the callous treatment in a family tomb of the beloved departed whose names were in a very real sense a potent force in the present. Ossilegium thus harmonizes with the attitudes of the ancients toward death, which did not mark in a strict sense an end to life. The practice of secondary burial, therefore, supports the Israelite conception of the totality of the individual.

There are numerous biblical passages which suggest the potential that man's bones possessed in death. Most notable perhaps is the resurrection of an unnamed man who comes in contact with the bones of Elisha (II Kings 13:21) or Ezekiel's vision of the resuscitation of the dry bones (Ezek. 37). If we cannot take Ezekiel's vision literally we can at least appreciate it either as an eschatological poetic vision of the realization of the potential which the bones of Israel possessed in Sheol or as a dramatic presentation of the return of exiled Israel to the Holy Land such as Moses and Aaron were promised when they were denied burial there. Perhaps we may now speculate that the bones of Saul and Jonathan were in fact buried in a communal ossuary.

In addition to this, the very idea that the deceased could interfere in the course of events of the living (I Samuel 28) is proof of a rather lively conception of Sheol. The biblical phrase "to be gathered to one's fathers" thus means to die and to descend to Sheol where the family of all Israel was assembled. The idiom may also reflect rather literally the MB I tombs discussed above. It would elucidate Abraham's preoccupation with proper burial, and it would explain the Iron Age innovation of the communal ossuary, the actual means by which one was joined to the common soul of his ancestors. In death and reburial the deceased gained a sort of corporate existence. No doubt the prevalence of subterranean tomb chambers also reflects the Israelite view of Sheol, often described as a nether world located beneath the earth (Num. 16:20), or in the cosmic waters (Job 26:7), or under the "roots of mountains" (Jonah 2:6), or more frequently as "pit" (Pss. 16:10; 30:10). These images and metaphors are adapted from ancient Canaanite and Mesopotamian mythology, and there is no reason to doubt that the Israelites drew from this language of mythology. For it was in the language of myth that Israel came to understand the full meaning of history which had been oversimplified by some of the historical writers.

The biblical conceptions of man and of Sheol thus do not conflict with Israelite burial customs. Though the equally important practice of single inhumation existed alongside secondary inhumation, there is no reason to believe it presupposed any different theological framework. In Israel where there is some cause to question such activity as would be involved in a second burial, namely corpse defilement and opening a tomb, it is all the more significant to find such correspondence between customs and views of man and afterlife. It may be that the Levitical laws which relate to treatment of the dead indeed may constitute an attempt to combat a cult of the dead. After all, of all the nations of the ancient world Israel alone emphasized the defiling nature of the dead.

Secondary Burials in Hellenistic and Roman Times

Just as earlier discussions of the Chalcolithic tomb materials focused on the phenomenon of ossuaries, so too have most of the discussions of Jewish tombs in the Roman period centered about the problem of Jewish ossuaries. Indeed, the most expert commentators have remarked: "It is not clear from whom the Jews took this strange custom, which is indeed alien to the spirit of the Semitic peoples to whom disturbing the deceased was prohibited," or "No proper interpretation has been given on the religious-historical plane of this burial-custom which is alien to the Jewish tradition."[19] It is our belief that it is precisely the failure to note the continuity in the custom of bone gathering in Palestine that has occasioned such views.

During the Second Temple period the diversity in the kinds of secondary burials which characterized earlier periods persists. It therefore becomes increasingly difficult to single out the Jewish ossuary as something which signals a change in belief and we are accordingly skeptical of those attempts at relating a given variant of ossilegium to a specific socio-economic stratum or to a particular religious sect.[20] Since the evidence for the later period is so considerable, we can only highlight it and allude to the new theological implications which become attached to this ancient and venerated practice.

It is significant to note the presence of secondary burials without ossuaries in *kokhim* or loculi in the Hellenistic-Roman tombs of Marissa and Beit Jibrin. These tombs represent the earliest of this sort in Palestine. It is of crucial importance to find such attestation in that the innovation of the loculus grave itself may be a result of foreign influence. So determined were the owners of these tombs to utilize the *kokhim* for collected remains that very often the walls between loculi were taken down so that the area could be used as a sort of bone chamber.[21] Secondary burials into small *kokhim* and niches are attested in the Roman tombs here as well.

The adoption of the loculus grave pattern thus seems only to have reinforced a native propensity to gather and preserve skeletal remains. Though this peculiar tomb arrangement may have come to Palestine via Egypt, where Hebrew and Greek names are found in such tombs as early as the 3rd century, it seems more probable that this pattern was ultimately borrowed from the Greeks.[22] Both the Jews and the Phoenicians by the end of the 3rd century B.C. in Egypt and Syro-Palestine employed this pattern. Since the Phoenicians were inhumators and the Jews practiced both primary and secondary inhumation, it is apparent once again that a typological feature has been adapted to the peculiar customs of a given people, and its adoption is ample testimony to Jewish borrowing in the Hellenistic period.

Separate bone chambers or charnel houses, similar to the Iron Age bone chambers of Tell Fara^c and Tell en-Nasbeh, turn up with increasing frequency in the late Hellenistic period. By far the most impressive of these is Jason's Tomb, which is dated to the Hasmonean period and is one of the most elaborate tombs of that period. Room A, a smoothly hewn rectangular chamber with ten *kokhim*, evidently served as the place of primary interment until decomposition. Room B was the charnel house, since numerous piles of skeletalized remains numbering twenty-five burials were found along the wall of the chamber. Proof of transfer was established when pottery fragments from Chamber B were matched with pottery fragments from the *kokhim*.[23]

Several generations, the earliest of which dates to the time of Alexander Janneus, are represented here. The manner of transfer, alluded to in the tannaitic tractate *On Mourning* (Semaḥot 12.8), was by means of a sheet or mat. From a somewhat later period comes a reed bag, preserved in the Bar-Kokhba caves, which was used to collect or transfer the bones of the dead.[24] The similarity of these examples with the practice of earlier periods is obvious and striking.

An important parallel to Jason's Tomb comes from the southern chamber of a tomb in the Romema Quarter of Jerusalem. It consists of two adjoining rectangular chambers. The one for primary burial contained two *kokhim*. The bone chamber had three small niches or *kokhim* for the collection of skeletal remains while the floor chamber was covered with a layer of earth on which bone piles were laid out on mats. In a later period the bone chamber came to be used as a depository for ossuaries which became much more frequent by the Herodian period.[25]

Another feature of Iron Age tombs which continues into later periods is the communal ossuary or central depression in the rectangular bench tomb. It now is certain that such a cavity was not purely functional, viz., to facilitate the burial process made difficult by the limited height of the chamber, as some have argued. Corroboration of this comes from a late Hellenistic tomb at Ramat Raḥel.[26] In burial hall A there was a central depression and five *kokhim*. The *kokhim* with ossuaries belong to the Herodian phase while the secondary burials in the depression belong to the earlier phase. In the depression three skulls were found separated from the rest of the bones, which were carefully arranged into neat little piles. Once again a much earlier practice occurs in a later context. The emphasis on the importance of skulls is not at all surprising and is now well-documented in the later periods. Such skulls are reburied, for example, in some Jewish ossuaries from Jericho in Tomb K23.

A tomb at Wadi Yaṣul, Jerusalem, is extremely interesting because it shows secondary burials occurring both in *kokhim* and in the central depression without any trace of ossuaries.[27] The pottery is inconclusive and it is impossible to tell which of the two variants of the custom is earlier or whether indeed they are contemporary. The important factor to be observed here is that two different typological features are being employed in the custom of ossilegium.

Another tomb from Jerusalem, called the Maḥanayim tomb, suggests that in many instances the communal assembling of bones predated the appearance of individual ossuaries. In chamber no. III, the introduction of ossuaries on the farthest bench caused the remains of earlier burials to be pushed aside.[28] A similar situation obtains in the Jerusalem tomb on Reḥov Ruppin. This tomb is a rectangular chamber with seven *kokhim* and a central depression. Only *kokh* no. 1 was found undisturbed with its sealing slab still intact. Within the loculus the remains of three individuals were found inside a single ossuary which was situated in front of a heap of disarticulated bones in the corner. Here is an excellent example of the loculus being used for a simple secondary burial and also for a secondary burial into an ossuary. It is quite possible that in this particular instance the introduction of the individual container replaced older techniques of secondary burial though the tomb features themselves were utilized in both cases.

In yet another Jerusalem tomb from the late Hellenistic period on Reḥov Nisan-Beq, the older Iron Age pattern of a rectangular bench tomb with central depression occurs together with four long *kokhim* and four smaller ones. The latter perhaps may be called repositories and might well descend from Iron Age prototypes. The small ones could serve either for the collection of bones or for the deposition of a single ossuary. In *kokh* no. 2, one of the larger ones, a pit as wide as the loculus itself was cut at the rear and was used as a repository for human remains.[29] It is quite clear that the owners of such a tomb went to considerable length to insure the proximity of the mortal remains of their family, and it is in such a light that we have viewed similar Iron age tomb features.

It has been observed that secondary burials into *kokhim* without ossuaries occur at the time of the adoption of the loculus pattern. This practice continues throughout the Hellenistic-Roman period and is also found at Beth She^carim, which is our latest major site for the study of Jewish tombs in ancient Palestine. This accords well with the view derived mainly from the linguistic evidence that the term *kokh* itself, an eastern Semitic loanword into western Aramaic, is regularly associated with secondary burials.[30] We need not be impressed by those who are hesitant to accept ossuaries as a Jewish phenomenon because of the Greek term *glossokomon*, which incidentally is not attested until a period after the adoption of the convention of the individual bone container. Jews did not lack a Semitic vocabulary appropriate to secondary burials.

Even at Qumran, where the vast majority of graves thus far excavated have been primary inhumations in shaft graves with a recess at the bottom, there are several examples of secondary inhumation. In a period when the loculus pattern was in wide usage, it is not strange to find the sectarian covenanters employing a different burial pattern to emphasize their separateness. For a community to which ritual purity meant so much, however, the occurrence of even a few secondary interments is all the more noteworthy.[31] It is quite possible that these burials belong to those Essenes who lived away from the settlement by the Dead Sea and who desired to be gathered to their true brethren at Qumran in death.

Consideration of the great necropolis of Beth She^carim (Sheikh Ibreiq) is an appropriate way to end this brief survey. A careful reading of all the excavation reports will reveal that secondary burial was in fact the dominant mode of inhumation there.[32] Catacomb no. 1 offers by far the most variegated picture of burial customs and arcosolia, *kokhim*, and pits all in simultaneous use. The arcosolium, the most frequent type of burial in catacomb nos. 1-4, was used for both primary and secondary inhumation and even for the deposition of ossuaries.

The *kokhim* at Beth She^carim are smaller than the longer Hellenistic ones, ranging from approximately two to four feet in length. Again many were used as repositories into which bones were collected and in many instances more than several individuals were interred. Whole chambers were also used to store collected bones (room 2 or catacomb no. 1) or to store ossuaries or coffins. The inscriptions, moreover, leave no doubt that the necropolis served as a center for reburial of Jews from all over the Diaspora.

One of the inscriptions bears directly on the problem of the use of the sarcophagus as ossuary. It is inscribed on sarcophagus no. 11 of catacomb 20 and reads: "This is the sarcophagus of the three sons of Rabbi..."[33] This confirms the view that coffins were indeed used for the collection of bones as it is impossible to assume that all three bodies were interred intact in one coffin. A wooden coffin, dated to late Hasmonean times, found in burial cave 4 of the Naḥal David in the Judean desert, also seems to have been used as an ossuary, for it contained seven skulls.[34]

Given our broad understanding of secondary burials it is now apparent why we cannot accept the overemphasis on the individual ossuary which represents only a single variant of the custom of ossilegium. The very fact that ossuaries have turned up in the Diaspora at Alexandria and Carthage and in Spain in the late Roman period gives some indication of how important this mode of inhumation was.[35] Though individual ossuaries diminish in number in Palestine after A.D. 70, the attestation of diverse secondary burials and individual receptacles in various parts of Palestine in addition to Beth She︨arim gives further reason to use caution in restricting so distinctive a burial custom to a short period. In the view of most scholars ossuaries appear *ca.* 40 B.C. and disappear after A.D. 70. Indeed, it would be most strange to find any burial custom as striking as this limited to so short a time span. Once we have a view which allows us to consider all variants of secondary burial on the same continuum, the necessity for determining precise dates for ossuaries is substantially reduced. To be concerned about whether the first Jewish ossuaries date to 100 or 50 B.C. is to miss the point.

Theology of Jewish Ossilegium

As we move on to consider the theological ramifications of this custom in Jewish sources it needs to be stressed that the sources do not differentiate between burial in an ossuary and any other type of secondary burial.

> The ossilegium of two corpses may take place at the same time, as long as the bones of the one are put at one end of a sheet and those of the other at the other end of the sheet. (So Rabbi Johanan ben Nuri.)

> Rabbi ᶜAkiba says: In the course of time, the sheet will waste
> away; in the course of time, the bones will intermingle. Let them
> rather be gathered and placed in ossuaries. (Semahot 12.8)[36]

In the first half of this mishnah we can imagine the deposition of
skeletonized remains in a variety of ways, while in the second half
the convention of the individual ossuary is required. Though there
is a disagreement here on the manner of second burial, both
techniques of ossilegium are acknowledged. In the former instance
we can also imagine the disarray that would occur in effecting a
transfer by means of some sort of bag.

The custom of secondary burial carries many theological
implications in addition to those in the biblical writings which have
already been indicated. Of signal importance is the persistence of
the conception of man as a unitary individual whose mortal
remains constitute the very essence of that person in death. It is no
wonder that men desired to be buried or reburied with their fathers.
It is difficult to pinpoint exactly when burial in Palestine took on
new and added meaning that would cause Jews in the Diaspora to
desire burial in the Holy Land. However, it is clear that from the
turn of the common era until the 4th century A.D., Diaspora Jews
buried the remains of their dead in Palestine. This fact is
established by an examination of the ossuary inscriptions from
Jerusalem and the sepulchral inscriptions from Beth Sheᶜarim.

It was not long before the rabbis understood final interment
on holy soil as having special atoning values; they took
Deuteronomy 32:43 as the proof-text for this notion.[37] Such a
conception met with a good deal of hostility amongst those who
lived their lives in Palestine and saw their bretheren return to Eretz
Israel in death. Still another interpretation was given by the rabbis
on the benefits which accrued to an individual after burial in
Palestine: "The dead of Eretz Israel will be the first to be
resurrected in the days of the Messiah."[38]

It was the positive value given to the period of decomposition,
however, which best explains why secondary burial was so
important in the later period. Both the Babylonian and Jerusalem
Talmuds are most explicit regarding decay of the flesh as necessary
to the forgiveness of criminals:

> Both death and [shameful] burial (i.e., in the criminal's graveyard)

are necessary [for forgiveness]. R. Adda b. Ahabah objected: They observe no mourning rites, but grieved for him, for grief is borne only in the heart. But should you think that having been [shamefully] buried, he attains forgiveness, they should observe mourning rites; the decay of the flesh too is necessary [for forgiveness].[39]

In time this view, coupled with the view of the special effects of burial in Palestine, came to provide the conceptual framework for all secondary burials in rabbinic times and was no longer confined to criminals alone.

Closely related to these ideas is the concept of *damnatio memoriae*. The parade example in rabbinic literature is the notice of the exhumation and dragging of the bones of King Ahaz by his son Hezekiah in order to cancel the evil decrees of his father with regard to idolatry and also to expiate his father's sins by degradation of his remains.[40] Perhaps the reinterment of the bones of King Uzziah around A.D. 50 as recorded in the Uzziah inscription ("Hither were brought the bones of Uzziah, king of Judah—Do not open"), is more than a prohibition against disturbing the second burial of the leper king and reflects more than a growing reverence paid to both graves and relics. It is possible that Uzziah was denied burial in the "sepulchers of the kings" (II Kings 15:7; II Chron. 26:23) because he was a leper or for some other reason not understood by a later generation. The desire of the pious to bring his remains to their rightful place thus is in harmony with the whole complex of ideas associated with secondary burials.

Though the archaeological evidence for the custom of ossilegium suggests its discontinuance at Beth She‘arim in the 4th century, the ongoing desire of pious Jews to be buried in Israel or even to have a clod of heavy soil thrown on their coffins, symbolic of their return to Zion, provides vivid attestation of continuation of this tradition in modern times.

Conclusion

To be sure, the placing together of human skeletal remains in a common pit or chamber might at first glance seem to be an indiscriminate or harsh way of joining one's family in the hereafter.

It might seem that secondary burial stands in contradiction to the frequent maledictions against disturbing the dead or in violation of the ordinances that relate to ritual purity. Analysis of all the data, however, now indicates that such a procedure for the disposition of human remains is far more common and in keeping with Semitic thought than has heretofore been recognized. In a secondary burial the emphasis is on the safekeeping of remains within the precincts of the family tomb, and this seems to be in close harmony with the Semitic conception of the nature of man. In light of this the biblical idioms for death and burial are quite apt.

Despite the apparent silence of the New Testament in regard to ossilegium, the preservation of a martyr's remains or the veneration of a Christian saint in a relic chest seems best explained as an outgrowth of ancient Near Eastern burial customs. Dramatic evidence that secondary burial continues in precisely the form in which we have described it comes from the monastery of St. Catherine's in Sinai.[41] There the monks first bury their dead in a beautiful garden cemetery just outside the monastery wall. After a year the bones and skulls are gathered up and piled separately in the charnel house. In areas where conservatism runs deep, it is not strange to find the practices of a later period rooted in the warp and woof of ancient tradition.

Notes

[1] J. Mellaart, *Çatal Hüyük* (1967), pp. 204ff. For more detailed reporting on the burials one may consult Mellaart's preliminary reports in *Anatolian Studies* XII (1961), 41-65; XIII (1963), 43-102; XIV (1964), 39-119.

[2] K. Kenyon, *Jericho* I (1960), 4, 22-25; cf. also her later views in *Jericho* II (1965), 3, 11, 550. For a general discussion of secondary burials in this period see D. Gilead, *Palestine Exploration Quarterly* C (1968), 16-27.

[3] R. A. S. Macalister, *Gezer* I (1912), p. 78.

[4] For the most recent discussion of this material see P. W. Lapp, *BASOR* No. 189 (Feb. 1968), pp. 12-41; *Jerusalem Through the Ages* (1969), pp. 26-33.

[5] For Tiberias see V. Tzaferis, *Israel Exploration Journal* XVIII (1968), 15-19; for el-Fûl see provisionally W. G. Dever's Hebrew Union College Jerusalem School Newsletter of January, 1968. For further references consult P. W. Lapp, *Dhahr Mirzbâneh Tombs* (1966), pp. 40ff.

[6] E. Stern, ed., *Bulletin of the Israel Exploration Society, Reader A* (1965), pp. 70-71 (Hebrew).

[7]See provisionally J. Perrot, *Syria* XLIII (1966), 50, and the forthcoming article of A. Furshpan of the University of Connecticut to whom I am indebted for this information.

[8]J. H. Illiffe, *Quarterly of the Department of Antiquities in Palestine* V (1936), 113-126; J. Van Seters, *The Hyksos* (1966), pp. 45ff.

[9]Notably in *Israel Exploration Journal* VIII (1955), 101-105 and XVII (1967), 67-100.

[10]G. Caton-Thompson, *The Tombs and Moon Temples of Hureidha (Hadhramaut)* (1944), pp. 81ff., 90ff.

[11]W. M. F. Petrie, *Beth Pelet* I (1930), Pls. XVIII-XIX; cf. J. Waldbaum, *American Journal of Archaeology* LXX (1966), 331-340.

[12]See C. F. A. Schaeffer, *Ugaritica* I (1939), pp. 77ff., 90ff. and Figs. 60-71.

[13]See A. J. B. Wace, *Archaeologia* LXXXII (1932), 1-146, and E. Vermeule, *Journal of Hellenic Studies* LXXXV (1965), 123-148.

[14]A. Sakellarakis, *Archaeology* XX (1967), 276-281.

[15]K. Ohata, ed., *Tel Zeror II* (1967), pp. 35-41.

[16]For all this material see *Gezer I*, pp. 321-325; 336-337.

[17]W. F. Badé, *Some Tombs of Tell en-Nashbeh Discovered in 1929* (1931), pp. 18-33; C. C. McCown, *Tell en-Nasbeh I: Archaeological and Historical Results* (1947), pp. 82ff.

[18]H. Frankfort *et al*, *Before Philosophy: The Intellectual Adventure of Ancient Man* (1961), p. 21.

[19]M. Avigad, *Sepher Yerushalayim* (1956), p. 321 (Hebrew); P. Kahane, *Israel Exploration Journal* II (1952), 127, n.2.

[20]L. Y. Rahmani, *ʿAtiqot* III (1961), 93-120; M. Avi-Yonah, *Oriental Art in Roman Palestine* (1961), pp. 25-27.

[21]E. Oren, *Archaeology* XVIII (1965), 218-224.

[22]So I. Noshy, *The Arts in Ptolemaic Egypt* (1937), pp. 19-20; cf. N. P. Toll, *The Excavations at Dura-Europas, A Preliminary Report of the Ninth Season of Work, 1935-36, Part II: The Necropolis* (1946), p. 7, who argues for a Syro-Phoenician origin.

[23]Rahmani, *Israel Exploration Journal* XVII (1967), 61ff.

[24]Y. Yadin, *The Finds from the Bar-Kokhba Period in the Cave of Letters* (1963), pp. 30-31, Pls. 6-7.

[25]Rahmani, *Eretz-Israel* VIII (1967), 186-192 (Hebrew). A summary of the finds in this tomb appeared earlier in *Israel Exploration Journal* XIII (1963), 145.

[26]M. Stekelis, *Journal of the Jewish Palestine Exploration Society* III (1934-35), 25ff. (Hebrew).

[27]Avigad, *Eretz Israel* VIII (1967), 133-35 (Hebrew).

[28]Rahmani, *ʿAtiqot* III (1961), 105-107.

[29]*Ibid*., pp. 108-109.

[30] Y. Kutscher, *Eretz Israel* VIII (1968), 279 (Hebrew).

[31] R. de Vaux, *L'archéologie et les manuscrits de la Mer Morte* (1961), pp. 37f.

[32] B. Mazar, *Beth She'arim, Report on the Excavations during 1936-40, I: The Catacombs I-IV* (1957), p. viii of the English summary.

[33] Avigad, *Israel Exploration Journal* VII (1957), 241ff.

[34] *Israel Exploration Journal* XII (1962), 181ff.

[35] For Jewish ossuaries in Alexandria see E. R. Goodenough, *Jewish Symbols in the Greco-Roman Period* (1953-69), Vol. I, 115; Vol. II, 63; and Vol. II, Fig. 113; for Carthage see J. Ferron, *Cahiers de Byrsa* (1956), pp. 105-17; and for Spain see H. Beinart, *Eretz Israel* VIII (1967), 298-305 (Hebrew).

[36] The translation is that of D. Zlotnick, *The Tractate Mourning* (1966).

[37] See in the Babylonian Talmud, *Kethuboth* 111a and *Berakoth* 18b; in the Jerusalem Talmud, *Kethuboth* 12.3=*Kiliam* 9.3.

[38] *Genesis Rabbah* 96.5.

[39] Babylonian Talmud, *Sanhedrin* 47b (Soncino Translation).

[40] *Mishnah Pesaḥim* 4.9; Babylonian Talmud, *Pesaḥim* 56a and *Berakoth* 10b; Jerusalem Talmud, *Pesaḥim* 9.1.

[41] B. Rothenberg, *God's Wilderness* (1961), p. 159.

7

THE NECROPOLIS FROM THE TIME
OF THE KINGDOM OF JUDAH
AT SILWAN, JERUSALEM

DAVID USSISHKIN

One of the impressive archaeological remains from the period of the First Temple in Jerusalem, when the city was the capital of the kings of the house of David, is the necropolis situated within the area of the present-day village of Silwan. The existence of the necropolis had been known for many years, and various tombs were studied by distinguished scholars, primarily C. Schick, C. Clermont-Ganneau, A. Reifenberg, N. Avigad and recently S. Loffreda.[1] In spite of its importance, however, a general systematic study of the necropolis was not carried out until last year. The reason for this is, perhaps, to be sought in the hostile nature of the villagers. Already in the 19th century their notoriety had spread among European travelers and scholars in Jerusalem. C. Warren, for example, wrote in 1876, "The people of Siloam are a lawless set, credited with being the most unscrupulous ruffians in Palestine."[2] Thus, the general survey of the site which we began in the summer of 1968 on behalf of the Israel Exploration Society, [3] gave us an overall picture of the graveyard for the first time. A careful study of the remains indicated the existence of a monumental necropolis, unique in contemporary Palestine, where nobles and notables of the kingdom of Judah were undoubtedly interred.

The village of Silwan and our necropolis are situated on the east slope of the Kidron valley, opposite and at short distance from the "City of David," sometimes called the "Hill of Ophel," or the southeastern hill, which is the site of biblical Jerusalem. The slope is very steep, and several long and vertical cliffs are situated there, one behind and above the other, like terraces constructed on the slope of a hill. The tombs are rock-cut burial chambers, whose entrances are hewn in the vertical cliffs. All the tombs are now open and empty and only partly preserved. During the late Roman period, at the time when Jerusalem became "Aelia Capitolina," or more probably during the early part of the Byzantine period when extensive building activities took place in Jerusalem, the cliffs of Silwan were turned into large stone quarries, which resulted in much damage to the tombs. Further damage was done during the Byzantine period when Christian monks settled in the burial-caves, widened the entrances, made niches in the walls, destroyed burial resting-places and engraved crosses on the walls. In addition, a few caves were converted into churches. Finally the necropolis suffered when the Arab village was built; tombs were destroyed, incorporated in houses or turned into water cisterns and sewage dumps. However, we still were able to locate nearly forty tombs which were at least partly preserved, and we know of the existence of a few others which are by now completely destroyed.

The tombs, or at least most of them, can be typologically divided into three different kinds, each of which will be dealt with below. A few tombs contain elements which are characteristic of two of these types. Significantly, all the tombs of each type seem to be concentrated in one cliff or area in the graveyard, a fact which undoubtedly is not accidental.

The Tombs with a Gabled Ceiling

The seven tombs of this group[4] are among the most beautifully rock-cut tombs known in the Jerusalem area even when compared with tombs of later periods. The stone-dressing of these rock-cut chambers is very fine. All tombs are made for a single or a double burial, and only one tomb contains resting-places for three bodies. The ground-plans and architectural elements are similar in all the tombs. The entrances were cut in the vertical cliff, and one probably needed a ladder in order to enter many of the tombs. The entrance is narrow and almost square, measuring only about 50 to 60 centimeters (20 to 24 inches). The entrance leads into a rectangular burial-chamber with a gabled, and in one case rounded, ceiling. The length of the biggest chamber is 2.40 meters, its width 1.31 meters and its height in the center 2.55 meters (over seven feet long, four and one-third feet wide and seven and one-half feet high). The resting-place is cut in the long wall of the chamber, to the left or to the right of the entrance. It has the shape of a rectangular trough, in which the dead person was placed on his back. A ledge, the width of which is about ten centimeters (four inches), was hewn along the upper edge of the trough; almost certainly it supported a lid placed on the trough after the burial. At the bottom at one end of the trough, a "pillow" was cut in the rock for the head of the dead person. A depression was cut in the pillow to support the head. It should be noted that all the pillows were cut at the end of the trough nearer to the entrance.

Two tombs contain a double resting-place. The shape of the double burial trough is identical to those described above but its width is doubled. Here also a pillow was cut in the rock, containing two depressions for the two heads. It must be assumed that here a man and his wife were interred, and this should explain the following curious fact: In each of the two double troughs the two pillows are not cut at one level, but one is a few inches higher than the other. Furthermore, the bottom of the trough which corresponds to the higher pillow seems to be higher than the other half. Thus it seems that one body, almost certainly that of the husband, was placed higher than the body of the wife, so that the woman's inferior status was also demonstrated after her death!

Finally, another interesting point should be indicated. We have already mentioned the similarity between the architectural elements of the various tombs of this group. A comparison between all of the resting-places in the tombs indicates that they have nearly the same measurements in such matters as the width and height of the trough, the width and height of the pillow, the width and height of the ledge. The only measurement which clearly differs is the length of the trough. While the longest one is 2.10 meters long (almost seven feet), the shortest one is only 1.75 meters (just under six feet). For various reasons it seems clear that the tombs were prepared by their owners while still alive, and thus we have to conclude that each tomb-owner ordered a tomb to fit the measurements of his own body.

The Tombs with a Straight Ceiling

This group includes tombs which mostly contain two or three burial-chambers hewn one behind the other. Some of the caves are relatively large and contain chambers of about three meters (ten feet) square. The chambers have straight ceilings, and most of them contain a right-angled cornice which is cut in the corner of the ceiling and the wall. A small number of resting-places for the dead were hewn in each tomb. These are either benches or a simpler version of the above described trough without the ledge for supporting a lid. Large entrances are also typical of these tombs and so far it is not clear how they were blocked.

In addition, there are a few tombs which seem to be a hybrid between the two above discussed types. Of special interest is one containing a large burial-chamber with a straight ceiling. At the back of the chamber an impressive resting-place was hewn out of the rock, resembling a sarcophagus placed on the floor. Undoubtedly, it was covered with a stone lid, the remains of which are not preserved.

The Monolithic Above-Ground Tombs

Three magnificent tombs of this type (as well as a fourth tomb which resembles them) are situated at the northern end of the village. In the case of all three, the rock section in which the burial-chamber is hewn was separated, in other words cut out, from the continuation of the cliff; this created an above-ground cube-shaped monolithic tomb. Hebrew sepulchral inscriptions were engraved on the façades of all three tombs; significantly, while the inscriptions were placed in all the tombs of this group they are absent in all other tombs in Silwan.

The most famous monolithic tomb is that called the "Tomb of Pharaoh's Daughter." Before two other monuments were identified as being above-ground monolithic tombs, the "Tomb of Pharaoh's Daughter" was the only tomb of that kind known to have existed in the Israelite period. It is not surprising, then, that it was studied by many scholars.[5] This monument is well preserved and is now cube-shaped with a flat roof. The tomb contains a small burial-chamber with a gabled ceiling and a bench for a single burial. The sepulchral inscription was almost completely destroyed when a Byzantine monk widened the entrance to the tomb. N. Avigad proposed that a pyramid must have crowned the tomb in antiquity[6]. He assumed that only the bottom of the pyramid was hewn in the rock and that the upper part was constructed with stones. In order to verify this point we cleaned from the present flat roof the accumulated debris.

To our amazement we learned that the original pyramid was turned into a quarry, probably in the Roman-Byzantine period, and we could see the impressions left by three straight rows of rectangular stones which had been removed in a planned and systematic manner.

The second monolithic tomb, the "Tomb of the Royal Steward," is situated in the main street of the village. In 1870, Clermont-Ganneau discovered two sepulchral inscriptions engraved in sunken panels cut into the tomb's façade. He bought the inscriptions, removed them from the tomb, and sent them to London where they are exhibited at present in the British Museum.[7] Only recently Avigad succeeded in deciphering them.[8] The longer inscription, engraved on the left-hand side of the façade above the tomb's entrance, tells us, "This is [the sepulcher of . . .]yahu who is over the house. There is no silver and no gold here but [his bones] and the bones of his slave-wife with him. Cursed be the man who will open this!" We thus learn that the tomb belonged to a high official of the kingdom of Judah, a royal steward or a royal chamberlain, whose title "who is over the house" appears several times in the biblical record. His name was only partly preserved and Avigad and Yadin suggested identifying him with "Shebna who is over the House" (Isa. 22:15), a high official of King Hezekiah (cf. below). The inscription also informs us that he was buried in the tomb with his āmāh (translated as "slave-wife" by Avigad).

A survey of the monument is not easy, as at present it is half buried under the modern houses of the village. In addition, the tomb was turned into a cistern at a later period and now its walls are covered with a thick layer of water-proof plaster. At present it serves as a store. A study of the exterior of the monument confirmed Avigad's suggestion that it is an above-ground monolithic tomb. A study of the inside of the tomb indicated that the original tomb contained two burial-chambers cut one beside the other. They were damaged beyond recognition and were connected to form one single chamber in the Roman-Byzantine period. Significantly, the original chambers had a straight ceiling with a cornice of the type discussed above. The remains of a resting-place for a single person could be discerned in the inner burial chamber. We reconstructed a double resting-place in the outer burial chamber but it must be borne in mind that this may have been a resting-place for one person (or even that there was no resting-place at all). The fact that the tomb contained two burial chambers necessitates, in our opinion, a new interpretation for the baffling shorter inscription which was engraved on the right-hand side of the façade.[9] It seems to us that this may be the sepulchral inscription of the person who was buried in the single resting-place of the inner chamber, while " . . . yahu who is over the house" and his *āmāh* may have been buried together in the outer burial chamber, probably in the double resting-place which seems to have been cut there.

The Newly Discovered Monolithic Tomb

The third monolithic tomb stands beside and to the north of the "Tomb of the Royal Steward." Its discovery is, undoubtedly, the most important achievement of our survey. Clermont-Ganneau had already discerned the dressed corner of the monument,[10] but it seems that the façade was then hidden, so that he did not see the Hebrew sepulchral inscription, which was discovered by Prof. A. Reifenberg in 1946.[11] During the survey, we found the section of the façade with the inscription, and unearthed the façade as much as we could. We could not uncover other parts of the tomb as it is situated under a courtyard of a modern house, while the burial chamber is blocked and serves at present as a cistern.

However, we were able to learn the following details. This above-ground tomb portrays the finest and most delicate stone dressing in the Silwan necropolis. Its width is *ca.* 4.75 meters (or fifteen and one-half feet) and its present height 4.23 meters (almost fourteen feet). The top of the monument was quarried in the Roman-Byzantine period and here we are inclined to reconstruct a pyramid like the one which crowned the "Tomb of Pharaoh's Daughter," in which case the original height of our tomb may have reached 5.50 meters (over eighteen feet). A step is cut in the rock along the lower end of the façade. A deep niche or recess, whose height is 2.42 meters, its width 1.50 meters and its depth fifty centimeters (about seven feet by five feet by twenty inches), is hewn in the center of the façade. The entrance to the burial chamber, now destroyed and blocked, was cut in the recess. Remains of a protruding cornice can be discerned in the upper part of the façade. The sepulchral inscription was engraved in the center of the façade, above the recess of the entrance, and below the cornice. It contained three lines, and according to our calculations, its width was 74 centimeters (about thirty inches). However, only small sections of the inscription were preserved. Cleaning it enabled us to suggest small corrections to Reifenberg's reading. It seems that both the text and the shape of the letters resemble those of the adjacent long inscription of ". . . yahu who is over the house." The word *qbrt.z* . . . was preserved in the first line, and in parallel to ". . . yahu's" adjacent inscription, it was probably preceded by the word *zʾt*, thus meaning "[This is the] burial of Z . . . ." In the second line we can discern the words *ʾšr yp[tḥ]* . . . meaning "(the one) who op[ens] (this tomb) . . . ." Nothing can be read in the mutilated and weathered third line.

The Importance of the Silwan Necropolis

We shall now discuss briefly the date, character and importance of our necropolis. It seems to be beyond doubt that all the tombs date to the pre-exilic period.[12] We believe, although it is hard to prove it, that the date of the tombs can be narrowed to the 9th to mid-7th centuries B.C. The suggested dating of the necropolis is based on arguments of differing kinds. We shall briefly mention two of them. Firstly, the tombs with a gabled ceiling are probably from the same period as the "Tomb of Pharaoh's Daughter" which has an identical ceiling. The tombs with a straight ceiling can be assumed to be contemporary with the "Tomb of the Royal Steward" which contains two chambers with a straight ceiling and a right-angled cornice. In turn, the remains of their sepulchral inscriptions date these monolithic tombs to the pre-exilic period. Secondly, our tombs bear strong architectural resemblance to other Iron Age tombs in the Near East, some of which will be mentioned later in this article. Therefore, if this dating is correct, we see in pre-exilic Jerusalem the phenomenon of about fifty monumental tombs hewn in the cliffs in a distinguished location opposite and near the "City of David." Their exclusiveness becomes more apparent if we consider the fact that tens of thousands of people were buried in Jerusalem in the period of the First Temple, almost certainly in tombs of types characteristic of the period.[13] Our tombs were prepared for the burial of relatively few people and they cannot be considered as "family tombs." It seems that here ministers, nobles and notables of the kingdom of Judah were buried. The architecture of the tombs and the burial traditions sharply differ from anything known from contemporary Palestine. Elements such as entrances located high above the surface, gabled ceilings, straight ceilings with a cornice,[14] trough-shaped resting-places with pillows, above-ground tombs, and inscriptions engraved on the façade appear only here. Only the resting-places shaped like benches and the small square entrances appear elsewhere in Judah.

In our opinion the origin of the Silwan tomb architecture should be looked for in Phoenicia, whence it was imported to Jerusalem as part of the Phoenician influence in Israel and Judah. It is difficult to decide whether the owners of the tombs were Phoenician nobles who resided in Jerusalem or were local nobles who adopted Phoenician burial customs. It may be that both suggestions are correct, as we have three different groups of tombs, each of which is mainly concentrated in a separate section of the slope. Shebna "who is over the house," the noble who was ferociously attacked by the prophet Isaiah (Isa. 22:15-19) is usually identified with ". . . yahu who is over the house."[15] Whether Shebna and . . . yahu were the same person or not it seems logical to assume that Shebna prepared a tomb for himself in our necropolis, an assumption which is supported by the fact that the prophet calls him *skn*, a Phoenician title. And in the prophet's reproach, "What have you to do here and whom have you here, that you have hewn here a tomb for yourself, you who hew a tomb on the height, and carve a habitation for yourself in the rock?" (RSV) one can hear his anger both about the exaggerated richness of the tombs and the foreign traditions embodied in them.

It should be mentioned that this monumental tomb architecture also seems to have spread from Phoenicia to other countries, and thus we can find tombs which resemble ours far from Palestine. We shall mention only the rock-cut tombs in Asia Minor[16] and the monumental tombs recently excavated in Salamis, Cyprus.[17] Most surprising is the resemblance between our tombs and the royal tombs of the kings of Urartu in Van, Armenia.[18] There too we see rock-cut tombs located in the cliffs, each consisting of a few chambers, and some chambers having a straight ceiling with a cornice similar to those which appear in our tombs. Thus in the 8th century B.C. we have a clear cultural link between the kingdom of Urartu and Judah.

Finally, we shall briefly discuss another relevant problem. The royal sepulchers of the house of David undoubtedly formed the most monumental and magnificent necropolis in biblical Jerusalem. The biblical text specifically states several times that the sepulchers were situated "in the City of David,"[19] in other words within the limits of the "Hill of Ophel" (i.e. the southeastern hill).[20] There R. Weill discovered [21] the remains of big rock-cut chambers or tombs which he, as well as other scholars who followed him later,[22] identified as the royal sepulchers of the house of David. In our opinion the Silwan tombs refute Weill's identification. The Silwan tombs are more monumental, and they portray a much higher standard of stone-dressing than that of Weill's tombs. And as it is highly unlikely that the tombs of the nobles were more beautiful and bigger than those of the kings, we have to conclude that the tombs discovered by Weill are not those of the kings of Judah. It seems, therefore, that the location and discovery of the sepulchers of the house of David remains as a challenge for future archaeologists working in Jerusalem.

Notes

[1] Cf. C. Schick, *Palestine Exploration Fund Quarterly Statement*, 1890, pp. 16-18, 67, 252-56; C. Clermont-Ganneau, *Archaeological Researches in Palestine* (1899), I, 305-13; A. Reifenberg, *Journal of the Palestine Oriental Society* XXI (1948); 134-37; N. Avigad, *Israel Exploration Journal* III (1953), 137-52, and V (1955), 163-66; S. Loffreda, *Studii Biblici* XVI (1965-66), 85-126.

[2] C. Warren, *Underground Jerusalem* (1876), p. 149.

[3] The survey was supported by Tel Aviv University, the Hebrew University, and the Municipality of Jerusalem. It was carried out with the assistance of Mr. G. Barkay.

[4] Some of these tombs were studied by Loffreda (see note 1), who erroneously dated them to the Hellenistic-Roman period.

[5]Cf. F. de Saulcy, *Voyage en Terre-Sainte* (1865), II, 307-13; G. Perrot and Ch. Chipiez, *History of Art in Sardinia, Judaea, Syria and Asia Minor* (1890), I, 272-83; Clermont-Ganneau, *Archaeological Researches*, I, 313-16.

[6]N. Avigad, *Palestine Exploration Quarterly* LXXXII (1947), 112-15.

[7]Clermont-Ganneau, *Archaeological Researches*, I, 305-13.

[8]N. Avigad, *Israel Exploration Journal* III (1953), 137-52; V (1955), 163-66.

[9]Cf. our study in *Bulletin of the American Schools of Oriental Research* 196 (Dec., 1969), 16-22.

[10]Clermont-Ganneau, *Archaeological Researches*, I, 309.

[11]A. Reifenberg, *Journal of the Palestine Oriental Society* XXI (1948), 134-37.

[12]For a different opinion, cf. Loffreda, *Studii Biblici* XVI (1965-66), 85-126.

[13]Since this article was written two large monumental tombs dating to this period were identified by G. Barkay and A. Kloner in the grounds of the monastery of St. Étienne in the northern part of Jerusalem (Cf. Notes and News, *Israel Exploration Journal* 26 [1976], 55-57). The tombs are cut in the rock, and significantly, their architecture bears much resemblance to the tombs in the Silwan necropolis.

[14]A straight ceiling with a cornice can also be seen in one rock-cut tomb in the area of Lachish (J. Naveh, *Israel Exploration Journal* XIII [1963], 74-92, Pls. 9-13). Naveh dated it to the 8th century B.C., but later, in following F. M. Cross's suggestion, has lowered its date to the 6th cent. (in *Harvard Theological Review* LXI [1968], 74). The latter date was also advocated by Loffreda *Studii Biblici* XVIII (1968), 249f. The architectural resemblance of this tomb to the Silwan tombs seems to indicate its unusual character.

[15]Cf. Avigad, *Israel Exploration Journal* III (1953), 150f., G. E. Wright,

[16]Cf. Perrot and Chipiez, *History of Art in Phrygia, Lydia, Caria and Lycia* (1928), pp. 78ff.; cf. esp. Figs. 64, 67-68, 72-74, 143-46.

[17]V. Karageorghis, *Excavations in the Necropolis of Salamis*, I (1967).

[18]Cf. C. F. Lehmann-Haupt, *Armenien Einst und Jetzt* (1926), II, 120ff.; B. B. Piotrovskij, *Il regno di Van Urartu* (1966), pp. 299-313, Pls. XII-XIII.

[19]Cf., for example, I Kings 15:24, 22:51; II Kings 9:28, 14:20.

[20]Cf. S. Yeivin, *Journal of Near Eastern Studies* VII (1948), 30-45; J. Simons, *Jerusalem in the Old Testament* (1952), pp. 194-225.

[21]R. Weill, *Revue des Études Juives* LXXI (1920), 1ff.

[22]Cf. J. Simons, *Jerusalem in the Old Testament*, pp. 194-225.

8

GEOLOGICAL STUDIES IN FIELD ARCHAEOLOGY

REUBEN G. BULLARD

The science of geology treats the crust of the earth in much the same way that archaeology considers areas of human occupation. This discussion seeks to explore this parallel relationship and to examine some aspects of excavation in which questions arise that apply to areas of specialty for geologists. The writer is aware of the problem of terminology which may be unfamiliar to the non-geologist. Minimal definitions are included in the discussion.[1]

Field study for this article was carried out on the site of Gezer in the central Shephelah of Israel.[2] The aim of the investigation conducted during the excavations has been a broader under-standing of the relationship between Gezer's inhabitants and their environment during the city's history. Certain areas of inquiry have proved useful in the initial phases of this research. A survey of the local and regional geology made from field studies and from the growing literature has provided information about the nature and origin of the rocks and minerals encountered in the excavation. Exposed soils and clays within five kilometers of Gezer were systematically sampled and analyzed for mineral and trace element content. Potential temper sources such as local stream channel and terrace deposits and Pleistocene and Recent sands of the Coastal Plain were studied mineralogically.[3] Randomly sampled discards from the daily pottery calls, together with oven wall fragments and mud brick remnants were collected. This material was analyzed for clay mineral content, firing history, and temper. A growing catalog of ceramic groups and temper suites is being assembled.

Stratigraphic relations and sedimentalogical data are areas of specialization for geologists who can contribute measurably to the understanding of the history of occupation at a site. Petrologic study of regional and local bedrock materials is providing a preliminary basis for determining the provenance of numerous

igneous, sedimentary, and metamorphic lithic artifacts and
building materials found in the historical phasing of a city-site.

Regional and Local Geology

The topographic features of the earth's surface take their form
mostly from the effects of bedrock composition, configuration,
and climate. The location of mountains and hills, valleys and
plains, rivers and streams, the ground water supply, the occurrence
of caves, the nature of the soil and the wealth of mineral resources
are all governed by geological factors.

A division of the southern Levant into geomorphic or
physiographic provinces is relevant to the work of the archaeologist and the historian. This is because each province is defined on
the basis of topographic or surface relief features which are caused
by geologic conditions in the crust of the earth. Local
environmental variation in each province has a significant effect on
the inhabitants even to the extent of affecting their way of life. The
inhabitants of the Coastal Plain, for example, lacked the hard rock
sources for wall and house construction which the Shephelah and
Judean hill areas had in abundance. Southeastern Galilee abounds
with basalt surface rock which is a highly durable grindstone
material and stands in marked contrast with the soft chalk and
brittle chert rock sources of the Shephelah. The high frequency of
basalt grindstones at Gezer means that the inhabitants traded or
traveled some distance to secure a material they preferred above
local resources.

The physiographic provinces of the southern Levant:[4]

1. *The Negev*. This portion of Israel extending from Beersheba
to the Gulf of Aqaba is bounded by Sinai on the west and the Araba
on the east.

2. *The Araba - Dead Sea - Jordan Valley*. The rift between Israel
and Transjordan is a long (400 km) and narrow (10-30 km) tectonic
depression (crustal deformation) extending from the Gulf of
Aqaba (Eilat) to the foothills of Mt. Hermon.

3. *The Emek Yizreel* (biblical Esdraelon). A graben structure
(down-faulted block of the earth's crust) trends northwest from the
central Jordan valley in the region of Beth-shan (Beisan) about 30
kilometers.

4. *Galilee Highland.* Galilee is situated between the Emek Yizreel on the south and the Lebanon border on the north.

5. *The Carmel Uplift.* Mt. Carmel is a folded upwarp which is a structural continuity with the Megiddo syncline and the Um el-Fahm anticline extending into the West Bank area.[5]

6. *The Judean - Ephraim Mountains.* "The Backbone of central Palestine" is the northward trending anticlinal mountain belt with three north-northeast *en echelon* (off-set parallel) structural components: the Hebron mountains on the south, the Judean mountains in the central area, and the Ephraim mountains on the north. This mountain system is bounded in the east by the rift valley faults and on the west by the dip of the bedrock (about 30°) under the Shephelah.

7. *The Coastal Plain.* This province extends along the eastern shore of the Mediterranean Sea from the borders of Sinai on the south to the Lebanon border near Rosh Ha-niqra. It is punctuated only by the cape which is the result of the Carmel uplift. Below the Carmel promontory, the coastal area is subdivided into the Philistine (Pleshet) plain on the south and the plain of Sharon on the north. Longitudinally the Coastal plain west of Gezer is marked with kurkar ridges (fossilized or cemented sand dunes) and hamra (deeply weathered Pleistocene red sands). The swamps the Romans began to drain have all been given outlets to the sea in modern times leaving swamp-deposits.

8. *The Continental Shelf.* This submarine extension of the coastal area of the eastern Mediterranean has a maximum width of about 15 kilometers. It exhibits numerous rock outcrops regarded as submerged kurkar. From the shoreline the area slopes gently westward to the shelf-break point at about the 110 meter depth west of the coast of Israel.

9. *The Shephelah.*

"Over the Plain, as you come up from the coast, you see a sloping moorland break into scalps and ridges of rock, and over these a loose gathering of chalk and limestone hills, round and featureless, with an occasional bastion flung out in front of them. This is the Shephelah—a famous theater of the history of Palestine—debatable ground between Israel and the Philistines, the Maccabees and the Syrians, Saladin and the Crusaders."[6]

Shephelah means *lowland*, or the subtle rolling foothill area bordered on the east by the Judean and Ephraim mountains and on the west by the Coastal plain. Morphologically the foothills province extends from the Carmel uplift in the north on Cretaceous limestones to the vicinity of Gezer from which it extends southward mostly on Eocene chalks and limestones to the northern Negev. Topographic highs persist under a protective armor of a caliche-like weathered residual bedrock crust termed *nari*.

It is upon such a topographic high that the city of Gezer was built giving it a commanding position over the coastal road (the *Via Maris*) which lay toward the eastern margin of the Coastal plain because of the swamp land to the west. In addition Gezer was suitably situated to control traffic to the Judean mountains along the route through the Aijalon valley lying to the north and northeast of the city. Moreover the inhabitants of Gezer were conditioned by the economic geological aspects of the central Shephelah, sometimes near, sometimes far: tools, building materials, weapons, and the raw materials for various enterprises and commodities.

Soils and Soil Clay Mineralogy

The term soil has been used with a variety of meanings by farmers, civil engineers, archaeologists and geologists. Soil scientists regard soil as that earth material which has been acted upon by physical, chemical, and biological agents to the extent that it will support rooted plants. Archaeologists sometimes use the term for any very fine-grained sediment in the excavation which has color as its only distinguishable feature. In this discussion we are considering a soil to be the weathered material on or at the earth's surface representing the naturally altered parent rock material. Weathering processes change the minerals of the bedrock which were formed under different conditions into minerals which are stable in the environment of the existing climate. Soils may be residual (existing on the parent rock from which they are derived) or transported (moved elsewhere by natural agencies).[7]

The composition of soils varies with different parent rock sources and with different climate regimes. In Israel bedrock characteristics and climate have produced two dominant soil types in the region about Gezer. The dense crystalline limestones of the Judean-Ephraim mountains weather to terra rossa soils[8] containing some clay components and especially iron oxide, which imparts the distinctive deep red coloration. The softer chalks and marls which underlie the central and southern Shephelah give rise to a brown soil containing clay, oxides of iron and manganese mixed with calcium carbonate residues—a rendzinate soil.[9] Local soil clays are frequently concentrated in the floodplain deposits of the streams in the area. At Gezer rendzinate soils and clays found use as floor surfacing, wine or olive press wall surfacing, sub-plaster stone wall filling, oven walls, terra cottas, and unfired and fired mud brick material.

A surprising discovery in the soil and clay studies of the Gezer environment is the occurrence of insoluble tests or shells of Eocene foraminifera in the soil derived from the parent chalk. Originally composed of calcium carbonate, these silica-replaced fossils occur in the rendzinate soil produced by the weathering of the rock under local climatic conditions. They are entrained in the soil clay matrix and become a part of any mud brick or pottery materials made from it. The occurrence of such fossil forminifera in statistically high numbers provides evidence for the locality as understood by the area of outcrop where a particular fossil bearing bedrock formation occurs. In Israel such areas may vary from one physiographic province to another.

Ceramics

Inasmuch as pottery may be considered the most durable and widely distributed packaging medium of antiquity, those shapes which were used over broad geographical areas become a valuable means of chronological interpretation. Pottery, from the viewpoint of a petrologist, is essentially a man-made (or in a special sense, a metamorphic) rock and is practically indestructible after its primary purpose is met. As such it is composed of heat-altered clays having a particular trace element chemistry along with temper (sand-size particles or straw) added by potters to give the mixture properties to resist failure during drying and firing.

The non-organic portion of soils of most importance to pottery makers is the clay mineral content. While potters knew nothing more about clays than whether they were plastic when wet and would become durable in shape when fired, we are in a position to understand just why some clays made fine pottery, some poor pottery, and some clays simply failed. Clays are natural fine-grain, earthy materials which become plastic when combined with water. Chemical analyses show that clays are composed of silica, alumina, and water and may also contain iron, alkalis, and alkaline earths. X-ray diffraction studies reveal that clay minerals are usually platy or fibrous in atomic structure, with groups of atoms repeating themselves to form layered crystalline sequences.

The plasticity exhibited by clays is the result of very thin films of water held on and between sub-microscopic plates or fibers. The slippery property of clays is a glide effect of these minute platelets on surface water. This response is the clay behavior sought by potters for workability in hand and on the wheel. After his vessel is shaped, the potter allows this "surface water" to evaporate during which the plastic effects diminish to the point where the vessel becomes "leather hard." Cohesion and electrostatic charges bond the clay mineral platelets and fibers together and the vessel is ready for firing.

The effect of heat is to remove internal water from the platelets and fibers.. This is the point at which the potter found the answer to the critical question about his clay vessel—will it crack? Trial and error (with good luck) led him to realize that certain clays would not crack and that the addition of temper would lessen the tendency to do so of those which did. We know that kaolinite, illite, montmorillonite, palygorskite (attapulgite), and sepiolite are the dominant clay minerals present in southern Levantine sources. These minerals seldom occur naturally in high purity except in isolated environments. Only the first two may yield a fine ceramic when available in the quantities used by the makers of certain Greek and Cypriot wares. While some local sources in stream deposits contain varying amounts of kaolinite and/or illite, Gezer potters learned that most local soil clay sources (because they are rich in palygorskite—a fibrous clay) required tempering additives to prevent vessel failure during drying and firing.

Pottery temper was found by potters in the sands of local beaches, in the stream beds of local wadis and from recent and geologically older sand dune sources. In the case of most mud bricks and some terra cottas (sarcophagi, baking oven walls, and a few storage jar handles and walls), straw and grass tempers were utilized. The mineralogy of sand tempers varies with the place of origin, and, assuming ancient potters did not transport their temper raw materials from considerable distances, the composition may yield information about the probable locality of origin.

The activity of a modern potter shows the importance of good clay sources, but it is probably not typical for potters because of transportation limitations. In 1968 a Palestinian potter at the Balâṭah refugee camp obtained his clay from the Moza Marl, which outcrops on the stone surface near el-Jîb. He drove to the Mediterranean beach and dune sands near Natanyah for his temper materials. The Gezer studies do not show such a wide-ranging combination in the same ware.

The Gezer staff recognized that the subjective nature of color values in ceramic description and study required the standardization of some recognized system from the beginning of the current excavations. We have adopted the Munsell Soil Color Charts for this purpose. Regardless of the nature of the illumination, essential color data are recorded for chroma, hue, and lightness value, using numbered terminology along with the designated common color name; for example 5YR 5/2, reddish gray.[10] This system has been the reference standard for field geologists and pedologists for a number of years in the United States. Color plates, not possible here, are highly desirable in comparative ceramic study..

We can observe in a number of illustrations distinct variations in gross temper compositions. Some of the areas where such sources occur today have been recorded, and we can say something about the probability of these sources being used in antiquity. Those categories appearing at the beginning of the list below are most likely materials made at Gezer from sources available very close to the city. All but the last two are very probably produced in what is Israel today from materials in the areas noted. Exotic or foreign ceramic materials are usually recognized on stylistic grounds, but analytic data can be useful here too, especially in the discovery of local copies.

Proposed Provenance for the Gezer Ceramics

A combination of clay texture, clay mineral and trace element content,[11] and temper data has led to a tentative proposal for the origin of the Gezer pottery materials. We have added analytical data from unfired and fired mud and clay structures found throughout the excavation providing a high degree of certainty about local clay materials available to Gezer potters—if they desired to use them—in the past. We have grouped the pottery into categories which matched the preliminary data derived from natural clay and temper occurrences. A neutral designation termed *Type I, Type II*, etc. was used in the initial phase of the research. The categories are as follows:

Type I Pottery (and mud bricks). The immediate area around Gezer with the local residual, colluvial and alluvial soil clays originating on the Zorᶜa formation (Middle and Lower Eocene). It includes material available today on the topographic saddle and on the foothills immediately to the south.[12]

Type II Pottery (and mud bricks). Residual, colluvial and alluvial soils derived from the Taqiye, Ghareb and Menuha Formations which underlie the lowlands immediately north and east of Gezer.

Type III Pottery. Soils and clays produced from the Turonian and Cenomanian (i.e., the Judean group) lithic strata which underlie the Shephelah to the north and the Judean mountains to the east.

Type IV Pottery. Residual, colluvial and alluvial soils produced by weathering of basalt flows such as Galilee.

Type V Pottery. A category at present somewhat general, but initial data suggest the following: alluvial soils and clays from the Aijalon valley, the Yarkon river valley and the Sorek valley together with associated lake and swamp deposits through which these streams cut on the Coastal plain in their courses to the Mediterranean.

Type VI Pottery. The Coastal plain with lake clays and hamra sands and silts and the Recent dunal sands.

Type VII Pottery. Possibly the Golan, as the clays show relic shards (volcanic tephra) in the ceramic paste. Pyroclastic deposits from the late Neocene cindercones observed on the Golan (and the Hauran) are a possible source. Data incomplete.

Type VIII Pottery. Exotic clays and tempers, the physical, mineral, and trace element chemistry of which are totally unrelated to that which is known in the literature, e.g., Cypriot, Aegean or otherwise.

We are proposing these tentative categories as a basis for discussion and refinement. They represent only a beginning in the study of Gezer materials.

Some Examples of Gezer Ceramic Paste and Temper

A maximum surface area of a potsherd may be obtained by cutting a section tangential to the curvature of the vessel so that the longest and intermediate particle dimensions tend to be exposed. Type I pottery is illustrated in this example. The clay mineral content and trace element chemistry compares closely with that of the central Shephelah. Chalk and nari temper are available in the sediment load deposits in the valley of the wadi just east of Gezer. The particles are subangular to rounded as a consequence of stream transport abrasion. Chert and siliceous chalk are present in minor amounts.

An unusual combination of clay mineral variation and temper technique is shown in a Late Bronze vessel. Type II clay is produced on the Paleocene marls (Taqiye Formation) underlying the lowlands east and north of Gezer. The temper used occurs in the wadi just east of Gezer and contains partially silicified Eocene faunal assemblages. The attached handle portion of this potsherd (A) is an example of straw temper usage which was added to the temper used in the body portion (B). A significant difference was noted in the trace element content between (A) and (B): The handle paste (A) gives values in the range of that observed for the rendzinate soil formed on the Eocene chalks higher in the local geologic stratification on the flanks of the tell and on the Shephelah to the south (Type I conditions). The body portion gave trace element values comparable to those found for Type II ceramics. Only a few examples of this unusual combination of materials have been found. The Gezer potters may have found that the straw temper made the palygorskite-rich soil clays more amenable to handle construction.

A number of examples were observed in which the pottery raw material was probably obtained from the local neighborhood to the north or east of the city, but in combination with a temper similar in composition to the sediments occuring in stream sorted deposits along the Aijalon valley. North of Gezer this valley contains sediments whch are eroded from the dark burnt lime deposits of kilns which were observed in considerable number along one of the local tributaries.

The appearance of lime kiln dross in pottery tempers may serve as an indication of the beginning of the firing of carbonate lithologies to make lime. Ancient kilns were observed along a stream where erosion had exposed limestone bedrock more suitable for firing than the local nari. This uninhabited valley occurs just west of the pre-1967 No-Man's Land where twenty-two remnants of kilns of various ages were counted. Some of the kilns consisted of nothing more than mass-wasted piles of rubble. Out-crops of hard Turonian limestone had been exploited by the kiln operators along the wadi which drains this "kiln valley." The chan-nel of this wadi, a tributary to the Aijalon valley, was choked almost to its banks with considerable quantities of fine sand-size to angular pebble-size dross fragments. Here the activity of water as a transporting, rounding, and sorting agent is impressed upon the sediment. This temper source, when incorporated in ceramics for the first time, would offer a basis from which to infer the existence of lime burning operations and the use of lime at the time the pottery was made. The data are incomplete, but late Early Bronze materials are the earliest ceramic evidence for this temper supply encountered at this point in the research.

A temper found frequently in the Gezer pottery is the red hamra sands which compose the highest Pleistocene transgressive deposits in the Coastal plain west of Gezer. Hamra is composed of sand-size quartz grains coated with the sesquioxides of iron and aluminum as a result of lateritic weathering and has the appearance of terra rossa.

Tempers exotic to the Gezer area are calcite and basalt. A frequent occurrence of calcite temper may be expected in ceramics originating in such areas as the Ephraim mountains where veins of calcite twelve centimeters thick were observed in Cenomanian formations. The calcite tempered examples tend to show a mineral and trace element content distribution of Type III ware. Ceramic materials (Type IV) which arise in areas where alkaline-olivine basalt flows constitute the bedrock (e.g., southeastern Galilee) usually show values which compare with data found for the soil clays which weather from this rock. These clays usually have a montmorillonite content and trace element chemistry which set them apart from soil clays formed on limestone in Israel. Basalt tempers are available in the sediments of streams which flow across the basaltic lava rock.

Stratification and Sedimentation

The task of interpreting the history of stratified remains from antiquity involves considerably more than the interpretation of the ceramic evidence. It goes beyond the recognition of the layered or stratified levels and the careful delineation of their geometry. This vital and highly important facet to the understanding of the history of a city which is undergoing excavation involves the examination of the sediments and the meaning of the configuration in which they are found.

"Digging is destruction." Even the casual observer of the glaring, gray-white dust which comes up under the trowel of the excavator is acutely aware of the fact that these deposits can tell their story only once. Afterward, they become refuse or spoil in actual fact. Geological research at an excavation is not the work of a laboratory technician whose job is merely analyzing those curiosities brought to him by the archaeologists from the field in the confines of research quarters. In the context of work done at Gezer (and also at Shechem) the research task is essentially a new way of looking at stratified sediments in historical deposits. This approach to the history of accumulation of sediments in ancient cities is that which has traditionally concerned the sedimentologist. Sedimentary petrologists add to the task of rock description that broader concern of understanding the geological history of a stratified unit, i.e., the mode of origin. The student of archaeology in similar manner stands to gain much by adding to the description all the genetic data he can assemble.

Attention is directed to those processes in the confines of the regime of human activity which produced the sedimentation of the archaeological context. Our primary aim or purpose here is an elucidation of human history by means of those methods proven successful in the hands of the earth scientist. The ultimate goal we seek is an understanding of the ecology controlling the life of the Gezer inhabitant and his dependency upon the environment in which he lived.

The problems of major concern in the course of this research were: 1) the primary composition of the sediment; 2) the manner or mode of deposition; and 3) the agency which was responsible for the occurrence of the sediment in the context in which it was found. Vital to this concept is the observation by the specialist of the sediments in their stratified position. Facies relationships[13] exist within each stratigraphic entity in the same real sense they do in the sedimentary basins within the geological regime of sedimentary environments, whether continental or marine.

There are a number of ways to study sediments. The central concern of this research has been to present the data in such a meaningful and significant way that it is useful to the archaeologist and historian in the integrated synthesis of the primary material. We made arrangements to obtain our own samples, observing the lateral and vertical relationships of that which was being cleared. Documentation included photographic recording of the deposits *in situ*.

We set up a field laboratory in the dig house at Gezer. This consisted of a work bench with north light in the staff room, a binocular stereoscopic microscope and standard sieves. A suite of reagents was prepared for special treatment such as the solution of carbonates, spot and stain tests for dolomite, potassium, phosphates, copper, tin, and silver. Other tools considered as basic to mineralogists were also included in the equipment.

Sedimentary analysis at Gezer involved the recording of the texture, considering particle size, shape and roundness, surface texture, porosity and permeability, and the packing and fabric. We determined mineral composition and analyzed primary and secondary mechanical structures such as bedding, bedding planes, irregularities, deformation, disruption and truncation, and distortion.

Classification of Sediments for the Archaeologist

Inasmuch as human history is the ultimate goal of the study of these materials, the primary objective and determining principle in this classification is a genetically meaningful designation of the sediments studied. We have used the following classification as a preliminary framework:

I. Occupational structures and associated sediments.

A. Features cut or hewn into the bedrock which provide evidence of their primary usage (hence they become models for understanding their constructional counterparts).
(1) Rooms or dwelling places cut in the bedrock, wine and olive presses.
(2) Storage vats, silos, magazines, drainage channels, cisterns, and water tunnels.
B. Primary structures built in each of the successive cities.
(1) City walls and gates, streets, and drains.
(2) The structures which make up the courtyards of houses (with associated sediments) along with plastered walls, wine presses, cisterns, cooking ovens, quarters for livestock, and refuse pits.
(3) House interior structures (where they can be distinguished from (2) above): Wall and roof materials, doorway structures, floor sequences with ovens, hearths, cooking stoves (some have been observed having a fired clay composition), refuse pits, infant burials, and other debris from human activity within the confines of such dwellings.
(4) Structures associated with crafts and with industrial activities such as pottery and lime manufacture, tools, and weapon manufacture with typical sediment.
(5) Structures built for cultic and ceremonial practices and associated sediment.
(6) Buildings serving man's aesthetic propensities such as the arts: theaters and circuses.
C. Primary sediment left *in situ* in surfaces as a result of human activity in the city as outlined in the contexts above. The composition and fabric of the accumulation and its subsurface makeup. Consideration of the specific origin or agent of deposition.

II. Exotic (non-local) pottery, lithic objects, and mineral artifacts.
  A. Mills, grinders, pounders, ballistae and stone and metal tools and weapons.
  B. Semi-precious and precious minerals and gemstones.
  C. Vessels fabricated from special rock and mineral materials, e.g., alabaster and basalt.

III. Destructional deposition.
  A. Debris resulting from the falling of structures.
  (1) The collapse of walls, the filling of cisterns and water supplies, the destruction of cooking facilities.
  (2) Skeletal remains of occupants and animals.
  B. Debris resulting from the burning of structures.
  (1) House roofs, the beams of which have burned with resultant structural failure.
  (2) Carbonate fortifications such as gate areas composed of limestone or nari which have been calcined by the use of fire.
  C. See V below from which these may be inseparable.

IV. Occupational hiatus.
  A. A minor occupational lapse within the city (may be explained on the basis of a plague or famine or a migration of a city's population or a destruction of the city which was locally incomplete—more data needed).
  (1) Sand, silt, and clay deposits from sheet wash and ponding on surfaces which are sites of normal occupational sedimentation.
  (2) Air-borne deposits which would normally be eroded by normal occupational activities.
  B. A major occupational gap.
  (1) The development of an incipient soil on domestic sediment or destructional processes of weathering.
  (2) The erosion of strata by natural processes (see below). Stratigraphic truncation and angular unconformities may occur.
  (3) The blanketing of streets and structures by loess (wind-borne silt) and sand (in semi-arid regions).

V. The processes of erosion which may remove any one or all of the above:
  A. Mass wasting (downslope movement of material under the influence of gravity).
  B. Running water.
  C. Deflation by wind (wind erosion).

VI. Naturally induced destructive agencies:
    A. Earthquakes.
    B. Volcanic eruptions with ash falls, mudflows, nuée ardente (hot dense gas clouds), caldera explosions (such as in the case of Thera).
    C. Earthquake tidal waves.
    D. Raising of sea level upon coastal sites.
    E. Floods.

Sedimentation Studies at Gezer

As the soft carbonates of the Central Shephelah undergo decomposition during weathering, an insoluble residue known as rendzinate soil is formed. The preservation of this soil is rare in the area of Gezer inasmuch as subaerial denudation (topsoil removal by erosion) has taken place since removal of the vegetable cover by man and animals, for example through possible deforestation. As a consequence, a residual profile of undisturbed or virgin soil was keenly anticipated in the excavations.

Such soil was in fact encountered first in the excavation of the MB II C glacis and the LB I outer wall structures. In this area as much as one meter of virgin soil was found undisturbed on the nari bedrock below. The position of this quantity of virgin soil points to the fact that this thickness was preserved when the glacis and the LB wall were constructed in an area ideally situated for mass-wasting processes. Such soil retention may suggest the presence of some manner of plant anchoring of the regolith (weathered bedrock and soil). If climatic conditions were very little differnt from that of today, arboreal retention probably would be required to hold the soil in place. Deforestation of the Shephelah, therefore, may have taken place after the Late Bronze Age, if indeed the area was ever under forest cover. Pollen and charcoal studies are being undertaken to understand the nature of the floral population.

Study of the MB II glacis constitutes another application of geological techniques to field archaeology. The section exposed by the Gezer Field I excavation trench is illustrated in section. The glacis was used as a defensive structure during the Hyksos period (Middle Bronze II B and C). Gezer has an example of this structure which may prove to be classic. Its location between the massive inner wall and the outer wall has prevented mass wasting from causing significant deterioration in its stratification.

The glacis represents massive amounts of earth movement. The striking interfingering of the relatively clean, unweathered chalk with that of occupational and destructional debris and quarried bedrock marks out a pertinent chapter in the ecology of Gezer. Stratigraphic relationships show a dark brown (10 YR 3/2, Munsell) virgin soil with shallow cultural intrusion on the nari-bedrock. Above this is a lens of Taqiye marl distinguished by the Paleocene foraminifera, *Globoconusa* sp., a light gray-green color (5 Y 6/2), and "limonite concretions" pseudomorphic after goethite. This marl outcrops to the east and north around the lowest parts of the hill upon which Gezer is situated. Two lenses about 2 meters from virgin soil are surface rendzinate soil derivations of the Eocene with occupational debris. After another lens of Taqiye marl, local surface soil materials were used to back-fill in front of the massive MB II nari wall.

The surface of the glacis gives evidence of the care used in the preparation of this defensive structure. The surface and supporting lenses (wedges) are composed of unweathered chalk quarried from the Maresha formation (contains Middle Eocene coccolitho-phoridae and foraminifera). The freshly quarried chalk was tightly packed to achieve a high degree of hardening. At the surface the chalk was worked into a paste giving it a firm smooth surface that has been virtually impermeable to ground water; as the water ran down the slope of the glacis it deposited about two to four inches of sesquioxide concentration of iron and aluminum immediately above the chalk paste.

It is important to realize that this degree of impermeability could be achieved only with the use of unweathered chalk materials, always in short supply because of the nari crust which locally attains a thickness of three meters. Moreover, siliceous chalk bedrock horizons were useless since the quarried aggregate of this material could not be packed hard and would easily be scaled by assaulting enemy soldiers. The construction of this sloping chalk apron about the city demanded a supply of fresh chalk which could be supplied from a nearby quarry. This material was available only from the excavation of such features as tombs, cisterns, rooms, and water tunnels. The relative inaccessibility of unweathered chalk created an economic supply problem that forced the glacis builders to go to the base of the local Shephelah to quarry raw material required for the surface.

The stratigraphic hiatus. Criteria which distinguish sedimentary processes other than those regarded as occupational accumulation or destruction sediment are as follows: (1) a stratified weathered zone in which there is gradational enrichment of clay mineral content vertically; (2) sediment of a clearly loessic character (wind-blown silt in the 0.03-0.08 mm. size range); (3) sheet wash deposits or ponded sediments across broad areas of the site. These deposits, occurring within the stratification of a tell, are usually devoid of facies which exhibit an occupational or destructional sedimentary character in their inherent fabric.

Weathering and soil zones. An occupational hiatus permits natural processes controlled by the climate to produce physical and chemical changes within the upper levels of exposed occupational features in destruction debris. Weathering has been estimated to proceed in the eastern Mediterranean area at the rate of 10 centimeters in 1000 years.[14] Anticipation of changes in abandoned cultural contexts is therefore not unreasonable. Soils in the true pedogenic sense of the world within the local stratification were encountered in an incipient state.

An example horizon with known vertical control may be observed in Field 1, Area 8 at Gezer. The latest pottery found on top of the MB II wall was Roman. No later contexts were found above this level. Macalister's dump is seen above the "soil" with the character-istic sorting of his tip lines. Samples were taken at five centimeter intervals throughout this stratum. Minor yet significant increases formed during the 1700 years of weathering were noted in the clay mineral content upward in this unit. Changes in the clay mineral composition show an increase in palygorskite, a mineral released by the action of weathering, over the illite, a major component of the unfired mud brick debris that reflects mineral concentrations of the alluvial clays of the Aijalon valley. This study of a "paleosoil" is intended as a model designed to serve as the basis for understanding the meaning of stratified sediment of this nature.

The occurrence of loess. No better place to observe the cessation of normal occupational activity in a city may be found than the street environment. Street surfaces inward through the entrance of the south-central gate have been delineated in the step-like demonstration of successive street surfacings utilized by the excavators.[15] This surface distinction may be made partly on the basis of the relative hardness or resistance of the street sediment to the trowel. A deposit of an unusual nature was discovered in the excavation of these street surfaces: A locally variable sixteen-centimeter thickness of finely divided sediment uniformly in the silt size range of .03-.08 mm. blanketed the area observed. Sieved portions of this stratum showed the absence of the usual occupational sediment ingredients: charcoal flecks, unweathered chalk particles, nari, pottery fragments of various sizes, and the field soil clay which is usually mixed with the street surface material.

Comparative analysis with loessic samples taken on field trips in the Beersheba area revealed a striking comparison of particle sizes in the concentration ranges typical of that of loess. An occupational hiatus of this form can be missed by anyone who is scraping only for hard surfaces.

Precipitation (rainfall) runoff. While the subject of surface water drainage is one familiar to students of geology, these features may not be initially recognized by untrained eyes. This form of sedimentation has been observed in a number of stratified contexts.

Areas where local ponding occurs give rise to a peculiar sediment known as graded bedding. A coarse to fine particle deposition occurs where surface water runoff cannot find an outlet. Sequences of graded bedding (coarse particles grading upward into finer sediments) imply repeated rainstorms which carry a sediment load to a local base-level in which the coarse particles settle out more rapidly than the fine. One can actually count the number of rainstorms from the graded couplets in the example from Field I excavated by Joe D. Seger of the Gezer Staff.

Occupational sedimentation: mud brick debris. Mud bricks have been observed with various compositions in varying states of preservation. The history of the use of mud bricks is documented in an usual way in a section cut through a Middle Bronze gate structure, excavated by J. Randolph Osborne.

The sediment is compositionally different in the various types of mud bricks used for the construction of the defensive wall and its gate. The frequency and distribution of the bricks serve to illustrate the fact that certain compositions played a key role in the structural stability of the walls.

The higher clay content of the Aijalon floodplain colluvial, alluvial, and residual soils provided a greater structural strength than the residual rendzinate soil materials near by. The wall, however, is an illustration of structural failure, for the inhabitants of the city found it necessary to add to the fired brick structure brick material of a far less competent composition. Several different compositions of debris brick material were used.

The effects of mass wasting and slump may be observed not only in the crescentic slip-plane scar observable on the surface above the wall but also in the lobate flow structures at the toe of the slip. Whether this represents a failure in the fortification structures of the city during the time of occupation or whether it is a subsequent failure of the wall, it took place before internal destruction afforded a buttress to prevent the inward slumping of the wall structure.

The two phases of wall construction signify different types of fortification activity: an orderly construction of a defensive wall built of the best materials available and prepared carefully to produce a durable structure (Locus 3012), followed by hasty additions to this well-conceived structure from occupational debris sediment (3020) taken from inside the city to repair or strengthen the former construction. The use of low strength occupational debris sediment in the construction of the brick defensive wall may have been an ill-conceived last resort to bolster a failing structure by means of materials available to the inhabitants of the city within the confines of their defenses. This section is an illustration of a potentially tragic incident in the history of the wall near the southwestern gate.

Occupational sedimentation: domestic surfaces. During times of continuous occupational sedimentation in those areas where houses exist as structural entities through long periods of time, thick occupational sequences have been found. These take the form of slow accretionary floor surfaces in domestic quarters. These sediments have been observed as thin layers composed of sand, silt, and clay-sized particles of chalk, nari, ash, pottery and field soil clay into which have been pressed olive pits, small bone fragments, and potsherds (usually with convex surface upwards).

Important differences in the nature of the occupational sediment exist as it is laid down in the dwelling floor context. The significant features to be noted are: (1) specially prepared flooring which may be composed of field soil or chalk and nari layers; (2) ash layers which are a facies continuum from a cooking or baking area; (3) the dust and sediment from the human and animal activity in the environment of a courtyard. This last may include animal pens, ovens, grinding implements such as saddle querns and mortars, and grain and water storage containers, along with refuse pits. The walls of these structures commonly were found to be composed of easily worked nari and rarely of siliceous chalk and limestone. Unfired mud bricks have been recorded for courtyard walls. Calcined lime with straw binder, occasionally layered from multiple redressing is characteristic of roofing construction which was supported with half-beam timbers. Specially prepared flooring materials include crushed chalk paste (some examples featured minor straw binder), crushed nari with a rendzinate soil matrix, fitted cobble/pebble stone floors, compacted field clay, hamra sand and bimodal[16] Recent beach sands. Specialized features constructed into these flooring surfaces were hearth depressions and store-jar receptables (especially in Middle Bronze houses).

Destructional sediment: defense structure failure. Among the means used to breach defensive structures was the form of attack which was quite effective against carbonate lithologies. This was a "breaching fire" or a "burning with fire" event. Since the gate structures were probably the most assailable of all the defense fortifications of the ancient city, this area usually came under attack. Such an incident may be recorded in the archaeological stratification of Gezer in the area of the south-central gate. This kind of assault could be very effective. Decomposition of the nari gatehouse structure resulted with the nari blocks being reduced to calcium oxide in a failure of the outside and part of the inside wall. Ceramic evidence found sealed in charcoal beneath the calcined wall rock material enables the probable date of deposition to be assigned to the time of Pharaoh Shishak whose Palestinian conquests are recorded in the literature.

Ceremonial practice sedimentation. R. A. S. Macalister had excavated the Gezer High Place area in his campaigns early in this century. Very little of the original sediment of this interesting area was left for the modern excavator to examine. Macalister did, however, leave the stratification immediately underlying the pillars untouched. This presented an excellent opportunity for the application of the critical analysis of modern stratigraphic technique. These small remnants of original stratification held the only remaining information which could tell a more accurate story concerning the events of man's activity in this place. The sediment was washed to remove the masking effect of fine silt and clay size material and sorted with a five millimeter, 250, and 74 micron sieve sequence so that the particles could be studied according to size category and composition.

The High Place was excavated in 1968 under the supervision of Mrs. Anita Furshpan. Initial phases of the excavation made clear that any structures connected with the use of this area had been destroyed. Speculations about the function of this area range from that of a burial and mortuary center in the city to that of an area of sacrifice (the nature of which ranges according to the viewpoint of the commentator from animal to human sacrifice).

Analysis of the deposits of the area near the "laver" or hollowed stone block determined that the sediments were of a unique character. Compositions of this nature were not observed in any other context of this or other excavations in which the writer has taken part. A typical excerpt from the field lab notebook follows:

G.68 7/31
V.7.188
LOC.7006 (soil under plaster surface next to basin)
        556 gm. sample

This material is composed of fine pebble to fine sand size nari, burned nari, scorched and burned bone splinters and fragments, burned teeth fragments, pottery fragments, terrestrial gastropod fragments, fine sand size clear quartz grains, and calcite fragments. Proportions were: unburned nari and chalk 50%; burned and blackened nari 30%; burned bone and teeth fragments 15%; pottery and miscellaneous 5%.

The nature of the sediment on this plaster surface connects the use of that level with burning in which there has been free ash and fire fall in the production of burned nari and scorched bones. The fire was not that of a hearth, but burned in such a way that its coals fell away from the point of burning before the nari was calcined and the bone material consumed. The burned teeth (four fragments showing enamel and dentine) show strong burning, together with the other bone fragments, suggesting that the animal involved in the burning included the head part(s) of (a) carcass(es). The pavement was made up of a chalk and nari pebble chip aggregate in a nari and chalk paste.

The presence of burned nari and bone in this chip pavement surface is atypical of any paved surfaces observed, including the streets of Field III (the Solomonic gate) and the floor and court paving surfaces in the makeup of Field I (domestic quarters) including MB and EB levels. A different kind of activity yielded the sediment of this area. Certainly a ceremonial sacrificial explanation is possible.

As a further commentary on the sediment of the High Place, analysis of the pillars is pertinent. The composition of these materials is nari, the partially weathered bedrock material amply available to Gezer inhabitants on the flanks of the Shephelah about the tell. The nature of one of these monoliths, No. 7, is exotic to the central Shephelah. It contains Upper Cretaceous, Campanian or Turonian megascopic shallow marine fauna. This facies of limestone is not locally expressed in the Turonian exposed in the Nesher Cement Quarry to the north of Gezer. The nearest available source known to the writer is the western flank of the Judean anticline.

A channeling not characteristic of natural solution has been cut into this pillar. The depth and position of this surface feature could afford a rope hold by which the stone was dragged to its present position.

Sedimentary structures and facies relationships. Lateral relationships within each stratum must be examined from the standpoint of facies relationships: the lateral variation within a given stratum of sediment caused by synchronous deposition of polygenetic agencies. This concept should be constantly in the mind of the excavator for whom it is critical to recognize the nature of each facies of a stratum or phase as it is being dug. Sedimentary structures may be recognized primarily on the basis of fabric and texture of the sediment body in addition to the mineral composition. Thus study of these features is critical while they are being dug.

Summary: Sedimentary Description

Analysis of the sediments in archaeological stratification is a vital feature of the historical elucidation of the data. A practice common among excavators involves a concise description of the sediment bodies shown in profile or section drawings of the stratification exposed along a trench face or balk. Here the genetic significance is almost completely lost unless otherwise described. The use of such color texture terms as "sticky black burnt," "green bricky," and "dark brown stony," is not only imprecise but unacceptable. Where color is a natural function of a deposit and germane to an understanding of its nature and function, a standardized reference term should be used in locus descriptions along with the correctly designated popular color name.

Each sedimentary entity should be carefully studied and analyzed to record not only the composition of its material, but also the agency, insofar as it can be determined, by which it was deposited. Notation essential to this aspect of description is a standardized size reference table. The use of such terms as "egg," "fist," and "melon," size is to be discouraged. As in sedimentology, particle sorting, size, composition, and fabric are important properties of deposits which are characteristic of given agencies in the total cultural activities of man. In the absence of the activities of man, i.e., in a stratigraphic hiatus, the depositional agencies of natural processes are quite distinctive. Destructive events of man are recorded in a fashion readily discernible to most observers. Chaotic fabrics, surfaces bearing shattered pottery, smothered and charred combustibles, collapsed roofs, and out-of-plumb wall remnants are some of the destruction facies encountered.

The Petrology of Artifacts

The role of tools and weapons in the occupational activity of the inhabitants of Gezer is one of considerable signficance. It shows the extent of man's utilization of the raw materials of his immediate and remote neighborhood. It is a reflection of his dependence upon the economic geology sometimes close, sometimes remote from the immediate environment of his way of life.

This phase of research concerns the petrology of the artifacts as a means directed to the understanding of the provenance of each of these entites. Petrographic study, the purely descriptive aspect of petrology, is relevant in two aspects of this discussion: (1) to ascertain the reason why a particular rock type or mineral was used for a specific function as a tool or a weapon, i.e., the essence of the physical properties, hardness, luster, fracture, cleavage, color, and ability to take a polish; (2) to suggest a potential provenance.

Consideration of the grinding stones used by the Gezer inhabitants constitutes a case in point. The unsuitability of the local bedrock is a critical issue. Chalk has neither the hardness nor cohesiveness required for this function. Chert (often referred to as flint), a nodular component of the local chalk, is far too brittle and unworkable to be shaped into a suitable grinding vessel. Some limestone mortars and a few kurkar saddle querns have appeared in stratification. There is a far greater number of basalt saddle querns at Gezer; obviously the inhabitants preferred this material, brought from a distance, for even mundane domestic activities.

In summary, the provenance of the rocks and minerals recorded at Gezer ranged from the chert (flint) available in the nodules which occur in the Middle Eocene horizons within the Gezer ground water tunnel to such very exotic materials as acid pumice which may have floated from an Aegean explosive source to the shores of Israel. The lithic catalogue is growing with each additional season of excavation.

The contribution of a geologist to the success of any archaeological excavation is proportional to his awareness of the petrology of the region of the site(s) he is working. Study in this area is far from complete, but an initial foundation has been laid upon which future research may be structured.

Notes

[1]A handbook and glossary of field terms for archaeologists is in preparation. An inexpensive useful source is the American Geological Institute, *Dictionary of Geological Terms* (1962).

[2]Since 1966 the author has served as consultant in geology, and since 1969 as member of the Core Staff of the excavations at Gezer; cf. *BA* XXX (1967), 34-62. This project is under the direction of William G. Dever with H. Darrell Lance as Associate Director; institutional sponsorship is provided by the Hebrew Union College, with financial support from the Smithsonian Institution. The writer wishes to express his gratitude to Nelson Glueck who first invited him to pursue geological research in the Near East.

[3]Residual soils are those from weathered bedrock *in situ*. The soil now exists in place of the rock from which it was formed. Colluvial soils and clays are those which have moved downslope from the place of origin under the influence of gravity. Alluvial soil clays are those eroded, transported, and deposited by the running water of streams. Temper is any coarse material added to pottery clay to prevent failure of the vessel. Geological time-rock terms, e.g., Pleistocene, may be found in any introductory text.

[4]See especially M. W. Ball and D. Ball, *American Association of Petroleum Geologists*, Bulletin 37 (1953), No. 1, pp. 1-113.

[5]A syncline is a fold in the rocks in which both sides dip inward toward an axis. An anticline is also a fold structure, but instead both sides dip outward from an axis.

[6]G. A. Smith, *The Historical Geography of the Holy Land* (1966) p. 143.

[7]Residual soil is considered virgin when there is no significant cultural material found in it. Transported soils are not found where they are formed but where they are redeposited by some agency of sediment movement, for example, mass wasting down slope or running water.

[8]M. Gal, *Proceedings of the International Clay Conference* (1967), Vol. II.

[9]*Ibid*, and the *Atlas Israel* (1955).

[10]The Munsell Color Company, Inc., 2441 North Calvert Street, Baltimore, Maryland 21218, publishes soil and rock color charts.

[11]Trace elements are those present in minor amounts in the earth's crust. Those used in this study are zirconium, strontium, nickel, titanium, copper, manganese. Iron and calcium were also recorded.

[12]The bedrock formations outcropping in the vicinity of Gezer are in sequence, older to younger, the Bicna limestone, Turonian in age; the Menuha formation, Senonian in age; Ghareb formation, Maastrictian age; Taqiye formation, Paleocene age; and the Zorca formation, Lower-Middle Eocene.

[13]A lateral (synchronous) subdivision of a stratified unit; it may be a change of agency of deposition, e.g., a street surface sediment is a facies of the courtyard sediment, both of which were deposited at the same time.

[14]D. H. Yaalon, *Bulletin of the Research Council of Israel*, IIG, No. 3 (1963).

[15]Excavations in Field III, the Solomonic Gate, were under the direction of John S. Holladay, Jr. of the University of Toronto.

[16]Bimodal sediment has two principal size categories derived from two sources and/or agencies contributing to its makeup. Coastal sands of Israel contain both quartz and sand grains (from the Nile) and larger waveworn marine mollusk shell fragments. Wind-blown sands are better sorted and exhibit a narrow range of size variation.

9

HYGIENE CONDITIONS IN ANCIENT
ISRAEL (IRON AGE)

EDWARD NEUFELD

[In the past, the BA *has printed articles of a cross-disciplinary kind, to illustrate areas yet to be opened up in full measure by archaeologists. The following article is reprinted from the* Journal of the History of Medicine and Allied Sciences XXV (1970), *with the kind permission of its editor Miss Elizabeth H. Thomson, to suggest the state of investigation on its subject at present. It should be pointed out that archaeologists have not often been asking these questions of their soil and artifacts; the subject of hygiene is in its infancy so far as archaeology is concerned. It is to be hoped that the printing of this introductory essay, with its valuable bibliography as well, will further encourage archaeologists to work with natural scientists to gain more information on the subject at issue in the article. — Editor]*

The aim of this paper is to present the essentials of hygiene conditions and practices in ancient Israel. The chief range of the inquiry is confined to the period of the early and middle Iron Age of the Near East, which roughly covers the 12th to early 6th centuries B.C. The main sources of information come from textual materials of the Bible itself, archaeological findings, and labors of previous scholars to whom references are made.

Though our knowledge derived from archaeological explorations and from the greatly advanced studies of the Old Testament is progressing at a very remarkable speed, the range of information concerning various aspects of hygiene is extremely limited. Data contained in the historical books of the Old Testament, the writings of the Prophets, and the Wisdom Literature reflect largely the day-to-day actual practices and usages; on the other hand, the legislative materials, and, even more, the ritual sections of the Bible which have a direct bearing on some of the subjects of hy-

Illus 11-5

giene remain a particularly baffling problem. In most instances we are at a loss to decide the extent to which they reflect real usages or merely serve a normative purpose.

Due to these and many other circumstances, the scope of this study was inevitably limited to those points which, broadly speaking, rest on evidence which is sufficiently understood to serve as a reliable historical source. The probability of definite conclusions depends upon the nature of the groundwork of solid facts on which it rests, and so far few of them—though respected— are definite; most of them can only be approximate. It is hoped that within these limitations maximum clarity has been achieved without falling into over-simplification.

Drainage and Sewerage Disposal

The notion of street drains for storm sewers is a modern development. Archaeological evidence from the Middle and Late Bronze Ages shows house drains in the homes of the wealthy. In Jericho a ruin of a masoned subterranean sewer was recovered which strongly suggests domestic sewerage,[1] and at Tell Beit Mirsim (most probably biblical Debir, about eleven miles southwest of Hebron) the excavated material looks like a channel, though it, also, was probably drainage for domestic waste.[2] At Bethel, the site of which has been identified as eleven miles north of Jerusalem, a very well built drainage system was found.[3] Here the stones are fitted more closely and the cross-section is much more regularly rectangular than those at Jericho. According to Albright, the drains of Bethel "discharged rainwater, and drainage outside the city wall."[4] This is possible, but it is most unlikely that these drains were built so as to conduct rain-storm water outside the city wall.

With the exception of the Iron Age drains through the gates of Megiddo and Gezer there is little evidence of house drains during the Iron Age in Palestine, but it is reasonable to assume that the few rich had them. Albright is of the opinion that during the period from the 9th to the early 5th centuries B.C., "subterranean drains were employed increasingly as time went on in order to keep the interior of towns as dry as possible."[5] This seems doubtful since in view of the small rainfall, the steepness of the hills on which most cities were built, and the absorbency of the soil in those areas, the need for such large drains was marginal.

As a rule, sewage was disposed of in the soil or in a nearby patch of ground, although there are ample textual references to mud or mire, and refuse (II Sam. 22:43; Isa. 57:20) in the alleys and out-of-door space (II Sam. 22:43; Mic. 7:10; Zech. 9:3; 10:5; Ps. 18:43). Waste was generally thrown into the streets to be removed eventually by animals or during the rainy season by the rain, and, similarly, there are allusions to carcasses in the "midst of the outdoors" (Isa. 5:25). These ill-defined conditions were not accepted as a matter of fact, but rather were referred to with a sense of shame and disgrace. It seems that the ideal standards of sanitation entailed keeping houses clean, scraping off the mud and mire, and clearing away the dust, particularly the coarse dust of the cities.

While there is no direct evidence, we may safely assume that Israel, like Egypt, Babylon, and Assyria, had an advanced appreciation and understanding of cleanliness, and a community concern for preserving it. The understanding of sanitation all over the ancient Near East seems, in fact, distinctly higher than that of early and even late Middle Age Europe, where the body was not a thing to be safeguarded, but rather something to be sharply subjugated and controlled. Fresh air, sunlight, communicable disease control, and personal cleanliness were all neglected, and drain pipes and aqueducts already built even fell into disuse. Practically the only public health principles that came down through the Middle Ages were those of isolation and quarantine, and they were very inadequately carried out.

Sanitation of the Home and Cooking Conditions

The general conditions were not conducive to personal, home, or public hygiene.[6] Notwithstanding the repugnance to filth, the immediate physical environment of village and city life presented several unsanitary elements, such as dirt, poisonous gases from decomposed sewerage, refuse of all sorts, garbage, infected food, and polluted water. These were breeding grounds for rats, rabbits, flies, cockroaches and various other insects, together with many varieties of micro-organisms which rapidly spread infections through the air, water, and food insect vectors.

In addition, the frequent crudeness of sanitary arrangements inside and outside the houses in all countries of the ancient Near East and, for that matter, in Europe of the early and late Middle Ages, is well known. As a rule, dwelling houses of the ordinary population throughout the Iron Age of Palestine were single-storied, one-family units. They were simple in their design, planning, structural elements, and appearance. The art of building in Israel was for a long time crude compared with that of Canaan of the Bronze Age. Houses were built on a low foundation with walls made from sun-dried clay bricks and irregularly shaped stones.[7] In the hill country, however, houses were usually made from stone, and were therefore more solid. Large houses like those excavated in Tirzah (probably identical with modern Tell el-Farᶜah, seven miles northeast of Shechem), which if completed would cover nearly 325 square feet of living space on the ground floor,[8] or those of similar dimension at Mizpah (generally identified with modern Tell en-Naṣbeh, seven miles north of Jerusalem), Shechem, or Hazor most certainly did not represent the average building for shelter or residence only.[9]

The average house was small, consisting of a single room covered with smooth clay; this adjoined a courtyard. Houses had flat roofs, the simplest and least distinguished of roof forms. A low entrance led from the narrow street or alley into the courtyard. Because of the glare of the sun and the dust of the streets, window openings were few and small (Hos. 13:3). They were sometimes latticed, letting the light in and the smoke out. Houses of the wealthy were more spacious, having several rooms on adjoining sides. As a rule, they had "upper rooms," constructed on the flat roof, to be used for living quarters (Isa. 22:1), or for guests (Isa. 9:25; I Kings 17:9; II Kings 4:10). These were reached by a flight of steps made of wood or stone set on the outside. Such a room provided the comfort of fresher, cooler air, and therefore was referred to as "the cool chamber" (Judg. 3:24). In such houses the ground floor was used as a family storeroom.

Housing and cooking sanitation were poor, though there is no doubt that within the limits of the existing conditions, cleanliness in moderation was observed.[10] The use of the primitive hearths found in the courtyards of most dwelling houses, and even the movable baking ovens or stoves were sources of offensive odors which attracted insects, and produced gases, vapors, and dirt precipitates.

Bread was baked over hot coals (I Kings 19:6; Isa. 44:19). Still later bread was baked on iron plates, iron griddles (Lev. 2:5; 6:21; I Chron. 23:29), or even in bread pans (Lev. 2:7, 7:9). Throughout the Bronze Age and particularly during the Iron Age (in fact up to modern times) most utensils were made of clay. The ovens referred to above, constructed of sherds and special clay, were two or three feet in diameter,[11] and were frequently built over a pit lined with stones.[12] As a rule they were kept in the courtyards and differed little from those still used in present-day Arab villages.[13] Usually, each household had its own oven, but not infrequently one was shared by several families (Lev. 26:26). "In most cases courtyards were east of the rooms so the prevailing west wind blew smoke odors away from the house."[14] In spite of this, the offensive odors must have been so strong that they caused people to move around, although the use of air-purifying agents brought some relief. These conditions promoted the breeding and spread of germs, giving rise readily to air-borne infections. In the excavations at Tell Beit Mirsim, ovens were found outside the houses, and similarly at Tell es-Saᶜidiyeh, apparently biblical Zarethan, five ovens were located in a cooking area, not in the courtyards.[15] This suggests how oppressive those odors must have been and what attempts were made to counteract them, however effective these may have been.

Fortunately, outdoor living, especially during the long summer, was a great part of the pattern of daily life; people moved to the open fields, to the gate of the city with its adjoining open areas of various market places, to the open spaces near the wells and the springs—all were main public gathering places where much time was spent—where the fresher air gave relief from the various conditions near the house. Obviously outdoor living brought other important benefits. In all seasons outdoor air is in greater motion than indoor air, and is therefore more stimulating. Although part of the benefit of outdoor life is due to the physical exercise that accompanies it, even when inactive outdoors, the same stimulating effect of coolness and air motion is felt.

A much more important factor in this connection is crowding, since there is indeed a definite relationship between numbers of people to a room and the occurrence of respiratory infections, a matter on which recent figures are available. However, we lack evidence on this point because at present it is impossible to ascertain figures of ancient populations, population growth, density of population (which obviously was not spread uniformly), size of families, or of collections of persons gathered closely together or forced into a confined space. So far we have not even reached the explanatory stage and lack the details to affect a coordination of the facts with regard to manipulation and interpretation. The only thing which can be stated with certainty is that all ancient populations were small in size, and equally so the size of their habitual areas. As a rule the areas, as well as the populations, have increased, but not significantly. We have, therefore, no basis whatsoever to approximate sizes of crowds, and any calculation of figures based upon evidence drawn mainly from the size of areas, while profitable in modern conditions, is misleading when applied to ancient populations, since the most important variables remain unanswered.

Hygiene and Infant Mortality

These health and sanitation conditions markedly affected the lives of the people; the gravest aspect was the very high maternal and infant mortality. Both were the direct result of sanitation conditions, and not, as frequently suggested, of undernourishment or malnutrition. As a rule, food scarcities do not seem to constitute effective checks of population size, though it should be noted that food scarcity does not invariably imply famine. For example, protein malnutrition is conducive to infant morbidity and infant mortality even though a state of actual famine may not exist. However, in most of Eastern Asia the birth rate has remained extremely high despite the fact that almost chronic undernourishment, as well as frequent periods of famine, have prevailed there throughout history. It was the appalling sanitation conditions, inevitably resulting in the spread of highly contagious diseases such as *puerperal septicaemia* (childbed fever), the various, most unhygienic, obstetrical practices of midwives, relatives, and friends who aided in delivery, and various customs of handling infants, that gave rise to the startling maternal and infant mortality.[16]

The frequent finding in excavations of numerous infant and child skeletons constitutes archaeological evidence which points to a high infant mortality rather than to a normative practice of child sacrifice.[17] It is true that references to human sacrifice abound in the biblical records, and bones unearthed in sanctuaries and elsewhere are supposed to attest to child sacrifices (although it can seldom be demonstrated that this is the case). The prophets' fierce condemnations of this custom as repulsive, and repugnant to Israel's sacrificial ritual, confirm its existence. The practice of human sacrifice was, in part, an inheritance from the Canaanites and Phoenicians, who continued it long after it was forgotton among the Babylonians and Egyptians, and in part an isolated reappearance of an ancient and widely spread custom in most areas of the ancient Near East. However, the burial of many infants in urns and jars under the floors of private dwellings, or nearby, as the well-accepted custom was, shows beyond a doubt that these were burials of infants who died other than by human sacrifice. In fact, in many instances, the scrupulous manner in which these babies were placed, or their actual interment in jars, reflects an act discharged with the reverence and grief attending the dissolution by death of parent-child relationships, rather than the disposition of bones left after sacrifices.[18]

Personal Hygiene Habits:
Body Cleanliness, Bathing, Clothing, and Table Manners

Faces were washed regularly and probably thoroughly, and hands, which tend to carry large numbers of bacteria, were frequently washed and generally clean. Metaphysically "clean (*bor*) hand (or) palms" denoted, as in our day, "innocence," "good faith," or "honor" (Deut. 21:6; II Sam. 22:21; Ps. 18:20, 24; Job 9:30; 22:30). Though our information regarding the meticulous observance of washing hands before any meal,[19] or the usage of daily bathing or at least of washing hands prior to recitation of morning prayers,[20] comes from late sources, there is no doubt that they reflect very early customs. In fact, careful washing of hands before and after meals is widely practiced among many primitive tribes of different cultures. In accordance with the widespread ancient Near Eastern custom great stress was laid on regular washing of feet (Gen. 18:4; 19:2; 24:32; 43:24; Judg. 19:21; I Sam. 25:41). The references to a "washpot" or "basin" (*sir raḥaṣi*— Pss. 60:8; 108:10) in connection with "casting off the sandal" clearly indicate their common use for the purpose of washing feet. Obviously washing the feet and hands for cultic purposes was an established religious commandment (Exod. 30:18, 19, 21; 40:31; Deut. 21:6; II Chron. 4:6).

There is little direct evidence that much body washing took place although personal cleanliness among women was particularly observed in connection with various solemn family occasions (Ruth 3:3; Song of Songs 5:3; Judith 10:3). It seems that the washing of the body, including the head, was performed in the homes of the ordinary population in an upright standing position, with the water being poured from a jar over the whole body. It is possible that, as in ancient Greece, the Israelites washed in warm water and scraped their skins with a strigil.

Everywhere in the ancient Near East young women were particularly concerned with cosmetic-hygiene standards. As it will be pointed out later, perfumes and incense have practically the same origin and great value was placed on both all over the ancient Near East. There is much archaeological evidence of cosmetic palettes of limestone from the Middle Iron Age in Palestine,[21] and of beautifully executed—principally in ivory and alabaster—jars[22] and ointment flasks from the 13th century B.C. from Lachish. Similar toilet articles have survived from much earlier times from Egypt[23] and from Mesopotamia.[24] We may possibly assume that some essence containing fragrant extracts of aromatic resin or gum, a kind of perfume, was concealed by young women in small scent bottles in their bosoms (cf. also Song of Songs 7:9; however, see Pope, *Song of Songs* [1977], 636). There is no doubt that refined personal hygiene was maintained among the upper social strata of the population. It may be safely assumed that royal families and the wealthy, in addition to bathing in rivers (cf. Exod. 2:5; 7:15), streams, bathing pools in the gardens, and in domestic bathtubs (II Sam. 11:2) as seen in the pottery figurine found at

Achzib and dating from the 8th-7th centuries B.C., also had luxurious bathrooms in their elaborate houses. They were probably similar to the bathrooms and also bathhouses of the pre-Homeric era discovered in Crete and Mycenae which were confined only to the tiny upper class of the society.

There is the archaeological evidence of enclosed Roman and Byzantine public baths in buildings, including a heating system, found at En-Gedi (an oasis of the west side of the Dead Sea, nearly thirty-five miles southeast of Jerusalem), and belonging to the late Herodian period.[25] Similar evidence comes from Masada[26] and a number of other places. Undoubtedly the very precise regulations in the Mishnah and particularly in the Talmud concerning the ritual bathing reflect old habitual practices, widely known long before the compilation of the Mishnah. In addition to the *miqwe* which is an immersion pool for ritual bathing or rather purification (*tebilah*), we learn from the Mishnah of the *merḥaṣ* or *beth merḥaṣ* which is a bathhouse confined to the purpose of physical cleanliness.[27] The latter were someties heated (*merḥaṣ nissoqeth—Shebiith* 8:11). As a rule the *batē merḥaṣ* were not very common; many cities and villages had no such bathhouses (*Ketuboth* 7:8). They seem to have been regarded as fairly important business property[28] often compared, in commercial value, to olive presses. These bathhouses were not luxurious establishments such as those in the palaces of the Aegean civilization (Knossos and Phaistos, 17th-14th centuries B.C.) but small, simple, and humble structures accessible to the bulk of the population, indicating that cleanliness occupied a fairly important place in ancient Israel. However, as far as textual evidence of the Bible is concerned, apart from the reference to ablution, there is no mention of ancient public bathing in Palestine prior to the Talmudic period except that of open-air bathing in the sea (II Chron. 4:6), and in the rivers, commonly widely practiced, no doubt, by the great mass of the ordinary people (II Kings 5:10-14; see also John 9:7).

As far as clothing and its effect on cleanliness and soundness of the skin was concerned, the following can be stated. Very few textiles have survived from ancient Palestine, and therefore our knowledge of these is mainly derived from textual material of the Bible and from ancient paintings and sculpture of adjoining countries.[29] Linens manufactured from flax fibers and wool were the principal fabrics used for clothing. Rather rough-textured garments made of leather, probably tanned, were used as girdles and footwear (Gen. 3:21; Lev. 13:48; II Kings 1:8).[30] All garments were primarily geared to the art of arranging them around the body. They were loose and roomy, and therefore permitted easy temperature regulation and satisfactory body movement and blood circulation. Tight-fitting clothes were unknown. The undergarment which was worn next to the skin was the *ketoneth* (Song of Songs 5:3). This was a long, half-sleeved, shirt-like garment reaching just above the ankles. As a rule the *ketoneth* was made of wool since linen fabrics were expensive. The "shirt" obviously was frequently moist from the high rate of perspiration which is absorbed from the surface of the body. Since moist clothing is a good culture medium for bacteria, there is no doubt that much bacterial infection and skin irritation resulted from soiled clothing, particularly the *ketoneth*. In addition, woolen clothes are difficult to launder, and therefore it is obvious that this garment was rarely clean. It may be mentioned also that with minor exceptions[31] the practice of "changing clothes" was almost unknown among the ordinary population. As a rule garments were handed down from parents to children. They were very valuable personal articles, and often served as pledges (Prov. 20:16; 27:13); this particularly applied to mantles or wrappers used for covering by night (Exod. 22:25-27; Deut. 24:10-13) and for other purposes (Exod. 12:34; Judg. 8:25; I Sam. 21:10). The practice of impounding garments is now confirmed by the discovery of a petition of a seasonal agricultural worker of the 7th century B.C.[32]

Table manners were rather primitive. Except for the use of knives, and probably ladles or stirring sticks, food was obviously prepared (and eaten) with the hands, under poor sanitary conditions. The frequent references to "fleshforks" (I Sam. 2:13-14) or "fleshhooks" (Exod. 27:3; 38:3) as well as the two- and three-pronged forks excavated in Gezer in a layer of the Late Bronze Age, describe sacrificial implements used by priests during sacrifices and have no bearing on domestic table manners. In the book of Proverbs (23:4) the use of knives was indicative of good table manners, particularly when dining with the upper class. Privacy of plates or bowls was unknown. Hands were dipped in the common bowl and food passed from mouth to mouth. Mouths were wiped on sleeves which thus became coated with food and converted into media for bacterial growth and decay. All eating, as everywhere in the ancient Near East and in Greece and in Rome, was done behind closed doors.[33]

Cleaning Compounds

The common method of cleaning utensils and implements used in cookery and in domestic work was to rub them with sand. For finer utensils, however, oil and the juices of some plants were used, as well as fuller's clays, called active clays, which easily absorb impurities from oil and fats. For body cleaning the bulk of the population used various chemical compounds. These were usually made from olive oil, possibly also from palm kernel oil, plant ashes containing much potash, or from salts of fatty acids. The upper classes used expensive and refined soap and oil mixtures.

Among the most well-known cleaning compounds were the *neter* (Jer. 2:22), probably a mixture of natron with some chemical properties of alkalis and fats, also the *borith* (Jer. 2:22; Mal. 3:2; Job 9:30), presumably made from some herbs, trees, and shrubs that bear fruit containing a soapy substance.[34] Possibly both terms refer to different types of soaps, namely, to "hard" soap and to "soft" soap. To the *neter* some must have added vinegar (*homeș*), the original function of which was to allow fermentation, but this practice was ridiculed (Prov. 25:20).

Cleanliness in Cooking and Food Preparation

There were various methods of cooking, baking, broiling, roasting, frying, and stewing; however, boiling and broiling were the most common methods. Throughout the Iron Age, as from time immemorial, different clays were the staple materials from which cooking utensils were made. Those made from metals were rare and obviously expensive. All cooking utensils and jars in various sizes and designs, including a fine variety of highly polished utensils with incised designs, paintings, or ornaments, were made of clay of various types fired at high temperatures. Their quality, appearance, or shape was obviously not homogeneous, as almost each period had its own characteristic pottery.[35] As a rule, pots, deep round-shaped vessels, and large bowls served as cooking utensils, while plates, pans, and dishes served more general domestic purposes, and were used primarily for preparing and serving food.

There is little evidence to suggest the standards of cleanliness observed in the handling of cooking utensils or in the preparation of food. It is doubtful whether there was an awareness that dirt had much to do with food-borne illness and food poisoning, though one textual reference clearly points to the observance of cleanliness of cooking vessels, and of protecting them from dust. Thus, the popular self-explanatory parable in II Kings 21:13 reflects the usages of washing and wiping plates, particularly shallow, round-shaped fine plates, used mainly for preparing and serving food; an example is the shallow round-shaped dish, usually referred to as ṣalaḥath (Prov. 19:24; 26:15; II Chron. 35:13). Plates were stored face-downwards for protection against dirt and dust. As mentioned, scraping and cleaning various cooking utensils with sand must have been common.

Contamination of food by various extraneous and poisonous materials was bound to have been common. It is questionable whether the dietary laws were ever strictly observed.[36] Similarly there is no evidence to strengthen the statement that "fruit and vegetables were washed and cleansed when they were added to cooked items." This is simply an assumption, not a fact.

On the other hand, some care was taken to protect the food being prepared from surrounding contamination. Textual references to "open vessels" with no lids fastened down clearly indicate that pots with fastened-down lids were used during preparation and storage to protect food from insects and various contamination. In fact, an ingeniously constructed lid of the middle 8th century B.C. was unearthed by Yadin at Hazor.[37]

Deodorants

In order to counteract the objectionable odors, or to control them, various deodorants were used in temples, public places, houses of the rich, and probably also of the poor, particularly on solemn occasions.[38] In ancient Israel, as in many ancient Near

Eastern countries, and for that matter in most tropical and semi-tropical countries, there was a widespread growth and use of various plants used as deodorants. They were adapted to the environmental conditions of the area, and were among the basic needs of daily life. According to Harrison,

> It is undoubtedly true to say that the majority of these fragrant substances whether imported or not, were by no means confined to the more wealthy members of the population, since the numerous references in the Old Testament and other literature testify to the widespread usage which these aromatic materials enjoyed in everyday life.[39]

The active components of the deodorants came from various plants with agreeable aromatic qualities. They emitted sweet penetrating odors during combustion. Many and various other ingredients which added fragrance to the air also came from various plants. They yielded incense, laudanum, spices (*besamin*, possibly *comiphora opobalsamum*),[40] resins, balsams (resins in fluid character), gums, myrrh, frankincense, spikenard, and others. Such plants provided the raw material to yield sweet odors, or, rather, "a blend of materials each with its own particular odor, resulting in one overall and pleasant impression." Some such substances were also used, chiefly by women, for cleansing the skin and enhancing the attractiveness of face and body. Although such usage probably injured the skin, it may be stressed "that their use was an essential part of general hygiene."[41]

Such cosmetics were made from locally grown plants, especially in the Jordan valley (Gen. 43:11), En-Gedi (Song of Songs 1:14),[42] and Gilead (Gen. 37:25; Jer. 8:22), but many were imported, most probably from southwest Arabia (Jer. 6:20) and Somaliland.[43] The unusually large number of specific names for these plants suggests that (a) most of them were indoor deodorants, which are in effect air deodorants; (b) they were of several types, depending on the specific function; and (c) more than one plant is involved. Their botanical identity is in doubt, and is subject to wide discussion.[44] Probably most of them belong to the wide range of small plants in the mint family, and some to the varieties of trees and shrubs noted for their natural aromatic exudations. Neither disinfectant nor antiseptic, these deodorants did not, of course, destroy the offensive odors, but only masked them with another odor less unpleasant, or with a perfumed smell that was probably stronger. Thus their use had a limited sanitary significance.

The art of preparation, blending, and compounding various extracts of these plants required great skill and craftsmanship. It was confined to experts in spice-mixtures and ointment-mixtures. These apothecaries (*roqeaḥ*) were, as in Ugarit,[45] organized in guilds (Neh. 3:8). Their work was in many ways related to boiling or rather steam distillation. It should be noted here that

> from early times apothecaries found it profitable to distill water in which fragrant herbs were immersed, and to condense the steam which passed over carrying with it the odorous principles to form fragrant "waters" for medicinal and cosmetic purposes. This method was effective in separating from other constituents of plants the pure "essential" oils (essences). From different plants were secured pure hydrocarbons of the type called by organic chemists *terpenes*, such as oil of tupentine, juniper, peppermint, and lemon. Certain plants yielded alcohols such as methanol. benzyl-alcohol, menthol, and geraniol. Some yielded cyclic hydrocarbons such as cymine, myrcine, and pinine; while still others yielded phenols such as thymol; or aldehydes such as geraniol, citronella, benzaldehyde, and vanillin; or ketones such as camphor and menthol. From valerian, valerianic acid was obtained and from certain plants were extracted acetate of benzyl-alcohol, cynnamyl-alcohol, and methyl-benzoate.[46]

These apothecaries were engaged in the manufacture of preservatives for mummification[47] which was allied to medicine. Obviously the nature of their work entailed a knowledge of various herbs and treatment of disease. We may safely assume that they were the general medical practitioners.

Insecticides

A very important use of plant extracts was as insecticides. Some possibly destroyed, but all drove away, vast numbers of insects which plagued people indoors and all the fauna of the Near East. As with the cosmetic-hygienic deodorants, there were several classes of insecticides, these depending on their mode of action,

season of the year, species of insects, speed of effect, and dosage
required for the type of organism that they were principally
intended to control. Most of these insecticides were of limited
effectiveness, but even today in spite of the rapid advances of all
sciences, control of insects is no easy matter.[48]

Many climatic factors are associated with insect ecology, but
tropical and subtropical conditions, especially, favor the proliferation of some varieties. Almost every species of plant and
animal is subject to attack by some insect or other. Some insects
beset cattle and sheep, transmitting the diseases of men and other
animals. Other insects disseminate bacteria, fungi, and viruses that
cause diseases among the plant life. The Bible abounds in
references to various species of insects, many of which cannot now
be recognized.[49] In Palestine, as all over the world, there was a
permanent painful apprehension of impending epidemic diseases,
insect pests, or other plagues originating from contact with
infected rodents, usually rats, and their fleas. The fleas take the
Bacillus pestis into the stomach with the blood of infected animals,
then regurgitate the organisms and pass them into the blood of
other animals they bite. Such plagues usually appear suddenly and,
though they do not last long, cause a very high death rate. Some of
them consume both the flesh of men and beasts (Zech. 14:12, 15,
18) or cause "a severe disease affecting your bowels so that your
bowels will come out day after day because of the disease"
(II Chron. 21:14-15). Solomon in his dedication prayer referred to
the disaster caused by some of them (I Kings 8:37).

From early times the commonest method of controlling insects
was by the smoke of frankincense and many other aromatics.
Smoke reduces the supply of oxygen required for life, and has a
chemical effect on the breathing organs, particularly those of
mosquitoes, flies, and other flying insects. Many small altars or
incense stands of various sizes, made of stone or pottery, some of
which were not necessarily part of sanctuaries, were unearthed at
Megiddo, Tell Beit Mirsim, Gezer, Beth-Shan, and Shechem from
the Iron Age.

From Iron age [of Palestine] private houses various small stone altars
were found, 1/2 to 1 m. (20 to 40 inches) high, rectangular in cross
section, which have an upper surface measuring 20-by-20 to 30-by-30

cm. (8-by-8 to 12-by-12 inches), often having a bowl-shaped depression in the top and as a rule having "horns" in the four corners. In view of their small size these items can only be incense altars which, because of the place where they were found, must have served as private censors, whereas the clay object from Iron age Taanach customarily considered an incense altar was more likely a brazier for heating in the cold season of the year; cf. Jer. 36:22-23.[50]

The smoke of incense or other aromatics, well known and widely employed in sacrificial ritual among the Egyptians,[51] Babylonians,[52] and Canaanites[53] served two purposes: (a) protection against diseases, and (b) the usual function of insecticides. From the earliest times it had been believed that certain substances had the power of protecting from diseases. This particularly applied to sweet-smelling herbs, balsams, and spices. The fumes arising from burning of these substances were held to be more effectual than the natural scent. On the other hand the purpose of the smoke of incense or other aromatics as insecticides is obvious. The widespread daily offering of incense in Israelite sacrificial ritual, which, according to the Bible, both accompanied other offerings and at times was made by itself, had precisely these aims. Noth, referring to incense burning, says that "the burning of incense seems to have been part of public and private cultic practice since very ancient times with an apotropaic purpose"[54] but de Vaux translates the *mizbah hazzahab* (I Kings 7:48) as "altar of perfumes"; referring to *qetoreth*, he maintains that "in liturgical language, it is applied to offerings of perfumes, the full expression being *qetoreth sammim*, which occurs frequently in the Priestly texts. Incense (*lebonah*) is only one constituent of the offering and Exod. 30:34-38 gives the recipe for the perfume to be used in worship: it contained equal parts of storax, onyx (obtained from certain shell-fish) galbanum and incense . . . they were imported into Palestine from abroad and were used in cultic worship as an added refinement."[55] It is useful and interesting to quote the opinion of Carrey P. McCord and William N. Witheridge who rightly point out that

In the literal sense, the words "incense" and "perfume" have practically the same origin. Perfume was the aroma given off with the

smoke of any odoriferous material as it was burned: *perfumare*—
fumigate, perfume; *incendere*—incendiate, incense . . . The function
of incense was probably threefold in early times—symbolic,
hypnotic, and hygienic. Even in the case of hygiene, the effect of the
heavy oriental fragrance was no doubt more psychologic than
physiologic or antiseptic. Combustion has long been associated with
purification, both in a religious and in a medical sense; and it is not
unusual that sacrificial and fumigating fires should be treated with
aromatic substances in an attempt to offset the acrid, pungent,
sickening odors of burning organic matter. Cremation of the dead
has been practiced throughout man's history; but even when present
methods of interment were used, the ancients burned incense at their
funeral and burial procession, a practice still followed in some parts
of the world. The development of sanitary techniques for the
handling of departed relatives did not and would not result in a
prompt discard of rituals having as strong an olfactory appeal as the
burning of aromatic woods, gums, spices, flowers, and seeds.[56]

Maimonides nearly eight hundred years ago explained clearly:

> Since many animals were daily slaughtered in the holy place . . . there
> is no doubt that the smell of the place would have been like the smell
> of slaughter-houses, if nothing had been done to counteract it.
> Therefore, (the Torah) commanded to burn incense there twice every
> day, in the morning and in the evening, in order to give a pleasant
> odor to the place and to the garments of those who officiate there
> (*Moreh Nebukim*, III, Vienna, 1864, Chap. 45, p. 321).

To sum up, while incense is effective in combating unpleasant
odors, it has to be emphasized again that smoke of incense or, for
that matter, of other aromatics did not effectively destroy insect
pests, but rather annoyed them, drove them away, or deflected
them and hence was of limited effectiveness.

Economic Importance of Insecticides and Deodorants

The plants from which spices were obtained were costly (Exod.
30:23-24; I Kings 10:10; II Chron. 9:1) and were a prominent
commercial commodity in domestic and in international trade all
over the ancient Near East (Gen. 37:25; 43:11; Ezek. 27:17).[57]
Hezekiah boasted because of his large amount of spices (I Kings

20:13; Isa. 39:1-3). International trade on an extensive scale and over wide distances—which was expensive and dangerous—required good organization and implied high profit. It was a large-scale enterprise for the state, and also for the small private merchant. There is no doubt that the problems of supply of these plants must have been serious matters of public concern. Along with precious stones, camels, gold, and silver, spices were offered as tokens among royalty (I Kings 10:2, 10). They were always in great demand, and were an important source of income for those who dealt in them. The popular and widespread use of these plants and their products constituted one of the major elements of national wealth controlled by the state. The conjecture of Mazar *et al.*, that "at the end of the Iron Age (i.e., in the reigns of Josiah and his successors) En-Gedi was a royal estate, and that the families of perfume-growers and manufacturers carried on their crafts in the service of the kings (I Chron. 4:23)"[58] is strongly supported by the documents from Mari of the 18th century B.C., which attest to the control and large-scale distribution of spices by the crown.

It may be added that plants from which spices were derived were economically very important throughout the realms of classical Greece and Rome[59] and also for several centuries during the Middle Ages were an item of extensive trade between Mediterranean cities and the Orient; western products were traded for spices which were widely distributed.[60]

Purification Ritual and Hygiene

The many and widespread customs and ceremonies concerning ritual purification by waiting periods, bathing, fire, quarantine, "constrictions or restraint of the personality,"[61] avoidance of contact with death-defiled "contaminated" persons and places, together with the apodictic food and other restrictions, fulfilled in ancient Israel, as in many other societies, a dual purpose. On the one hand they served to protect people and communities from moral impurity or ritual unfitness; and, on the other hand, especially among communities of a primitive level, their sole aim was regeneration (II Chron. 29:12-19; Ezek. 43:20-22; 45:18-20; Neh. 13:9; I Macc. 4:36-58), or as Gaster puts it, "to seek periodically to renew its vitality and thus ensure its continuance."[62]

Thus they served a very useful and functional purpose in the general system of social control. Most of them are rooted in taboos or notions very similar to taboos. They are closely related to very primitive religious ideas and go back to times immemorial. Generally they refer to actions barred by rules of manners or morals, rather than of law. In practice taboos are the negative precepts, or prohibitions in connection with certain objects, dress, persons, foods, acts, burial grounds, parts of one's person, sick persons, and so forth. These are set apart as harmful and unclean, and by extension dangerous. They are not to be touched. Taboo objects are marked in many ways, and in many cultures tabooed things were looked on as sacred. Edward Westermarck rightly says that "when a thing is taboo, in the strict sense of the word, it is supposed to be charged with mysterious energy which will injure or destroy the person who eats or touches the fobidden thing, whether he does so willfully or by mistake."[63]

In ancient Israel, at a relatively late period—during the Monarchy and after the Exile—most of these very old cultic rites were prescribed in the large body of legal rules found in the first fifteen chapters of Leviticus, though many rites are referred to in much earlier and later parts of the Bible. The composition of these regulations is a product of the priestly circles who were the strong central power with the jurisdiction to carry through the task of codification (Lev. 10:10-11; 11:47; 20:25-27; Ezek. 22:26; 44:23). Eissfeldt rightly points out that

> Even if in their present form they are for the most part fairly late and are likely to reflect the practice normal in the Jerusalem temple towards the end of the pre-exile period, they, or at any rate the material on which they are based, are by no means to be regarded as purely literary constructions, but as ordinances taken from the actual practice of the cult. . . . Even if the surviving collections of cultic laws are fairly late, we may nevertheless assume with complete confidence that such laws existed already at an earlier period, even much earlier. For the cultic ideas and customs which are regulated in the material which survives are practically all old, and even very old, and must therefore at an earlier period already have been regulated by appropriate instructions. Thus it is certain that the examples which

we have go back in content to ancient times, and in many respects also in form, and there is nothing against the assumption that they even go back into the period of oral tradition.[64]

These ritual laws and their techniques had nothing to do with physical cleanliness of the human body or with daily health habits, or general environmental sanitation. Even the ritual bathing was not connected with care of the body, but was rooted in the very ancient taboos;[65] it was linked up primarily with regeneration.[66] However, in most instances these customs and laws tend directly and indirectly to relate to objects and actions which were significant for the welfare of the social order. In the field of physical cleanliness, as the late Robertson Smith pointed out,

> the impurities which were thought of as cleaving to a man, and making him unfit to mingle freely in the social and religious life of his community, were of various kinds, and often of a nature that we should regard as merely physical, e.g., uncleanness from contact with the dead, from leprosy, from eating forbidden food, and so forth.[67]

Though there is no evidence, I am confident that by the period of the Monarchy and the Exile, while these cultic laws had obviously not lost their original functional significance, they were also understood to serve the purpose of prevention of disease, constituting laws of personal hygiene, home hygiene, and public hygiene. At that state this interrelationship was very close if not in every way coincident. This is beautifully expresed in the Mishnah (*Soṭah* 9:15) where it says that "heedfulness leads to physical cleanliness (*nêqiyoth*) and physical cleanliness leads to ritual purity (*tohorah*)." Accordingly, the content of some of these rules was "intended for oral transmission to the laity"[68] with obvious purpose of their promotion and wide adoption.

Purification Ritual and Control of Disease

This close interrelationship is particularly and distinctly evident in the frequent precepts concerning washing hands and feet, and body-bathing, laundering of clothing, prohibition of association with "impure" persons (i.e., those suffering from communicable diseases, or with objects used by them) (Lev. 15:1-28; cf. Lev. 14:45), with filthy garments (Zech. 3:3; cf. Deut. 23:14), contact with corpses (Num. 19:11ff.), or with carcasses even of "clean" animals (Lev. 11:39-40).[69] Precisely the same is true with reference to the prohibition of eating flesh of some animals, which under existing climatic conditions was dangerous to human health, to rules concerning menstrual "impurity" (Lev. 15:19-20; cf. II Sam. 11:4) or prolonged vaginal bleeding (Lev. 15:25-30), childbirth (Lev. 12:2-8), regulation concerning a variety of skin ailments, infectious diseases including that which is traditionally translated as "leprosy" (Lev. 13-14; cf. II Kings 5) as well as to the disposition of human excrement outside the living area.

Of particular significance is the quarantine "purification" procedure for the prevention of epidemics which harassed men. The quarantine period usually lasted one week (Lev. 13:4, 21, 26, 31, 33, 50) but sometimes, after exposure and development of the first signs of infection, the isolation period was extended to two weeks (Lev. 13:54). As a rule this isolation applied only to the persons exposed to the communicable disease. However, in the case of the spread of a *negga* (probably an infectious disease which caused a very high death rate), the following alternate rules are prescribed: (a) emptying the house; (b) shutting the house for a period of seven days; (c) removal of some of its bricks outside the city; (d) disinfection of the house, and even removal of the substance disinfected outside the city. Should the same infectious disease spread again after the disinfection, the house and all its carpentry and bricks had to be destroyed and discarded outside the city (Lev. 14:38-48). Of great significance is the fact that "purification" techniques involved also the rinsing or burning of the garment of the diseased person, shaving the hair of the head, beard, and even the eyebrows (Lev. 14:8-9) and sterilization by means of fire (Lev. 13:55-58). Thus, in effect, the ways to fight communicable diseases were to destroy the germs, or prevent their being carried to healthy people. This leads us to the conclusion that although germs which directly cause certain infections and diseases were obviously unknown in those days, there was an awareness of the notion that some diseases were caused by the entry into the body of some infective agents.[70] There was obviously no concept of bacteria, but there was a full realization that an infectious disease can be defined in the broadest sense as a sickness that is passed along from a sick person to a healthy one, directly or through some third person or object. It is clear that the understanding of the differences between acute, chronic, and contagious illness were well known.

Many of these ritual purification laws and their techniques reflect for their time a remarkable understanding of hygiene, and closely related subjects, which was acquired empirically. They presuppose a fairly well-developed system of hygiene. None of the known rituals of the ancient Near East, as illustrated in mythological texts, incantations, and descriptions of festivals, can be compared to the vast scope of detailed topics, extent of knowledge, systematic elaboration, and clear identification of spiritual "purity" with community responsibility, as exemplified in the textual materials of the Bible. It is safe to assume that in ancient Israel, and for that matter, everywhere in the ancient Near East, the compulsory exercise of many agencies affecting the physical well being of man, such as cleanliness of person and clothing, consideration of food, arrangement of dwellings, removal of waste material, prevention of disease, maternal health, disposal of the dead, and general sanitation, as well as the exercise of compulsion for hygiene, was to a considerable extent born out of these cultic customs, techniques, and practices.[71]

Notes

[1] K. M. Kenyon, *Archaeology in the Holy Land* (1960), p. 187 (cf. pp. 160f., Pl. 36a); also *Digging up Jericho* (1957), p. 229 (Pl. 45b).

[2] W. F. Albright, *AASOR* XVII (1936-37), Pl. 12.

[3] Albright, *BASOR* No. 56 (Dec 1934), p. 8, Fig. 5.

[4] Albright, *The Archaeology of Palestine* (1963), p. 101.

[5] *Ibid.*, p. 210.

[6] For archaeological evidence regarding hygienic conditions and diseases in Palestine referred to in studies of human remains, see A. Hrdlicka in P. L. O. Guy, *Megiddo Tombs* (1938), pp. 132-208; R. A. S. Macalister, *The Excavation of Gezer* (1912), I, 58-69; D. L. Ridson, *Biometrika* XXI (1939), 99-166. See also A. Keith, *Palestine Exploration Quarterly* LXXII (1940), 7-12; M. Giles in O. Tufnell, *Lachish III* (1953), pp. 405-9; F. Fenner, *Die Krankheiten im Neuen Testament* (1930); A. Gemayel, *L'hygiene et la medicine á travers la Bible* (1932); J. Preuss, *Biblisch-*

Talmudische Medizin (1911); P. Humbert, *Revue d'Histoire et Philosophie Religieuses* XLIV (1964), 1-29; E. W. G. Masterman, *Palestine Exploration Quarterly* L (1918), 13-20, 56-71, 112-19, 156-71; LI (1919), 27-36; P. Tournier, *Bibel und Medizin* (1953); H. N. and A. L. Moldenke, *Plants of the Bible* (1952), pp. 149f.; and H. Nathan and N. Haas, *Israel Journal of Medical Science* II (1966), 171ff.

[7] B. Mazar (Maisler), *BA* XIV (1951), 46; for detailed information concerning changes between Middle Bronze and Late Iron Age construction, see Albright *AASOR*, XVII (1936-37), 22f., 32f., 39f., and XXI-XXII (1943), 19ff., 49ff. See also R. de Vaux, *Revue Biblique* LXII (1955), Pl. 6, and U. Jochims, *Zeitschrift des deutschen Palästina-Vereins* LXXVI (1960), 86ff.

[8] De Vaux, *Palestine Exploration Quarterly* LXXXVIII (1956), 133.

[9] G. E. Wright, *Shechem* (1965), pp. 158ff.; E. F. Campbell, *et al.*, *BASOR* No. 180 (Dec. 1965); and Campbell and J. F. Ross, *BA* XXVI (1963), 19.

[10] H. K. Beebe, *BA* XXXI (1968), 50.

[11] For archaeological evidence regarding ovens and silos in the Early Bronze Age see de Vaux, *Cambridge Ancient History* (rev. ed.), Chap. 13 (1966). For evidence for Late Bronze and Iron Ages, G. A. Barrois, *Manuel d'archéologie biblique* (1939), I, 320ff.; and M. Noth, *The Old Testament World* (1964), pp. 159f.

[12] L. Köhler, *Theologische Zeitschrift* IV (1948), 154ff. Cooking on pits lined with stones was a widespread primitive custom; see R. H. Lowie, *An Introduction to Cultural Anthropology* (1934), p. 59. J. Kaplan, *Bulletin of the Israel Exploration Society* XVII (1950), 49-51 (Hebrew), convincingly suggests that Hebrew *kerah* was a pit, and that ovens found at the bottom of such pits represented the original *kerah* where heating and cooking took place. Kaplan convincingly compares these pits with those used from the end of the 4th millennium B.C. down to the 6th century B.C.

[13] G. Dalman, *Arbeit und Sitte in Palästina* (1928-35), IV, 88ff.

[14] Beebe, *BA* XXXI (1968), 57.

[15] *Ibid.*, p. 52.

[16] E.g., the widespread practice of dressing the umbilical cord of the newly born infant with dirty rags, rubbing its slippery skin with salt as an antiseptic (Ezek. 16:4; cf. Job 38:8). According to Reiske (quoted in R. Smith, *Kinship and Marriage in Early Arabia* [1907], p. 181), the Arabs were accustomed to hide a newborn child under a cauldron till the morning light. Granquist reports: "I myself saw a new-born boy, after he had been swaddled immediately after birth, on a plaited straw tray . . . such as the fellahin use for a table, on which had been spread some rags. Nowadays one generally uses a market basket for the first part of the time." H. Granquist, *Marriage Conditions in a Palestine Village* (1931), I, 27, n. 2.

[17]On the basis of a series of Punic votive inscriptions where a sacrifice named in Phoenician *molkomer* (meaning "votive offerings") occurs, Eissfeldt suggests that the Molek (*mulk*) referred to in the Bible, to whom human sacrifices were made (literally, "leading children through the flames of Molek," Lev. 18:21; 20:2-5; II Kings 23:10; Jer. 32:35) was not a divinity at all, but a particular type of sacrifice, simply a "votive offering." See O. Eissfeldt, *Molk als Oberbegriff im Punischen und Hebräischen und das Ende des Gottes Moloch* (1935). This is an ingenious theory but not entirely convincing to everyone; see W. Kornfeld, *Weiner Zeitschrift für die Kunde des Morgenlandes* LI (1952), 287-313; and E. Dhorme, *Anatolian Studies* VI (1956), 57-62. For further literature on this question, see Eissfeldt, *The Old Testament: An Introduction* (1965), p. 70, n. 1.

[18]Guy, *The Excavations of Armageddon* (1929), p. 4; C. C. McCown, *The Ladder of Progress in Palestine* (1943), pp. 59, 176; de Vaux, *Studies in Old Testament Sacrifice* (1964), pp. 60ff., 82ff., and *Ancient Israel* (1961), pp. 441ff. For similar evidence in different cultures, see C. Wells, *Bones, Bodies and Disease* (1964), pp. 176-82.

[19]*Soṭah* 4b: "Whoever eats foods without previously washing the hands is as though he had intercourse with a harlot," and "Whoever eats a loaf of bread (a piece of bread) without wiping his hands is as though he eats impure food." See also Matt. 15:2; Mark 7:3; Luke 11:38.

[20]Sybilline Book III, 591-93; Josephus, *Antiquities*, XVI.10.23.

[21]R. S. Lamon and G. M. Shipton, *Megiddo I* (1939), pp. 108-11, Pl. 96; Albright, *AASOR* XXI-XXII (1943), 80f. See also Dalman, *Arbeit und Sitte,* IV, 259-68; V, 266, 276, 286f., 334, 339, 346, 352f.

[22]I. Ben-Dor, *Quarterly of the Department of Antiquities of Palestine* XI (1944), 93-112.

[23]A. Erman and H. Ranke, *Ägypten und ägyptisches Leben in Altertum* (1923), pp. 257f. Cf. A. Lucas, *Ancient Egyptian Materials and Industries* (1966), pp. 353, 355, 359-64.

[24]C. L. Woolley, *Ur Excavations II: The Royal Cemetery* (1934), p. 245. For documentary evidence see B. Meissner, *Babylonien und Assyrien*, I (1920), 242ff., 353, 403, 411f.; II (1925), 82, 84, 239; E. Ebeling, *Parfumrezepte und kultische Texte aus Assur* (1950).

[25]Mazar and I. Dunayevsky, *Israel Exploration Journal* XIV (1964), 128-30, and XVII (1967), 142f.

[26]Y. Yadin, *Israel Exploration Journal* XV (1965), 29-36; see also his *Masada* (1966), pp. 75ff.

[27]*Taʾanith* 1.6; *Nedarim* 5.3, 5; *Aboda Zarah* 3.4; see also *Megillah* 3.2. Notwithstanding the basic differences between the *miqbeh* and the *merḥaṣ,* terms are not infrequently interchanged (*Shabbath* 1.2; *Pesaḥim* 7.8; *Nidah* 9.3; *Makshirin* 2.2.5).

[28] *Baba Meṣia* 8.8; *Baba Batra* 4.4, 6, 7; 10.7; *Aboda Zarah* I. 7.9; *Megillah* 3.2.

[29] L. and J. Heuzey, *Histoire du costume dans l'antiquité classique: L'Orient* (1935), pp. 22ff.; H. Frankfort, *Sculpture of the Third Millennium B.C. from Tell Asmar and Khafajah* (1939), pp. 49-55; F. Boucher, *20,000 Years of Fashion* (1967), pp. 57ff.; R. Pfister and L. Bellinger, *The Excavations at Dura Europos. Final Report IV, Part II: The Textiles* (1945), pp. 15ff.; Bellinger, *Working Notes*, II (1950), 24ff. For analysis of some of the textiles which have survived in Palestine, see Bellinger, *BASOR* No. 118 (April 1950), pp. 9-11; G. M. Crowfoot, *Palestine Exploration Quarterly* LXXXIII (1951), 5-31, and *Les grottes de Murabaat (Discoveries in the Judean Desert,* II) (1961), pp. 72ff.; E. Crowfoot in Kenyon, *Jericho I* (1960), p. 662.

[30] See on this point M. L. Ryder in D. Brothwell and E. Higgs, eds. *Science in Archaeology* (1963), pp. 529ff.

[31] Among royalty (I Sam. 28:8; II Sam. 12:20; II Kings 22:14=II Chron. 34:22); priests (Lev. 6:4; Ezek. 42:14; 44:19); and probably the very rich. Giving "fresh outfit of clothing" was of great significance (Gen. 45:22; Judg. 14:12f.; II Kings 5:5, 22, 23).

[32] Regarding this document, see J. Naveh, *Israel Exploration Journal* X (1960), 129-39; F. M. Cross, *BASOR* No. 165 (Feb. 1962), pp. 42-44; J. D. Amusin and M. L. Heltzer, *Israel Exploration Journal* XIV (1964), 148-57; S. Yeivin, *Bibliotheca Orientalis* XIX (1962), 3ff.; and the valuable remarks of S. Talmon, *BASOR* No. 176 (Dec. 1964), pp. 29ff.

[33] According to the Talmud (*Qiddushin* 40b), "He who eats in the market place is like a dog, and some say that he is unfit to testify." According to Rashi, he is unfit to testify because he has no self-respect.

[34] I. Löw, *Simonsen-Festschrift* (1923), pp. 158ff.; also his *Die Flora der Juden* (1924), I, 637-50; Dalman, *Arbeit und Sitte,* I, 263; Moldenke, *Plants of the Bible,* pp. 215f., 280; M. Levey, *Chemistry and Chemical Technology in Ancient Mesopotamia* (1959), p. 122. In passing it may be mentioned that the reference in Job 9:30 to "snow water" is rather a reference to a kind of fine body soap, cleaning lotion or ointment; for evidence, see M. H. Pope, *Anchor Bible: Job* (1975), p. 72, and Löw, *Die Flora der Juden,* I, 648. For *ashlag* in the *Mishnah*, as a kind of mineral used as soap, see *Shabbath* 9.5 and *Niddah* 9.6.

[35] This is well known, but for a recent excellent study on the subject available now in English from the Rutgers University Press see R. Amiran, *The Ancient Pottery of the Holy Land* (1970).

[36] Judg. 13:4, 7; I Sam. 14:32ff.; Ezek. 4:14. The biblical dietary laws are very old. They are presented in a negative way insofar as they refer to the prohibited foods. The available evidence indicates that with one exception

(a kid not to be seethed in its mother's milk, Exod. 23:19, 34:26; Deut. 14:21) they are the product of the sharp contrast with the Canaanite food customs. It may be added that during the Hellenistic period the dietary laws were disputed in cases of emergency, as seen in Tobit and Judith. From Maccabees it appears that in many instances these laws were taken lightly, though in this very period it became decisive, for being a true Israelite, to observe these laws (I Macc. 1:62ff.). See Mark 7:14-23; Acts 10:9-16, 11:1-10; but cf. Gal. 2:11-13; Col. 2:16; and Acts 15:20, 29.

[37]Yadin, *Hazor I* (1958), Pls. CLIII, 15 and LXXIII, 9. (In relation to this, see the vessel of the Early Bronze Age found by de Vaux and interpreted by him as a "strong box." *RB* 68 [1961] 583, pl. XLVIa.)

[38]Prov. 7:17; 27:9; Psalm 45:9; Song of Songs 3:6; see also Luke 7:46. Similar was the case in the Mishnaic and Talmudic period; *Berakoth* 6.6; *Sanhedrin* 109a; *Shabbath* 18a.

[39]R. H. Harrison, *Healing Herbs of the Bible* (1966), pp. 52f.

[40]Called in the Mishnah *aparsemon*. See Y. Feliks, *Agriculture in the Period of the Mishnah and Talmud* (1963), p. 297, n. 56 (Hebrew). On the derivation of *aparsemon* from *peršanti* used in the Amarna tables, see Mazar, *et al.*, *Ein-Gedi Excavations in 1961-62 = Atiqot* V (1966), 8-9.

[41]R. J. Forbes in C. Singer, E. J. Holmyard and A. R. Hale, eds., *A History of Technology* (1956), II, pp. 52f. Some of them, particularly laudanum, were used for centuries as opium and morphine; they served as pain relievers and were valuable as an anti-diarrheic. See on this point K. Herfort, *Graefs Archiv Ophthalmologie* CLXIV (1962), 312f.; see also Moldenke, *Plants of the Bible*, p. 77.

[42]Mazar, *et al.*, *Atiqot* V (1966).

[43]J. M. A. Janssen, *Jaarbericht 'Ex Oriente Lux'* XIV (1955-56), 63ff.; J. Vergote, *Joseph en Egypte* (1959), pp. 10ff.; G. W. van Beek, *Journal of the American Oriental Society* LXXVIII (1958), 14ff.; also van Beek and A. Jamme, *BASOR* No. 151 (Oct. 1958), p. 15.

[44]Löw, *Die Flora der Juden*, I, 196, 298-313, 362ff.; II, 240, 643ff.; III, 389; Feliks, *Plant World of the Bible* (1957), pp. 231ff. (Hebrew); Moldenke, *Plants of the Bible*, pp. 77, 84ff., 177ff.; van Beek, *BA* XXIII (1960), 70ff.; Harrison, *Healing Herbs of the Bible*, p. 22; M. Zohary, article "Flora," *Interpreter's Dictionary of the Bible* (1962), II, 290f.; O. Warburg, *Pflanzenwelt* (1916), II, 182.

[45]C. H. Gordon in *The Aegeans and the Near East: Studies Presented to Hetty Goldman* (1956), pp. 140ff.; see also Gordon, *Ugaritic Literature* (1949), p. 130, Text 12 plus 97, and 120; and *Ugaritic Textbook* (1965), Sec. 17.2, VI 2.

[46]E. V. McCollum, *A History of Nutrition* (1957), p. 137; see also Forbes, *Short History of the Art of Distillation* (1948); and Levey, *Chemistry and Chemical Technology in Ancient Mesopotamia*, pp. 31ff.

[47]If this may be concluded from the Chronicler (II Chron. 16:14), according to whom Asa, king of Judah, was buried "in the crypt which was filled with spices blended with spice-mixtures of all kinds of aromatic spices."

[48]There is an enormous literature on the subject, for a general survey see C. L. Metcalf, *et al., Beneficial and Injurious Insects* (1951); see also, W. B. Herms, *Medical Entomology* (1950); C. B. Symes, et al., *Insect Control in Public Health* (1962).

[49]On some of the insects in ancient Palestine, see F. S. Bodenheimer, *Animal Life in Palestine* (1935), and his article "Fauna," in *Interpreter's Dictionary of the Bible*, II, 254-56. See also the articles published in *Studies in Agricultural Entomology and Plant Pathology*=Z. Avidor, ed., *Scripta Hierosolymitana* XVIII (1936). See now Edward Neufeld, *Apiculture in Ancient Palestine (Early and Middle Iron Age) Within the Framework of the Ancient Near East (Beitrag, Ugarit-Forshungen*, X, 1979) and by the same author "Insects as Warfare Agents in the Ancient Near East" (*Orientalia* XLIX, 1980, pp. 30-57).

[50]Noth, *The Old Testament World*, p. 179. See also Nelson Glueck, "Incense Altars," *Essays in Honor of Herbert G. May*, eds. Harry Thomas Frank and William L. Reed (1970) 325ff.

[51]Lucas, *Ancient Egyptian Materials*, pp. 90-97; R. O. Steürer, *Uber das wohlriechende Natron bei den alten Agyptern* (1937); V. Lortet, *La résine de térébinthe* (sonter) *chez les anciens egyptiens* (1949).

[52]According to Herodotus (*History* I, p. 183) the Babylonian temple of Bel consumed annually a thousand talents of incense.

[53]In a private communication, M. Dahood kindly informs me "The best known instance of incense being used for sacrificial use (in the home very probably) is 2 Aqht:1:28-29; *mšsu qtrh l^c pr* 'who sends out his incense from the dust' (here *^c pr* is merely a poetic synonym for first colon *arṣ*). Cf. Gordon, *Ugarit and Minoan Crete* (1966), p. 122. On the term *dgt* in 1 Aqht 185, 186, 192, 193, where it is parallel to *dbh*, see H. A. Hoffner, *Journal of Near Eastern Studies* XXIII (1964), 66-68." Professor Dahood adds in his letter that "on the use of plants for cosmetic purposes, one text that springs to mind is *^c nt* II: 2: *kpr šb^c bnt, rh gdm wanhbm*. Though scholars disagree in rendering this line, I prefer Gaster's version in *Thespis*, p. 211, henna as of seven maidens, a scent of coriander and perfumes (?). His note on the verse is also useful, giving references to the use of henna, or camphor, in antiquity. In Song of Sol. 1.14 *koper* occurs with *^c en gedi* though *gedi* is normally derived from 'goat.' I suspect that the poet wanted also to elicit the concept of 'coriander.' Cf. also J. C. de Moor, *Orientalia* XXXVII (1968), 212-15, and n. 4 on p. 212."

[54]Noth, *The Old Testament World*, p. 179; see also M. Haran, *Vetus Testamentum* X (1960), 123.

[55]De Vaux, *Ancient Israel*, pp. 411, 423.

[56]C. P. McCord and W. N. Witheridge, *Odors, Physiology and Control* (1949), p. 187; see also M. C. Buer, *Wealth, Health, and Population in the Early Days of the Industrial Revolution* (1926), pp. 164ff.

[57] In addition to literature quoted in note 43, see Albright in G. E. Wright, *The Bible and the Ancient Near East* (1961), p. 451.

[58]*Atiqot* V (1966), 21.

[59]In addition to the literature quoted by Mazar, *et al., Atiqot* V (1966), 8, n. 27, see W. W. Tarn, *Hellenistic Civilization* (1965), pp. 260-361; and L. B. Jensen, *Man's Food, Nutrition and Environment in Food Gathering Times and Food Producing Times* (1953), pp. 85ff.

[60]Note the words of L. Worrell in M. B. Jacobs, ed., *The Chemistry and Technology of Food and Food Products* (1951), II, 1706f.: "They [spices] have occupied an important place in world commerce for many centuries. In fact, the exploration of many parts of the world was due to attempts to find easier and shorter routes to the Orient for the purpose of obtaining spices. It has been pointed out repeatedly that America was accidentally discovered by Columbus in his search for an all-water route to India and the East Indies. During the period of the early explorations the demand for spices was great in western Europe, when strong flavouring agents were needed to disguise the odors and tastes accompanying the partial decomposition of foodstuffs which often occurred."

[61]This excellent translation of *inna nepeš* in Lev. 16:29 comes from Gaster, *Thespis* (1951), p. 65.

[62]Gaster, *Thespis*, p. 23.

[63]E. Westermarck, *The Origin and Development of the Moral Ideas* (1912), I, 233.

[64]Eissfeldt, *The Old Testament: An Introduction*, p. 30.

[65]J. G. Frazer, *Adonis, Attis, Osiris* (1961), pp. 179ff.

[66]S. Gierdion, *Mechanization Täkes Command* (1948), pp. 628ff.

[67]R. Smith, *Lectures on the Religion of the Semites* (1914), p. 428; see also H. E. Sigerist, *Landmarks in the History of Hygiene* (1956), p. 8.

[68]Eissfeldt, *The Old Testament: An Introduction*, p. 31. Note the following quotation (by permission) from G. Rosen, *A History of Public Health* (1958), p. 27: "Cleanliness and personal hygiene are to be found among present-day primitives and were unquestionably practiced by prehistoric and early historic men. Primitive peoples generally dispose of their excretions in a sanitary manner, but their reasons for this behavior are not necessarily identical with ours. Throughout large periods of human history, cleanliness has been next to godliness because of religious beliefs and practices. People kept clean so as to be pure in the eyes of the gods and not for hygienic reasons. Cleanliness and hygiene were emphasized on such

grounds among the Egyptians, the Mesopotamians, the Hebrews, and other peoples."

[69] For details, see F. E. König, *Geschichte der alttestamentliche Religion* (1915), pp. 560ff.; J. Pedersen, *Israel: Its Life and Culture* (1940), III-IV, 8ff., 22, 273ff., 294, 364ff., 437, 451ff. As to priestly conditions of cleanliness all over the ancient Near East see Gaster's article "Sacrifices," in *Interpreter's Dictionary of the Bible,* III, 156.

[70] Father Roland de Vaux kindly drew my attention to the paper by J. Levin, *Expository Times* LXXVI (1964-65), 154-57. Garrison is probably right, in *Bulletin of the New York Academy of Medicine* V (1929), 899f., when he states that "the rules in Deut. 23:11-14 for policing of a camp contain the germinal idea of the military latrine (Lev. 15:16)."

[71] Sigerist, *Man and Medicine* (1932), p. 278.

10

THE PRACTICE OF WRITING IN ANCIENT ISRAEL

A. R. MILLARD

The epigraphic discoveries of recent decades have shown beyond any doubt that writing was well-known in Palestine during the period of Israelite rule. The intention of this paper is to examine the use made of writing there at that time and the extent of its practice. Two sources are available on which any conclusions will rest: on the one hand, references in the surviving literature, mainly the Old Testament; on the other hand, extant specimens of writing or evidence for the former existence of documents now perished. In the Old Testament, so D. Diringer has informed us recently, are found "as many as 429 references to writing or written documents,"[1] but divergent views on the origins and dates to be attributed to many of the books containing these references lay use of their information open to question. Accordingly, we shall concentrate upon the ancient material recovered from Palestine and the neighboring lands.

The total number of written documents surviving from antiquity in this area is very large, ranging from Egyptian hieroglyphs to the scribbles of Nabatean travelers. Whilst we can find occasional examples of the hieroglyphic and cuneiform scripts within the borders of ancient Israel and the time-span of the Monarchy, our interest is limited to writings in the alphabetic script inherited by the Israelites from the previous inhabitants of the land. Accidents of preservation and discovery have provided far more material from ancient Israel than from her neighbors; the greater intensity of exploration and settlement in Palestine is a contributory factor, too. However, enough is known of writing in Phoenicia, Aram, Ammon, Moab, and Edom to imply that a picture could be painted for each of these states similar in many respects to the one we shall compose for Israel.

Illus. 19

The Documents

For the present purpose the known texts may be placed in three categories according to their content and destiny: monumental, professional, and occasional. While the form of script is involved to some degree in this study, it is not the basis of the division, although Old Hebrew or Phoenician does exhibit slightly divergent tendencies, formal in the "monumental" texts, cursive in the other two groups, as J. Naveh has shown.[2]

The *monumental* inscriptions need only brief mention here. These are texts intended for public display as enduring records. As it happens, the Siloam Tunnel Inscription alone can be counted a worthy representative of its class in Hebrew. And when admiring its calligraphy, it should be remembered that the engraver had only the light of oil lamps or torches to illumine his work some six meters from the end of the tunnel. The meager remnant of a stele from Samaria and perhaps a dedicatory plaque of ivory carried off as booty to the Assyrian arsenal at Nimrud may be adjudged "official" and placed beside the Siloam text. With these three can be associated the epitaphs from tombs in the village of Silwan in that they were written, apparently, for the king's officials.[3] In 1978 a piece of a large stone plaque bearing another early Hebrew text was discovered during excavations in Jerusalem. The script dates from about 700 B.C., but, unfortunately, only a few letters of four lines remain.

Most early Hebrew texts fall into the category of *professional*. Use of this term indicates at once that a trained class was responsible for their production. In part this remains an assumption, for no piece is signed, nor has any material such as exercises survived from a scribal school, unless the Gezer Calendar is one such product. At this juncture the literary sources help with their frequent use of the word *sopher*, "scribe," basically one who wrote, whatever other functions he may have had.[4] A single archive testifies to the activity of scribes in the palace, the Samaria ostraca from the reign, it seems, of Jeroboam II.[5] They represent only the lowest grade of secretarial duty, the noting of goods received at the palace, in this case wine and oil from the countryside around. More exalted products of the Hebrew chanceries have vanished. Sad witnesses to their former presence in the excavated area of the Samaria palace are the fifty or so clay sealings bearing on the reverse the imprint of the fibers of papyrus sheets to which they were once attached, and which, we may surmise, were letters or legal deeds.[6] Nine of the bullae were impressed by the matrix showing a scarab-beetle design and may be the royal seal of Judah, for Y. Yadin has recognized the scarab-beetle as the royal emblem of the southern kingdom.[7]

Sole survivor of the once numerous papyrus documents is the fragment from a cave in the Wadi Murabbaᶜat. We may assume that papyrus was the preferred material for any texts of importance or length, although the re-use of the Murabbaᶜat piece three times implies that it was not commonly available, at least not at the outposts of the Dead Sea shore.[8]

Other clay sealings have been found, notably at Lachish where the two from the Wellcome-Marston Expedition are now joined by seventeen from Y. Aharoni's excavation beneath the Persian period shrine. They were in a clay juglet where they had been put for some unknown reason after the papyri to which they were attached had been opened.[9] A hoard of similar sealings is to be published by N. Avigad, who has also published a group of post-exilic date.[10]

Ostraca are our best evidence of the scrivener's work, simply by reason of their greater durability. Our division of Hebrew inscriptions into three categories leads us to narrow the use of "ostracon" to potsherds inscribed with continuous text, thus excluding those bearing a simple statement of ownership. Letters and accounts make up the content of the two hundred and fifty or so known ostraca. A valuable translation and commentary of the majority has been published by André Lemaire (see n. 5). The absence of legal deeds results from the use of papyrus for these more important texts as shown by the situation at Elephantine where both papyri and ostraca survive; and the ostraca are used only for ephemeral records.

Other objects falling into this class of "professional" products are the inscribed weights and the numerous seals. In each case the letters were engraved on the stone, sometimes a very hard stone, usually with considerable skill. Whether the engravers were scribes or literate lapidaries cannot be said, although the fluency of the script makes it likely that the engravers knew their letters. We shall return to this question.

Occasional denotes a class of writings frequently disregarded in surveying Hebrew inscriptions. These are the pottery vessels and other objects on which the names of their owners or a note of content have been written, and a miscellany of scribblings on all sorts of stone surfaces.

The Writers and the Readers

Clearly, professional scribes were responsible for the bulk of Hebrew written documents. Some traces of their activity in Samaria have been mentioned. Had the Hebrew monarchs not employed scribes at their courts in daily tasks and in making records for the eyes of their subjects and for posterity, they would have been unique among their contemporaries. When a king is said to have written a letter, it is to be understood that a secretary performed the physical task.[11] Certainly this was the case in Babylonia, Assyria, and in Egypt.

Israel shared so many material and cultural aspects of her life with these nations that we should give a little attention to them. Various literary texts laud the scribal art in both regions. Egypt seemingly had an even higher regard for the scribe than Babylonia, but we can rely only on the opinions of the scribes themselves for that! Schooling at all grades and the various specialties are frequently described. Afterwards many avenues were open to qualified scribes, for they were indispensable as masters of the complicated writing systems of Egypt and Babylon. The most accomplished served in the imperial govenments; in Egypt the most modest might accompany the gangs of laborers hewing royal sepulchres.[12] Numerous as they may have been in the civilized centers, scribes were less common in the provinces and border lands. So in the Amarna era when Palestine lay firmly within the sphere of cuneiform writing, petty rulers there might share the services of the same scribe.[13] Given the dominance of the complicated systems of hieroglyphic and cuneiform, the following words can be applied to the situation: "While the art of writing was well known . . . it was by no means universal, and was largely confined . . . to a professional class."[14]

The question is, did the same state obtain in Israel, of which in fact the words cited were actually written? An affirmative answer would be given by many scholars. One has stated lately, "Indeed in ancient Israel it was probable that the ability to read and write did not extend outside the professional scribes and ruling class."[15] Others dissent. Forty years ago, E. Dhorme observed that writing was not confined to the upper classes in Israel.[16] The primary reason for such an opinion has been well expressed by W. F. Albright: "The 22 letter alphabet could be learned in a day or two by a bright student and in a week or two by the dullest; hence it could spread with great rapidity. I do not doubt for a moment that there were many urchins . . . who could read and write as early as the time of the Judges, although I do not believe that the script was used for formal literature until later."[17]

Incomplete and unrepresentative as the epigraphic evidence already summarized may be reckoned, we will argue that is adequate to support Albright's claim and dispose of the view maintaining a very limited use of writing in ancient Israel.

Monumental inscriptions have their simple analogies in Egypt, Syria, and Mesopotamia; whether they could be "known and read of all men" or by the literate elite alone was immaterial to their authors so long as they could be read by someone. The class of professional products can be assigned to the same body of scribes with some confidence. Army commanders at Lachish and Arad are likely to have had personal secretaries, or at least a scribe attached to their important fortresses. Here, too, the expert would read or write as required; but how far did this system extend? Is it necessary to assume the presence of a scribe at every military outpost of the small kingdom of Judah? If so, there was a very large number of scribes in that state; if not, either military stations were without any means of written communication for sending or receiving orders or reports, or the military included some undesignated person who possessed the appropriate skills. (We cannot tell whether the Lachish letters from Hoshayah were themselves brought from him by couriers, or whether they are copies made at Lachish from other written texts or from oral messages. That five [Nos. 2, 6, 7, 8, 19] are written on parts of the same pot might favor the second alternative.)

The question of the extent of literacy looms larger in the light of the numerous Hebrew seals recovered. No comprehensive survey of seals from Iron age Palestine is available for estimating a ratio of inscribed to uninscribed, but a glance through various excavation reports leaves the impression that it is higher than in Syria or in Mesopotamia. A catalogue begun by F. Vattioni in 1969 and brought up to date in 1978 reaches a total of 452 Hebrew seals and impressions.[18] (His list of Aramaic seals reaches a total of 178, of which only a few bear no design or picture beside the writing.[19]) Some of these are not strictly Hebrew in so far as the personal names are compounded with alien theophoric elements, or are known to be foreign, or the script is not Hebrew, or the seals were found in a content implying a non-Hebrew source[20]; some may date from after the end of the Monarchy, but there are others which should be added.[21] Of course, some seals can never be satisfactorily assigned, the divine names ꝰEl and Ba‘al being common to several Semitic languages, e.g., *l‘zꝰ bn b‘lḥnn* (Vattioni, no. 36). However, a round figure of some 350-400 for the known number of Hebrew seals or their impressions cannot be far wrong. Noteworthy is the occurrence of the Tetragrammaton (YHWH) as an element in personal names in the forms *yhw*, *yh*, or *yw* over 200 times.

It is clear that the seals were applied to clay in sealing letters or legal deeds and also to large jars and other objects. In the first case they served as seals, authenticating and securing documents which would contain the names of the parties and the witnesses in the text proper (cf. Jeremiah 32). In the latter case, when applied to jars and the like, they seem to have acted as marks of ownership and identification. When the seal carried a pictorial design as well as the owner's name, little difficulty would arise in recognition. However, as many as one third of the Hebrew seals are engraved solely with the owners' names and patronyms, and any attempt to identify these seals obviously demanded reading ability.[21] Moreover, many of the stones are very small, down to half an inch in length, not always easy for the modern Hebraist to read! But was it necessary to read the impressions made by the seals at all? Seals were fastened to documents for security; the seals impressed on jars may have served only as guarantees of capacity. Their function is bound up with the still uncertain use of the "royal" (*lammelek*) stamps which have a pictorial symbol to facilitate recognition beside the relevant and often illegible inscription, "the king's: Hebron/Ziph/Socoh/ *Mmsht*."[22] If they were simply guarantees of a fixed capacity, they may be compared with the guarantee contained in the royal bust or device stamped on coins by the issuing authority; and the rare pre-exilic and more common post-exilic seal impressions combining official and private forms[23] have a remote analogy in the early medieval English coins bearing the king's name on one face and the name of the responsible mint-master on the other as a warranty of the coin's integrity. If the seals impressed on jars were marks of identification which were required to be read, they have a parallel in the roughly scratched notes on jar-handles from Gibeon which, there can be no doubt, were written to be read.[25]

Two seal-stones proclaim their owners "the scribe" (*hspr*), but both are Moabite in origin.[26] A larger number belonged to members of the royal household, yet this is still a small proportion of the whole corpus. (Vattioni, Nos. 72, 110, 209, and 252 bear the title *bn hmlk* "the king's son;" Nos. 69, 70, 71, and 125 ʿbd hmlk "the king's servant.") Are the majority of seals to be attributed to government officials, despite the absence of titles? As an explanation of two seals known in duplicate and another in triplicate this is attractive.[27] It would seem hard to assume, then, that those officers were unable to read the names on their own seals, even if they had secretaries. Illiterate nobles would surely require a design they could distinguish easily, as in Babylonia (although it may be remarked that many Babylonian stamp seals of the 7th and 6th centuries B.C. bear designs of a figure before divine emblems which are often barely distinguishable from each other), whereas the small inscriptions might be confused easily. Accordingly, the well-to-do and the royal officials are likeliest to have owned inscribed seals—their very nature made them costly— exemplified in families like Jeremiah's.

One limitation inherent in the use of inscribed seals is their particularity. Pictorial seals might be passed from generation to generation or even sold without alternation; seals only naming owners and their fathers could be less simply handed on over long periods or alienated, and therefore had a more limited lifetime. In Babylonia a seal could be employed by more than one individual or generation even when inscribed with a personal name. All, however, carry other designs, too.. Dynastic seals passed on over long periods are no exception, for they name the place as well as the king who first commissioned them beside the royal device.

The merchant class may or may not be represented amongst the seal owners, but they are relevant when we turn to the inscribed weights. While learning simple ciphers for multiples of a shekel or other unit hardly demands literacy—and many weights were uninscribed—and the unlettered might recognize *nṣp, pym,* and *bqᶜ* by their distinctive labels, the shuttle-shaped weight marked *rbᶜ šql,* or the bronze turtles with *plg rbᶜt šql* and *ḥmš* are more demanding in that respect as are the jars inscribed "royal *bath* measure" (*bt lmlk*). Still literate traders need not have been numerous; the inscribed weights are all of low denomination, therefore reserved for the more precious goods sold in small quantities.

In surveying Hebrew inscriptions uncertainty was expressed about the engraving of the stones, whether they were passed, cut and polished by the lapidary to some scribe who incised the legend, or whether one man carried out the whole operation. The directions for making the priestly regalia in Exodus 28 imply that an engraver did all this work. Scrutiny of photographs reveals comparatively few seals with a design and a name where the name is obviously later, or made with different tools.[28] Of course, an engraver may have copied the writing traced for him by a scribe; but the high quality of script evident in most of these tiny inscriptions, the frequent ligature of *h* and *w* (e.g. Vattioni No. 144, contrast 161), and the rarity of error (perhaps original omission of *p* in Vattioni No. 150) combine to suggest that many of the engravers were familiar with their letters. Thus a very specialized class of craftsmen, "seal-cutters or engravers," can be counted among those who could read in Israel.

The Evidence of the "Occasional" Texts

Seals and weights are small, easily transported to an engraver's bench. The objects in the third category of text are not of the same nature. Did Pekah write his name on the storage jar found at Hazor, or did he invite a scribe for the purpose?[29] If the same question is asked of each potsherd or vessel bearing a name the answer may be "Yes, he called in a scribe" on a few occasions (perhaps, for example, the jug from a ritual desposit at Jerusalem with $Plyhw$ pecked on the body, and the sherds inscribed before baking from the same place[30]); but it is hard to accept for all of the three-score or so known today. Apart from plausibility, comparison with Babylonia plays a part in reaching this conclusion. There the number of potsherds or ordinary objects inscribed in cuneiform with personal names—admittedly a more difficult process—is very small indeed; and there writing was widely known but its practice limited, as noted above, to the scribe and the academic. A name written on a vessel served to distinguish it from others: if only one were uninscribed, it could be identified instantly; if several bearing their owners' names were brought together, identification could be made only by someone who could read, or by each owner recognizing the form of his own name. Again, such graffiti as the partial alphabet on a palace step at Lachish,[31] or the couplet on a tomb-wall nearby[32] could be the work of scribes; equally they could be the idle scratchings of a waiting petitioner or mourner. The inscriptions in the tombs at Khirbet el-Kôm, also near Lachish, are clearly not the work of the most expert hands either.[33] However, the difficulties of a scribe accustomed to writing with pen and ink when faced with a stone surface need to be borne in mind.

Of much earlier date are the copper arrowheads found near Bethlehem, generally agreed to belong to the 12th century B.C. They bear the words $ḥṣ$ $ᶜbdlbᵓt$, "Arrow of ᶜAbd-lebaᵓat."[34] Whoever wrote on these objects was not a professional engraver; many of the letters were impressed with the sharpened end of an instrument like a narrow chisel, accounting partially for their eccentric shapes. Was it a scribe called in haste to write on an unusual substance who made these marks, or the owner who used the tool most ready to hand to write in the easiest way?

These are speculations, yet the motley remnants of early Hebrew writing warrant them. The tenor of the Old Testament books is to treat reading and writing ability as an ordinary accomplishment, and the surviving examples of "occasional" texts especially support that literary evidence. For a society comparable with Israel in this aspect we should turn not to Babylon or to Egypt, but to classical

Greece where the same simple script was the possession of every citizen.

The Antiquity of Writing in Ancient Israel

A glance through the texts cited will show a great majority dating from the late 8th to the 6th centuries B.C. So it is legitimate to ask whether it may be extended backwards into earlier times. Documents from before *ca.* 750 B.C. are limited to the Samaria ostraca, witnessing a very mundane use of writing, the record of names and deliveries;[35] an odd seal placed in the 9th century B.C. on epigraphic grounds;[36] a few scattered ostraca and graffiti such as those from Hazor Stratum VIII; and the Gezer Calendar, a lonely monument from the Solomonic era.

Although merely isolated survivors, these pieces show at least some use of writing; and even were a use on the scale postulated for the subsequent period predicated for this, there could be no assurance that many examples would be unearthed. The factor of preservation has to be taken into account, a factor very much responsible for the uneven representation of relics from ancient Palestine in modern museums. Generally, the spectacular finds are made in the ruins of cities abandoned in haste, whether the cause be a natural disaster or hostile action, or in the tombs of notable persons. Remains of earlier cities, inhabited then superseded in peace for reasons of obsolescence or fashion, yield comparatively little. This is a commonplace of archaeology, and it applies equally to the recovery of ancient written documents. With few exceptions, the archives of ancient western Asia known today belong to the closing decades of the lives of the buildings in which they were found, a matter which has only rarely received mention in considering the contents of such archives.[37] In his recent classification of the Elephantine Aramaic papyri and ostraca J. Naveh has been able to use this fact to good effect.[38] It follows that even if examples are few, the employment of writing on as wide a scale in the early period of the Monarchy as in the later cannot be ruled out—"absence of evidence is not evidence of absence."

The Purpose of Writing in Ancient Israel

Most of the specimens of Hebrew writing now available were

made for mundane and ephemeral purposes. The monumental texts and tomb inscriptions alone were intended to endure, and obviously the best professional scribes would be brought to engrave the most important of these, or to trace the characters. Was the service of writing limited otherwise to matters of daily life—accounts, letters, and legal deeds—the work of scribes in busy centers? These were surely its most common end, and the documents which it was invented to record. Next to them may be placed the dedications and memorials required by ordinary folk from time to time, a class of text comprising almost the whole of our earliest group of alphabetic material, the Proto-Sinaitic Inscriptions,[39] and the recently found tomb notices of Khirbet el-Kôm of the Judean monarchy, the work of craftsmen less skilled than those of Jerusalem (see n. 32). Yet Israel would be unique in the ancient world had nothing else been written down. By the same broad analogy Albright's belief, noted earlier, that the script was not used for formal literature until after the time of the Judges may be disputed. The witness of lengthy texts from early in the history of other scripts (e.g. the Pyramid texts of Egypt, the Abu Salabikh and Fara tablets from southern Babylonia) suggests that the alphabet, too, could have been put to the same use soon after its invention. Ugarit has given examples of Canaanite myths, legends, and other compositions in the cuneiform alphabetic script of *ca.* 1400 B.C. which appears to owe its inspiration to the Canaanite alphabet. The scribal habits of Ugarit borrowed much from Babylonian models, but it is an open question whether the latter alone gave the impetus to record local literature in writing. Canaanite tales roused sufficient interest to be translated and preserved in Egyptian and Hittite,[40] a process which is hard to understand as strictly pedagogic, even if Babylonian literary texts were confined to scribal schools. Moreover, once a script has established itself no bounds can be set on its use. If kings of Byblos could have funerary and dedicatory inscriptions set up in the 11th and 10th centuries B.C., there seems little reason against positing even longer texts written less laboriously on papyrus in the same alphabet. (Notice the access Josephus claims to Phoenician records in *Antiquities* VIII ii 8; *Apion* I 17, 18.) And as far wider circles than the professional scribes could understand the writing,[41] they could read any such texts to which they had access, the last being the controlling factor.

It is submitted, therefore, that the indications of ancient usage contradict any idea of writing not being used for "formal literature" at a date as early as the Judges in Israel and allow, rather, the conclusion that both Canaanites and Israelites had the means to record and read anything they wanted, from brief receipt to lengthy victory poem, from a private letter to a state treaty. Whether they actually did so is not within the power of epigraphic evidence cited to reveal; but it does allow the possibility.

Here we reach the limit of our study. The questions of literacy and its extent inevitably follow from thoughts on the use of writing, but we have been concerned to show simply that writing was theoretically within the competence of any ancient Israelite, not the prerogative of an elite professional class alone, and to show that it was, in fact, quite widely practiced.

Notes

*This paper was read to the Society for Old Testament Study in January 1972 and has benefitted from comments made by many friends.

[1] *Cambridge History of the Bible,* I, ed. P. R. Ackroyd, C. F. Evans (1970), p. 13; some examples are given by D. J. Wiseman *ibid.*, pp. 37f; see further H. Michaud, *Sur la Pierre et l'Argile* (1958), Chap. 1. A selection of early Hebrew texts is now available in J. C. L. Gibson's *Syrian Semitic Inscriptions*, vol. I (1971).

[2] *Harvard Theological Review* LXI (1968), 71. D. Diringer has a slightly different, five-fold, grouping in his essay cited above.

[3] On the tombs themselves see now D. Ussishkin, *BA* XXXIII (1970), 34-46 and *BASOR* No. 196 (1969) 16-22.

[4] My colleague, K. A. Kitchen has drawn my attention to the fact that *sopher* when written as a Canaanite loanword in Egyptian is accompanied by three determinatives, one specifically indicating his function as a writer; see Papyrus Anastasi I ii 7. See also M. Burchardt, *Die alt-kanaanäischer Fremdwörter*, part 2 (1911), no. 1147.

[5] For the reattribution to this date in place of the reign of Menahem proposed by Y. Yadin in *Scripta Hierosolymitana* VIII (1961), 17-25, see Y. Yeivin, *BASOR* No. 184 (1966), 13-19, who utilizes the testimony of the Arad ostraca that Egyptian numerals were employed in Hebrew writing. For a detailed treatment of the Samaria ostraca see A. Lemaire, *Inscriptions Hebraiques* (1977).

[6] J. W. and G. M. Crowfoot, and K. M. Kenyon, *Samaria-Sebaste* III (1957), pp. 2, 88.

[7] *Scripta Hierosolymitana* VIII (1961), pp. 13-17. For another view, that it is the royal emblem of Israel, see A. D. Tushingham, *BASOR* No. 200 (1970), 71-8; No. 210 (1971), 23-35; a view I have opposed in *BASOR* No. 208 (1972), 5-9.

[8] J. T. Milik in R. de Vaux, *Discoveries in the Judean Desert of Jordan* II (1961), pp. 93-100, Pl. XXVIII; F. M. Cross, *BASOR* No. 165, (1962), 34-42.

[9] *Israel Exploration Journal* XVIII (1968), 165-8, Pl. 11.

[10] See N. Avigad, *Israel Exploration Journal* XXVIII (1978), 52; *Bullae and Seals from a Post-Exilic Judean Archive (Qedem* 4, 1976).

[11] Cf. H. Michaud, *Sur la Pierre et l'Argile* (1958), pp. 12f.

[12] E.g. J. Cerny, "Egypt from the Death of Ramesses III to the End of the Twenty-first Dynasty," *Cambridge Ancient History*, 3rd Edition, vol. II, part 2 (1975), pp. 620ff.

[13] For example, Zimrida of Lachish (letter 329) and Widia of Ascalon (letters 320-6); see E. F. Campbell, *The Chronology of the Amarna Letters* (1964), pp. 112f.

[14] T. H. Robinson, *A History of Israel* (1932), p. 231.

[15] A. J. Phillips in P. R. Ackroyd, B. Lindars, *Words and Meanings* (1968), p. 194.

[16] *Revue Biblique* XXXIX (1930), 62 = *Recueil Edouard Dhorme* (1951), p. 541.

[17] In C. H. Kraeling, R. F. Adams, *City Invincible* (1960), pp. 122-3.

[18] *Biblica* L (1960), 357-88, supplemented by *Augustinianum* XI (1971), pp. 447-54 and *Annali dell'Istituto Orientali di Napoli* XXXVIII (1978), pp. 227-54.

[19] *Augustinianum* XI (1971), 47-65.

[20] Ammonite: Vattioni Nos. 29, 94, 98, 135, 159, 164, 225, 229, 347, 383, 386, 442 on onomastic grounds; Nos. 117, 157, 165, 166, 194 by provenance; Nos. 103, 115, 116, 170 (?), 195, 201, 217, 221, 259, 262, 263, 264, 297, 298, 317, 318, 382, 384, 385, 387, 388, 389 (?), 390, 391, 440, 441, 443, 444, 445, 446, 447, 448, 449, 450, on onomastic and or epigraphic grounds; Nos. 41, 439 by style; Moabite: Nos. 111, 112, 113, 114, 146, 265, 266, 451, 452 on onomastic grounds; Nos. 74, 209, 267, 269 (?) on epigraphic grounds; perhaps No. 102, found at Kerak; Edomite: Nos. 118, 319, 320 by provenance; Nos. 119, 395 on onomastic grounds; No. 227 on both grounds. Similarly, Nos. 81, 82, 84, 129, 130, 138, 160, 180, 193 may be called Aramean, and Nos. 126, 127, 128, 158, 219, 234 Phoenician. No. 73 belonged to an officer of a Philistine city; cf. H. Tadmor, *BA* XXIX (1966), 99.

[21] Notably, the seals published recently by N. Avigad which may have belonged to men named in the Bible, see *Israel Exploration Journal* XXVIII (1978), pp. 53-56.

[22]Cf. already A. R. Millard, *Tyndale House Bulletin* XI (1962), 7, and J. Naveh, *Harvard Theological Review* LXI (1968), 72f.

[23]On these stamps see P. W. Lapp, *BASOR* 158 (1960), 11-22; F. M. Cross, *Eretz Israel* IX (1969), 20-22; A. D. Tushingham, *BASOR* No. 200 (1970), 71-78; No. 201 (1971), 23-35; H. D. Lance, *Harvard Theological Review* LXIV (1971), 315-32, has important observations on the dating. D. Ussishkin has now produced evidence that these stamps were current at the end of the 8th century B.C., see *BASOR* No. 223 (1976), pp. 1-14. P. Weiten, *Die Königs-Stempel* (1969) argues that the stamped jars brought supplies from four royal estates to various military garrisons; see further T. Mettinger, *Solomonic State Officials* (1971), pp. 93-97.

[24]Discussed by F. M. Cross, *Eretz Israel* IX (1969), 24-26. See now the work of N. Avigad, n. 10.

[25]J. B. Pritchard, *Hebrew Inscriptions and Stamps from Gibeon* (1959), and *BASOR* No. 160 (1961), 2-6.

[26]Vattioni, *Biblica* L (1969), Nos. 74, 113; see n. 17.

[27]Diringer, *Le iscrizioni antico-ebraiche palestinesi* (1934), pp. 122f., No. 5a, c *šbnyhw*/ / *czryhw*; Vattioni, Nos. 198, 199 *jhwḥl/šḥr* and *jhwḥjl/šḥr* from Ramat Rahel; Vattioni Nos. 231, 232, see Y. Aharoni, *Eretz Israel* VIII (1967), 101-03, Pl. 13, and *BA* XXI (1968), 15, Fig. 10, two seals inscribed *lʿlyšb/bn* *ʾšyhw*, and one *lʾlšbn/ʾšyh*, fascinating variants in presumably contemporary writings.

[28]E.g. Vattioni Nos. 16 (= Diringer no. 16), 137, 138 (= Moscati, Nos. 17, 18).

[29]Y. Yadin, *Hazor* II (1960), p. 72, Pl. 159, 5.

[30]For the graffiti from Jerusalem see J. Prignaud, *Revue Biblique* LXXVII (1970), 50-67 and in P. R. S. Moorey, P. J. Parr, eds., *Archaeology in the Levant* (1978), pp. 136-48.

[31]D. Diringer in O. Tufnell, *Lachish* III (1953), pp. 357-8.

[32]J. Naveh, *Israel Exploration Journal* XIII (1963), 74-92, Pls. 9-13. F. M. Cross in J. S. Sanders, *Near Eastern Archaeology in the Twentieth Century* (1970), pp. 299-306 leans to a date in the sixth century B.C. for these texts, and J. C. L. Gibson also favors a date as late or even later in his *A Textbook of Syrian Semitic Inscriptions* (1971), p. 57.

[33]Khirbet el-Kôm texts: W. G. Dever, *Hebrew Union College Annual* XL-XLI (1969-70), 139-204.

[34]On these and similar items from Syria and Lebanon see F. M. Cross, *Eretz Israel* VIII (1967), 19ff.

[35]For the date see n. 4. The date P. W. Lapp would set them in the reign of Ahab on archaeological grounds: *Vetus Testamentum* XX (1970), 255.

[36]Vattioni No. 40; see F. M. Cross, *BASOR* No. 168 (1962), 15, n. 12.

[37]E.g. W. G. Lambert, *Revue d'Assyriologie* LIII (1959), 123; A. R. Millard, *Tyndale Bulletin* XVIII (1967), 17.

[38] *The Development of the Aramaic Script* (1970), p. 37.

[39] See W. F. Albright, *The Proto-Sinaitic Inscriptions and their Decipherment* (1966).

[40] "Astarte and the Sea," James B. Pritchard, *Ancient Near Eastern Texts* (1955), p. 17; "El, Ashertu, and the Storm-god," Pritchard, *The Ancient Near East: Supplementary Texts* (1969), p. 519.

[41] A warning such as that engraved in the shaft of the tomb of Ahiram would have had no meaning to an illiterate rober or a casual laborer: photography, etc., in M. Dunand, *Revue Biblique* XXXIV (1925), Pl. VIII; text in H. Donner, W. Röllig, *Kanaanäische und Aramäische Inschriften* (1968-69), No. 2.

11

THE EARLY DIFFUSION OF THE ALPHABET

P. KYLE MCCARTER

It is well known that our alphabet is descended more or less directly from a writing system perfected by the Greeks in preclassical times. The quality of that ancient alphabet is amply demonstrated by its durability: centuries of use have required only small adjustments. Indeed an early Greek scribe would recognize most of the uppercase letters used to print these pages, and he in turn could draw only a few forms which would not be familiar to an untrained modern reader.

It is less well known but now widely agreed that the Greek alphabet was a modified version of a much older system devised under some measure of Egyptian influence centuries earlier. But neither to the Egyptians, who inspired it, nor to the Greeks who perfected it, should our thanks go for the invention of the alphabet. This was the achievement of another people, certainly Semitic and almost certainly Bronze Age Canaanite, of whose culture the coastal states of Phoenicia preserved the highest form in the Iron Age. The Greek historians themselves used to tell the story of Cadmus, a Phoenician prince, who, though better known as the founder of Thebes and ancestor of Oedipus, was said to have brought the letters from his homeland and instructed the rude Boeotians in their use.

Evidence for the earliest history of the alphabet, therefore, is to be sought in Syria and Palestine—the ancient Canaanite domain—and, after the Phoenicians ventured there, throughout the Mediterranean basin. Modern discovery and excavation in these areas have clarified this history in increasing measure. Inquiry into the subject in the present generation, however, has probably benefited more from refinements in methodology than from fresh evidence. These refinements have placed us in a better position than ever before to trace the critical early steps in the

Illus. 32-4

diffusion of the alphabet and its development from a tentative, semipictographic, Middle Bronze signary to the sophisticated national scripts of the Iron Age. In addition, we can now reckon with some precision the time and general circumstances of the crucial transmission of the alphabet from Phoenicia to Greece.

A Note on Method

The discipline of archaeology is sometimes subdivided into epigraphic and non-epigraphic branches. This classification must have been first proposed by an epigrapher. Written remains are characteristically the most meager product of an excavation and can hardly be balanced against the combined yield of architecture, pottery, jewelry, weaponry, and so on. It might be supposed that the information recorded in inscriptions justifies our special regard for them. The handsome catalogue of a recent exhibition of inscriptions at the Israel Museum in Jerusalem is entitled *Ktwbwt Msprwt* or, in English, *Inscriptions Reveal*. But as a matter of fact it is an unusual inscription which reveals more than the name of the owner of a broken jug or—at best—the livestock he brought to market on a particular morning in antiquity. This is especially true of texts in alphabetic script. The great stelae are exceedingly rare and reluctant—or so it seems—to come to light unbroken. Yet more than a few scholars are quite happy to spend their time brooding over such cryptic, unsatisfying graffiti.

There need be no apology for this. The written word permits an intimacy between the archaeologist and his subject as no other artifact can, and the task of decipherment appeals to the most elemental nature of the scholar. In addition—and more to the point—the trained epigrapher can now by the rigorous application of modern methods derive appreciable information from the most insipid inscription. Language, spelling, and the forms of the letters themselves are all important clues. Since the last of these is the special concern of this report, a few comments on paleographic method are in order.

The shape of the letters—or, more correctly, of the graphic signs representing the letters—did not remain the same throughout the early history of the alphabet. Instead they changed gradually in time. The reasons for this process are straightforward enough, as explained below; but in brief the change in letter-forms is motivated by the principle of economy that is inherent in the alphabetic system of writing. That is, the direction of change is generally towards simplification in the scribal execution of the various signs and elimination of ambiguities in stance and direction.

This process of morphological development is the good fortune of the paleographer, for although the rate of change cannot be predicted nor its direction anticipated, the shapes of the signs can be charted for any period from which sufficient inscriptions have survived. The developing sequence of letter-forms has already been mapped out for considerable expanses of time in the early history of the alphabet, though important gaps remain. The result is that new inscriptions as they are recovered can usually be dated quite securely on the basis of the appearance of the incised letter-forms alone. Of course this happy situation, arising as it does from such simple principles, is greatly complicated in practice, not only by the irksome gaps in our evidence but also by the frequent branching of the alphabet into subdivisions or, occasionally, by the existence of distinct scribal traditions even within a single script. Nevertheless, it is the refinement of the typology of the early letter-forms which more than anything else has advanced our knowledge of the history of the alphabet as described below.

Alphabetic Origins

The oldest known specimens of writing which certainly belong to the direct ancestry of our alphabet are still the so-called Proto-Sinaitic inscriptions. These comprise a small group of rock-cut graffiti from the ancient turquoise-mining community of Serābîṭ el-Khâdem in the Sinai peninsula. Less than thirty have survived in a condition satisfactory for modern epigraphic study, and even these are badly eroded.

The Proto-Sinaitic material can hardly be listed as a recent discovery. In fact it was apparently these inscriptions which were viewed and recorded by the sixth-century adventurer Cosmas of Alexandria (who navigated as far as India, earning his surname "Indicopleustes") and even earlier travelers. In his monastic old age, Cosmas described the inscriptions as the earliest form of the letters of the alphabet, taught by God to the Hebrews on their journey through the Sinai and later learned from Israel by Cadmus of Tyre (!), who carried them to Greece and thus, eventually, the rest of mankind. This opinion was so widely accepted that still in the nineteenth century Serābît el-Khâdem was seldom omitted from guidebooks to the Holy Land. It was not until 1905 that the site received a modern archaeological evaluation during the Sinai explorations of Sir Flinders Petrie, the great British Egyptologist. By his own account it was only in spite of high winds, lumbago, and desert rats with an appetite for his luggage that Petrie managed to recover the bulk of the Proto-Sinaitic material in one season. His assignment of the mysterious inscriptions to a period some two centuries earlier than current dates for the Exodus was fatal to the hypothesis of Cosmas Indicopleustes.

Petrie himself seems never to have regarded the Proto-Sinaitic writing as more than "a local barbarism," as he later styled it. Instead it was Sir Alan Gardiner who first (in 1915) recognized the genuine significance of the system and its essential character. It was alphabetic. The individual signs were pictographs assigned to discrete phonemes according to an acrophonic principle. That is, a drawing of a familiar object was used to represent the sound with which its name began. Thus, for example, a picture of a house denoted b since the word "house" (*$bayt$-) began with that sound. The language was certainly Semitic (the Egyptian word for "house" being pr), and Gardiner was able to make enough identifications to read at least one word with confidence.[1]

He went on to suggest—correctly as it now seems—that the first alphabet was similarly pictographic in design and acrophonic in operative principle and that it might have been derived under Egyptian influence, since the hieroglyphs exhibited similar characteristics, though in a much more complicated system. Gardiner's interpretation of the Proto-Sinaitic inscriptions has since been confirmed and considerably extended, especially by the late W. F. Albright (see the bibliography), though much of Albright's decipherment must be regarded as tentative, and, in any case, much remains to be learned.

To the inscriptions collected by Petrie and subsequent expeditions to Serābît two more were added in 1961 by Dr. Georg Gerster, who recovered them from the nearby Wâdi Naṣb.

One of these new texts seems very archaic, showing the pictographic character of the script especially well. There is, for example, an "ox-head" and a "fish" in column 3 and a "(human) head" in column 4. This may well be the oldest known example of our alphabet and cannot, in any case, stand far after the invention of the system.

The Serābîṭ materials date to the beginning of the Egyptian New Kingdom and the transition from Middle to Late Bronze cultures in Palestine. Scattered inscriptions of a similar character and from about the same period have been found in Palestine itself; and, although a few older curiosities have been proposed as alphabetic, there is really no sound evidence for the existence of our alphabet long before the beginning of the sixteenth century B.C. We ought now to regard the Proto-Sinaitic inscriptions as a very early use of an old Canaanite alphabet which must have been devised much in the fashion described by Gardiner sometime late in the Middle Bronze Age.

The use of a Canaanite alphabet in an Egyptian mining community in the Sinai should come as no surprise. The participation of Asiatics, apparently as state slaves, in the operations is well documented. Already in Middle Kingdom times Egyptian hieroglyphic texts from Serābîṭ and other Sinaitic sites listed workers specifically from Syria and Palestine. On the other hand, the suggestion that Asiatic servants in Egypt or their kinsmen in the Canaanite homeland were responsible for the invention of the alphabet ought to prompt reflection. Historians unanimously praise the appearance of the alphabet as a singular advancement in civilization, antiquating as it did the clumsy excesses of older systems. This view, though vindicated by the passage of time, is in many respects anachronistic. The great merit of alphabetic writing is its economy, to be sure, but at the time of its invention it must have been viewed as a completely practical expediency, a modest resource to correct the lack of an indigenous writing system. While it is true that both Egyptian hieroglyphic and Mesopotamian cuneiform required hundreds of distinct signs to represent their languages and the Canaanite alphabet less than thirty, it is difficult to imagine that the new contrivance was regarded as an improvement over the sophisticated and elaborate systems of the great powers. The immediate advantage of the alphabet's economy was accessibility. In Egypt or Mesopotamia the art of writing was necessarily confined to professional scribes with extensive training, but there is no reason to believe that either of those societies desired a more generally accessible way of writing and every reason to believe that they did not. If the long-range political significance of the alphabet is immense, insofar as it has made written communication and the means of preserving articulate records available to the ordinary man, it would nevertheless be hardly proper for us to trace its origin to an egalitarian impulse. Instead the first alphabet should be described as a makeshift device of inconspicuous genius. Besides, early alphabetic writing, since it was purely consonantal in character, admitted ambiguities which the older systems avoided by one means or another and which would not disappear entirely until the Greek introduction of vowels centuries later. So it is neither incorrect nor even excessively romantic to describe the origin of our alphabet as humble.

The Emergence of the National Scripts

The alphabet entered the Late Bronze Age as an unceremonious gathering of pictographs and emerged as a highly conventionalized procession of shapes. The stages of regulation and abbreviation that were passed are incompletely known, but materials for study are steadily coming to light, and we can now trace the refinement of the old Canaanite alphabet tolerably well in general and very well in some particulars. In broad outline, it was as follows. As in the case of Egyptian hieroglyphic, the old pictographs could be written in vertical columns or in horizontal rows. The rows might proceed from left to right or right to left. Of these options, only the last would remain in the eleventh century, but the elimination of first the vertical and then the left-to-right directions was quite gradual. Inscriptions from the transitional period, especially the thirteenth and twelfth centuries, exhibit confusion in the orientation of particular letters. The individual signs were supposed to face in the direction of writing, but the variability of this direction created problems. The epigrapher often finds a form that is reversed, sidelong, or even inverted with respect to its neighbors.

There seems to have been a tendency from the beginning to conventionalize and simplify the pictographs themselves for facility in drawing. The result was that many of the characters quickly became more abstract than pictorial. This process was so nearly complete by the beginning of the Iron Age (*ca.* 1200) that features reminiscent of the old pictographs already seem quite archaic.

By about 1100 B.C. a distinctively Phoenician national script was in use in the great port cities north of Palestine. The emergence of new cultures in the rest of Canaan had left Phoenicia the chief heir to the high Bronze Age civilization and therefore the legatee of the Canaanite alphabet. To this extent the Phoenician alphabet is not to be considered as a new branch of the old system but instead, its purest Iron Age expression. It is also true that the other great national scripts of a later period—Aramaic, Hebrew, and so on—seem to have been mediated to some extent by the Phoenician[2] in spite of the fact that the Canaanite alphabet had been at home, of course, in the regions occupied by Aram and Israel as well. It follows, then, that except for Phoenician the national scripts of the Iron Age are to be described as new branches of the alphabet.

By studying the early development of these national scripts, we can see that the advent of such a new branch was not a sudden occurrence. First of all there was a period of preparation during which a particular society would adopt and employ an existing tradition. Then at some later time the writing of the same group would begin to display distinctive features. The new script can soon be distinguished from the parent tradition not only by its innovations but also by any features it may have preserved from the moment of its independence which have subsequently disappeared in the parent tradition itself. Such archaisms are a great aid to the paleographer in estimating the time when a particular national script emerged. The Hebrew script, for example, though the details of its origins remain somewhat obscure, retains features in its early history which recall tenth-century Phoenician forms. On this basis (and others) we should suppose that the national script of Israel, after an initial period of preparation and Phoenician influence, diverged as an independent tradition sometime in the tenth century B.C. The old Aramaic script, incidentally, seems to have had a similar timetable. At least this is suggested by the earliest Aramaic inscriptions which, when they begin to appear in the ninth century, already display features distinctive with respect to Phoenician.

The history of the Ammonite script provides an excellent illustration of the development described above. Indeed the recovery of the Transjordanian national scripts is one of the busiest frontiers of the modern investigation of the diffusion of the alphabet. As recently as 1961 George M. Landes, reporting in this journal on the evidence from modern archaeological activity for the study of Ammonite culture, could only lament the lack of pertinent written remains. "Our knowledge of the Ammonite dialect," he wrote, "is . . . solely dependent upon a few words, mostly personal names, found inscribed on a small collection of Ammonite seals."[3] In the few years since the appearance of Professor Landes' article, at least three major Ammonite inscriptions have come to light, giving us a complete, if undetailed, picture of the history of the Ammonite script from its divergence to its demise.[4] These include: (1) the so-called Ammān Citadel Inscription, apparently a fragment of a royal (?) temple dedication of the ninth century B.C.; (2) an interesting wall inscription from Tell Deir ʿAllā to be dated early in the seventh century B.C.; and now (3) the inscribed copper bottle from Tell Sīrān on the campus of the University of Jordan as reported in the issue before last of this journal, dating to the early sixth century. To these we shall soon be able to add an eleven-line docket of provisions for the royal house from Heshbon. This inscription, Heshbon Ostracon No. 4, was found last year and will soon be published by F. M. Cross. (See Cross, "Ammonite Ostraca from Heshbon," *Andrews University Seminary Studies* XIII, 1975, pp. 1-20). These new materials clarify many things which were quite opaque only a few years ago. For example, it is now beyond doubt that the affiliations of the Ammonite language were purely Canaanite—that is, Ammonite belonged to the same language group as Phoenician and Hebrew.

The Ammonite appropriation of the alphabet is now thoroughly understood. As the Ammān Citadel Inscription shows, the Ammonites in the ninth century still used the standard Aramaic lapidary script. After this period of preparation, a distinctively Ammonite national script diverged from the Aramaic parent tradition sometime in the mid eighth century, as surviving archaic forms in the seventh-century script of the Deir ʿAllā inscription suggest. There then began an age of independent development of which the Sīrān bottle is a late exemplar, displaying a number of Ammonite peculiarities. Finally the Aramaic script returned in the late sixth century as the imperial hand of the Persian age, and the Ammonite episode in the history of the alphabet was over.

It was surely no accident, incidentally, that the use of a national script corresponded to the period of greatest Ammonite prosperity, as the contents of Iron II tombs in and around Ammān had already suggested to Landes and as recently confirmed by the discovery of pottery of high quality at Heshbon. This period in Jordanian history must have been one of considerable political independence, in spite of the nominal suzerainty of Assyria. We expect *a priori* that the features peculiar to a distinct national script would be most likely to develop in a society with sufficient cultural autonomy to suspend scribal adherence to external models. Indeed it is reasonable to suppose that the growth of a national script was a natural by-product of the rise of national identity. Thus the emergence of national scripts in Iron Age Syria and Palestine may have corresponded directly to the new nationalism that was supplanting the old city-state ideology of the Bronze Age. It is true, at least, that our paleographic estimates of the antiquity of the various national scripts seem to correspond in general with important junctures in political history. These correspondences include: (1) the derivation of a distinctively Phoenician script to the rise of imperial Tyre at the beginning of the Iron Age; (2) the divergence of the Hebrew script to the period after the transition from tribal league to nation-state in Israel; and (3) the divergence of the Aramaic script to the consolidation of the Aramaean kingdom in Damascus after the demise of the Solomonic Empire.

The Transmission to Greece

The propagation of the Canaanite alphabet in Syria and Palestine and its variety of early expressions in the national scripts of the Iron Age are relatively new areas of research. Until about a generation ago, in fact, early inscriptions in any of the Northwest Semitic languages—Phoenician, Hebrew, Aramaic, and so on—

were commonly regarded as specimens of a single, more or less homogeneous script. Scholars have learned to distinguish these only lately. The refinement of modern paleographic method to the extent that an early inscription might confidently be dated within general boundaries is almost as recent a development. As might be expected, these new areas of research have greatly influenced older areas. One of the constant stumbling blocks of Semitic and Hellenic epigraphers alike has been the origin of the Greek alphabet, and here the influence of recent research has been especially salutary.

That the Greek alphabet was borrowed from the Phoenician at some point in antiquity has never been in serious doubt. The Greek letters are arranged in the Phoenician order and bear the Phoenician names. Early inscriptions from the two alphabets display clear similarity in the forms of corresponding letters. Moreover, the ancient Greek historians freely acknowledged this debt to the Phoenicians, and the letters themselves were sometimes called *phoinikēia*. On the other hand, there has never been general agreement about the precise time of the transmission of the alphabet to Greece or, until recently, any basis for such an agreement.

The scholarly community of the nineteenth century entertained an exaggerated view of the role of the Phoenicians in the development of Mediterranean civilization. In particular, Hellenic culture was believed to be derived largely from oriental forerunners, especially as mediated by Phoenician mercantile activity in the Aegean. Early intercourse between Phoenicia and Greece was taken for granted, and the transmission of the alphabet was assumed to have occurred sometime in the second millennium B.C. The recovery of Mycenaean civilization beginning late in the century, insofar as it revealed a high culture indigenous to the Aegean, sparked a reaction to these assumptions so explosive that its reverberations are still being felt. Scholars, especially Hellenists, began to the deny the presence of Phoenician vessels in the Mediterranean until well into the first millennium. The date of the transmission of the alphabet was lowered accordingly in the popular estimation. Finally in 1933 the distinguished Hellenist and classical archaeologist Rhys Carpenter introduced the opinion that the Greek alphabet had existed no earlier than about 700 B.C. and argued the position persuasively on the basis of a comparison of letter-forms combined with a sobering reminder that after generations of excavation no Greek inscription antedating 700 B.C. had yet come to light.[5] Carpenter convinced many of his colleagues, and his followers have remained numerous though most would now revise his date of 700 B.C. upward by as much as half a century on the basis of new evidence. Others, including many Semitists, who found Carpenter's original proposal extreme have long defended dates only somewhat higher. Indeed it would not be unrealistic to say that a consensus of scholarly opinion has begun to emerge favoring a date for the introduction of the Greek alphabet sometime early in the eighth century B.C.

Recent archaeological activity and especially modern epigraphic method (since only recently has it been possible to identify specifically Phoenician inscriptions and date them securely) seem now to suggest that this consensus viewpoint, while accurate in certain respects, may be incomplete. The recovery of new Phoenician inscriptions from several Mediterranean sites has facilitated the interpretation of older materials so that we now have major inscriptions, well understood and firmly dated, of the eighth and ninth centuries and earlier from Cyprus, Sardinia, and Malta as well as the coastlands of Anatolia, North Africa, and Spain. The oldest of these (discounting small fragments) is a badly weathered gravestone from Cyprus, first published in 1939 by A. M. Honeyman but recently rephotographed in the Cyprus Museum at Nicosia for fresh examination.[6] The preserved portion is a tomb curse, and the main clause reads: "Let him who [dese]crates this p[lace] perish, whether by the hand of Baᶜl or by the hand of ꟸEl or by [the hand of the As]sembly of ꟸEl!" The new photographs reveal paleographic features much more archaic than previous estimates have suggested. Indeed certain forms find good parallels only in the famous royal inscriptions of tenth-century Byblos. In short, the inscription can hardly be dated later than the early ninth century B.C., and a complete new study is badly needed.

The maritime Phoenician inscriptions not only give eloquent testimony to early Phoenician presence in the Mediterranean but also enrich our evidence for the development of the alphabet in the ninth and eighth centuries. It is clear that the point in their history when the forms of the Phoenician letters most closely resemble those of their earliest Greek counterparts must be the time of the transmission of the alphabet. Thus the developing Phoenician series arranged in chronological sequence will provide a framework into which the earliest Greek alphabet may be interpolated.

It is difficult, however, to speak of a single "earliest Greek alphabet." The oldest surviving Greek inscriptions already exhibit the variety of forms which later differentiate them into local or epichoric scripts. Certain letters have different shapes in different localities. So, in fact, there are several "earliest Greek alphabets." Nevertheless, all of these share certain outstanding features which distinguish them from the Phoenician parent script. In particular, all employ the signs for five of the Semitic consonants—ʾalep, he, waw, yod, ʿayin—as the vowel letters *alpha, e(psilon), u(psilon), iota,* and *o(micron).* Since it is not reasonable to suppose that such a radical departure occurred more than once independently, we may be sure that there was a single earliest Greek alphabet after all. This earliest alphabet may be reconstructed to a great extent from a comparison of later forms.

A detailed paleographic discussion of the place of the Greek scripts in the Phoenician sequence has been provided elsewhere (see the bibliography) and is out of place here. The sporadic elongation of the Greek letter-forms, sometimes to an extreme degree, is especially striking. This corresponds to an early eighth-century scribal fashion common to the Northwest Semitic scripts during which the stems or tails of the letters were sometimes drawn with long, graceful strokes in contrast to the compact ninth-century forms. Most of the individual Greek forms also fit best into the Phoenician sequence in the early eighth (or late ninth) century. Especially important are the fourth and eleventh letters. Greek *delta* never shows any trace of the short stem which has already developed in Phoenician *dalet* by the eighth century. On the other hand, the old trident-form Phoenician *kap* of the tenth century and earlier finds no parallel in Greek *kappa*, which shares the stem of the late ninth- and eighth-century *kap*. Numerous other instances can be cited to support the contention that the earliest Greek alphabet reflects a Phoenician model of the late ninth or early eighth century B.C. It comes as no surprise, incidentally, that these years encompassed the reign of the fabulous Pygmalion of

Tyre (831-785 B.C.) and the meridian of Phoenician mercantile expansion.

There are, however, complicating factors. In the first place a few of the Greek forms occur regularly in stances different from their Phoenician counterparts. *Alpha* has been rotated ninety degrees and "set on its feet." Greek *beta*, when it most closely resembles Phoenician *bet*, has been inverted. *Lambda* occurs in a variety of stances unfamiliar to *lamed*. *Sigma*, even when it preserves the four-stroke shape of *šin*, has been rotated ninety degrees. This brings us to an important characteristic of early Greek writing which is not apparent from our script charts. In the earliest inscriptions the letters might be arranged in rows from right to left or from left to right or even *boustrophedon*, that is "as the ox plows," in alternating rows. Eventually, of course, a uniform left-to-right tradition prevailed in Greece.

All of this might be attributed to idiosyncratic inner-Greek development were it not for the results of recent research in the development of the old Canaanite alphabet. As explained above, the Canaanite alphabet went through a phase after the demise of vertical writing when precisely these directional options—sinistrograde, dextrograde, or *boustrophedon*—were available to the scribe.[7] We also noted earlier that the occurrence of single letterforms "out of stance" was common in the same period. Indeed old Canaanite *ʾalep, bet, lamed,* and *šin* in the stances of Greek *alpha, beta, lambda,* and *sigma* are all attested in inscriptions from the 12th or 13th centuries B.C.

These data become even more suggestive when we add the evidence of a few formal oddities in the Greek alphabet. Most striking is the dotted *omicron* common to the Greek scripts of the Doric Isles (and occasionally elsewhere). Semitic ʿ*ayin*, the model for *omicron*, lost its center dot—a vestige of the pupil in the old "eye" pictograph—late in the second millennium but, as shown above, frequently preserved it in the twelfth century. Other early Greek forms such as "box-shaped" *eta* and the stemless *xi* or *epsilon* also seem more at home in Phoenicia *ca.* 1100 than *ca.* 800.

Similar evidence has recently been marshalled by Joseph Naveh of Hebrew University in Jerusalem in behalf of a vigorous argument for an early transmission of the alphabet to Greece.[8]

Many may dismiss his position as eccentric or even regressive insofar as it superficially resembles nineteenth-century ideas. But Professor Naveh is an epigrapher of unimpeachable qualification, and his conclusions are reasonably drawn and must be acknowledged. Still, the unqualified assertion of an early borrowing seems as inadequate as the simple affirmation of a ninth/eight-century borrowing. As noted above, the evidence for the latter is considerable. Even Naveh is obliged to admit the instance of *kap* and *kappa*.

It is reasonable to suppose at least—and perhaps at most—that the Greeks, though their script did not diverge as an independent tradition before *ca.* 800, had experimented with the Semitic alphabet as early as *ca.* 1100, that is, at the time of the collapse of Mycenaean civilization with its own system of writing. The memory of the earlier experimentation survived long enough—perhaps in an isolated moribund tradition somewhere— to exert a limited influence upon the final formulation of the Greek alphabet years later. The similar influence of older indigenous writing systems upon the borrowing of the Asianic alphabets (such as Carian) from a Greek model is well documented.

The historical implications of this discussion of the Greek alphabet are several but not altogether clear until combined with other information. The chronology of early contact between East and West in the Mediterranean is the subject of much current research and, for that matter, controversy. The need is great for systematic analyses of the kinds of empirical data which archaeology can provide. In particular, we await an accommodation of Mediterranean pottery chronology to that of the more securely dated ceramic industry of the Levant. The increase in archaeological activity at many Phoenician and Punic sites scattered about the Mediterranean basin, including the current excavations of the American Schools of Oriental Research (with the Institute for Cypriote Studies of the State University of New York at Albany) at Idalion, Cyprus, and the projected ASOR expedition to Carthage in Tunis, offers much hope for the raw materials of such investigations. The student of the diffusion of the alphabet in the Mediterranean is both enabler and beneficiary of this enterprise.

Further Reading

The definitive study of the origin and early evolution of the alphabet is an article under that title by F. M. Cross, published in *Eretz Israel* 8 (1967), *8-*24. Cross has also been the leading figure in the isolation and description of the national scripts of Syria and Palestine. His forthcoming study of the Ammonite script was cited in a footnote. Albright's work on the Proto-Sinaitic inscriptions, alluded to above, is published as *The Proto-Sinaitic Inscriptions and Their Decipherment*, Harvard Theological Studies No. 12 (1969). The already classic study of the epichoric Greek scripts is Lillian H. Jefferey's handsome volume *The Local Scripts of Archaic Greece* (1961). No complete treatment of the maritime Phoenician scripts exists, but the major paleographic issues are reviewed along with a full discussion of the transmission of the alphabet to Greece in my monograph entitled *The Antiquity of the Greek Alphabet and the Early Phoenician Scripts*, published in the Harvard Semitic Monograph series (1975). Finally, since many readers of this journal will be interested in ASOR excavations related to the issues raised above, they are referred to the "Annual Report to the Trustees, the Corporation, Members and Friends" for 1974 of President G. Ernest Wright (1973-74 Newsletter No. 9), especially pp. 10-12.

Notes

[1] Or rather one word combined with a preposition: *lbᶜlt*, "to Baᶜlat," that is, "to the Lady/Mistress. . . ." This accorded splendidly with the abundant Egyptian hieroglyphic inscriptions from the site, which included many votive inscriptions to the goddess Ḥathor, who presided over the temple at Serābît and was routinely referred to as "the Mistress" of one thing or another, including turquoise. Ḥathor's identification with the Semitic deity Baᶜlat, especially of Byblos, is now amply attested.

[2] This is clear for a variety of reasons. For example, Hebrew preserved in the Iron Age twenty-three of the Semitic consonantal phonemes but Phoenician only twenty-two. The alphabet used by both had only twenty-two signs. This meant that Hebrew had to use one sign to represent two distinct sounds (viz., $s̀$ and $š$, which in Phoenician had fallen together as $š$). Presumably, if the Hebrew alphabet had been derived directly from the older system without Phoenician mediation, it would have kept the signs for both phonemes.

[3] *BA* 24 (1961) 65-86; reprinted in *Biblical Archaeologist Reader* 2 (1964), pp. 69-88, esp. 83.

[4] These discoveries are reviewed with bibliography and a full discussion of the Ammonite script in *BASOR* 212 (1973), 12-15 by F. M. Cross,

My brief sketch here is heavily dependent on this article, entitled "Notes on the Ammonite Inscription from Tell Sīrān," which Professor Cross has kindly made available to me in manuscript form.

[5] *American Journal of Archaeology* 37 (1933), 8-29.

[6] Honeyman's original publication was in *Iraq* 6 (1939), 104-108. See now Olivier Masson, *Bulletin de Correspondance Hellénique* 92 (1968).

[7] Note for comparison that the ancestral alphabet of the South Semitic scripts diverged from the main Canaanite branch about this time and that the same variety in direction of writing was preserved in its descendants.

[8] *American Journal of Archaeology* 77 (1973), 1-8.

12

THE BIBLICAL POTTER

ROBERT H. JOHNSTON

So I went down to the potter's house, and there he was working at his
wheel. And the vessel he was making of clay was spoiled in the potter's
hand, and he reworked it into another vessel, as it seemed good to the
potter to do.

Jeremiah 18:3-4

The serious study of the pottery from a given site began in
1891 when Sir W. M. Flinders Petrie published the results of his
excavation at Tell el-Hesi. He realized the chronological value of
sherds from a stratified site and began to establish a corpus of
pottery forms arranged in relative chronological sequence. Since
that time, every expedition report has contained photographs and
drawings, with detailed descriptions and comparative typological
studies, of the pottery forms found. Since fired clay is almost
indestructible, the greatest proportion by far of the artifacts found
at a site consists of thousands of pottery fragments, along with
some whole vessels. Petrie wrote in *Tell el Hesy* (1891), p. 40:

Once settle the pottery of a country, and the key is in our hands for all
future explorations. A single glance at a mound of ruins ... will show as
much to anyone who knows the styles of the pottery, as weeks of work
may reveal to a beginner.

When G. Ernest Wright wrote his doctoral thesis in 1937, he
observed that, while Petrie's use of ceramics was basic and of great
value in establishing chronology, there was more that could be
learned from the study of ancient pottery. As he puts it on the first
page of his *The Pottery of Palestine from the Earliest Times to the
End of the Early Bronze Age*:

But a detailed study of the value of pottery for the history of human
culture has yet to appear. Its greatest value at present is undoubtedly

Illus. 38-40

chronological; yet more expert studies in the future will perhaps allow the student of ethnology, commerce, and related subjects to make far-reaching deductions from ceramic evidence, for which at present there is so little solid ground.

Dr. Wright had a vision of conducting an excavation of major importance on which specialists of all types could study excavated material and each add his expertise, leading toward a more complete understanding of the data unearthed. This would involve ethnologists, pollen analysts, geologists, paleo-zoologists, paleo-botanists, ceramic technologists, and all their special tools. The vision was to set a precedent for future excavations in the Mediterranean world. I had the privilege of working with Dr. Wright in the capacity of ceramic specialist for four years, studying material from Idalion, Bab edh-Dhra, Shechem, and other sites.

Another influence has also played its part in calling forth studies such as those I shall describe here. Frederick R. Matson of Penn State University developed a new thrust to the study of ancient ceramic materials built around an ecological approach. He has taught a small number of devoted students to use their ceramic studies to better understand the cultural context in which the vessels were produced. He puts it this way in *Ceramics and Man* (1965), p. 202:

> Ceramic ecology may be considered as one facet of cultural ecology, that which attempts to relate the raw materials and technologies that the local potter has available to the functions in his culture of the products he fashions.

In what follows, I want to carry on a conversation both between the potter and his culture, and between the ancient potter and his modern equivalent in the villages of such places as Cyprus, where age-old techniques are still practiced, informed by long tradition. In all probability the techniques are much the same, so I shall move back and forth without apology.

The Potter and His Clay

The potters of ancient Palestine played a major role in the life of their times. The role of the craftsman was to produce a variety of objects needed for daily life—the pots and pans of antiquity—as well as special vessels for ceremonial occasions. He also assisted in the production of bricks, roof tile, drain tile, bee hives, cultic stands and other cultic objects, writing materials, kilns, and ovens. The ancient craftman must have been an important member of his community, although he probably never achieved great political status by practicing his craft. We get a sense of the craftmen's status from a passage in the Apocrypha, where in Ecclesiasticus (Ben Sirach) 38:31-34 this is said about a variety of craftsmen:

All these rely upon their hands and each is skillful in his own work. Without them a city cannot be established and men can neither sojourn nor live there. Yet they are not sought out for the council of the people, nor do they attain eminence in the public assembly. They do not sit in the judge's seat, nor do they understand the sentence of judgment; they cannot expound discipline or judgment, and they are not found using proverbs. But they keep stable the fabric of the world, and their prayer is in the practice of their trades. (All biblical and apocryphal quotations in this article are from the RSV.)

The clay used by the biblical potter was an earthenware clay usually found in the immediate vicinity or brought in from no great distance. Village potters in Jordan and adjacent areas today still secure clay from nearby beds. Clay is a material of secondary origin, resulting from the weathering and disintegration of certain types of primary rocks. It is a hydrated aluminum silicate mixed with small proportions of iron compounds, calcium carbonates, quartz, sand, organic matter, and alkalies. The iron compounds bring about the colors of the fired ware and the varying amounts of impurities condition the nature of the clay.

Almost all of the village potters I have studied for nine summers, who produce village functional ware, seek and use "thixotropic" clays, clays that are extremely plastic in the forming stage and set up almost immediately when the piece is completed. This immediate hardening of thixotropic clays is very important to the potter, who must work briskly and expeditiously to produce the daily quota of functional pottery. Additives are mixed with the clay as binders or to slow the drying of attached parts such as handles. The materials so used today are threshing-floor straw, dung, cat-o-nine tail fuzz, and ashes. When one studies ancient sherds with a binocular microscope these same additives can be identified. The addition of non-plastic material to plastic clay reduces excessive shrinking and helps prevent cracking in the pottery during the drying phase. The non-plastic additives also open the clay body and increase the porosity of the ware, an important factor in the storage of water, since it allows cooling by evaporation. The effects of thermal shock when the vessel is fired are also lessened by these additives.

The biblical potters and brick makers added threshing floor straw to their clay as noted in Exodus where the Israelites had to go out and search for stubble to add to clay:

> You shall no longer give the people straw to make bricks, as heretofore; let them go and gather straw for themselves.
>
> Exodus 5:7

> Thus says Pharaoh, "I will not give you straw. Go yourselves, get your straw wherever you can find it; but your work will not be lessened in the least." So the people were scattered around throughout all the land of Egypt, to gather stubble for straw.
>
> Exodus 5:10-12

The practice of adding these materials is continued today, the technique passed on from potter to potter, brick maker to brick maker, over several thousand years. The clay of the ancient potters was used as it was found in nature, except for the removal of large stones. This material sufficed for the manufacture of heavy functional ware and ovens, but for finer, burnished ware a finer clay was needed and this was secured by letting the clay stand in settling basins where the heavier particles would sink to the bottom and the upper layers of fine clay could be skimmed off. After repeated settling, a very fine, watery clay, called "slurry," resulted, which, after the excess water had evaporated, became an excellent clay for throwing and for slip-decorating. Today, village potters sometimes mix several clays from different sources to get just the right clay "body" for the manufacture of the ware they wish to make. Presumably the ancient potter did the same thing. Potters seek, and would have sought in ancient times, colored clays on the slopes of nearby hills where it is the product of the disintegration of certain sedimentary rocks. Red ocher, an earthy form of hematite mixed with clay, was one of the types sought, as were kaolin and white marl, a mixture of clay and calcite useful for making a white slip. Incidentally, this mixing of clays from several sources can cause problems for the modern researcher who is testing ancient sherds for the so-called trace elements of the clay, hoping to be able to find the original clay bed by matching the pattern of trace elements in the sherd with what occurs in the modern beds. The ancient potter may have mixed up modern scientists by mixing his clays!

Decoration of Palestinian pottery was done by applying clay slips—watery solutions of clay—before firing; slips were less liable to rub off or chip than would paint or "wash" applied after firing. Information about the locations of clay beds and deposits of clays good for colored slips was passed from potter to potter, and the rights to beds probably became an important aspect of the potter's survival. When a clay bed was exhausted, the potter might have to make radical changes in the amount of ware he produced, as well as in the form of the vessels he could satisfactorily make.

Some special clays were no doubt transported over considerable distances, and therefore constituted an aspect of commerce. An example from modern times is the shipping of "Ball clay" from England to the American colonies. In fact, Ball clay got its name from the fact that it was sold by the ball. Some clays will produce a burnished surface when rubbed with a bone or stone at the leather-hard stage of drying. During the rubbing a fine micro-layer of clay is brought to the surface and forms a sheen. The potter would sometimes get himself a surface for burnishing by dipping wares made of coarse clay bodies in a suspension of clay in water, thereby giving the entire surface a slip. This slip could then be burnished or polished whereas the coarser clay without the slip could not have been.

After a satisfactory clay was secured and mixed to the plastic consistency wanted, the potter had to "wedge" or de-air it. Unless this was done, the water distribution would have become uneven in the clay and air pockets would have remained; on firing, these pockets would gather and hold steam, and eventually blow out, shattering the fired ware. One of the ways of wedging clay is fast foot treading, an activity described by two Old Testament prophets. In Isaiah 41:25, we sense this part of the potter's work in a striking word-image: "I stirred up one from the north and he has come from the rising of the sun, and he shall call on my name; he shall trample on rulers as on mortar, as the potter treads clay." Similarly, but here in the brick-making process, Nahum 3:14: "Draw water for the siege, strengthen your forts; go into the clay and tread the mortar, take hold of the brick mold!"

Village potters still wedge their clay by treading or by kneading or clapping balls of clay together. It is the first step in the manufacturing process and one of the most important if breakage is to be averted (there will be some anyway, as any potter knows). Potters and their apprentices often pride themselves in treading the clay in a rhythmic fashion, forming exact patterns in the clay as they work it.

During the wedging process, large stones or pieces of other foreign matter are removed, since they would cause cracking as the plastic clay dries and shrinks. The tempering ingredients—threshing-floor straw, animal dung, cat-o-nine tail fuzz, shell or sand—are added at this point and worked into the clay to improve the workability and reduce shrinkage. As the potter or his apprentice-helper wedges the clay, he also brings it to the final consistency he wants. If it is too wet and too sticky he can add dry clay. To clay that is too dry, he adds more water and kneads it into the mixture. The potter gauges the consistency of his clay by the way it feels.

The Making of Pots

The biblical potter used a variety of methods to build and shape his pottery. The earliest evidences of the potter's techniques indicate that hand-building was the means used. Some ware was made by the pinch-pot method: A piece of clay is held in the palm of one hand and the walls formed by pinching the clay with the other hand until the walls have been raised and thinned. This method was used for making small containers, such as votive dishes or miniature pots. An experienced potter can work very swiftly with this technique and produce a large variety of small forms. The process is described by Henry Hodges in his 1964 book called *Artifacts*, p. 25, as follows:

A ball of clay is formed and this is held in the palm of one hand, the thumb of the other hand being dug into the clay ball. The ball is then rotated slowly while the clay is gently squeezed between the thumb and fingers of the shaping hand. The process is continued until a pot is formed.

Pottery made in this manner was usually scraped down to refine the form when it was leather hard, and sometimes burnished or polished. A layer of slip could be applied, as we have noted, to take the burnish.

Another early technique used to form vessels was the coil method, or a combination of the coil method with a paddle and anvil process. A base of fairly thick clay was laid down on a "bat" made of woven material, bark, stone, or even a piece of broken pottery. This bat allowed the potter to move the piece around as he worked and to carry it to the drying area later. Ancient sherds have been found with the impression of woven material in the base—the imprint of the bat on which the pot was made.

Alfred Lucas (see the 1962 edition of his *Ancient Egyptian Materials and Industries*, edited by J. R. Harris) suspects that this technique may have had an early start in Egypt:

> In the early days of pottery making in Egypt, that is during neolithic, Badarian and predynastic times, pots were made by hand, though it is possible that in shaping some predynastic pottery the clay was placed on a mat which could be rotated on the ground. Such a technique was still in use during the Middle Kingdoms at Kerma, where pots were also built up inside a basket or bag (pp. 368-9).

The interrelationship of technique and pottery style between Egypt and Palestine during the Early Bronze Age is emphasized by J. B. Hennessy in his *The Foreign Relations of Palestine during the Early Bronze Age* (1967). The flow of craft and craftsmen between Egypt, Palestine and Cyprus is noted in a number of excavation reports and can still be observed in the study of village potters.

To return to the coil technique itself, the potter rolls coils of clay and applies them to the base, adding coils and working them into the clay until the desired height and shape are achieved. The walls of the vessel being formed can be thinned and altered by paddling, using wooden or clay paddles and clay or stone anvils. This technique is used in many villages throughout the Middle East today. Sometimes the wooden or clay paddles have designs carved in them which when used on the soft clay vessel decorate the piece as it is being formed and thinned.

Another variation used in the hand-building process is the "stroking method." This is usually done on a slow wheel or tournette. A "pug" of clay is placed on the bat which is in turn fastened to the head of the tournette. The pug is opened by pushing the fist down inside while patting the exterior in order to keep the walls more even and to prevent stretch cracks. A stick is used next to draw up and thin the vessel through stroking the soft clay from the base upward. The piece can be made quite thin and the technique lends itself to the making of juglets or tall, thin pieces. The early pottery found at Bab edh-Dhra in Jordan from Early Bronze I (around 3150-2850 B.C.) was formed in this manner, judging by the forming marks visible on the pieces studied. I have studied and photographed village potters on Cyprus in the villages of Phini and Ayios Dhimitrios using this method to manufacture non-functional ware that made use of trees, birds, and snakes as decorative elements—all symbols recalling motifs of the Bronze Age. This is not the proper occasion to go into full detail about the stroking method, but an exploration at greater length is called for because of its important pertinence to the Early Bronze period.

So far, we have been looking at processes of hand-building. Studies made both by Frederick R. Matson and by me have noted that in villages where hand-building processes are still used it is the women who make the pottery. Women also usually fire the ware, and men take care of selling it. When a mechanical device is introduced, such as a stick-turned wheel or a kick wheel, men take over the manufacturing. Our studies in other areas of the Middle East, by the way, have noted that itinerant potters go from village to village, changing clay bodies and style of pots made depending on the available supplies of materials and the needs and wants of a given region.

Now we turn to pottery made on the tournette; here the potter uses a combination of techniques varying from hand-building, paddle and anvil, coiling, and stroking, to the technique using in full measure the centrifugal force of the true potter's wheel. Many pieces of hand-built pottery, it should be noted, have marks that look like wheel marks and are misleading to the archaeologist studying the ware.

The tournette or slow wheel was the device used to produce pottery prior to the development of the true potter's wheel. It is a simple turntable made of stone or wood, either round or square, which is rotated by hand or with the foot on a vertical point or shaft. It has a limited momentum and usually does not make great use of the centrifugal force of the potter's wheel in the throwing process.

Let me describe the slow-wheel process in terms of the way a village potter in Cyprus now does it. She places a lump of clay on the bat and opens the piece by forcing her hand down inside while patting the outside. When the base is opened and formed, coils of clay are formed by rolling clay between the hands. The coils are added around the pot as the tournette is slowly turned and the vessel increased in height. When several coils have been added the walls are again patted with the hands in a hand-paddle and anvil method to thin and shape the form. When the height of the vessel reaches the point where the sagging of the wet clay causes a problem, the outside of the vessel is wound with cord or strips of cloth to prevent slumping. This allows the potter to keep on building even though the clay is still soft and wet. Later, when the clay "sets up," the cords can be safely removed to enable an assistant to finish the piece. After the potter has built the vessel in the manner described she will usually rub the upper part of the vessel with a stick to make the piece round, to improve the form and to eliminate the forming marks.

The piece is next wet-smoothed using a piece of cloth. This brings a fine layer of clay to the surface and again eliminates the marks of the manufacturing techniques. At this point, the opening is shaped into a trefoil spout with the fingers and the handle or handles added. This is done either by fashioning a coil into the final handle shape and leaving it to dry to leather-hardness before attachment, or, where especially plastic clay is being used, attaching the coil at once and "pulling" the handle right on the pot. Re-enforcing coils are added to strengthen the handles and smoothed down. Later the bottom of the piece is trimmed, using an iron tool to thin the lower area and to refine the form of the vessel. When the potter or her helper thins the piece, she thumps the walls with a finger and judges the thickness by sound—notice how all the senses play their part in good pottery-making! Using the thumping method, potters rarely cut through the bottom of pots or make them too thin.

The finished pieces are wet-smoothed again and rubbed down with a round stick or stone to smooth and polish the exterior. They are set aside in the shade to dry slowly, so as to reduce cracking as the shrinking takes place. The thixotropic, or very plastic, clays these village potters use are easy to form, set up rapidly so as to permit fast finishing, but have very high shrinkage—as much as 30%. Additives such as sand retard this degree of shrinkage somewhat, but potters using this type of clay lose much of their product to cracking and breaking.

The Potter's Wheel

Now a closer look at the Jeremiah passage with which I began. The potter's wheel mentioned in 18:3 was undoubtedly the kick wheel still used by potters in many parts of the world; see also Ecclesiasticus (Ben Sirach) 38:29: ". . . The potter sitting at his work and turning the wheel with his feet." In his very useful study, *The Ceramic Vocabulary of the Old Testament* (1948), James L. Kelso observes "Jeremiah 18:3 . . . is the only specific [Old Testament] reference to the potter's wheel and oddly enough the word is in the dual. . . ."

Perhaps the dual is pertinent, however. The potter's wheel consists of a shaft with a throwing head on top and a heavy wheel that the potter turns with his feet until the proper momentum is achieved. Double wheels are known, which were spun by an assistant, but usually the potter sits and kicks his own wheel as he forms, or "turns," his pieces. The biblical potter's wheel would probably have been made of clay, wood, and, for some parts, stone. The heavier the flywheel, the longer the wheel would keep turning once it was kicked into motion.

As he sets to work, the potter takes a quantity of clay, a pug, proportionate to the size of the piece to be made, and adheres it to the bat which in turn has been adhered to the wheel's throwing head with a coil of clay. Sometimes he throws the clay lump onto the bat with great force, or he may pat it into place while he slowly turns the wheel. The clay must be firmly attached to the bat or it will come loose during the throwing process. The wheel is started by kicking the lower wheel. The potter wets his hands and "centers" the clay by forcing it to rise and fall several times. When the clay is turning on the wheel with little or no wobble the potter opens the form with his hands and draws up the sidewalls to the desired height and thickness. Most potters complete the drawing height in three steps so as not to overwork the clay or to make it too wet. If the clay becomes too wet, the piece will sway and collapse and the process will have to start again with a new piece of clay. The wheel is usually turned or rotated in a counter-clockwise direction since most people are right-handed; the vessel is formed with the left hand on the inside supporting the clay and the right hand pressing inward, usually with the knuckles, against the centrifugal force of the spinning clay mass. This drawing up technique leaves tell-tale finger or knuckle ridges spiraling upwards on the inside and outside of the piece. The potter sometimes removes the outer throwing marks, by trimming or wet smoothing, but usually some evidence remains of the throwing method. The skill of the potter is judged by his production rate, the thinness of his pieces, and the aesthetic beauty of the forms he throws.

After the piece has been thrown and allowed to dry for a time, it is turned upside down, and the lower half of the vessel trimmed and the base formed. On some pieces, the spiral cut-off marks remain from the use of a cut-off string to force the completed piece from the wheel (what the archaeologists call a "string-cut" base). On other pieces, after careful tooling, the base will be domed inward so as to compress the clay base and reduce the possibility of cracking during the drying and firing processes. This indentation of the base allows the finished piece to stand better on a flat surface. Much pottery of the biblical period, however, was finished with a rounded or even pointed bottom, and was used on tripods or in holes in the ground. Indeed, large store jars were often set in the ground, or even in rocks with pointed concavities, quite likely to be reused door socket stones. Some of the smaller pieces were probably placed on woven fiber rings that would allow the user to lean them over for easier access to their contents.

For throwing small pieces such as lamps, the potter could "throw off the hump." A good-sized piece of clay is centered on the wheel, and a number of pieces are made, each from the top of the column of clay; as each is finished, it is cut off with the potter's fingers and his cutting string. With this technique, the potter does not need to center a pug of clay for each small vessel. It is possible to throw ten to a dozen lamps off one piece of clay using this technique.

For larger, more complicated pieces, the biblical potter could throw several sections of his piece and join them together. This was a common practice for necks, handles, spouts, platform bases (as on a chalice), etc. Potters used molds to form elaborate decorative elements, which were then sprigged onto the vessel. Usually thin slip was wiped on the pot area and on the decorative attachment and the two joined together, pressing firmly so as to remove any trapped air. Stamp-seals could be pressed into the clay to denote ownership, volume, or as a trade mark of the potter.

After careful drying the pottery was fired in a kiln—usually an up-draft kiln using camel-thorn, wood, or dung cakes as fuel. The firing would take two to three days, since the temperature had to rise very slowly so as not to crack or break the pieces. The fire was begun very slowly so as to "steam" the ware—to get the remaining moisture out of it. Since the fuel and kilns used usually produced a smoky fire, the ware was at least partly "reduction-fired," an atmosphere which draws some of the oxygen out of the clay itself as well as using up the oxygen of the draft; reduction-firing produces a harder clay body at lower temperatures—a savings in time and fuel. Pottery was usually fired in the 700-900° Centigrade temperature range, producing a porous fabric in a vessel. This porosity would have served to keep drinking water cool in vessels made for that purpose; the potter could seal the pores by smoking the interior or coating it with bitumen.

Other Work for the Potter

Clay was used for many other purposes, and the potter was called upon to provide the raw material for tablets and simple maps, for molding figurines, etc. His clay would be used to make spindle whorls and loom weights, plaster for walls and roofs, dye vats, smelting furnaces, bricks, and tile. Even what we can think of as the ultimate end-product of his craft, the broken potsherd, was useful. Sherds were used as ostraca, bearing messages written in ink on subjects from military dispatches to contract memos; they could be used for dipping water, for carrying hot coals, or as a strigil. Consider Isaiah 30:14:

> And its breaking is like that of a potter's vessel which is smashed so ruthlessly that among its fragments not a sherd is found with which to take fire from the hearth or to dip up water out of the cisterns.

And notice Job 2:8: "And he took a potsherd with which to scrape himself, and sat among the ashes." As for map-making and the implied purpose of conveying military intelligence, see Ezekiel 4: 1-2:

> And you, O son of man, take a brick and lay it before you, and portray upon it a city, even Jerusalem; and put siegeworks against it, and build a siege wall against it, and cast up a mound against it. . . .

* * * * * *

"They keep stable the fabric of the world." The potter had an important role to play in his locale. Potters taught their sons and daughters their technique and artistry, passing on one of the few unbroken traditions from its beginning down to the present day. The opportunity to observe village potters at work in Palestinian villages or on Cyprus, or in many other parts of the world, will soon pass with the inroads of modern technology. While the opportunity remains, one can still relate the past and present together to help form a more complete picture of biblical life.

> These were the potters and inhabitants of Netaim and Gederah; they dwelt there with the king for his work.
>
> I Chronicles 4:23

Further Reading

Ruth Amiran, *Ancient Pottery of the Holy Land* (Rutgers University Press, 1970); Emile Bourry, *Treatise on Ceramic Industries* (New York: Van Nostrand, 1901); R. Hampe and A. Winter, *Bei Töpfern und Töferinnen in Kreta. Messenien und Zypern* (Bonn: Habelt, 1962); Robert H. Johnston, "The Cypriot Potter," in L. Stager, *et al., American*

Expedition to Idalion, Cyprus: First Preliminary Report, Seasons of 1971 and 1972 (Cambridge, Mass.: ASOR, 1974); James L. Kelso and J. Palin Thorley, "The Potter's Technique at Tell Beit Mirsim," in *AASOR*, 1943; Paul Lapp, *Palestinian Ceramic Chronology* (New Haven: ASOR, 1961); Anna Shepherd, *Ceramics for the Archaeologist* (Washington, D.C.: Carnegie Institute Publication 609, most recent edition, 1971). Consult also the various works cited in the text of this article.

13

KING SOLOMON'S PALACES

DAVID USSISHKIN

King Solomon's reign over Israel and Judah from approximately 970-930 B.C. was characterized by peace and great prosperity, and his kingdom stretched from the borders of Egypt to the Euphrates. This period forms a cornerstone in the archaeology of the Holy Land. On the one hand, long and detailed descriptions of Solomon's glorious reign and building activities appear in the Old Testament. On the other hand, substantial remains of the Solomonic period have been uncovered during the excavation of various sites in Israel; and much comparative material has been discovered in the neighboring countries. It is the existence of these two sources of information, the texts and the archaeological remains, which makes this period so fascinating in the study of biblical archaeology; for although these sources are based on different concepts, they are mutually dependent and combine to form a coherent picture. As we shall see throughout this study, the biblical descriptions corroborate the archaeological data recovered in the excavations, throw light on them, and help in their dating and interpretation; and conversely, the archaeological remains illustrate the biblical text and help clarify the obscure parts. The famous illustration of this corroborative parallelism is the verse in 1 Kings 9:15: "And this is the record of the forced labor which King Solomon conscripted to build the house of the Lord, his own palace, the Millo, the wall of Jerusalem, and Hazor and Megiddo and Gezer." This passage was the focal point in the discovery and interpretation of the Solomonic monumental city-gates at Hazor, Megiddo, and Gezer. Another fascinating illustration of the parallelism between the biblical and material sources can be found in the case of King Solomon's royal palaces. With Professor Y. Yadin's discovery of a new palace in Megiddo—described for the first time in *BA* 33 (1970)—it seems

Illus. 21-8

appropriate to re-evaluate the problems of the palaces and describe them in detail for the readers of *The Biblical Archaeologist.*

The Royal Palace in Jerusalem

When King Solomon ascended the throne, Jerusalem stretched along the ridge labeled by scholars the "South-East Hill,"the "Hill of Ophel," or the "City of David." At present, the ridge is situated to the south of the Turkish city-wall, in the section between the Dung Gate and the south-east corner of the Old City, or in other words, to the south of Haram el-Sherif where the Dome of the Rock and el-Aksa mosque were subsequently built. Solomon increased the area of the walled city on its northern side by incorporating in it the hill of Moriah on which the Haram el-Sherif is now situated. There he constructed a royal enclosure or royal acropolis which contained the temple and his royal palace. As is the case in other royal cities in the Ancient East, the Solomonic enclosure was built at the edge of the city rather than in its center, and at its highest point, thus dominating the entire capital. The area of the Solomonic enclosure is now covered by the Haram, and it is agreed by most scholars that the temple was built on the very spot where the Dome of the Rock now stands. The royal palace seems to have been built to the south of the temple. Archaeological investigations cannot be carried out in the area of the Haram; and in any case, it is very doubtful whether Solomonic remains are preserved at all as the whole hill was leveled and rebuilt by King Herod the Great. Hence our evidence on Solomon's royal palace in Jerusalem, which obviously was the largest building constructed by that king, is confined to the biblical descriptions combined with comparative archaeological material.

In I Kings 7:1-12 the biblical narrative gives a brief account of the palace in question. The shortness of the account may be due to the attitude of the editors of the Book of Kings, who included in the text a detailed description of the "house of the Lord" while hardly paying attention to the neighboring secular palace, though the latter was larger in size and took a longer period to build. The record appears to be accurate, but its briefness and the use of technical terms make it difficult to comprehend the text fully. The measurement used in the description is the ancient local cubit, which is either the shorter cubit, *ca*. 44.5 cm. or 17.5 inches, or the longer cubit, *ca*. 52.5 cm. or 20.65 inches in length. We shall start our discussion by quoting the biblical verses mentioned above, but we must remind the reader that a translation of a biblical text—and in particular a somewhat obscure text like this one—tends to be an interpretation as well. The description runs as follows:

(1) Solomon had been engaged on his house for thirteen years by the time he had finished it. (2) He built the house of the forest of Lebanon which was a hundred cubits long, fifty broad, and thirty high; and it contained four (=three, in the Septuagint translation) rows of cedar columns crowned with cedar capitals (?). (3) It was paneled with cedar beams which extended over the beams (?), which in turn rested upon five columns, arranged fifteen in a row. (4) There were *šequpim* in three rows, and *meḥezah* against *meḥezah* three times. (5) And all the doors and the jambs and the *šequpim* (?) had right angles, and *meḥezah* against *meḥezah* three times. (6) He made the hall of columns, fifty cubits long and thirty cubits broad, and a hall and columns with a cornice in front of them. (7) He built the hall for the throne, which is the hall of judgment where he was to give judgment; this was paneled in cedar from one side of the floor to the other. (8) His own house where he was to reside in the other court behind the hall was made in the same way; and he made a house for Pharaoh's daughter whom he had married, constructed like the hall. (9) All these, on the inner and outer sides, from foundation to coping, and from outside (?) to the great court, were (constructed) of measured (?) ashlar stones of good quality (?), dressed with chisel (?). (10) The foundations were of large stones of good quality (?), stones of ten cubits and stones of eight cubits. (11) And above were measured (?) ashlar stones of good quality (?) and cedar. (12) And the great court around, built of three courses of ashlar stones and one course of cedar beams (?). . . .

It seems clear from the description that the palace—often labeled "the king's house"—was constructed within a "great court" which probably separated it from the temple and other structures in the acropolis. Inside the great court were built six units which were introduced consecutively:

1. "The house of the forest of Lebanon." This unit alone was nearly the same size as the temple.

2. The "hall of columns," a rectangular hall which was about 75 feet long and 45 feet wide.

3. The "hall for the throne," also called the "hall of judgment." This was the main ceremonial hall of the palace in which the king's magnificent throne to be described below was undoubtedly placed.

4. "The other court," which was "within the hall." The living quarters of the palace adjoined this court.

5. "His own house where he was to reside," which obviously was the king's private abode.

6. "A house for Pharaoh's daughter," which was a separate dwelling unit within the palace built for Solomon's famous wife, who probably was the daughter of Pharaoh Siamun.[1] This unit may also have included the living quarters for other wives and concubines as well.

What did the palace look like? The biblical description is so brief that it is impossible to reconstruct the edifice and its ground plan solely on the basis of the written evidence, and we have to turn to the aid of the archaeological data. Several scholars have attempted to interpret the text and reconstruct the palace using comparative archaeological material;[2] our own attempt to do so which is published elsewhere[3] forms the basis for the discussion below.

When studying the problem of reconstruction of the edifice, it seems that two assumptions concerning the interpretation of the text should be adopted. A few attempts at reconstruction assumed that the palace contained several separate buildings, each comprising one of the above units. "The house of the forest of Lebanon" was undoubtedly a prominent, detached building. But it seems (following Benzinger and Watzinger) that the other five units listed above were incorporated into one single structure. The second assumption, based on the first one, is that the biblical account discusses the different units of the palace consecutively, beginning at the entrance and working toward the far side in the order in which they would be seen by anyone entering and passing through the building. In other words, we assume that the main entrance to the palace was through the "hall of columns"; from there one entered the "hall for the throne," then "the other court," and finally the living quarters surrounding the latter. It may be added that the biblical description of Solomon's temple seems to introduce the three units of the temple in a similar sequence, namely, the outermost first and the innermost last (I Kings 6; II Chron. 3).

When looking for comparative architectural data generally contemporaneous with the description of the palace, we turn northwards to Syria and southern Anatolia where Phoenician, Aramean, and Neo-Hittite kingdoms flourished during the 10th-8th centuries B.C. The biblical record describes in great detail how Solomon—whose people did not possess an architectural tradition of their own nor the necessary technical knowledge—brought masons, craftsmen, and building material from the Phoenician kingdoms of Tyre and Byblos for the construction of the temple. The biblical descriptions of the temple accord well with our knowledge of contemporary Phoenician architecture and art, and it can be safely assumed that the architects and builders of the adjacent palace complex were also brought from Phoenicia. All the above-mentioned kingdoms were undoubtedly connected with the Phoenician culture which inspired Solomonic architecture. Therefore, let us change the course of our discussion and turn for a while to survey the palaces in the northern kingdoms.

The Bīt-ḫilāni

A common type of ceremonial palace, universally labeled today by scholars as the *bīt-ḫilāni*, was built by the rulers in southern Anatolia and northern Syria during our period. This type of building already appears in northern Syria during the Late Bronze Age, and the royal palaces of Alalach and Ugarit are built in this fashion.[4] It became very popular during the Iron Age, and several *bīt-ḫilāni* palaces dated to the 10th-7th centuries B.C. have been unearthed in Tell Halaf (biblical Gozan), Karatepe, Sakçagözü, Zincirli, and Tell Tayanat. It is reasonable to assume that the royal palaces in southern Syria and Phoenicia, unexcavated so far, are based on a similar ground plan.

The architectural principles of the *bīt-ḫilāni* can be best introduced in connection with the ground plan of a typical example. The *bīt-ḫilāni* is a self-contained building which is generally characterized by a number of specific features. The entrance to the building is through a portico which may have one, two, or three columns. The entrance to the building is set in the long wall of a rectangular hall. A small side-room is built beside the

entrance hall. The main hall of the building is located behind the
entrance hall and the side-room; and in this case, the length of the
main hall is similar to the combined length of the entrance hall and
the side room. A few small rooms are built behind and beside the
main hall, forming the back of the building. A staircase, or a square
tower which probably supported a staircase, is built to the right or
left of the entrance hall. The shape and the construction of the
superstructure of the building are open to conjecture, and hence we
can only guess how the main hall was lit. The main hall was
undoubtedly roofed, and it served as the throne room in the royal
palaces. The hall may have been lit by clerestory lighting; its ceiling
being higher than that of the adjoining rooms.

Although nowadays the whole building is called a *bīt-ḫilāni*, it
seems that in antiquity the term *ḫilāni* denoted only the
magnificent porticoed entrance which is so typical of that kind of
building. This term apparently stems from the Hittite term
Hilammar which appears in the Hittite texts of the Late Bronze
Age. During the Iron Age the *ḫilāni* is mentioned several times in
the inscriptions of the Assyrian kings who—influenced by "western
fashion"—incorporated such a porticoed entrance into their own
buildings in Assyria.[5] Sennacherib, for instance, records that "... a
room with windows like (that) of a Hittite palace, which in the
language of Amurru is called *bīt-ḫilāni*, I built. . . ."

The best comparative archaeological material for our purpose
comes from Zincirli, the site of the capital of the kingdom of
Sam³al. The ruling house of Sam³al was founded during the 10th
century, and Sam³al remained an independent kingdom till the end
of the 8th century B.C. Zincirli was excavated by a German
expedition about eighty years ago. The royal acropolis of the city
was unearthed, and it contained several *bīt-ḫilāni*s built by the
kings of Sam³al.[6] Palace J was built by King Kilamuwa during the
third quarter of the 9th century B.C. The palace continued to be in
use for another century, during which time it was partially
modified. It combines within one building the ceremonial *bīt-
ḫilāni* and the living quarters of the ruler. Adjoining it, King
Barrakib constructed Palace K during the third quarter of the 8th
century B.C. Here the palace proper does not include any living
quarters. Four other ceremonial *bīt-ḫilāni*s were uncovered in the
acropolis, but their exact function remains obscure. The biggest of

them is Hilani I, also labeled "The Old Hilani" by the excavators. Hilanis II and III are very similar to one another. The fourth *bīt-ḥilāni*, which is the smallest in Zincirli, adjoins Hilani II on the northern side. All four buildings were very badly preserved above foundation-level, and the position of the inner doorways and windows is unknown.

Solomon's Palace as a *Bīt-ḥilāni*

Turning back to Jerusalem, it seems that the architects adopted the ground plan of a *bīt-ḥilāni* for Solomon's royal palace. Watzinger has already suggested the comparison of the "hall of columns" with typical *bīt-ḥilāni* from Zincirli, the "columns" of the biblical description being the columns of the portico at the entrance to the *bīt-ḥilāni*. Galling followed him and suggested that the "hall for the throne" was a *bīt-ḥilāni* as well. However, he considered each of these units to be one complete *bīt-ḥilāni*, and thus his reconstruction of the palace shows several separate buildings. It seems that a satisfactory solution lies in a combination of these suggestions and our above-mentioned assumption that the palace formed one single building. In other words, it seems that both these "halls" should be identified as parts of one single *bīt-ḥilāni*.

Let us compare Solomon's palace to the royal palaces in Zincirli. In Kilamuwa's Palace J one enters the building through a portico which has one single column. The portico leads to a front hall, and together they form the hall corresponding to the "hall of columns" (J1). From there one proceeds into the throne room (J3), the largest hall in the building, which corresponds to the "hall for the throne." From the throne room one proceeds to the far side of the building which formed the living quarters of the royal household (units J4-J12). It seems that either unit J7 or the north-east half of unit J6 (or, perhaps, both) was an open courtyard, as otherwise it would have been impossible to arrange the lighting in all rooms in this part of the palace. Furthermore, the square tower J10 which is situated between these rooms probably supported a staircase leading to another floor, meaning that the rooms on the ground-floor could not have been lit from above. The plastered floors with

drainage systems built underneath which we found both in J7 and
the north-east half of J6 were considered by the excavators to be
facilities for washing, but they can also be interpreted as arrangements to prevent the formation of mud in winter and drain away
the rainwater. We have here, then, an inner courtyard which is
parallel to the "other court" in Solomon's palace, and also as in the
latter, living quarters that adjoin this court. In the neighboring
Palace K, which was built by Barrakib, the main entrance is
through a magnificent portico approached by a flight of seven
steps. The entrance hall is the hall corresponding to the "hall of
columns," and behind it the throne room is situated (K2), in
parallel to the "hall for the throne."

The above comparisons give us a general idea what the main
edifice of Solomon's royal palace looked like. A clearer idea of the
building and its reconstruction can be gained by studying the
palaces uncovered at Megiddo. However, before turning to
Megiddo, let us first discuss a few more problems connected with
the palace in Jerusalem.

The "Hall for the Throne" and the Throne

The "hall for the throne" was undoubtedly the most important
room in the palace. Here King Solomon—as well as his
descendants—gave audience and received official visitors. The hall
was also called the "hall of judgment" where Solomon—
considered by "all Israel" to have "the wisdom of God in him to
render justice"—pronounced judgment. The king's throne, which
stood in a prominent position inside the hall, symbolized royalty,
the king's reign and power, and his dynasty. A good example of its
symbolic meaning and importance is the case of the *coup d'état*
which the priest Jehoiada carried out in Jerusalem *ca.* 836 B.C. The
event is discussed in detail in II Kings 11. Following the declaration
of the infant Joash as king and his anointment in the temple, Joash
was rushed "to the king's house, and he sat on the throne of the
kings"—almost certainly Solomon's throne, placed in our hall![7]

The layout of this hall must have been similar to that of the
throne rooms in the Zincirli royal palaces, a layout typical in fact of
all contemporaneous throne rooms in Syria as well as in Assyria.

Thus, almost certainly it was a rectangular hall with the official
entrance in its long side. The throne was placed on a rectangular
dais or raised base, constructed at the far side of the hall adjacent to
its short wall and centrally placed. In nearly all the throne rooms of
that period the throne was placed at the side left of the entrance, so
that upon entering the room one had to turn left in order to face the
king. The dais for the throne was found in Barrakib's throne room,
and it should be reconstructed near the north-west wall in
Kilamuwa's throne room. Another feature typical of contemporary throne rooms is an open hearth near and in front of the
throne. Kilamuwa's throne room had a rectangular brazier and
Barrakib's a round one. Other throne rooms contained "movable
hearths," a small metal "cart" with wheels which could be moved
nearer to or further from the throne on a specially built platform or
"stone-rails." The remains of such a "movable hearth" were indeed
discovered in the palatial *bīt-ḥilāni* at Tell-Halaf.[8] It seems
reasonable to assume that such a hearth—whether fixed or
movable—was in use in Jerusalem as well. This conclusion is
strengthened by the story of King Jehoiakim (608-598 B.C.) who sat
in the winter house in the ninth month, "and there was a fire on the
hearth burning before him" (Jer. 36:22). The ninth month of the
Hebrew calendar, Kislev, falls about December in mid-winter; and
it is not surprising that a fire was lit in the hearth. Incidentally, the
fact that the royal palace in Jerusalem was called—at least at a later
date—a "winter house," probably to distinguish it from the royal
summer residence, provides another parallel with the palace of
Barrakib. The latter boasts in his building inscription that "my
fathers, the kings of Sam'al, had no good house. They had the
house of Kilamuwa which was their winter house and also their
summer house. But I have built this house." Lastly we have to
mention that the walls of Solomon's throne room were "paneled in
cedar from one side of the floor to the other." Correspondingly, the
walls of the entrance hall and the throne room in Barrakib's palace
were covered with wooden beams; and their reconstruction
probably presents a clear picture of the appearance of the walls in
Solomon's throne room.

Solomon's throne was placed on a dais which was approached
by six steps. It was so magnificent that apparently "nothing like it

had ever been made for any kingdom." Following is its description in I Kings 10:18-20: "And the king made a great throne of ivory and overlaid it with fine (?) gold. The throne had six steps, and the top of the throne was round behind. There were arms on each side of the seat with a lion standing beside each of them; and twelve lions stood on the six steps, one at either end of each step." This description resembles the throne portrayed on a Canaanite ivory from the 13th century found in Megiddo and the throne portrayed in relief on the sarcophagus of Ahiram, king of Byblos, Solomon's Phoenician contemporary.[9] In both cases, the throne is equipped with arm-rests and its top is turned back and downward, neatly rounded. Both thrones are flanked by winged sphinxes, corresponding to the lions on Solomon's throne. The throne was probably made of wood, partly overlaid with sheets of gold and partly decorated with carved panels of ivory veneered to the wooden parts. The ivory decoration was the reason why it was known as "a great throne of ivory." The application of ivory panels, often elaborately carved, as veneer to expensive furniture was in fashion in the royal courts of Canaan and Phoenicia; and Solomon's case is no exception. Such a throne, decorated with beautiful ivories in Phoenician style, has only recently been discovered in a royal tomb in Salamis, Cyprus.[10]

"The House of the Forest of Lebanon"

The last unit to be discussed in Solomon's monumental palace complex is a large detached building with an unusual name, "the house of the forest of Lebanon," described in the few unclear verses cited above. The building was 100 cubits long, 50 cubits wide, and 30 high (about 150 feet long, 75 feet wide, and 45 feet high). The building probably contained three, or possibly even four rows of columns, composed of fifteen columns each. They were made of cedar, and undoubtedly the appearance of a large number of cedar columns, densely placed and resembling a forest, explains how the building acquired its peculiar name. Cedar capitals—probably of the proto-Ionic order which will be discussed below—crowned the columns and supported the ceiling which was paneled in cedar beams. If the columns extended to the full height of the building, they would have been extremely high; and we have to consider the possibility (after Vincent) that they supported a second floor rather than a roof. Doorways and windows were arranged in an obscure, though symmetrical manner. The biblical record does not inform us about the function of the edifice. Nevertheless, it is stated in I Kings 10:21 that "all the vessels (?) of the house of the forest of Lebanon are made of pure (?) gold." In addition, Solomon made five hundred shields of two types, all of gold, and kept them there. It may be inferred (from I Kings 14:26-28) that these ceremonial shields were held by the guards at the gate of the palace complex.

When looking for comparable archaeological material for our edifice, we find that no similar building has thus far been excavated in Palestine or Syria. One such building, however, which seems to bear some resemblance to "the house of the forest of Lebanon" turned up recently in distant Altintepe, a site in eastern Anatolia. Altintepe represents a royal citadel of the kingdom of Urartu and it was excavated by a Turkish expedition headed by Professor Tahsin Özgüç of Ankara University. The kingdom of Urartu flourished in the hilly country of eastern Anatolia from the 9th to the 6th centuries B.C. The Urartians developed a prominent culture of their own; their architecture, metal-craft, and art are impressive. Prior to the 9th century the Urartians seem to have been wandering tribes, thus not possessing an architectural tradition of their own. As with Solomonic architecture it seems reasonable that Urartian monumental architecture was influenced by the architectural traditions crystallized in the important centers of Syria, south Anatolia, and Assyria with whom the Urartians had much contact. The citadel of Altintepe is dated by Özgüç to the 8th-7th centuries B.C. An analogy between the building there and our edifice in Jerusalem can be drawn if we consider both to represent the Phoenician architectural tradition, namely a type of building developed in Phoenicia and "exported" by the Phoenicians to the neighboring countries.

The building in Altintepe stood beside the citadel's temple, and only its foundations were preserved.[11] The building is rectangular and contains one hall only. Its length is about 150 feet and its width about 94 feet. The stone foundations are deeply set and about 9 feet thick. Remains of an adjoining building were uncovered near one of the narrow sides, and here Özgüç reconstructs the main entrance. The position of the doors and the windows is generally unknown. The walls were built of bricks and the interior was decorated with wall paintings. Inside the hall, eighteen stone column-bases were found *in situ*, arranged in three rows, six in a row. They were four and a half feet in diameter and apparently supported huge columns.

Summarizing the possible analogy between the Altintepe building and "the house of the forest of Lebanon" we see that both are rectangular buildings of a similar size. The height of the Altintepe building is unknown but the thickness of the foundations and the column-bases indicates that it was considerable, like the building in Jerusalem. In both buildings three rows of columns supported the roof, though the Urartian building had only 18 columns as compared to 45 in Solomon's edifice. Özgüç considers the Altintepe building to have been a royal reception hall, which formed a prototype for the *Apadana*, the royal audience hall of the Achaemenid kings of Persia a quarter of a millennium later. On the basis of this analogy, may we consider "the house of the forest of Lebanon" as having a similar function in Solomon's palace complex? And may we then trace a line of development from Phoenicia and "the house of the forest of Lebanon" to Urartu, and thence to the royal palaces of Persia?[12]

The Southern Palace in Megiddo

Solomon's palace in Jerusalem was his central and most magnificent palace but not his only one. The data hint at the existence of another palace in Gezer,[13] and other palatial buildings are probably hidden elsewhere. Two palaces, however, were excavated at Megiddo, one in the southern part and one in the northern part of the mound. It is interesting to note that while all our information on the palace in Jerusalem is derived from the written text, everything we know about the palaces in Megiddo is learned from the archaeological data.

The massive foundations of the southern palace (No. 1723) were uncovered by the expedition of the Chicago Oriental Institute.[14] The monumental palace was set in a wide square court (No. 1693) which was reached through a prominent gate-house (No. 1567).

Adjacent and to the west of the court, another building (No. 1482), probably of administrative character, was built. The stratigraphical position of this palatial compound (labeled Stratum IVB by the excavators) remained uncertain after the termination of the excavations, but it was clarified during Yadin's recent excavations in Megiddo. Hence it seems that the southern palace compound— as well as the northern palace complex which will be discussed below—were constructed by King Solomon.[15]

The structures of the palace compound were destroyed during the 9th century B.C. when most of the building stones were taken for re-use in the buildings of Stratum IVA, but the preserved remains are sufficient to give us a clear idea of what the palace looked like. The gate of the court opened to the north toward the center of the city. The large courtyard did not contain any buildings other than the palace, and it was paved with a layer of hard lime plaster. The palace was not built at the center of the court but nearer to its west side. The back wall of the palace was in line and joined the back wall of the court, and both were probably incorporated into the city's fortifications.

The plan of the palace proper was nearly square, roughly 69 feet by 64 feet. The reason for the formation of a recess in the southeastern corner is not clear. The foundations of the building are heavy and deeply set, indicating the massive character and the considerable height of the palace. Ashlar stones were incorporated in the foundations and in particular in the two northern corners of the building. Only a few dressed stones of the superstructure remained, enough to show that at least the lower part of the superstructure was built of ashlar masonry rather than of bricks. The position of these stones and marks incised by the builders on the foundation stones indicate that the walls of the superstructure were slightly narrower than the foundations. Of special interest is unit No. 1728 which adjoined the eastern wall of the palace and extended almost exactly halfway along this wall. Although it is bonded to the palace proper it is clearly a separate unit; it forms an "addition" to the square palace and it is constructed in a different fashion. The walls of this unit are built solely of ashlar stones laid in headers (i.e., laid lengthwise across the wall). Significantly, the space inside this unit was filled with rubble, and the large stones were placed evenly to create a platform.

The excavators attempted to reconstruct the edifice, even though none of the doorways and windows were preserved, and their location is unknown. They interpreted unit 1728 as an open porch leading to the main entrance which opened into K. A side entrance was reconstructed at the western side.[16] Unit A was considered to be an open court, and room M, and possibly room G, to have supported a staircase leading to a second story and to the roof. They suggested that the square foundation in the center of room M supported a square tower that rose above the rest of the building. The excavators published a perspective view of the suggested reconstruction which has since been reproduced in many books.

The Southern Palace—A *Bīt-ḫilāni*

It seems to us, however, that the palace should be reconstructed in a different way. Our starting point is the striking resemblance between the Solomonic gates at Hazor, Megiddo, and Gezer, which led to the conclusion that all "were in fact built by Solomon's architects from identical blueprints, with minor changes in each case made necessary by the terrain."[17] It occurred to us that the same might have been done in the case of Solomon's palaces, though the palace in Jerusalem was obviously a bigger and more monumental edifice than the provincial palace at Megiddo. We expected, then, that the southern palace would be a smaller version of Solomon's "house" in Jerusalem and based on a similar ground plan, namely, that it would incorporate on the one hand a *bīt-ḫilāni* of the Zincirli pattern, and on the other all the units of Solomon's palace in Jerusalem in their respective order.

Our expectations seemed to materialize when we studied the data on the palace. It is difficult to accept the excavator's suggestion that unit 1728 formed a porch leading to the main entrance, as in this case the entrance would not be in front of the building, opposite the main gate of the court which encompassed the palace, but in a side-wall, compelling the entrant to change direction when approaching the building. We would have expected then that the main entrance would be in the facade of the building, and there the only suitable room where the entrance could be reconstructed is room H.

It seems that rooms H, J, K, and probably the adjoining "filled" unit 1728, constitute a typical *bīt-ḫilāni*. H is the entrance hall with the portico, parallel to J1, K1, and A in the palaces of Kilamuwa and Barrakib, and to Hilani III at Zincirli respectively. J is the adjoining side-room corresponding to C in Hilani III and J2 in Kilamuwa's palace. K is the main hall of the *ḫilāni*, parallel to J3, K2, and D in the palaces of Kilamuwa and Barrakib, and Hilani III respectively. As in the *bīt-ḫilāni*s at Zincirli, the length of the main hall is similar to the combined length of the entrance hall and the side-room. Unit 1728 might have been a tower parallel to towers K4 and B, built beside the entrance hall in Barrakib's palace and Hilani III.

More details of the portico at the entrance of the palace may perhaps be reconstructed. The excavation report describes a wall, labeled wall 1444, which was built above the palace compound in a later period.[18] It adds, nevertheless, that "the northern half of wall 1444, that is, the part built of hewn stone, existed originally in Stratum IVB and appeared to have formed a footing along the north wall of the palace. . . . The south face of the row of squared stones fell exactly along the line of the north face of the superstructure of the palace. . . ." It is obvious that the "northern half of wall 1444" formed a step which was built in front of the portico at the entrance to hall H. This part of the step which was preserved, when redrawn on the plan of the southern palace, stretches along the eastern part of the portico and beyond it, along the wall of side-room J. Symmetrically, the step probably extended for a similar distance beyond the west side of the portico. A step or a row of steps built of hewn stones in front of the portico is typical also of the *bīt-ḫilāni*s of Zincirli. Of special interest is a row of seven steps leading to the entrance of Barrakib's Palace K. In this case as well, the steps are wider than the entrance, extending along the wall beyond the right and left sides of the portico.

The pilasters and pillars of our portico seem to have been decorated with proto-Ionic capitals. This type of capital probably originated in Phoenicia, and various examples have been found in several Iron Age sites in Israel. They are stone rectangular capitals which were mounted on rectangular pilasters or rectangular columns, and their faces bear a typical carved design. Two unusu-

ally large proto-Ionic capitals were found at Megiddo not far from
the southern palace. The excavators reconstructed them in the gate
leading to the court of the palace, but it seems more likely that they
should be assigned to the portico at the entrance to the edifice. One
of the capitals was carved on one side only and was probably
mounted on one of the pilaster-jambs of the entrance. The second
capital does not bear a design, but it is worked and smoothed on all
four sides. Therefore, it probably crowned a column in the center
of the portico. If this reconstruction is correct, the columns in the
portico must have been rectangular and about four and a half feet
long. The portico can be arbitrarily reconstructed with two such
columns.

As in Kilamuwa's palace, further rooms, probably living
quarters, were built behind the *ḥilāni* proper in the southern
palace. Unit A was probably an open court as suggested by the
excavators. This is indicated by the size of the unit and its central
position, surrounded by other rooms. This court is parallel to J6 or
J7 in Kilamuwa's palace. It seems that the palace in Megiddo had
two staircases leading to a second floor. G is a long and narrow
room, too narrow to be used for any other purpose than a staircase.
Such staircases, commencing in the entrance hall to the right or left
of the portico, were typical of the *bīt-ḥilāni*. In Kilamuwa's palace
room GK probably formed an identical long and narrow staircase
built at the side of the portico. Room M in the palace of Megiddo
probably contained another staircase built around the central
square column. It seems that room M is parallel to J10 in
Kilamuwa's palace; the latter also seems to be a square staircase
situated in the living quarters behind the main hall of the *ḥilāni*.

This suggested reconstruction of the southern palace at Megiddo
corresponds well with the biblical description of Solomon's palace
in Jerusalem, which was analyzed above, and thus it seems that our
palace at Megiddo reflects the ground plan and probably the
appearance of the larger edifice in Jerusalem. The palace at
Megiddo was encompassed on three sides by a large open court
which is parallel to the "great court" in Jerusalem. The entrance
was through entrance hall H, a rectangular hall which is parallel to
the "hall of columns" in Jerusalem. From hall H one proceeded to
hall K, which corresponds to the "hall for the throne" in Jerusalem.
The position of the entrance to hall K supports our conclusion that

in Jerusalem the throne was placed at the far end of the hall, on the left-hand side. From this hall one approached court A, which is parallel to the "other court" in Solomon's palace. The living quarters adjoined court A as in Jerusalem. It seems that here also it is possible to discern two separate units within the living quarters, similar to "his own house where he was to reside" and the "house for Pharaoh's daughter" in Jerusalem. One unit was formed by the rooms on the west of the palace—B, C, D, E, F, and staircase G—while the second unit included the rooms on the south side—L, N, O, P and staircase M.

The Northern Palace at Megiddo

The newly discovered northern palace (No. 6000)[19] increases our admiration for the magnificence of Solomonic Megiddo. It is rectangular in plan and larger in size than the southern palace (*ca.* 84 by 63 feet). Its walls were built of ashlar stones which were mostly robbed after the destruction of the palace. The ground plan of the building was reconstructed by the late architect I. Dunayevsky, and the excavations proved the reliability of his attempt. Yadin's identification of the palace as a *bīt-ḫilāni* is indeed convincing, and its ground plan can best be compared to that of Hilani I from Zincirli. The latter is considered by the excavators of Zincirli to be older than the other *ḫilāni*s and may have been built in the 10th-9th centuries B.C. In the northern palace (as well as in Hilani I) there is an entrance hall through which one enters the central, large rectangular hall.[20] Unlike the case of the *ḫilāni*s discussed above, the entrance hall and the central hall are similar in length and both are situated in the center of the building. Undoubtedly, the entrance to the palace was through a magnificent portico set in the center of the building's facade, and here the foundations were *ca.* 6 feet thick, thicker than those of the other walls. The central hall was surrounded by small rooms. To the right of the entrance hall was found a "filled" unit, almost certainly a staircase on the *ḫilāni* pattern.

The reconstruction of the northern palace as a *bīt-ḫilāni* follows the trend of thought which had previously led us to suggest the reconstruction of the Jerusalem palace and the southern palace in

Megiddo discussed above. And indeed, the reconstruction of the northern palace strengthens our argumentation. So far, the appearance of the *bīt-ḫilāni* in Palestine as part of the Phoenician artistic and architectural influence in that period was a mere assumption used as part of our argumentation, but now it seems to be an established fact. Hence, we now have two Solomonic *ḫilāni* palaces in Megiddo which, nevertheless, differ from one another. The southern palace had living quarters in it, and—as suggested by several scholars—it might have been the residence of Baana, the son of Ahilud, who was Solomon's governor in "Taanach and Megiddo and all Beth-shean" (I Kings 4:12). The northern palace, on the other hand, was solely a ceremonial palace.

The layout of the two *ḫilāni* palaces at Megiddo generally resembles that of the palaces in Zincirli as well as those found at Tell Tayanat. At both Megiddo and Zincirli one sees contemporaneous *ḫilāni* palaces of a different kind, probably having different functions. On the one hand, there are the residential *ḫilāni* palaces, and on the other hand the large ceremonial ones. Significantly, Hilanis I and III in Zincirli were built at the edge of the mound, facing the center, with their back wall built near and perhaps forming part of the fortification wall of the acropolis. Similarly, the two Solomonic palaces at Megiddo are facing the center of the mound with their back wall forming part of the city's (inner?) line of fortifications; and it seems within reason to indicate the possibility that Solomon's palace in Jerusalem might have adjoined the Solomonic city-wall (I Kings 3:1, 9:15) in a similar fashion.

Turning briefly to Tell Tayanat, possibly the site of Kunulua, the capital of the kingdom of Hattina, we see several *bīt-ḫilāni*s unearthed by an expedition of the Chicago Oriental Institute.[21] More than one building level was discovered in the acropolis, but the main architectural concept did not change. Here again we see a central palatial *bīt-ḫilāni* which probably contained an official section as well as living quarters (Buildings I, VI), and in addition another ceremonial *bīt-ḫilāni* (Building IV). It is noteworthy that behind the central palace (Building I) a small royal shrine (Building II) was uncovered. The latter is universally regarded as being strikingly similar to Solomon's temple, which was built in Jerusalem not far from our palace![22]

A few words must be added here about the constuction of the palaces. The heavy stone foundations of the Megiddo palaces which were largely composed of ashlar masonry have already been mentioned. The walls of the gate to the court of the southern palace, the heavy proto-Ionic capitals whch must each have been supported by a large stone column, a few ashlar stones found in their original position above the foundations of the southern palace—all indicate that at least the lower part of the superstructure of the Megiddo palaces was built of ashlar stones. This conclusion corresponds well with the biblical description of the palace in Jerusalem which was constructed "from foundation to coping" with "ashlar stones of good quality (?), dressed with chisel (?)," some being ten and eight cubits in length! The walls of the palaces were almost certainly built in the Phoenician style with the stones placed meticulously, one beside the other, and arranged in a pattern of "headers" and "stretchers." In part, the walls must have been composed of plain smoothed stones, while others probably contained stones with a drafted central boss.[23]

Of special interest is the biblical description which informs us that the superstructure of the palace was composed of "ashlar stones of good quality (?) and cedar" of Lebanon, while the great court was built of "three courses of ashlar stones and one course of cedar beams (?)." Such a construction in which wooden beams were horizontally placed between courses of ashlar masonry is very typical of the Phoenician architectural style. This feature can be seen at Megiddo in the Solomonic city-gate and in the gate to the court of the southern palace. The wooden beams—long decayed— are now represented by a wide "gap" filled with earth which separates two courses of ashlar masonry in the wall.

At the end of our discussion we see that the scanty remains of Kings Solomon's palaces so far allow us but a glimpse of the magnificent buildings of this glorious king. Nevertheless, perhaps we can now understand the reactions of Solomon's most illustrious royal visitor. I Kings 10:4-5 tells us that "when the queen of Sheba saw all the wisdom of Solomon, *the house which he had built*, the food on his table, the courtiers sitting round him, and his attendants standing behind in their livery, his cupbearers, and the whole-offerings which he used to offer in the house of the Lord, *there was no more spirit left in her*"!

Notes

[1] On Solomon's Egyptian father-in-law, see K. A. Kitchen, *The Third Intermediate Period in Egypt* (1973), pp. 280-283.

[2] See, for example, the studies which are cited below: I. Benzinger, *Hebräische Archäologie* (3rd ed. 1927), pp. 211ff.; C. Watzinger, *Denkmäler Palästinas* (1933), Vol. I, pp. 95-97; K. Galling, *Biblisches Reallexikon* (1937), p. 411; H. Vincent and M. Steve, *Jérusalem de l'Ancien Testament*, Parts II-III (1956), pp. 423-431.

[3] D. Ussishkin, *Israel Exploration Journal* 16 (1966), 174-186; 20 (1970), 213-215.

[4] On the *bīt-ḫilāni* see H. Frankfort, *Iraq* 14 (1952), 120-131.

[5] *The Assyrian Dictionary* (Chicago), Vol. VI, pp. 184-185.

[6] All the *bīt-ḫilāni*s are described in detail in the excavation report. See F. von Luschan and others, *Ausgrabungen in Sendschirli* II (1898), III (1902), IV (1911).

[7] Significantly, biblical Hebrew uses the term *throne* as the symbol of monarchy. For example: "I will establish the throne of your kingship upon Israel for ever as I promised to David your father" (I Kings 9:5).

[8] M. Frh. von Oppenheim and others, *Tell Halaf*, Vol. II (1950), pp. 45-50.

[9] J. B. Pritchard, *The Ancient Near East in Pictures* (1954), Nos. 332, 456, 458.

[10] V. Karageorghis, *Salamis: Recent Discoveries in Cyprus* (1969) pp. 92-93, Pls. IV-VI, 42.

[11] The building is described in detail in the excavation report. See T. Özgüç, *Altintepe*, Vol. I (1966), pp. 44-46, Pls. V-VI, XVII-XIX.

[12] Another comparable building published after the present article had been written is the Phoenician temple of Astarte in Kition, Cyprus. It dates to the 9th century B.C. The great hall of the temple, which adjoined the Holy of Holies, contained four rows each of seven columns. The columns were made of wood, possibly cedar of Lebanon, and rested on square stone bases. See V. Karageorghis, *Kition, Mycenaean and Phoenician Discoveries in Cyprus*, London 1976, pp. 96-100, fig. 18, pls. 69-74.

[13] D. Ussishkin, *Israel Exploration Journal* 16 (1966), 186, note 36.

[14] The palace complex is described in detail in the excavation report. See R. S. Lamon and G. M. Shipton, *Megiddo*, Vol. I (1939), pp. 11-27.

[15] A different opinion has recently been expressed by Y. Aharoni. See his argumention in *The Journal of Near Eastern Studies* 31 (1972), 302-311.

[16] Here a few ashlar stones were found in their original position in the floor of the court (No. 1617). They may represent the remains of a stone platform which adjoined the west wall of the palace.

[17] Y. Yadin, *Israel Exploration Journal* 8 (1958), 85-86.

[18] *Megiddo*, Vol. I, p. 21.

[19] Y. Yadin, *BA* 33 (1970), 73-75; *Israel Exploration Journal* 22 (1972), 162-164.

[20] And not an open court as interpreted by Yadin.

[21] These buildings are described in detail in the excavation report. See R. C. Haines, *Excavations in the Plain of Antioch*, Vol. II (1971).

[22] It should be noted that the Solomonic palace complex in Jerusalem as interpreted above seems to differ in one respect from the pattern of the palaces at Megiddo, Zincirli, and Tell Tayanat. In Jerusalem a single *bīt-ḥilāni* building is described, and it should be compared to the main palace building in the above sites. In these sites we find additional *bīt-ḥilānis* which are unparalleled in the description of the palace in Jerusalem. And instead, the Jerusalem palace contains a unique structure, "the house of the forest of Lebanon."

[23] The best example of Israelite walls constructed in Phoenician style can be seen in Samaria. See J. W. Crowfoot and others, *Samaria-Sebaste I: The Buildings* (1942), Pls. XII-XXXII.

14

LIFE IN THE DIASPORA: JEWS AT NIPPUR IN THE FIFTH CENTURY B.C.

MICHAEL D. COOGAN

In 594 B.C., some three years after the deportation of King Jehoiakin and several thousand craftsmen and military and court officials to Babylonia, Jeremiah advised the exiles: "Build houses to live in, and plant gardens and eat their fruit. Take wives and beget sons and daughters. . . . Multiply there and do not decrease. Seek the peace of the city to which I have sent you, and pray for it to Yahweh, for in its peace you will have peace" (Jer. 29:4-7). Apart from the fragmentary cuneiform records listing rations provided to Jehoiakin in Babylon,[1] little is known of the life of the deportees of 597 and 587 B.C. But they and their descendants must have followed Jeremiah's advice, to judge from a remarkable collection of documents dating from the following century in which Jewish names frequently occur.

This collection, the most important single source for our knowledge of the Babylonian Diaspora during the Persian period, was found in 1893 during the excavations at ancient Nippur by the University of Pennsylvania.[2] It is a corpus of some seven hundred and thirty tablets dating from the reigns of Artaxerxes I (464-424 B.C.) and Darius II (424-404 B.C.). Known as the Murashu documents, after the head of the banking family whose records they were, these tablets, although prosaic in content, have proven to be of considerable interest for orientalists. In the following pages we will examine some of the documents in which the Jews are mentioned in order to sketch the life of the exiles in Nippur.

The Murashu documents are written in Akkadian cuneiform. On many of them a brief inscription written in Aramaic with ink has also been preserved. Called dockets or endorsements, these inscriptions usually contain a brief summary of a document and the name of the person with whom the banking firm was doing business; they served as filing labels. (The practice of enclosing a

Illus. 29

tablet in a clay envelope inscribed with a duplicate contract had been discontinued by the Neo-Babylonian period.) Most of the tablets also have seal impressions (or occasionally fingernail marks) of one or more of the principals and witnesses.

The names of the principals and witnesses in the various contracts show that Nippur was a cosmopolitan city under Persian rule. Apart from the large number of individuals with Babylonian names there were also many Persians, Medes, Egyptians and West Semites; the last group included Jews with biblical names such as Hanani, Shabbatai and Jonathan.[3] An initial problem is to isolate those individuals and families which were Jewish. The fact that a name which occurs in the Murashu documents is also attested in the Bible is not significant, for many of the names in use in Jewish communities at various periods are not exclusively or identifiably Jewish. As we shall see, many of the Jews at Nippur had names which we can identify linguistically as Aramaic or Babylonian, but such names were naturally not restricted to Jews. Notorious biblical examples of this practice are Esther and Mordecai, whose names are derived from the Babylonian deities Ishtar and Marduk; further examples of this kind of religious syncretism are discussed below. In addition, because of the close relationship between Aramaic and Hebrew, it is often impossible to identify the language of a name more precisely than to say that it is West Semitic. This is especially true in the case of nicknames and abbreviated names, generally called hypocoristica. Despite such ambiguities, however, we can isolate with certainty several Jewish families in the Murashu documents by combining linguistic and genealogical data.

One example is the family of Tob-yaw. The only published contract in which it occurs is X.118, unfortunately too fragmentary to translate here; from what remains of the tablet we can establish the membership of this family as follows:

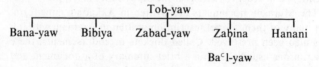

Four of these names, Tob-yaw, Bana-yaw, Zabad-yaw and Ba^{c}l-yaw, have as their second element -*yaw*, the form of the divine name Yahweh used in final position in personal names at Nippur in this period (and elsewhere in other periods, notably in the Samaria ostraca some three centuries earlier); these individuals were certainly Jews. The biblical equivalents of their names are Tobiah, Benaiah, Zebediah, and Bealiah. It is thus reasonable to assume that the rest of the family was Jewish as well. Of the remaining names, Hanani is a common hypocoristicon of names such as Hananiah; Minahhim is the equivalent of biblical Menahem; Zabina is Aramaic, but was used by Jews, for it is one of the names of the returning exiles (Ezra 10:43); and Bibiya is an Akkadian name meaning "baby" which occurs in the form of Bebai in Ezra 2:11.

In IX.45[4] several Jewish principals have jointly made a contract with the sons of Murashu:

> Yadi^c-yaw, the son of Bana-^ʔel; Yahu-natan, Shama^con and Ahi-yaw, the sons of Yadi^c-yaw; Satur, the son of Shabbatai; Baniya, the son of Amel-nama; Yigdal-yaw, the son of Nana-iddin; Abda, the son of Apla; Nattun, the son of Shillim; and all their partners in Bit-gira; spoke freely to Ellil-shum-iddin, the son of Murashu, as follows: "Rent to us for three years the Mares' Canal, from its inlet up to its outlet, and the tithed field which is on this canal, and the field which is to the left of the Milidu Canal, and the three marshes which are to the right of the Milidu Canal, except the field which drinks (its) waters from the Ellil Canal; and we will give you annually 700 *kur* of barley according to the standard measure of Ellil-shum-iddin, and, as an annual gift, 2 grazing bulls and 20 grazing rams.

The rest of this typical contract quotes Ellil-shum-iddin's acceptance of the terms, describes the mutual responsibilites of the lessees, and concludes with the usual list of witnesses and the date formula (year 36 of Artaxerxes, or 428 B.C.).

By combining the data of this tablet with those found in another tablet, IX.25, we can reconstruct the following genealogy:

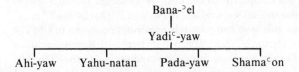

Four of the names of the members of this family are Yahwistic, and all have close biblical parallels from the post-exilic period (as do most of the Jewish names in the Murashu documents): compare, respectively, Benaiah, Jedaiah and Jediael, Ahijah, Jehonathan, Pedaiah and Shimeon.

Of the other principals in the contract, Yigdal-yaw is certainly Jewish; his name, like its biblical parallel Igdaliah, means "Yahweh is great." It is interesting to note that his father, Nana-iddin, has a Babylonian name. Nattun and Satur may be Jewish, but the genealogical and linguistic evidence is not conclusive.

In this document Yadi^c-yaw, his sons and his partners have agreed to lease certain properties with irrigation rights from the Murashu firm for three years at a rate of 700 *kur* of barley per year plus a small surcharge (the bulls and the rams). Since money was not generally used for local transactions in Nippur, payment in kind was the ordinary medium of exchange used by tenant farmers such as Yadi^c-yaw and his group. A *kur* was about four bushels, so they were renting a sizable acreage. The land was not owned by the Murashu firm itself, but belonged to absentee landlords who invested their property with the firm in exchange for a guaranteed rate; the firm was thus primarily a middleman.

Neither in this tablet nor in any of the others which mention identifiable Jewish individuals is there any hint of discrimination or of restriction on religious or ethnic grounds.[5] Jews are engaged in the same types of contractual relationships, at the same interest rates, as their non-Jewish contemporaries at Nippur. Thus, Mattan-yaw, the son of Shulum-babil (UM 148), was a sheep and goat herder; ^cAqab-yaw, the son of Bau-etir (UM 27 and 89), was a date-grower; Zabad-yaw, the son of Ḥinni-bel (UM 208), was a fisherman. Another (?) Zabad-yaw was a partner of Abi-yaw, the son of Shabbatai (UM 218), in the cultivation of "bow-land" (*bīt qashti*); this was a type of fief originally granted to military colonists of the Persian Empire who had to provide an archer and/or his equipment to the army in exchange for the grant of land. (Similar fiefs were called "horse-land," "chariot-land," etc.)

At least two Jews had relatively important positions. In UM 121 El-yadin, the son of Yadi^c-yaw, is associated with Rimut-ninurta, a member of the Murashu firm, as co-creditor in a transaction. The reason for this association is not clear; since the tablet was not written at Nippur but at Sin-belshunu, it is possible that El-yadin was the representative of the firm in that (unidentified) locality. Secondly, in X.65 and UM 205, Yishrib-yaw, the son of Pilli-yaw, is mentioned; the former tablet speaks of him as the chief officer (*shaknu*) of the serfs of the royal treasury, apparently a temporary or rotating position, since the latter tablet, written the following year, ascribes the same title to a certain Ismun.

As we have observed, not a few of the Jewish exiles mentioned in the Murashu documents have non-Yahwistic names. Since they occur in legally binding documents, they must have been the names actually used by their bearers, at least in public. Both extra-biblical and biblical sources suggest that after the exile the use of Babylonian names by Jews became more and more common not only in Babylonia but in Judah as well. One group upon whom pressure to adopt foreign names must have been strong was the remnant of the royal house of Judah; three members of this family who figure prominently among the first returnees in 538 B.C. have Babylonian names: Shealtiel and his son Zerubbabel, and the latter's uncle Sheshbazzar (assuming that Sheshbazzar [Ezra 1:8; 5:14] and Senazzar [I Chron. 3:18] are identical). Others with Babylonian names among the exiles returning to Judah include Bilshan, Hattush, Mordecai and Nekoda. (We should also allow for the possibility that some of the Jews in exile had two names: one Babylonian, used for legal purposes, and a specifically Jewish name as well. Knowledge of such a practice is attested in the story of Esther, who is introduced in Esther 2:7 as Hadassah, and also in Daniel 1:7.)

In the Murashu documents, Jewish individuals with names containing a Babylonian deity include Shamesh-ladin, the son of Yadi^c-yaw (X.94), Bau-etir, the father of ^cAqab-yaw (UM 27, 89), and Bel-uballit, the father of Mattan-yaw (UM 53). Other examples could be listed, especially of Jews whose fathers had more neutral types of Babylonian names, but those we have seen prove our point—it was not considered a serious compromise of one's Jewish identity to give a child a name which was not Yahwistic, nor even of Hebrew or Aramaic stock.

In fact, there is some evidence which suggests that at least a few fathers deliberately gave their sons names which were intentionally ambiguous: to a Jew they would sound Jewish, but to a Babylonian they would seem to be Babylonian. One example is derived from the West Semitic root ᶜ*qb*, "to guard, to protect." While well-attested in personal names of the second millennium (as in the name Jacob), this root was generally restricted during the first millennium to milieus in which Aramaic was the spoken language; it was especially popular at Nippur, where it is used in the names of eighteen individuals in the Murashu documents. This popularity may be explained by the frequency with which the similar sounding (but unrelated) Akkadian verb *qabû* is used in personal names of the Neo-Babylonian period. With this background it is striking to note a sudden increase of the root in biblical names of the exilic period, especially in the name Aqqub (borne by six individuals in Chronicles, Ezra and Nehemiah). It seems that Jews in Babylonia started to use the root in naming their children, and that the practice spread from Babylon to Judah with the returning exiles.

A similar influence of the biblical onomasticon may be observed in the increased use of the divine element ᵓ*ēl* in personal names during the latter half of the first millennium. Although used frequently during the second millennium, ᵓ*ēl* occurs only sporadically in names of individuals who lived during the time of the Israelite and Judean monarchies, and undergoes a sudden increase in popularity after the exile. This revival of an older style, while not unrelated to the general renewal of interest in Israel's past which characterizes much of the post-exilic literature, may also have been due to a conscious intent to be ambiguous. Since the Hebrew word ᵓ*ēl* was almost identical in sound to its Akkadian cognate *il(u)*, its use by the post-exilic community in Judah in their childen's names may reflect a tendency to assimilation to the Babylonians with whom they had frequent contact. This hypothesis is strengthened by a comparison of the contemporary communities at Nippur and at Elephantine in Egypt, the island far up the Nile, from which Aramaic papyri belonging to a Jewish military colony of the 5th century have come. While the element ᵓ*ēl* is used frequently in the names of individuals in the Murashu documents, it occurs only twice in names found in the Elephantine papyri; at Elephantine, of course, the potential for capitalizing on similar-sounding name-elements we have described would not have been available.

Finally, the frequency with which the Hebrew root *škn*, "to live, to dwell," occurs in post-exilic sources may also have been influenced in part by Babylonian contacts. Its use was in harmony with the developing priestly theology of the presence of God,[6] but may also have been affected by ambiguity with the common Akkadian verb *šakānu*. The name Shekeniah, borne by six individuals in Chronicles, Ezra and Nehemiah, should be compared with the name Shikin-ʾel in the Murashu documents.

Other influences, especially syntactic ones, of the experience of the Babylonian Diaspora upon Israelite namegiving could be added, but the point has already been sufficiently made. Names are only clues to beliefs and customs, and to social pressure and language.

Although they are neither great literature nor important historical sources, the Murashu documents do provide a significant glimpse into the social and commercial life of a Babylonian city under Persian rule, and thus help to augment our knowledge of the onomastic practices, occupations and circumstances of the Diaspora. Like their contemporaries at Elephantine, by the fifth century B.C. the exiles at Nippur had become fully integrated into the economic life of their society, fulfilling the injunctions of Jeremiah 29:5ff. perhaps even more thoroughly than the prophet had intended!

Notes

[1] See W. F. Albright, *BA* 5 (1942), 49-55.

[2] For a brief account of the discovery of the tablets, see H. V. Hilprecht, *Explorations in Bible Lands During the 19th Century* (1903), pp. 408-12. Most of the tablets were edited by Hilprecht and A. T. Clay, and were published as Cols. IX and X of *The Babylonian Expedition of the University of Pennsylvania*, Series A (1898 and 1904), and as Vol. II, Part I of *Publications of the Babylonian Section of the Museum of the University of Pennsylvania* (1912). Henceforth we shall cite these volumes as IX, X, and UM, respectively.

[3] In one of the Aramaic endorsements this name is written in alphabetic script as *yhwntn*; its cuneiform spelling was *ya-(a)-ḫu-u-na-ta(n)-nu*.

[4] This tablet, along with twenty-four others, most of them previously unpublished, was found in a trunk belonging to H. V. Hilprecht's wife after her death, and was re-edited by Oluf Krückmann in 1933. Other

translations of the Murashu documents into English may be found in J. B. Pritchard, *Ancient Near Eastern Texts Relating to the Old Testament* (1969), p. 221, and in D. W. Thomas, *Documents from Old Testament Times* (1961), pp. 95-96. The most complete study of the tablets is G. Cardascia, *Les archives des Murašu* (1951). See now also M. D. Coogan, *West Semitic Personal Names in the Murašu Documents* (Missoula, MT: Scholars Press, 1976).

[5]It is worth noting, however, that none of the scribes of the more than 500 published tablets has a non-Babylonian name. This is doubtless due to the indigenous character of the scribal schools, as well as to the difficulty of acquiring fluency in the Neo-Babylonian syllabary.

[6]See M. Noth, *Die israelitischen Personennamen in Rahmen der gemeinsemitischen Namengebung* (1928), pp. 194, 215; and F. M. Cross, *BA* 10 (1947), 65-68, reprinted in *BA Reader* I (1961), pp. 224-27.

15

THE WORKS OF AMMINADAB

HENRY O. THOMPSON AND FAWZI ZAYADINE

The third-year students majoring in archaeology at the University of Jordan are required to do 100 hours in field work. Fulfilling this requirement, they made a strong contribution to the staff of Tell Hesban in 1971 and to Dornemann's excavation on the Amman Citadel in 1968. In considering their assignment for 1972, Dr. Adnan Hadidi of the University's Department of History and Archaeology suggested we look at Tell Siran on the University grounds. This tell appears on an antiquities map in Arabic and on a 1932 road map of Jordan. A surface survey netted sherds from five periods: Mameluke, Umayyid, Byzantine, Hellenistic, and Iron II (7th/6th centuries B.C.). All five periods need additional archaeological information in the East Jordan area and when you have student excavators to train, a tell on campus is about as convenient a site as one can find!

The excavation ran from April 17 to May 16, 1972. The students gained practice in all facets of the work. They received training in site layout, stratigraphic excavation, and the washing, recording and drawing of artifacts. Unfortunately, only two loci were Umayyid (7th-8th cents. A.D.) and all the others were Mameluke (post-Crusader), so apart from quantities of sherds, they did not experience the excavation of the five different periods of which the surface sherds gave promise. We hope these can be found elsewhere on the mound. The Mameluke remains, especially the cisterns and underground rooms, are interesting in themselves and give ample reward to the excavators; a report on the excavations was published in the *Annual of the Department of Antiquities of Jordan* 18 (1973), 5-14.

Among the artifacts was a bronze, bottle-shaped object about four inches or ten centimeters long. When it was discovered on April 27, it excited curiosity, but its heavily corroded surface gave

Illus. 30-1

no hint of what was to come. When the metal objects were cleaned at the end of the excavation, the bottle turned out to be inscribed! Dr. Fawzi Zayadine made the initial translation of what proves to be the first complete Ammonite inscription ever discovered. Its eight lines of text contain 25 words and 92 letters; this compares with the 93 letters of the Amman Citadel inscription,[1] so the Siran inscription ranks as one of the longest as well.

The fourth line runs the longest; its last word bends around the bottom of the bottle. This bending slightly distorts the last three letters, which can probably be identified as *t, ḥ,* and *r*, though with some question remaining. Apart from these three, all the letters are clearly legible. In fact, they are so clear that several have asked if the inscription is really ancient. Since major museums are being fooled by fakes, one hesitates to be absolute about this. However, most copies or modern forgeries imitate or repeat known inscriptions. So far at least, there is nothing comparable to the Siran writing, though we will observe some standard formulae when we get to the translation below. Further, forgeries tend to mix letter forms of various periods. The forms of the Siran letters cluster in a fairly narrow period, centering around 700 B.C., judging from our paleographic analysis, about 100 years later according to Frank Cross. Historical considerations place the date of the inscription *ca.* 600 B.C., but official records often archaized in the way letters were formed. The figure of 700 is based on comparison with Aramaic, the script which is closest to our Siran inscription, but there may have been some cultural lag between developments in Syria and the impact of that development in the area of Amman; indeed, the only sure way to draw chronological conclusions from the study of writing is to have a good deal of datable material from the same general region and belonging to the same language.

In comparing an inscription with other writings, one begins with the ethnic group at hand, which in this case is the Ammonites. Most of the known Ammonite inscriptions are short names or phrases found on seals. They in turn have often been dated in relation to a king of the Ammonites named Amminadab, whose name appears on two seals from Amman, the seals of Adoni-Nur and Adonipelet.[2] This Amminadab is often equated with the king of the same name mentioned by Ashurbanipal, king of Assyria, about 667 B.C. We will return to this shortly, but here we can say that since Siran now gives us *two* Amminadabs as kings of the Ammonites, we must ask which one is referred to on the seals—or could each be represented by one of them? In any case, this means that no Ammonite inscription is dated to an absolute year; we can only date the Theater inscription,[3] the Citadel inscription mentioned above, and the others, relative to one another.

For the time being, then, we have to go outside of the Ammonite corpus. There are comparisons to be found with Moabite, Edomite, Hebrew, and Phoenician scripts, but the closest comparisons are found in materials written in Aramaic.[4] Let us give only a few examples to show what we mean. Ten of the eleven *b*'s in the Siran inscription have a head which is open, so that the letter looks like the English "y"; a good example is the fifth letter from the left of the first line on the Siran bottle. Now in the Aramaic script, the change from the closed head to the open one took place about 700-675 B.C. Just the opposite is the case with *d*; on the Siran bottle it is virtually closed—see the fourth and eighth letters from the right on line one of the bottle; in Aramaic script it opened up between 700 and 675. Another example: the hard "h"-sound (*ḥ*) is shaped like a ladder with two bars, as in the fourth letter from the right of line 5. This two-bar form appears in Ammonite and Moabite around 850 B.C.; in Aramaic script it appears about 750, but moves rapidly to a one-bar form about 700 B.C. Similar examples could be drawn from eleven other letter forms in the inscription, all pointing to around 700 B.C., if comparison to Aramaic scripts is the indicator.[5] As we have noted, such comparison has its perils, whether we think in terms of cultural lag or think instead that any script in relative isolation can develop its own peculiarities at its own pace. As we shall see, the attempt to date the kings named on the Siran bottle will point toward a later date.

The Words

The first word of the inscription is *m^c bd* which is derived from the verb "to do or make." The noun is probably in the construct state so it means here, "the works of." The "works" are those of Amminadab, king of the Ammonites. Note the frequent appear-

ance of this name in the Bible (Exod. 6:23; Ruth 4:19f.; etc.) and its
assumed meaning "my kinsman is generous (or noble)." A south
Semitic deity is named ꜥAmm, which raises the possibility that the
name means "my (god) ꜥAmm is generous." The name could be
applied to the people of Ammon. Their god is usally called Milcom
but this could be a royal title while the personal name, ꜥAmm, has
been lost to view.

The second line tells us that Amminadab was the son of Hiṣṣal-
ꜣEl—the reading was proposed to us by Cross—who was also king
of the Ammonites. He in turn was the son of another Amminadab,
king of the Ammonites. Hiṣṣal-ꜣEl may mean "El delivers or
protects."

The works of the first Amminadab include a vineyard and
gardens and something called ꜣthr and cisterns. In Isaiah 5, God is
described as planting a vineyard. While the work of a farmer is not
normally considered royal or divine in today's world, it was
apparently an activity worthy of ancient kings and deities. The
author of Ecclesiastes claims

> I made great works ($m^c sy$); I built houses and planted vineyards for
> myself; I made myself gardens and parks, and planted in them all
> kinds of fruit trees. I made myself pools from which to water the
> forest of growing trees. (Eccles. 2:4, RSV)

Our word ꜥthr is probably a new Semitic root—so Cross. A
South Arabic word for throne dias is ꜣthn. If the final r is a badly
misshapen n, or if we have Aramaic influence here with an original
n changed to r (as bn for "son" changed to br—a proposal made by
Mr. Christian Robin), we have an attractive translation for our
word. A throne dias in the midst of the king's garden would be an
attractive place to hold court. However, the term is quite different
from the other three "works" and the Aramaic did not influence a
change of bn to br in the first three lines of the Siran inscription.
Another possibility is the hollow verb ḥr, "to be white or hollow,"
with a derived noun meaning hole or hiding place. The hole(s) may
have been storage places for the fruit or additional water.

The word for cisterns, ꜣšḥt, is interesting because it appears in
the singular in the Mesha Stone from Dhiban. This famous
Moabite inscription dates from about 850 B.C. The term probably

derives from the root for "sink down," hence a reservoir or cistern as sunk in the rock.

Line six expresses a joyous wish for Amminadab: "May he (or, let him) rejoice and be glad." The phrase occurs several times in the Bible, for example in Psalms 31:7 and 118:24. Lines 7 and 8 close with the hope that Amminadab will have a life of "many days and long years." The inscription as a whole can be translated:

> The works of Amminadab, king of the Ammonites,
> the son of Hiṣṣal-ʾEl, king of the Ammonites,
> the son of Amminadab, king of the Ammonites,
> a vineyard and gardens and the ʾthr and cisterns.
> May he rejoice and be glad
> for many days and long years.

The Kings of Ammon

The Ammonite kings between 750 and 580 B.C. are known from Assyrian and biblical sources as follows: Shanipu (733 B.C.), (?) Zakir, Yeraḥ^cazar, Bod-ʾEl (700), Amminadab (667), (?) Ḥanan-ʾEl (620), Ba^clys (580). Shanipu paid tribute to the Assyrian king, Tiglath-pileser. He may also be the Ammonite king who rebelled against Jotham when Israel was ruling the area, according to 2 Chronicles 27:5. Zayadine has now read the Amman statue inscription as Yeraḥ^cazar, son of Zakir, son of Shanib. The last is identified with Shanipu.[6] A prism of Sennacherib (704-681) refers to his third campaign and a king named Buduili. A fragmentary text of Esarhaddon (680-669) mentions Puduil as king of Beth-Ammon. The Assyrian king, Ashurbanipal (668-627) refers to Bod-ʾel as king of the Ammonites. All three of these references are thought to be to the same king. This is crucial to the historical dating of the Siran inscription. Ashurbanipal's Cylinder C inscription refers to "Ammi-nabdi" as king of Ammon about 667. Thus one would assume that Bod-ʾEl was already old when Ashurbanipal started as king and Amminadab succeeded him within a year. He was probably, although not certainly, the son of Bod-ʾEl. The Ḥanan-ʾEl in the above list is found on an Ammonite seal and he is assumed king partly by analogy with the older name Ḥanun (990 B.C.). Ba^clys was the king who plotted with Ishmael to kill Gedaliah, the governor of what the Babylonians left of the kingdom of Judah (Jer. 40:14).

Hiṣṣal-ʾEl is a completely new addition to our knowledge of Ammonite kings. If the list on the Siran bottle is complete, he would eliminate Ḥananʾel as a king, perhaps making the latter a government official. However, if one assumes that the Siran listing, like other lists of ancient kings, is not complete, Ḥanan-ʾEl could still be considered a king of Ammon. The Siran list may simply jump from Amminadab's father to an ancestor Amminadab, rather than to the immediate biological "grandfather" Amminadab. Following Cross's dating, he would be a descendant.[7] Cross (op. cit.) suggests the 667 Amminadab (the seals and Ashurbanipal) is the father of an unknown son, and grandfather of Siran line 3 Amminadab, whom Cross dates to ca. 635 B.C. Cross puts Hiṣṣal-ʾEl ca. 620 and line 1 Amminadab ca. 600.

Summary

The addition of the Siran bottle inscription to the Amman Citadel and Theater inscriptions, and possibly the Deir ʿAlla writings, as well as the continuing contributions of the seals and other inscriptions, means that we are gradually filling out our knowledge of the ancient Ammonite language. In the meanwhile, excavations such as those at Hesban, Khirbet el-Hajjar, Rujm el-Malluf South, Rujm el-Mekheizen, Sahab, and Amman, fill out our picture of their material remains. Archaeology is once more living up to its purpose in making ancient people come alive in the pages of history.

Notes

[1] S. H. Horn, *BASOR* No. 193 (Feb., 1969), pp. 2-13.

[2] C. C. Torrey, *AASOR* 2-3 (1931-2), 103-8; G. L. Harding, *Quarterly of the Department of Antiquities of Palestine* 11 (1944), 67-74, and G. R. Driver, *ibid.,* pp. 81f.

[3] R. W. Dajani, *Annual of the Department of Antiquities of Jordan* 12-13 (1967-68), 65ff. Cross calls this inscription cursive Aramaic in an editorial comment. Cf. Henry O. Thompson and Fawzi Zayadine, "The Tell Siran Inscription," *BASOR* 212 (1973), 5-11, n. 2. Cf. also William J. Fulco, "The Amman Theater Inscription," *Journal of Near Eastern Studies* 38.1 (1979), 37-38.

[4] J. Naveh, *Israel Exploration Journal* 17 (1967), 256-8, and *Proceedings of the Israel Academy of Sciences and Humanities* 5, No. 1 (1970); Franz Rosenthal, *Die aramaistische Forschung,* Leiden, 1939, Schrifttafel; B. L. Haines, *A Paleographic Study of Aramaic Inscriptions Antedating 500 B.C.,* an unpublished dissertation for the doctoral program of Harvard University, Cambridge, 1966. On the Ammonite material, see especially F. M. Cross, *BASOR* No. 193 (Feb., 1969), pp. 13-19. Dr. James A. Sauer has collected many of the Ammonite materials in an unpublished paper, "Ammonite Inscriptions," which he has kindly made available to this study. This has been extremely helpful and his assistance is gratefully acknowledged. We also owe a debt of gratitude to Frank M. Cross for several proposals credited to him in the course of the study of the text. Cf. also Pierre Bordreuil, "Inscriptions Sigillaires Ouest-Sémitiques," *Syria* 50 (1973), 181-95.

[5] A more complete paleographic study is published in *Berytus* 22 (1973), 115-40.

[6] Fawzi Zayadine, "Note Sur L'Inscription de la Statue D'Amman J. 1656," *Syria* 51 (1974), 129-36.

[7] He says the script of this seal is advanced. "Notes on the Ammonite Inscription from Tell Siran," *BASOR* 212 (1973), 12-15, n. 23.

Part III

ARCHAEOLOGY AND
THE RELIGIOUS LIFE

16

THE "GHASSULIAN" TEMPLE IN EIN GEDI AND THE ORIGIN OF THE HOARD FROM NAHAL MISHMAR

DAVID USSISHKIN

The culture predominant during the Chalcolithic period in Palestine is known as the "Ghassulian Culture," named after Teleilat el-Ghassul in the Jordan valley, where it was discovered in 1929.[1] Ghassulian settlements were later discovered at many sites, mainly located in the peripheral areas of the country. They are found in the Jordan valley, the Judean desert, the coastal plain, the northern and western Negev, and even in southern Sinai. On the other hand, the Ghassulians (as we shall call the bearers of the Ghassulian culture) rarely settled in the hilly and northern parts of the country. For various reasons we can safely conclude that the Ghassulians immigrated into Palestine, bringing with them a well-defined culture of their own. No distinctive connections between the Ghassulian culture and those which characterized Palestine at the end of the Neolithic period[2] can be discerned and the early stages in the development of the Ghassulian culture seem to be missing in Palestine. The typical features of the culture evidently point to external connections and developments which occurred elsewhere, and the Ghassulian settlements are found particularly on sites which previously had not been settled. It is difficult to date accurately the Ghassulian immigration and settlement in Palestine, but they should probably be generally dated to the second half, or even the third quarter of the fourth millennium B.C.

A few points characterize the Ghassulian settlements and culture. The settlements were relatively small, dependent on primitive agriculture, and they lasted for a relatively short period.[3] It seems to have been a peaceful era as none of the settlements were fortified. They were finally abandoned, and no signs of deliberate destruction or conflagration indicating an enemy conquest were found in them. The same culture with its typical imaginative pottery predominates in all the Ghassulian sites, but in each area

Illus. 8-10

we observe a local trend or specialization in the architecture, crafts, and art. These merit our special attention. The Ghassulians introduced to the country crystalized architectural and artistic concepts and traditions, developed due to an evident aesthetic flair, unusual gifts, technical knowledge and experience in working with various new raw materials. In each area, a special branch of the culture was developed, sometimes reaching achievements unparalleled in later periods in Palestine. And here we should stress one point: the Ghassulian art is strongly connected with the yet unknown Ghassulian religious cult. In other words, the craftsmen and artists were not motivated by pure artistic inspiration but their creations were applied to the Ghassulian cult, and were meant to be used in the rituals. Finally, it should be stressed that it was the Ghassulians who introduced the manufacture of copper to Palestine. Their mastery in metalwork, which will be demonstrated in course of this article, undoubtedly contributed to the general prosperity of the culture.

We shall briefly mention a few aspects of the Ghassulian architecture and art. Most impressive in Teleilat el-Ghassul are the paintings which decorated the plastered walls of the houses.[4] In Bir-Matar and Bir-Safadi near Beersheba the Ghassulians first lived in large subterranean "houses," sometimes containing a few chambers, and only later changed first to semi-subterranean houses and then to above-ground houses.[5] In Bir-Matar the remains of a copper industry were discovered[6] while the inhabitants of the adjacent site, Bir-Safadi, specialized in the art of ivory carving, manufacturing figurines and other objects, probably talismans.[7] In Beersheba, as well as at other sites, large, meticulously carved basalt bowls and chalices,[8] as well as beautiful flint implements,[9] were found. On the coastal plain many burial caves were discovered, in which the dead were given "secondary burial" in clay ossuaries.[10] The ossuaries were individually shaped and decorated, in some cases imitating houses; they present another curious aspect of the culture.

The Temple in Ein Gedi

We shall now turn to the Judean desert, where the discoveries which form the main subject of this article were made. The oasis of

Ein Gedi, situated beside the western shore of the Dead Sea, forms one of the most beautiful spots in the desolate region. Not far from and parallel to the shore stretches a ridge of high cliffs, rising to a height of about 1000 feet. On the lower slope of the cliff, but at a considerable height above the lake (though still more than 600 feet below sea level), is situated the spring of Ein Gedi, the main source of water in the oasis. Another spring can be found but a few minutes' walk to the north, in the gorge of Nahal David. At a distance of about 150 yards to the north of (and some 100 feet higher than) the Ein Gedi spring, between it and Nahal David, a prominent rock terrace was chosen by the Ghassulians to build a temple.

Our temple is the main Ghassulian shrine known to us in southern Palestine. No remains of a Chalcolithic settlement were discovered in the area, and one has to conclude that the temple formed a focus for pilgrimage. The site chosen for the construction of the temple fits well the concept of a central isolated shrine. The rock terrace lies nearly underneath the barren, vertical cliff, ominously rising behind it, and high above the Dead Sea. A large section of the sea can be seen from the site, with the hills of Moab looming beyond. We can imagine the Ghassulian worshippers traveling to Ein Gedi from far away, climbing the cliffs and, arriving at the temple, stunned by the inspiring view.

The main lines of the edifice were visible without excavation. The site was discovered by Y. Aharoni in 1956, but the absence of pottery on the site prevented him from dating it.[11] The same year J. Naveh dug a small section in the lateral chamber; he dated the structure and suggested that it was a public building, "perhaps a sanctuary."[12] The temple was excavated in 1962 by the Hebrew University expedition to Ein Gedi, directed by B. Mazar and the late I. Dunayevsky.[13] The clearing of the courtyard was completed in 1964. Following the dig, the walls were skillfully strengthened, and the circular installation restored by M. Jaffe, thus preserving the remains of the edifice from further destruction.

It seems that the structures of the temple were adapted to the topography, since on three sides the walls reach the edges of the rock-terrace on which the edifice was constructed. The temple includes four separate structures: the main gate-building, the secondary gate, the lateral chamber, and the sanctuary. The four structures were connected to one another by a stone fence, thus forming an enclosure or courtyard. A circular installation was built in the center of the enclosure. The lower part of the walls of the structures was built of stones, fitted with care into the walls, with clay and small stones filling the gaps. The upper part of the structures was built of sun-dried bricks which, following the collapse of the structures, disintegrated and formed the debris accumulated around the lower parts of the walls. As a result the walls were mostly preserved to a height of one to three feet. Only the fence surrounding the enclosure and the circular installation seem to have been built solely from stones.

We shall start our description with the main gate-building. This formed the main gate of the enclosure, situated at the edge of the rock terrace and facing the spring of Ein Gedi. It contained outer and inner entrances, and a door was constructed in the former. A stone bench, about nine to twelve inches high, was built in the gate-chamber along all the walls except the section of the wall to the right of the outer entrance. The bench consisted of a row of large stones with flat tops, with smaller stones and clay filling the gaps. The secondary gate was oriented towards Nahal David, probably for the use of those who came from that spring. This gate was simpler in plan although finely constructed, and, amazingly, it could not be closed, since no door was constructed in it (cf. below)! The lateral chamber measures 7.5 by 4.5 meters (about 25 by 15 feet). The entrance was built in the center of the long wall which formed the chamber's facade. A paved path, 2.25 meters (about 7 1/2 feet) long, leads to the entrance of the chamber from the courtyard. A stone bench or step, composed of one row of stones about a foot wide and six to eight inches high, stretches along the facade. The chamber had a plastered floor and was found almost empty. Presumably it was used as a store for the temple's equipment or as a room for the use of the priests.

The sanctuary forms the largest and the most important building in the enclosure. It is a rectangular stone structure, 19.70 meters long and 5.5 meters wide (about 67 by 18 feet). Its width was probably limited by the ability of the architects to roof over the sanctuary without using pillars. A stone bench or step, mainly composed of one row of big stones, with small stones and clay filling the gaps, about eight inches high and a foot or more wide, was constructed on the outside around the walls of the sanctuary. Like the lateral chamber, the sanctuary is of the broad-house type, and its entrance was built in the center of the long wall, with the bench mentioned above forming a step in front of it. Two big stones placed in front of the bench form a second, lower step. In the sanctuary, opposite the entrance and adjacent to the rear wall, was constructed the sole altar of the temple. It has the shape of a horseshoe and is marked by a row of large stones. The altar contained a thick layer of ashes, the accumulated remains of ritual ceremonies. In the ashes were found burnt twigs and tiny bones, pieces of bitumen, many non-marine mollusca, beads, and broken clay figurines. In the right back corner of the altar was found a stone base, well carved but a little asymmetrical, and about ten inches high. It is round and it has a flattened top, while its bottom was left in the rough. Significantly, the base was carved from crystalline limestone, a kind of stone not available in the immediate vicinity of the temple. Thus the base is white in color, and it stands out in a temple built of darker local stones. We believe that it formed the base for the statue or cult-symbol of the deity whose cult was performed in the temple. In the central part of the sanctuary, stone benches were found similar to those in the gate-building. They are constructed from large stones with flat tops along the rear wall on both sides of the altar, along the front wall on both sides of the entrance, and in the central part of the chamber on both sides of the altar. On two sides of the sanctuary, between the benches and the lateral walls, small, round pits were dug in the floor. These are about twenty inches deep and seem to have been refuse pits into which the remains of the offerings were thrown. The pits were found full to overflowing with these remains, and most of the pottery discovered in the excavation was found in them.

Noteworthy is the construction of the entrances to these structures. Wooden doors seem to have been installed in the outer entrance of the gate-building, as well as in the entrances to the lateral chamber and the sanctuary. A stone socket for the support of the door-hinge was found in the inner, right-hand corner of the entrances. That part of the wall behind the stone socket formed a recess in the wall, into which the door fitted when opened inwards at an angle of 180°. In the outer entrance of the gate-building there was no such recess; instead, the stone bench was absent along this section of the wall. On the opposite side, the inner left-hand corner of the entrances, another recess or double-corner, some six to eight inches in width and depth, was constructed. This recess was probably meant to contain a wooden door-frame or a lock for the door. Significantly, no such arrangements were found in the secondary gate and thus it could not be closed with a door. Here the gate passage, in other words, the threshold of the entrance, was paved with flat stones stretching beyond the inner edge of the gate. The stone threshold was found intact, and it did not contain a stone socket for supporting a door hinge.

A word must be said at this point on the possibility that the structures were decorated with wall-paintings, like many buildings in Teleilat el-Ghassul.[14] This possibility is based on the discovery of a tiny fragment of painted plaster in the channel which is mentioned below. The fragment is only about an inch long and its surface is not even—which suggests that it belongs to an installation rather than a wall. The decoration of the main surface consists of a few parallel wavy lines, one thick pink, and three dark blue ones. Significantly, this fragment was plastered and painted twice beforehand, as in the case of Teleilat el-Ghassul, where Hennessy discerned a wall which was replastered and repainted more than twenty times.[15]

Finally, we turn to the circular installation, ten feet in diameter, built in the highest part of the courtyard. In its center a round basin, about sixteen inches deep and a foot in diameter, was constructed. At present, seven large flat stones form the wall of the basin, the bottom being the natural surface; but, assuming that the basin was meant to contain liquids, it must have been plastered. In fact, it can almost be proved that the basin contained liquids. In the section of the stone fence between the secondary gate and the lateral chamber a built outlet of a channel was discovered.[16] The orientation of the channel and the fact that its bottom is built at a level eight to nine inches lower than that of the bottom of the circular installation indicate that it was used to dispose of the liquids, probably water, from the basin, although it seems clear that they were not directly connected. The channel was not preserved and it was probably constructed of mud-bricks and clay.

The date of the temple and its cultural affinities were determined by the pottery, mainly the remains of the offering-vessels found in the refuse pits in the sanctuary. Since they were used for offerings, it is no surprise that the inventory mainly includes three types of vessels, namely, small and medium bowls, cornets, and also a few bowls standing on a hollowed-out foot.[17] In addition, a clay model of a bull laden with a pair of churns was found in the altar. Generally speaking, the material, techniques, shapes and decorations of the pottery are late Ghassulian. The only find of importance apart from the pottery is a fragment of an alabaster vessel found during the clearance of the circular installation. The fragment forms part of a cylindrical vessel which has nearly vertical walls as well as a flat round bottom. The preserved fragment, *ca.* 6.9 cms. long and *ca.* 5.5 cms. wide (less than three inches by about 2 1/2 inches), includes a large part of the bottom which shows conspicuous marks of drilling, and the lower end of a section of the side. It is the earliest alabaster vessel so far found in Palestine.[18] It seems to have been imported from Egypt, where cylindrical alabaster vessels of that kind were manufactured. A few such vessels are reported from the Pre-dynastic period,[19] and with the establishment of the first dynasty they became very common.[20] Furthermore, our fragment was checked by Dr. Z. Goffer from Tel Aviv University, who found it to be calcium carbonate like the Egyptian alabaster vessels. Our fragment is but another link in the evident cultural connections which the Ghassulians maintained with Egypt. These cultural connections are primarily expressed in the beautiful ivory figurines which were discovered in Beersheba.[21]

Very little can be said on the nature of the cult performed in the temple. Almost certainly it was connected with water. This is indicated by the location of the temple between and above two springs, with the gates oriented towards them. Furthermore, the circular installation and the reconstructed channel were probably connected with water. The alabaster vessel, whose base was found nearby, may have been used to fill the basin with water or to empty it. The "water cult" performed in the temple may, perhaps, be connected with eleven undated cup-marks, that is, small, round depressions, cut on the surface of four rocks near the Ein Gedi spring. Seven of these cup-marks are cut on one rock; they are two to six inches deep and four to eight inches in diameter. We should also mention that our temple bears a strong architectural resemblance to the sanctuary of Megiddo Stratum XIX.[22] The latter is also of the broad-house type with a courtyard in front of it. It was used, as indicated by the pottery, by the Ghassulians as well as by the bearers of the culture labelled "Proto-Urban" by K. Kenyon. Most interesting are a few broken cornets found in the area of the Megiddo temple—exactly as in the case of the Ein Gedi temple.

The archaeological data give a clear picture of the history of our temple. It was built on bed rock and was in use during one relatively short period. When it was deserted, the site was never resettled. All the data indicate that the temple met its end when it was abandoned by the Ghassulians, and not as a result of destruction by an enemy. No traces of fire, or any other signs of deliberate destruction could be found. On the other hand, in parallel to other Ghassulian sites, everything seems to point to the fact that the structures slowly crumbled owing to desertion and the effect of weather. Furthermore, the temple was found empty with all its cultic equipment missing. Hardly any objects, with the exception of the alabaster fragment, were found in the enclosure. The absence of such equipment becomes even more conspicuous when we remember the relative richness of the finds in the Ghassulian sites. One has to conclude that when the temple was abandoned its equipment was carried away by the priests. Unfortunately, they were rather thorough, and nothing was left behind. What happened to the temple's equipment and whence was it taken?

The Hoard from Nahal Mishmar

Ghassulian remains were found in many sites, open settlements and caves, in the Judean desert. Of special interest is the evidence of Ghassulian habitation in the caves at the western edge of the desert near the Dead Sea, north and south of Ein Gedi. Many of these caves open onto the barren vertical cliffs of the canyons, the approach to them being difficult or even dangerous. Among the Ghassulian finds from the caves, particular mention should be made of objects made of organic material, such as wood, textiles and baskets, which were preserved in the arid climate of the desert.

The cave relevant to our subject was excavated by P. Bar-Adon[23] and labelled by him "The Cave of the Treasure." The cave is situated in the canyon of Nahal Mishmar, about six miles south of Ein Gedi. The cave opens onto the vertical cliff, about 150 feet below the cliff top with an abyss of nearly 800 feet below it. Access to the place was made possible during the excavations with the aid of ropes and rope-ladders. The cave was inhabited twice, first by the Ghassulians and later in 135 A.D., when Jewish rebels of the Second Revolt against the Romans took refuge there. Bar-Adon and his assistants made their main discovery when they removed a stone covering a natural niche beside one of the walls in the cave. Its removal revealed a unique Ghassulian hoard which was hidden in the niche.[24] The hoard comprises 429 articles which were carefully wrapped in a straw mat. Most of the articles, 416 in number, are of copper. The hoard includes the following: about 240 metal as well as one stone and six hematite mace-heads of various sizes and shapes—rounded, flattened, egg-shaped and disc-shaped; about twenty chisels and axes; about eighty "wands" or "standards," some hollow and some solid, which vary in ornamentation and size; ten "crowns" differing in size and ornamentation; five sickle-shaped, perforated objects, made from hippopotamus tusks; and one concave "box" made of elephant tusk.

The articles portray the mastery of the Ghassulian artisans in the manufacture of copper objects, and their discovery drastically changes the earlier idea that the manufacture of metal was still in its infancy during that period. The articles are individually shaped and decorated, again manifesting the versatile ability of the Ghassulian artists and artisans, briefly discussed in the first part of this article. The objects, with the possible exception of the chisels and axes, could hardly have been tools or articles for daily use. It seems almost certain thay they were used in the Chalcolithic cult, and that their interpretation and function have to be sought in the sphere of Ghassulian rituals. Thus the copper articles form yet another class of Ghassulian art or craft, similar to the wall-paintings, ivories, basalt vessels and clay ossuaries mentioned

above, in which the talents of the artists and artisans were applied
to produce articles needed for the rituals.

The Origin of the Hoard

The origin of the hoard and the clarification of the circumstances
of its being hidden in the cave are the foremost problems which
concern us here. It seems, unless future research alters the present
picture, that these problems have but one logical solution. The
hoard contains an usually rich series of articles, together forming a
unique collection of equipment for use in the Ghassulian ritual.
The articles of the hoard must have been in use in a central Ghassulian sanctuary,[25] and it seems that the Ein Gedi temple, being a
central shrine and a place for a pilgrimage, is the only candidate to
which the articles of the hoard can be attributed. All data fit this
conclusion and we can attempt the following reconstruction. The
articles of the hoard formed the cultic equipment of the temple, yet
their ritual use so far remains enigmatic to us. When the decision to
abandon the temple had been reached, the "priests" methodically
assembled all the ritual equipment without leaving even one article
behind, and left for good. They traveled only a few miles until they
reached the Nahal Mishmar cave, where they stayed for a while.
There they decided to continue their journey, and, considering
their future return to be certain, chose to leave the ritual equipment
in the cave. They carefully wrapped the articles in a straw mat and
hid them in a niche, never to see them again.[26]

The above reconstruction of events must be considered in the
light of the wider problematical aspects of the end of the
Ghassulian culture, briefly touched upon in the first part of this
paper. The final abandonment of the settlement is not only typical
of the Ein Gedi temple, but it is also a general phenomenon in the
Ghassulian sites. Assuming that the temple was a center of
pilgrimage, one has to conclude that its abandonment probably
coincided with that of the settlements such as Teleilat el-Ghassul.
The data at our disposal is incomplete and we do not know what
form the process of abandonment took. The reasons for the
abandonment remain obscure as well. It may have been due to a
severe drought or, alternatively, it may have been a flight before an
oncoming enemy. The latter could have been the new settlers in

the country, the bearers of the "Proto-Urban" culture, or, as some authorities believe, the invading Egyptian army of king Narmer.[27]

The flight-before-an-oncoming-enemy theory gains weight from the Ghassulian habitation in the desert caves. The desolate nature of the area, the difficulties in obtaining food and water, the difficult access—all these indicate that the inhabitants of the caves were refugees in flight, exactly like the Jewish rebels of the Second Revolt who followed them a few millennia later. This theory can also explain the abandonment of our temple and the hiding of the hoard; one can imagine the priests receiving information on the arrival of the enemy, deciding to leave, meticulously packing the temple's equipment and traveling to the Nahal Mishmar cave, staying there for a time. There they may have received more alarming news about the enemy and hid the equipment before traveling further afield and finally passing into oblivion.

Notes

[1] For recent summaries of the Ghassulian culture, see R. de Vaux, *Cambridge Ancient History* (rev. ed.), I, Chap. IXb (Fasc. 47, 1966); J. Perrot in *Supplément au dictionaire de la Bible* VIII (1968), Cols. 416-39.

[2] They are termed "early Chalcolithic" by several authorities.

[3] Except, perhaps, Teleilat el-Ghassul and the Beersheba sites, where several levels or phases were discerned in the settlements.

[4] A. Mallon, *et al.*, *Teleilat Ghassul I* (1934), pp. 129-43, frontispiece and Pls. 55-72.

[5] Perrot, *Israel Exploration Journal* V (1955), 17-40, 73-77; M. Dothan, *Atiqot* II (1959), 4-12.

[6] Perrot, *Israel Exploration Journal* V (1955), 79-80.

[7] Perrot, *Syria* XXXVI (1959), 8-19.

[8] Perrot, *Israel Exploration Journal* V (1955), 78-79 and Pl. 18; Ussishkin, *ibid.* XVIII (1968), 45-46 and Pl. 3B.

[9] Perrot, *et al.*, *Israel Exploration Journal* XVII (1967), 203-16 and Pls. 38-41.

[10] E. Sukenik, *Journal of the Palestine Oriental Society* XVII (1937), 15-30; Perrot, *Atiqot* III (1961), 1-83; J. Kaplan, *Israel Exploration Journal* XIII (1963), 300-12.

[11] Y. Aharoni, *Bulletin of the Israel Exploration Society* XXII (1958), 39-40 (Hebrew).

[12] J. Naveh (Levi), *ibid.*, 46-48 (Hebrew), and in *Israel Exploration Journal* VII (1957), 264.

[13]The excavation of the temple was supervised by the present author. He is indebted to Prof. Mazar for his kind permission and encouragement to discuss the temple here, in advance of the detailed report now in preparation. A short description of the temple appeared in *Archaeology* XVI (1963), 107, and in the *Encyclopedia of Archaeological Excavations in the Holy Land,* English Edition, Vol. II (1976), pp. 371-72.

[14]See n. 4 above.

[15]B. Hennessy, *Levant* I (1969), 7.

[16]The circumstances of its discovery should be mentioned. It was not noticed during the excavation but found later by I. Dunayevsky and A. Kempinski. They looked for such a channel, deducing that the water basin which they assumed was in the circular installation must have had an outlet.

[17]See the pottery published by J. Naveh in *Bulletin of the Israel Exploration Society* XXII (1958), Fig. 2 on p. 48.

[18]Except perhaps two alabaster mace-heads found in Teleilat el-Ghassul; see Mallon, *et al., Teleilat Ghassul I,* p. 71, Pl. 35:4.

[19]G. A. Reisner, *Mycerinus: The Temples of the Third Pyramid at Giza* (1931), pp. 130ff.

[20]W. B. Emery, *Great Tombs of the First Dynasty,* I (1949), 130ff. and esp. Figs. 69A-71 there; W. M. F. Petrie, *The Royal Tombs of the Earliest Dynasties,* Part II (1901), Pls. LIH-LIIIA.

[21]Perrot, *Syria* 36 (1959), 16-18.

[22]G. Loud, *Megiddo II* (1948), p. 61 and Fig. 390. The stratigraphy and ground-plan of the temple, and its resemblance to our temple, are treated by Dunayevsky and Kempinski in *Zeitschrift des Deutschen Palaestina-Vereins* 89 (1973), 167-68, by Kempinski in *Israel Exploration Journal* 22 (1972), 10-15, and by C. Epstein in *Eretz-Israel* 11 (1973), 54-57 (Hebrew).

[23]P. Bar-Adon, *Israel Exploration Journal* XI (1961), 25-35; XII (1962), 215-26; *Archaeology* XVI (1963), 251-59.

[24]For various reasons, the attribution of the hoard to the Ghassulian culture seems to be established. For a different opinion, see Perrot, *Supplément au dictionnaire de la Bible* VIII (1968), Col. 441.

[25]Incidentally, some of the articles show signs of considerable use, such as the "crown" published in *Israel Exploration Journal* XII (1962), 221 and Pl. 41, whose projecting ornamentations are mostly broken.

[26]If this reconstruction is correct, the dates provided by carbon-14 analysis of the mat which covered the hoard also indicate the date of abandonment of the temple. Two samples of the mat yielded the dates 5390 ± 150 (3429 ± 150 B.C.) and 4880 ± 250 (2919 ± 250 B.C.).

[27]On the possible campaign of Narmer in Palestine, see Y. Yadin, *Israel Exploration Journal* V (1955), 1-16; Yeivin, *ibid.* X (1960), 193-203.

17

A PHILISTINE TEMPLE AT TELL QASILE

AMIHAY MAZAR

A unique Philistine temple was discovered last summer at Tell Qasile, a small site of about four acres on the northern bank of the Yarkon river, about 2 km. east of its mouth. The site had first attracted attention when two Hebrew ostraca of the Iron II Age were found there. Four season of excavations carried out by Prof. B. Mazar showed that the site was first settled in the twelfth century B.C. by the Philistines (Stratum XII). During the period of the Judges, the Philistines built there a well-planned city (Strata XI-X) with straight parallel streets and dwellings of similar plan.[1] This city was destroyed in the early tenth century. However, the settlement was renewed during the United Monarchy (tenth century B.C., Strata IX_2-IX_1) when the ruined houses of the Philistines were rebuilt and a large public building was erected. The town derived its importance mainly from the nearby inland port on the Yarkon. According to Mazar, this port can be identified with "the Sea of Joppa," where cedarwood from Lebanon was brought for use in building the Temple in Jerusalem, both in Solomon's and in Zerubbabel's time. The settlement at Tell Qasile continued to exist until its destruction by the Assyrians in the eighth century (Strata VIII-VII). The site was resettled in the Persian period and continued to be occupied intermittently until the Early Arab period.

Work was resumed at Tell Qasile in 1971, and in June-September of 1972 extensive excavations were carried out over an area of 500 sq. m.[2] It soon became clear that the area chosen for excavation was the cult center of the Philistine city, and the unique Philistine temple came to light, containing cult vessels and a wealth of other objects. The temple is built of sun-dried mudbricks laid on stone foundations and plastered over. The walls, whose average width is 1.20 m., have been preserved to a height of about 0.80 m.

The temple is a long house oriented towards the west, measuring 14,5 by 8 m., and consisting of two main parts, the antechamber and the main hall. The antechamber (inside measurements 6 by 3.70 m.) is entered through a wide opening taking up the entire width of its north wall, with a threshold made up of three elongated stone slabs. Stepped plastered benches line the walls, and the floor is of beaten earth. An opening in the northern half of the wall subdividing the building leads into the main hall, so that the visitor who entered the temple had to make a 90 degree turn in order to enter the main hall. The hall (inside measurements 7.20 by 5.65 m.) is a long room whose roof was originally supported by two wooden pillars set on round, well-made stone bases, placed along the center axis. Here too, stepped plastered benches were built against the walls. A long narrow compartment (3.20 by 1.35 m.) is partitioned off the hall by a thin wall running parallel to the west wall at a distance of 1.35 m. A raised platform (*bama*) built against this partition wall projects into the hall. Built of mud-brick and plastered over, it is raised about 0.90 m. above the floor. In the north, the *bama* abuts on the plastered benches, while in the south, two plastered steps lead up to it. The lower step is built around the western wooden pillar and covers its stone base. The imprint of the pillar is still so clearly visible in the step that its diameter can be measured. The *bama* served as the focal point in the temple ritual, and its location, exactly opposite the center of the entrance hall, appears to have been carefully chosen. Both *bama* and the entrance-way lie on a line north of the central axis, while the roof pillars are aligned on that axis, so that a visitor had an unobstructed view of the *bama* from the entrance to the main hall. At the same time, since the entrance to the building was placed at a right angle, people outside could not look into the main hall. There are no close parallels in Palestine to the temple plan as a whole, though there are similarities to several features of the temples at Lachish and Beth-shan, and to a small temple recently excavated at Mycenae.[3]

To what extent do the components of this temple correspond to the division of Solomon's temple into "porch" (*ᵓulam*), "sanctuary" (*hekhal*) and "Holy of Holies" (*debir*), a division also known in several Canaanite temples? The antechamber may perhaps be interpreted as the "porch," the main hall as the "sanctuary," and the raised *bama* as the "Holy of Holies." However, it should be emphasized that the temple at Tell Qasile is basically different from Solomon's temple and from related Canaanite temples, and it is therefore doubtful whether the biblical division can apply here.

Brick debris, burnt wooden beams, and heaps of ashes found in the temple bear witness to its destruction by fire. On the floor of the temple, under the brick debris, two large groups of finds came to light. One was found on and around the raised *bama* and the other in the compartment behind the *bama* which served as a store room. Both assemblages were very rich and contained numerous objects. Of great interest and rarity are the cult vessels found in the vicinity of the *bama*. These include two cylindrical pottery cult stands. One has two rows of windows, and its upper part is decorated with four human figures walking in profile, arms stretched to the sides, while the other is ornamented with two lions facing heraldically. At the foot of the *bama* a pottery plaque was found, bearing an Egyptian-style building facade enclosing two standing figures of deities modeled in relief, of which only the legs remain. Another cult vessel may have served for libations or for holding sacred plants. The vessel, which has one central and four lateral openings, has a red burnished slip and is decorated with plant designs. Among other objects found near the *bama* are a bird-shaped bowl, the head of a swan, a lion-shaped pottery rhyton, and a socketed bronze axe.

The store room behind the *bama* contained, besides many pottery vessels, a *kernos* bowl decorated with a bull's head. The rich assemblage of cult vessels gives us a glimpse of the ritual practiced in the temple.

The destruction of the temple can be dated by the pottery found on the floor near the *bama*. This pottery is identical with that found in previous seasons on the floors of the houses in Stratum X, the destruction of which was attributed by Prof. B. Mazar to David's conquest of the city in the early tenth century B.C. The pottery assemblage found in the store room behind the *bama* is somewhat different—in addition to vessels identical with those found near the *bama* it contained also earlier pottery, types attributed in previous seasons to Stratum XI. The deposit in the store room appears to have accumulated during a long period of time, and some of the vessels found there should be attributed to the earliest period of the temple's existence.

Excavations in the vicinity of the temple showed that to the south it was attached to a much larger building of which seven rooms were partly uncovered. The walls of both this building and the temple run parallel to the walls of the buildings exposed in the previous seasons, indicating that the town was laid out according to a preconceived plan.

East and north of the temple a wide courtyard with a beaten earth floor was uncovered. A square stone structure (1.20 by 1.20 m.) in this courtyard may have served as a foundation for an altar of burnt offering. The numerous animal bones found in the courtyard indicate that sacrifices were offered there.

Philistine strata antedating the temple were examined in the 1972 season only in a few trial pits, but there are some indications that an earlier temple may lie underneath. When the courtyard floor north of the temple entrance was removed, a pit came to light which was dug through earlier strata down to bedrock. This pit (or *favissa*) contained cult vessels of which the most outstanding was a 33 cm.-high pottery vase fashioned in the shape of a woman, probably a goddess. The top of the head served as the mouth of the vase, the breasts are sprouts through which libations can be poured out, and the arms of the figure are crossed on the body of the vase. Another interesting find is a lion-shaped pottery rhyton painted in black and red. A number of Philistine pottery types were found in the *favissa*, such as bottles, bowls, and horn-shaped vessels, all decorated in the characteristic Philistine style. The pit probably served as a cache for cult vessels which may have belonged to an earlier temple, destroyed before the present temple was built.

A few building remains attributed to Strata IX_2 and IX_1 provide some indications concerning the history of the temple in the tenth century. A lime floor was laid in these strata over the ruins of the temple and the courtyard. Some of the temple walls were rebuilt, and two building phases can be clearly distinguished. Though no cult vessels were found in Stratum IX, the inhabitants appear to have made an effort to repair the building, and it is reasonable to assume that the place continued to serve as a cult center.

The temple at Tell Qasile is the only Philistine temple excavated up to the present. The little we know about Philistine temples comes to us from a few biblical passages, the best known of which refers to Samson's destruction of the Gaza temple: "And Samson took hold of the two middle pillars upon which the house stood and on which it was borne up, of the one with his right hand, and of the other with his left" (Judges 16:29). The temple at Tell Qasile indeed has two pillars supporting the roof which are an integral part of the temple construction.

Who was the deity worshiped in the temple at Tell Qasile? One of the ostraca found on the site bears the inscription "gold of Ophir to Beth Horon . . . thirty shekels." Already in the preliminary report of his excavations, Prof. Mazar put forward the suggestion that the Beth Horon of the inscription is not a place to which the gold was dispatched, but that it refers to the house (Temple) of the god Horon whose temple he assumed to have existed in Tell Qasile or somewhere in its vicinity.[4] Horon is known to have been worshiped in the Hellenistic period at Yamnia (Yavne), and consequently this great Canaanite god must have been known and revered in Philistia. The connection between the ostracon inscription and the temple now uncovered poses a difficult problem since the script on the ostracon is characteristic of the ninth-eighth centuries B.C. Nevertheless, perhaps it can be suggested that the ostracon belongs to the latest renovation of the temple and that from the time of its foundation, the temple was dedicated to the god Horon. This question, however, must be left open.

Notes

[1] B. Maisler (Mazar), *Israel Exploration Journal* 1 (1951), 61-76; 125-40; 194-218.

[2] The Tell Qasile project, headed by Prof. B. Mazar, is carried out on behalf of the Israel Exploration Society, the Ha'aretz Museum, and the Archaeological Institute of the Hebrew University, Jerusalem, and is financed by the Municipality of Tel Aviv-Yafo and contributions of Friends of the Ha'aretz Museum. The excavations were directed by the author, assisted by M. Megiddon (administrator), Z. Maoz (surveyor), and a staff of students from the Hebrew University. Dr. Trude Dothan and Mr. E. Netzer (architect) advised the expedition.

[3] W. Taylour, *Antiquity* 176 (1970), 270ff.

[4] Mazar, *Israel Exploration Journal* 1 (1951), 210.

18

THE EXCAVATION SOUTH AND WEST OF THE TEMPLE MOUNT IN JERUSALEM: THE HERODIAN PERIOD

BENJAMIN MAZAR

Since the days of Wilson and Warren—a hundred years ago—the topographical and archaeological study of Jerusalem has developed extensively and is reflected in a considerable bibliography. Many problems however, remain concerning the history and topography of the Holy City, including basic questions of its character, development and extent in various times, which are still vague and hotly contested. The objective difficulties in the study of Jerusalem are enormous, especially because of the many destructions and, in certain cases, razing to the very bedrock, but also because only very limited areas are free of medieval and modern buildings and thus available for excavation. Moreover, it has been only during the present century that archaeological techniques have become more and more refined, enabling a far more accurate chronological determination of the remains of buildings and fortifications, and thus clearing up several of the basic problems through modern methods of stratigraphical diggings in the various parts of the city as well as putting to the acid test the plentiful material which has been gathered and analyzed over so many years of research.

Proceeding to discuss the recent discoveries from the glorious period in history of Jerusalem, from the reign of Herod the Great down to the destruction of the city and the second temple in A.D. 70—a period well known to us from ancient literary sources, especially the writings of Josephus Flavius and the Mishnaic-Talmudic literature, as well as the New Testament—we must note that it is especially in our own times that important results have been obtained. The uncovering of remains of the third wall, the limited excavations in the citadel, at the Damascus gate, within the old city proper and on the "Ophel," the study of the ancient water supply, and the extensive work on the various ancient burial-grounds surrounding the city have all greatly advanced research and have placed it on a firm basis. In spite of the basic differences in opinion concerning the city walls and the various topographical riddles in Jerusalem, today we are gaining a far more realistic picture of Jerusalem in Herodian times than that imagined by the scholars in previous generations.

Without going into the numerous general problems which directly or indirectly concern ancient Jerusalem, and the attempts to solve them, we shall limit ourselves to several conclusions stemming from the excavations of the last twenty months, south and west of the walls of the temple platform. This excavation, under my direction, with the assistance of Mr. Meir Ben-Dov and a rather small archaeological and technical staff, including the late architect I. Dunayevsky, eng. A. Urweider, Miss E. LeFrak and graduates and students of the Hebrew University, is being carried out under the auspices of the Hebrew University and the Israel Exploration Society. Work has been concentrated mainly in the open area delimited on the north by the southern wall of the temple platform and on the east and south by the Turkish walls, as well as in an area adjacent to the southern part of the western wall, in the region of Robinson's arch.

These areas are of special interest in regard to the ancient topography of the city. Here, where bedrock descends eastward from the western hill, down to the Tyropoean Valley and then rises up again to the "Ophel" hill, drastic changes occurred as a result of Herod's tremendous undertaking in doubling the extent of the *temenos* by filling up the Tyropoean valley as well as the western slope of the Kidron valley. The leveling-off of this enormous area was achieved by means of huge walls founded on bedrock, containing vast amounts of fill. In the outer temple courtyard, along its southern edge, Herod built his "royal stoa," reaching high above it. This construction is described by Josephus as one of the greatest architectural feats of mankind (*Antiquities* XV, 412). It was possible to reach this stoa directly from the upper city to the west by means of the viaduct spanning the eastern slope of the western hill. Robinson's arch, jutting out slightly from the western wall some 12 meters north of the southwestern corner of the temple platform, is a fragment of the eastern arch which supported this viaduct.

In planning our excavations, we leaned mainly on the results of Charles Warren's explorations of a hundred years ago, whose work consisted of digging narrow shafts and galleries around the walls of the temple platform. He published the results of his investigations, including important and accurate data on the lie of the bedrock, on the courses of the huge walls, on the pavements, water channels, etc.

In the first stages of our excavation, we paid special attention to the stratigraphy of the strip of land running along the southern wall, from the southwestern corner up to the buildings adjoining the "Double Gate," one of the two gates in the southern wall called in the Mishna the "Hulda Gates" (*Middoth* 1.3), which led up to the outer temple courtyard, under the "royal stoa." Our excavations enabled us to establish the stratigraphical sequence dividing the levels into four periods: the Early Arab (8 phases), the Byzantine (4 phases), the Roman (2 phases) and the Herodian (from Herod the Great down to A.D. 70). During this entire period till the "Double Gate" was closed, a street ran along the southern wall, leading from the southwestern corner up to the gate. In the Omayyad period this street was paved with cobblestones. A gate on the southern side of the street led to a magnificent building located on that flank. Without going into the problems presented by this building, we can state that it is similar in plan to the well known palaces of the Omayyad period. For the construction of this building ashlars, columns and other architectural remains from earlier periods were used. In the subsequent periods, in Abassid and Fatimid times, there were various attempts to restore the huge building partially, both by clearing debris away and through further construction. From the end of the Fatimid period on, the area of our excavations, south of the southern wall, remained uninhabited.

As for the Roman and Byzantine periods, we can note in passing that structures, some of them well preserved, have only been found adjacent to the southwestern corner, and to the east, next to the Turkish wall. The central area here apparently was reserved for gardens. The many finds of the Roman period include a stone slab on which is engraved a Latin monumental inscription from the time of Septimius Severus, many bricks and tiles bearing stamps of the Legio X Fretensis as well as of Colonia Aelia

Capitolina, an abundance of coins, fragments of marble sculptures, bronze figurines and large quantities of pottery and glass. Not less plentiful and interesting are the finds from the Byzantine levels.

Let us return to the Herodian period. Our excavations along the southern wall have revealed an impressive sight—the well preserved courses of the Herodian wall comprising huge ashlars, some of which are 10-11 meters long. The ashlars of the upper courses have careful margins surrounding flat bosses, whereas the lower ones have much cruder, bulging bosses.

The latter should be regarded as the foundations of the wall, for they were not intended to be exposed to view. The further we uncovered the wall, the clearer became the outstanding planning and workmanship involved in the construction. In a section next to the southwestern corner, we found a part of the Herodian street, paved with large, squared flagstones, with two flights of three steps each leading up to the east. This section of the street was entirely engulfed in debris from the destruction of the Temple wall in A.D. 70, including ashlars with flat bosses from the highest courses of the wall itself, and architectural fragments from the top of the wall and possibly also from the "royal stoa," including fragments of a Corinthian capital, columns, decorated stones and two sun dials, as well as many coins (the latest of which are from the fourth year of the First Revolt) and fragments of pottery and stone vessels typical of the Herodian period. Of special interest are the top cornerstone from the southwestern corner, as well as other fragments, which enabled the expedition's architect, the late Immanuel Dunayevsky, to make a reconstruction of the top of the southwestern corner of the wall. Later, we found in the debris ashlars with pilasters which were jutting out from the wall; these, together with remains of a small section of the western wall found many years ago beneath Bâb es-Saray, enable a comparison of the upper structure of the walls of the temple platform with those of the Herodian walls surrounding the cave of Machpelah in Hebron.

The study of the Herodian street was not without difficulties, for further to the east the flagstones of the pavement had been removed, apparently in the Roman period, at least in the few excavated areas. Surprisingly we discovered below the estimated level of the pavement two rows of masonry chambers built in the fill. In the easternmost section we even found a blocked opening between the two rows, with another opening slightly higher leading to the next chamber to the east, towards the "Double Gate." Here, we came to two conclusions: that these chambers were built in the fill in a continuous series the entire length of this part of the southern wall, and that two building phases are to be distinguished in the Herodian period. The latter point is evident in other areas, as well. These facts fit in well with what we know from Josephus, i.e., that construction work in the temple area went on until the time of the Procurator Albinus (*Antiquities* XX, 219-220; B. J. 5.36-38).

The Herodian street was bordered on its southern side by a wall, beyond which there was a plaza, c. 12 m. wide, sections of which we have uncovered recently. The plaza, which probably served as a gathering place for the crowds of pilgrims coming to Jerusalem on the festivals, is built over the fill and is paved with large flagstones, properly squared and trimmed, above a foundation of stones. On the south, the plaza was supported by a massive wall 3 m. wide, resembling Herodian masonry in Samaria and Jericho. All in all, we have clarified to a certain degree the character of this area south of the Temple Platform in the Herodian period. Even so, we still hope that in the future we shall be able to solve some additional problems for a better understanding of this area.

As for the finds so far examined, including those from the Herodian street and the small chambers, on the plaza, as well as in the area adjacent to Robinson's arch, and which are clearly to be ascribed to the Herodian period, first we must mention the abundance of coins, from Alexander Jannaeus down to the fourth year of the First Revolt—mostly coins from Jerusalem, but some few also foreign, such as two silver Tyrian shekels and a gold coin of Tiberius. Of the pottery, of special interest are the variety of the so-called Herodian lamps, and the small painted "pseudo-Nabataean" platters. A thorough study of the rich corpus of pottery should yield valuable results concerning our understanding of daily life in this area, close by entrances to the temple area. This is true also of the various types of stoneware, mostly fragmentary, including pieces which bear short Hebrew inscriptions. The stoneware includes vessels of various sizes and types often decorated in the Herodian style, as well as a large number of stone weights, some of which are inscribed. One stone vessel fragment is of special interest, for it bears the inscription *Qorbân*—"sacrifice," alongside and upside-down from the carved depiction of two bird figures. This inscription brings to mind what is stated in the Mishna: "If a man found a vessel and on it was written *qorbân* . . ." (*Maaśer Sheni* IV. 10). The depiction of the two birds may be connected with the offering of the woman in confinement (Leviticus 12:8). Of no less interest are two stone objects which may be of ritual origin: one is flat and square on top, with a sunken area in the middle, and a drain-like hole in one corner. The other seems to be similar to some Nabataean incense altars. Apropos, very few Nabataean coins and sherds were discovered in the excavations. It is worthwhile to mention that in the fill there was a considerable quantity of sherds from the end of the pre-exilic period, including handles bearing the *lmlk* stamp, together with sherds of the Herodian period, and a very few of the Early Hellenistic (including a handle bearing a *yhd* stamp) and the Hasmonean periods.

In trying to sum up the excavations to the west of the western wall, from the southwestern corner of the temple platform almost up to "Barclay's Gate," the first feature is "Robinson's Arch" which, according to common opinion, is a fragment of the viaduct spanning the space between the Upper City and the entrance to the "royal stoa" on the southern part of the court of the Temple. We had the opportunity in this area of solving several important stratigraphical problems and of somewhat clarifying the overall picture concerning the building phases in the Byzantine, Early Arabic and Crusader periods, as well as of discovering a building from the period of Aelia Capitolina in a reasonable state of preservation. A unique find was a Hebrew inscription carved into one of the stones of the western wall beneath "Robinson's Arch." Undoubtedly from the Byzantine period, and possibly from the days of Julian the Apostate, it quotes a passage in Isaiah 66:14—"And you shall see, and your heart shall rejoice, and your bones (shall flourish) like herbs."

As for the Herodian period: foremost is the fine preservation of the western wall up to a considerable height in this area. At a distance of 12.40 meters to the west of Robinson's arch, we came across the well preserved lower part of the finely constructed pier which supported the arch. It is 15.25 meters long—the length of Robinson's arch. We have found that the pier has four small rooms built into it, with their openings on the east, facing the Herodian paved avenue which passed beneath the arch. These rooms may well have served as shops, for the finds within them included stoneware, weights and coins, mainly of Agrippa I. Beneath the avenue, paved with large slabs, which was found to run north-south along the western wall down the Tyropoean valley, there is the grand Herodian aqueduct, already discovered by Warren. It is hewn into the bedrock and is vaulted over with stone voussoirs. So far, we have traced it for a length of some 200 meters, and it will become one of the major objectives in our future work, along with the channels leading to it—one of which, in the plaza area south of the southern wall, has already been cleared for a considerable length.

We are also pushing forward the exploration of the cisterns, reservoirs and other water installations hewn into the bedrock in the area to the west of the pier. It is now apparent that in some instances what were at first considered cisterns are actually older, subterranean tombs, of the Iron Age II. Moreover, it is quite certain that these tombs were hewn into the bedrock according to a well thought-out plan, on terraces of the eastern slope of the western hill, quite close to the original valley bed. In other words, they lie opposite the southern part of the temple mount, where it is supposed that the royal citadel of the Davidic dynasty stood. The tombs are of the Phoenician type found in the southern necropolis at Achzib, excavated by Dr. M. Prausnitz; according to the finds, these latter were ascribed to the ninth and eighth centuries B.C. They are also quite similar to some Iron II tombs in the village of Silwân. Their chief feature is a shaft which leads through a doorway to the plastered burial chamber, over which is hewn a *nefesh*, resembling a chimney covered with slabs or a gabled roof. Only in the finest of these tombs was there found a dromos leading to the shaft. Till now we have examined only a few of the tombs, of which examination suggests that they were cleared already in ancient times and remained unused until re-exposed in the Hasmonean (one of them contained an abundance of Hellenistic pottery and Hasmonean coins) and in the Herodian periods. Some were incorporated into the Herodian aqueduct.

Of course, these discoveries raise important problems concerning the expansion of Jerusalem in the period of the Judaean

Kingdom. It seems that this burial ground is from the ninth-seventh centuries B.C. It probably remained in use from the time of Joram until the days of Manasseh, i.e., the middle of the seventh century B.C., when—according to the recent archaeological evidence—the expansion of Jerusalem towards the west began, and the new quarters—the Mishneh and Maktesh—were established (cf. 2 Chronicles 33:14; Zephaniah 1:10-11). A new door has obviously been opened for restudy of the problems involving the royal tombs and the common burial ground in pre-exilic Jerusalem (cf. Ezekiel 43:5-9; Jeremiah 31:37-39). And indeed, this is a subject to which I hope to return in the near future.

19

STANDING STONES IN ANCIENT PALESTINE

CARL F. GRAESSER

Standing stones (*maṣṣēbôt;* singular *maṣṣēbāh*) were well-known objects in ancient Palestinian culture and are mentioned often in the Old Testament. (Hereafter masseba and its plural massebot will be used as English words.) Jacob erected his pillow-stone as a masseba at Bethel (Gen. 28:18). Moses set up twelve massebot at Sinai before the altar at the ratification of the covenant (Ex. 24:4). Yet at a later period a very different atttitude obtained. Massebot were no longer proper, but violently denounced (Deut. 16:22). King Josiah led a reformation in which these standing stones were destroyed from all the "high places" (II Kings 23).

The masseba was basically a stone "set up," as its etymological origin (from *nṣb* "to set up") indicates. In this position it served as a marker, jogging the memory. It would arrest the attention of the onlooker because it stood in a position it would not take naturally from gravity alone; only purposeful human activity could accomplish such "setting up." The study of massebot, therefore, is the study of those purposes that led to that "setting up."

Palestinian Tradition of "Plain Stones"

Biblical descriptions and the growing number of excavated massebot indicate that a wide variety of stones could be used as a masseba, ranging from any unworked natural slab to fine-hewn stones. As a rule it was a "plain stone," that is, it bore no inscription and had no relief or figure inscribed on it, however nicely it may have been shaped. In this the Palestinian stones differ markedly from those of the empires of Egypt and Mesopotamia. There inscriptions and reliefs were an almost unbroken rule. Long excavation in those areas has unearthed only a small handful of "plain" stones. On the other hand, plain stones predominate by far

Illus. 16-8

in Palestine in the Bronze and Iron Ages. The few inscribed stones found in Palestine are virtually all of demonstrably foreign origin or influence. It becomes clear, therefore, that there was a specifically Palestinian tradition of avoiding inscription or figure. It might more properly be called a Syro-Palestinian tradition, since many stones in Syria and Phoenicia were also "plain." Notable examples are the obelisks of Byblos and certain stones in the Phoenician colony of Carthage.

The causes and origins of this tradition can only be conjectured. Some sort of religious conservatism preserving the tradition of preliterate times would seem to be the key factor. Surely it was not due to lack of technical stone-cutting competence, since many of the Palestinian massebot are finely shaped and worked. This tradition may partly reflect a rejection of foreign or imperial customs, since the use of inscription and figure presumably originated and was common in the imperial cultures of Egypt and Mesopotamia. The stubborn persistence of this anepigraphic tradition is all the more surprising in view of the obvious borrowing from surrounding literate cultures of the custom of carefully shaping the massebot. Whatever the origin, the "plain stone" tradition was regnant in Palestine.

Therefore, we reserve the biblical (and thus Palestinian) term "masseba" for these plain, uninscribed, unfigured stones. The term "stele" will be used technically for *inscribed* standing stones.

Interpretation of Massebot

Precisely this absence of inscription on Palestinian massebot is the prime source of difficulty hindering our understanding of the meaning and function of these stones. The inscribed stele is at least partly self-explanatory; its inscription suggests the nature of the stone's function. Massebot, unfortunately, are mute. They offer no verbal hint of their meaning to the modern scholar, or for that matter to the ancient onlooker. Indeed, without any specific indication by an inscription, different individuals could easily attach *diverse* meanings to the *same* stone. Nor would it be at all difficult for the understanding of a given masseba to change over the course of changing generations. The diverse opinions regarding massebot in the Old Testament offer a good example of this fluidity and shift of meaning. The blankness of the massebot not only aided this fluidity but makes the present task of recovering the sundry ancient interpretations of these stones more difficult.

We possess three basic avenues leading to an understanding of the massebot. Firstly, it is reasonable to assume that these uninscribed standing stones in Palestine fulfilled some of the same functions that *inscribed* standing stones in other countries served. An analysis of the functions of Near Eastern steles can thus form the general background of the study of Palestinian massebot. Secondly, the *archaeological context* of an excavated masseba offers direct evidence of the use of that stone. Careful observation of the stone's position in relation to structures, altars, other massebot, offering vessels, and the like will suggest possible functions. Here it is crucial that excavation be done accurately— and reported completely! Finally, ancient *documents* mentioning massebot, primarily the Old Testament, show how certain ancient individuals conceived these stones. Unfortunately, many of the Old Testament authors branded them as highly improper without disclosing the significance ascribed to them by their users. One must take this disapproval into account when using this evidence.

We have here reached the most crucial point in any attempt to study massebot. What is our basic understanding of the masseba? By what principle shall one devise the categories of a typology by which we describe the uses of these stones? The decision at this point will inexorably shape what follows. In the late 19th century, some described the large rude stones known then, existing above the surface, as phallic emblems. These were said to symbolize the fertile powers of Baal, consort of the goddess Asherah, whose symbol was the sacred tree standing beside the masseba. Subsequent excavation of a host of massebot carefully shaped into flat slabs clearly disproves such phallic theories. Many scholars viewed the masseba as a *sacred* stone, the abode of some animistic spirit, either of a deity, demon, or dead man. Animism has fallen into disfavor and the sacredness inhering in a masseba is described today in terms more similar to *mana*. The stone is conceived as a medium of power, as charged with a concentration of divine power operative in the whole sacred area. Still others described the masseba as a variety of idol, a representation of the deity, effecting his presence in that place.

The present writer takes a different point of departure. (Indeed, the observant reader will note that it has shaped this discussion from the very first paragraph.) It will be assumed here that the ancient Palestinians thought of massebot as *standing stones* and that these stones served as markers, reminders, jogs for memory. The etymology of the term suggests this; and, much more significantly, most excavated massebot have been shaped and worked to resemble the steles, the *inscribed* standing stones, of the surrounding countries which clearly served this function. This is the crucial assumption.

Briefly stated, the masseba may perform four functions: *memorial*, to mark the memory of a dead person; *legal*, to mark a legal relationship between two or more individuals; *commemorative*, to commemorate an event, and more specifically to call to mind the participants in all the honor and glory of that event; and *cultic*, to mark the sacred area where the deity might be found, or more narrowly, to mark that exact point where the deity is cultically immanent, where worship and sacrifice will reach the deity. It is important to note that a single stone was not limited to a single function but often carried out several at one and the same time.

One other very important point. This typology does not intend to say that the idea of "marker" exhausts the functions of all standing stones. First of all, steles are not only standing stones but also bear inscriptions, symbols, or figures. The stele functions not only as a standing stone, but also as document and likeness. In fact, it is actually these elements which most directly execute some of the total functions of the stele! Furthermore, the plain massebot undoubtedly had other functions attached to them, functions which were actually proper to images, holy stones, or the inscriptions and figures on steles. The present writer feels that precision is best served if we speak of such functions as being *transferred* to massebot, not inherent in them. Thus while our typology is based on the masseba as a *marker*, it allows that other functions were transferred. In some cases these transferred functions even became primary. Certain biblical writers, for example, considered the massebot as a variety of idols (Lev. 26:1, Micah 5:13). Cultic stones had a special tendency to assume transferred functions so that for many these stones "enabled" or "effected" the deity's presence. The precise conception of a function transferred to a plain masseba is not only difficult to recover, but likely varied considerably according to period, culture, and even individual.

Legal Stones: Marking a Legal Relationship

Certain stones were intended to call to mind *legal relationships* existing between individuals or groups. The most common examples of this category are boundary and treaty stones. These functions were known already in early 3rd-millennium Sumerian city-states.

The war between the cities of Lagash and Umma began officially when the stele marking their boundary was thrown down. When king Eannatum of Lagash was subsequently victorious, he set up another stele at the border. This one recorded the treaty between the cities and spelled out the boundaries as well as commemorating his victory.[1] The text of the Stele of Vultures erected by Eannatum inside the city of Lagash includes lists of fields and lands such as may have been part of the text of the stele he set up out in the fields at the border. (See James Pritchard, *The Ancient Near East in Pictures* [Princeton, 1954], numbers 298-302. Later references to this most useful collection of pictures will employ the abbreviation *ANEP*, followed by the number of the *picture*, not the page number.)

The *kudurru* stones of Babylon were a type of boundary stone. (See *ANEP*, 454, 518-21.) Shaped like oval boulders, they recorded (a) titles to land, often by royal grant, (b) curses on anyone who might destroy the stone, (c) reliefs depicting the ceremony of the king's grant, and more interestingly, (d) symbols of the gods. These symbols apparently were meant to function like the curses—to invoke the protection of the deity and so to preserve the stone, since it was dangerous, presumably, to destroy the symbol of a god. Many ancient cultures shared this concern for preserving boundaries and boundary stones by some sacred sanction. The Old Testament, for example, prohibits moving landmarks (Deut. 19:14), and the imprecatory liturgy of Deuteronomy 27:17 pronounces a curse on the boundary-stone mover.

The royal steles erected by Assyrian kings served a legal function among others. These were markers proclaiming their dominion, and, when set up at the farthest point of their campaigns, noted also the limits of that control (*ANEP*, 442-44, 447).

The relief on an intriguing stele from Ugarit depicts two men with raised arms before a table with several objects on it (*ANEP*, 608). Lack of inscription renders certainty impossible, but it may well mark a contract or treaty and depict the moment of the oath confirming the contract recorded in the cuneiform tablets lying on the table.

Legal functions are well known among Old Testament massebot. Jacob and Laban set up a masseba—as well as a cairn according to the present text—at the border of Aram and Gilead on the occasion of a treaty (Gen. 31:45-52). The stone marked both the terms of the contract and the border between these lands. Moses erected twelve massebot at Sinai, one for each tribe (Ex. 24:4). We are not told whether they circled the altar of Yahweh or stood in a line. In any case, they marked both the relationship of each tribe to Yahweh and the fact that the relationship of the tribes was founded on their common commitment to Yahweh. Joshua set up a "great stone" at the Shechem covenant renewal, and its function is specifically explained: "It will be a witness against us, for it has heard all the words of Yahweh which he spoke to us" (Josh. 24:26-27).

The use of a plain stone to mark a legal agreement naturally depends on memory and oral tradition to preserve the precise terms of the covenant. A typologically later development of legal stones was the custom of inscribing the terms of the contract on the stone. The stone thereby serves also as a document. The covenant massebot of Shechem in Deuteronomy 27:1-8 and Joshua 8:30-35 are examples of this development; for they bore, written upon them, "the law of Moses." The 8th-century Syrian stele found at Sefire bears a lengthy text of a treaty between KTK and Arpad.[2] This documentary function has become primary in the most famous Near Eastern stele of them all, that bearing the Hammurapi Code (*ANEP*, 246). The use of a stone in the shape of a standing stone as the writing material for this document ultimately reflects the legal function of steles, that of marking relationships between parties.

Memorial Stones: Stones Memorializing the Dead

Standing stones were commonly used to mark the memory of the dead and often also to mark the position of his grave. The use of memorial stones was most fully developed in the thousands upon thousands of funerary steles in Egypt.[3] Such a stele did much more than memorialize the dead and mark his grave. It marked the proper spot for funerary offerings on the offering table so often set at its base. It was covered with pictures and inscriptions: the name which would effectively invoke the deceased in ritual, a picture of the deceased which would lend him a sort of existence and form a channel of his communication with the living, and food and furniture listed and pictured for use in the other world. In short, the stone and the figures and inscriptions upon it served to supply the needs of the dead, especially by expediting his funerary cult.

Memorial stone tradition was firmly rooted in Syria-Palestine, though their functions were usually considerably less complicated. Many Phoenician and Mediterranean memorial stones bear short funerary inscriptions. In fact, almost every use of the term *mṣbt*, the Phoenician cognate of the Hebrew *maṣēbāh*, occurs in these funerary inscriptions, referring to the inscribed stone itself.[4] The inscriptions regularly bear the name of the deceased and usually also that of the donor. These not only memorialized the deceased, but also the donor, as well as commemorating the donor's pious care for the dead.

There was a strong tradition for memorial stones among the Arameans of early first-millennium Syria. Many bore reliefs depicting one or two deceased sitting at a banquet table, sometimes with a servant in attendance (*ANEP*, 631-33). One of these was found at a tomb beside the royal *hilani* palace at Zinjirli, marking the burial spot (*ANEP*, 630). The banquet scene suggests the importance of food for the dead and the possibility that, as in Egypt, offerings were made for the dead. One cemetery near Carchemish has in fact yielded several offering tables in addition to two banquet-scene funerary steles, though in mixed contexts.[5] Ekrem Akurgal theorizes that the Arameans borrowed these banquet scenes from the Hittites for whom they depicted offerings to the gods.[6] Perhaps the ancient Aramean did not draw so careful a distinction between them. We know the Hittites considered their kings to have been deified on death. The category of ²elōhîm, "gods," included many sorts of more-than-human spirits. When the witch of Endor "raised" Samuel from the dead for Saul she cried out because she saw a "god" rising from the earth (I Sam. 28:13). Memorial steles with banquet scenes were still in use in the 5th century B.C. (ANEP, 635).

This Aramean tradition for memorial stones forms the backdrop to the two memorial stones specifically mentioned in the Old Testament. When Jacob buried Rachel, the wife he had labored for in Syria, he set up a masseba to mark her grave (Gen. 35:20). David's son, Absalom, also set up a memorial masseba; and he was born of a princess of Geshur which is just north of Syria. Absalom set up his own memorial stone while he was yet alive, "because he said, 'I do not have a son to cause my name to be remembered'; and he called the masseba after his name so they call it 'Absalom's monument' to this day"(II Sam. 18:18). Not having a son to be called "ben Absalom," he insured the continuance of his name and memory in Israel by a masseba that people would call "Absalom's monument." This is superb indication of the basic function of a memorial masseba—to mark the memory of the dead person. A less likely alternative is that the phrase "cause my name to be remembered" is a technical term referring to the use of Absalom's name in a funerary cult of some sort, such as might be fulfilled by a son.

Such *funerary* stones were not common in Babylonia-Assyria, though the memorial function of steles was well known. (Lack of stone in the alluvial plain of Babylonia limited the use of costly standing stones to those few of considerable means.) The Assyrian royal steles had the explicit secondary function of proclaiming the famous memory of the king beyond his death. One of the most remarkable set of steles in the Near East was found at Assur.[7] More than 130 stones were set in two rows facing one another just within the city walls. One memorialized kings, the other important officials. These steles differ from most steles in this area (which are regularly covered fully by figure and inscription) in that they bear only a brief inscription, "Image of NN," set within a small niche on the stone. In addition to the obvious memorial function, these rows were apparently meant to serve as a sort of "walk-in calendar." Not only were the stones arranged in a generally chronological order from east to west, but the individuals memorialized were those named in the eponym lists, the lists used by the Assyrians for computing dates.[8]

Commemorative Stones: Commemorating an Event and Honoring the Participants

A large proportion of steles extant serve a *commemorative* function. There are two aspects to this function. One or the other may be more prominent, but both are present. The stone commemorates an event, yet not for the sake of event in itself, but for the significance it lends to the participants. Most often the stone serves primarily to honor an individual or individuals by marking them in the distinction and glory they bear because of the part they played in the event commemorated.

The most obvious example of this function is the victory stone, commonly set up all over the Near East by monarchs to remind posterity of their accomplishments. Several have been found in Palestine, erected there by campaigning conquerors: Pharaohs Seti I and Ramses II at Beth-shan (*ANEP*, 320-21), Shishak at Megiddo, and Sargon the Assyrian at Ashdod.[9] King Saul set up a victory stone at Carmel after victory over the Amalekites (I Sam. 15:12). The biblical author judges this to be a bad thing, apparently because he set it up "for himself" rather than giving the credit for the victory to Yahweh. Samuel, on the other hand, is not chided for erecting the stone named "Ebenezer," "stone of help," after the rout of the Philistines. The name of the stone is clarified as meaning "Hitherto Yahweh has helped us" (I Sam. 7:12), though a case can be made that the original text read "It will be a witness that Yahweh has helped us."

The royal Assyrian steles, mentioned twice above, were primarily commemorative. The figure of the king in relief was bigger than life, and the text reinforced this impression by recounting his conquests and accomplishments. The king's gods, at whose command he conquered, were thereby also honored; and their symbols were included in the relief (*ANEP*, 442-44, 447).

To this class also must be assigned those stones set up in sacred precincts to commemorate a sacrifice or some other ritual act.

First-millennium Phoenician colonies of North Africa and the Mediterranean islands have yielded a whole series of steles commemorating *mlk*-sacrifices,[10] known in the Old Testament as sacrifices to "Molech" (Jer. 32:35; II Kings 16:3). Since these involved the sacrifice of an infant or some substitutionary animal, we can understand why this cultic event was worthy of commemoration! Other examples are offered by two simple steles from Ugarit. They are nicely hewn but bear only a short inscription noting the sacrifices (*ANEP*, 262).

"Votive" steles form an important group of steles commemorating cultic acts. The term "votive" is here used in a technical sense of those stones erected specifically in fulfillment of a vow (*ndr*) and/or in answer to prayer. The vow was a well-known religious practice of the Syro-Palestinian area, including ancient Israel. When seeking a certain boon from the deity, the worshipper would promise that upon the granting of this boon he would "repay" his vow by offering a sacrifice, erecting a stele, or some such appropriate act of thanksgiving (Psalms 54:6, 66:13).

A close study of the *form* of votive stele inscriptions is informative. Typical is that of the Bar-Hadad stele (*ANEP*, 499): (the brackets indicate illegible portions)

A stele which Bar-[Ha]dad, son of [. . .], the king of Aram, set up for his lord, for Melqart, which he vowed to him, and (then) he heard his [voice].[11]

This illustrates the five main parts of the votive-inscription form, to which a sixth is often appended.

1. Name of the object offered and inscribed: "Stele" (Relative clause) "which"
2. Verb: "vowed" [in above case, "set up"]
3. Name of donor, with identification (lineage, position, etc.): "NN, son of N, X"
4. Deity to whom offered: "for N" (Added clauses)
5. Benevolence commemorated: "because he heard his voice"
6. Prayer for future benevolence: "may he bless."

This analysis indicates two fundamental functions for the votive stele. First, it commemorated the benevolent action of the deity, his answering the donor's prayer. The stone proclaimed the deity's mercy before the community in the sanctuary. Characteristically, the specific benevolence is not spelled out. Not the details of the event but the glory which it lends to the deity is the issue. Secondly, the votive stele commemorated the ritual act of the donor's repayment of his vow. It marked the donor as a pious and thankful servant of his divine master.

The third function of these votive steles is signaled by the prayer "may he bless." The stele calls for *future* benevolence. It does this by standing before the deity as a constant reminder, commemorating both his earlier attitude of mercy towards this donor as well as the donor's piety and devotion. In effect the stone draws out and perpetuates the value of the donor's original ritual act of sacrifice and prayer.

This third function may also said to be a *transferred* function. For it is the proper function of a "dedicated" gift to call for the deity's benevolence. A "dedicated" gift often bears a dedicatory inscription quite similar to the votive inscription. It names the object offered, the donor, and the deity and includes the crucial part, a petition; but there is no mention of a vow or answer to prayer. The dedicated object is a gift intended to foster the deity's goodwill.

Now it is a striking fact that in the two best-known collections of North-west Semitic inscriptions[12] the overwhelming majority of votive inscriptions is on *steles*. On the other hand, simple dedicatory inscriptions are not found on steles, but always on other objects. Why was the stele especially suited as a votive gift? Perhaps the Old Testament practice of vows supplies the answer. The Israelite repaid a vow by reciting a "thanksgiving psalm" in the sanctuary. Thanksgiving psalms emphasize the duty of repaying God by proclaiming his goodness to the worshipping community. This is precisely the function for which the stele was fashioned! It is a *marker*. It was a *public* monument, marking the answer to prayer, thereby glorifying the deity before the worshipping community.

On the other hand, the dedicated gift was not intended for the community, but to gain the god's favor. Size and visibility to human eyes were not crucial, but rather proximity to the sacred precinct and usefulness and value to the deity. Thus dedicated gifts tend to be objects of cultic furniture—altars, statues, etc.—and are often made of precious materials, gold, silver, marble, etc.

To sum up then: This third function of the votive stele, that of calling for a future benevolence, may be viewed also as a transferred function. The stele is not only a marker but also a gift dedicated to his further favor towards the donor.

Sir Flinders Petrie discovered a curious series of small tablets in the Temple of Ptah in Memphis, inscribed with from one to as many as 376 human ears.[13] Inscribed petitions, adoration scenes, and figures with upraised arms suggest that these are "stones of petition," that is, steles raised in the sanctuary to commemorate a petition and continue the suppliant's appeal for aid. The multiplication of ears appears to be an attempt to effect a positive hearing. Their size is striking. The smallest stones measures less than 2 cm. high (one inch is 2.54 cm.), and all but one are less than 30 cm. high. Now a stele only 2 cm. tall is remarkable on any theory! Yet the size suits their "private" function. Since the petition was not a public matter and the stones were meant only for the eyes of the god, a miniature stele was sufficient.

Cultic Stones: Marking the Cultic Immanence of the Deity

Cultic stones mark the place where the deity is in some manner immanent so that worship offered there reaches him or her. They may mark this immanence either generally, by being placed at the entry or boundary of the holy place, or more specifically, by being set beside the altar or offering table, the exact spot of cultic intercourse between worshipper and deity. The small stele-with-offering table, bearing a sun disc symbol of the deity, from Ugarit is the clearest example of such a cultic function for a figured stele.

Royal Assyrian steles also fulfilled cultic functions. The Bronze Gate of Balawat depicts sacrifice before a royal stele (*ANEP*, 364 and p. 292). A small altar was found before a royal stele at Nimrud.[14] Presumably the symbols of the deities regularly found on royal stones served as the focus of the worship. In fact, the worshipper probably conceived himself to be joining the king in his worship (and recognizing his rule!), since the king is himself depicted in an attitude of devotion towards these symbols of the deities (*ANEP*, 442-44, 447). Thus these royal Assyrian steles could serve all four basic functions: legal, memorial, commemorative, and cultic. The many Egyptian funerary steles also served a cultic function in the mortuary cult, marking the spot where offerings to benefit the deceased pictured on the stone should be offered.

The cultic function is perhaps less common among steles than the other three functions: memorial, legal, and commemorative. Presumably these extra-Palestinian cultures focused their ritual more often on images. There is, however, a notable series of steles in north Syria and surrounding areas which served cultic functions. They bear a large figure of the deity in relief, often without any inscription (*ANEP*, 489-92, 532), but sometimes with a dedicatory or votive inscription such as the one quoted above from the Melqart stele. Such a large figure of a deity on display surely marked his cultic immanence in the area and could easily serve as a focus of worship. The stone at Jekke had this function, for its inscription states that this stone *and an altar* were dedicated together by the king (*ANEP*, 500). Unfortunately, the precise archaeological context of these stones is rarely known. They were often abused by invaders and provided prized building material for later generations. Enough have been found in debris around temples or entryways, however, to assure a cultic function generally.

It is intriguing to note that these figured stones, usually without any inscription, are most common in Syria on the fringes of the plain stone tradition. It is tempting to see in these stones a fusion of the tradition for plain cultic massebot with the artistic traditions of Mesopotamia and Egypt which filled the stele with figure and inscriptions carefully using all space. The depiction of the diety on the stele would thus explain the significance of unfigured cultic massebot. They were stones proclaiming the deity's cultic immanence. This same end was accomplished rather differently, of course. The masseba was not a likeness but a marker, and likely enough also a medium of the divine power. What other functions were transferred to them by those who worshipped before them at various times and places is difficult to determine.

This northern tradition of figured steles may have found its way into Israel among those Canaanite traditions imported by Jezebel and Ahab. In the temple of Baal in Samaria Ahab erected a masseba defined with curious precision as "the masseba of Baal," which is probably one of these figured steles (II Kings 3:2; 10:26-

27). Perhaps Hosea refers to such a relief when he complains that Israel "improved" their massebot (Hos. 10:1).

Cultic markers were common at the entryway of temples. There were of course many other kinds of furniture there to aid in the activities at this busy place. All this offered real opportunity for transferral of function. The pillars before Solomon's temple (called ᶜammûd, not maṣṣēbāh) may well have had transferred to them the cultic function of marking the sacredness of the area. If their names, Jachin and Boaz, are actually the first words of dynastic oracles inscribed on them, one may say they also had the legal function of marking the relationship of Yahweh and the Davidic dynasty (I Kings 7:21).

Jacob set up the classic cultic masseba at Bethel to mark the presence of Yahweh there who appeared in the dream. "Surely Yahweh is in this place. . . . how fearful is this place. This is the very house of God; this is the gate of heaven" (Gen. 28: 16-17). The other account of the erection of this stone also stressed communication between God and man: "Jacob set up a masseba in the place where he [God] had spoken with him" (Gen. 35:14). Jacob anointed the stone, presumably to dedicate it, and poured out a libation before it, the only ritual before a cultic masseba ever explicitly mentioned in the Old Testament (Gen. 28:18; 35:14). In addition, the stone served other functions. It commemorated the theophany. There is also a hint that it had some votive significance: "I am the God of Bethel where you anointed a masseba and made a vow to me" (Gen. 31:13; cf. 28: 18-22). Presumably the stone served as the focus of the ritual of Jacob's vow, but the close connection of stone and vow hints at an Israelite custom of votive massebot, perhaps even used as "stones of petition."

Interest has usually centered on Jacob's description of this masseba: "This stone, which I have set up as a masseba, will be a house of God" (Gen. 28:22). "House of God" is the usual term for "temple." Just how far are we to press this term in understanding massebot? In some way this stone symbolized or was a temple in miniature. Now some ancients probably did conceive of the deity "dwelling" in the stone in the literal sense of the term. Yet in this context it is also a pun on the name of the place, Bethel, which means "house of God." Likewise, since the stone was the only object here, it is true in a sense to say that it *was* the sanctuary/temple.

Jacob's phrase apparently echoes a Semitic idiom, however. Curiously, it is one best attested in late classical literature. The Greek *baitylion* is transparently derived from a Semitic word for "house of God," such as *bēt ᵓil*. It occurs in accounts of Syro-Phoenician (!) stones of meteoric origin, which have remarkable powers of locomotion and of working wonders.[15] This is a far cry from the simple standing stones of the Bronze and Iron Ages! One might write off as pure coincidence any connection between Jacob's stone and these *baitylia*, save for the lone Aramaic attestation of the phrase "houses of the gods," used of the steles bearing the treaty inscriptions at Sefire.[16] Whatever connection there is in terminology, there is clearly a great development in meaning.

Many French and some English writers use the term "betyl" to refer to venerated sacred stones, especially of certain stones and symbols of stones in reliefs from Syria, Petra, and Carthage.[17] There are continuities between these "betyls" and Bronze and Iron Age standing stones, but the discontinuities are also impressive. These "betyls" date to a period of massive extra-Semitic cultural influences which brought great opportunities for transferral of functions. An extreme example is the omphaloid *"idole bétylique"*[18] which was clothed in garments and jewelry and transported in procession, treatment typical for an idol but hardly a standing stone. Furthermore, these "betyls" tend to be squatter, more block-like, which suggests a certain loss of feeling for them as standing stones. In sum, these later betyls deserve a special study of their own to define more precisely their functions and relationships with earlier standing stones.

Typology of the Form of Massebot

Paul Lapp was the first to attempt a broad typology by which to describe the forms of massebot.[19] Enlarging on his work, five categories may be distinguished: *rude*, either in a natural state or only roughly worked; *slab*, of uniform thickness, the most common form, often with rounded top and sometimes tapering; *round*, usually with a single flat face, as if to receive an inscription, very rarely a true cone; *obeliskoid*, common at Byblos, with all four faces tapering, yet not exactly equal, so not a true obelisk; *square*, rare, with width equal to or only slightly greater than the thickness.

Unfortunately as clear as these categories of form appear, no significant correlation between form and function suggests itself. One geographical distinction is to be noted. The obeliskoid form is limited to Byblos. It is hardly surprising that the earlier stones, such as those of the Middle Bronze alignment at Gezer and the earlier stones known from Transjordan, tend to be larger, rough-hewn "rude" types. Presumably this is due to more primitive quarrying tools.

Excavated Massebot

The very beginning of archaeological work in Palestine at the turn of the century uncovered rows of standing stones. Excavators were eager to claim that these stones were sacred massebot—though in a surprising number of cases they had to admit that the stones had been "reused" structurally, rebuilt into later walls.[20] This eagerness was partly due to ideas about primitive religion popular then which made much of "sacred stones." According to the theory of animism, primitive men believed that spirits and demons "dwelled" or "had their abode" in such massebot. Another popular theme was that of evolutionary development to higher stages. Massebot neatly suited this theory; early (primitive) Israel used sacred stones but later proscribed them under the influence of (higher) ethical monotheism. Further excavation, however, led to a recognition that Israelites often used lines of stones structurally to support ceiling and roof. Most of the early excavators' "massebot" were not sacred pillars but structural posts! In fact, "From Pillar to Post" was the happy title Millar Burrows gave his 1936 article detailing the scholarly reanalysis of these "massebot!"[21] Recent excavations have proven much more productive, however, yielding many genuine massebot.

We begin out discussion of massebot excavated in Palestine and Syria-Lebanon with the single obeliskoid stone from Byblos. By good fortune offering vessels were found still in place on the altar or offering table before it. Thus far we have only the report that this was found "on a street."[22] We eagerly await the excavator's final report, but even that will not answer all the questions that rush to mind. This was clearly a cultic stone, marking the offering place. But did it also function as a commemorative or legal stone? What was the nature of the offerings—and other cultic acts here? To which deity were they offered? Why was it set up here? For a semi-private cult or for official acts? Were the buildings in the vicinity private or public? All this illustrates the difficulty involved in interpreting massebot.

The cultic basalt slab at Hazor,[23] erected in Stratum XIV, was reused in the last Canaanite stratum, XIII, which was presumably destroyed by invading Israelites. An offering still sits before this cultic stone and two small massebot beside it, likely commemorating some offering or petition. The group stood beside the entry of a fine "palatial building," subtly proclaiming the piety of the occupants and the importance of the area. In the likely case that this was a public building, we can imagine that the stone figured in oath ceremonies for contracts and other administrative business.

The pair of stones flanking the entrance of a temple at Shechem (quite likely the temple of Baal-berit, "lord of the covenant," Judges 9:4, 46) served an additional cultic function. They marked the border and entrance to the most sacred area. Undoubtedly they also formed the focus for much of the ritual we know took place in the court at the entrance of the temples. (Psalms 24, 95, and 118:19-20 are examples of psalms rehearsed at the entrance to the Jerusalem temple court.)

The striking broken slab in the court of this same temple is the largest slab masseba excavated in Palestine. The large altar which once stood between it and the temple suggests a cultic function. On the other hand, it is very difficult to avoid associating this splendid stone in some way or other with the "great stone" of Joshua 24:26-27. This Joshua erected as a legal stone after the Shechem covenant ceremony as a witness "because it had heard all the words of Yahweh." Intriguingly, the excavators date the erection of this masseba to this period, namely sometime after 1400 and before 1100 B.C.[24] Unlike most other massebot, this stone does not stand against a wall but alone in an open court. A large group of worshippers could thus stand about the stone as they would likely do in covenant renewal ceremonies. Such possible identification with Joshua's stone lacks proof, of course. Yet it may be worth noting that of all excavated massebot, this stone can lay the strongest claim, weak as it is, to being an actual stone mentioned in the Old Testament.

The entry to cities and buildings was a favored spot for massebot. First of all, the masseba could serve as a boundary marker to remind one of the nature of the area to be entered. For example, a warning at the boundary of a sacred area would be quite useful. Secondly, as a marker the masseba was meant to be seen. Therefore men tended to set them in large open public areas frequented by crowds and affording a good view. Open squares were rare within the precious space inside city walls except perhaps before a governor's palace and regularly at the gateway. Everyone had to pass through the gate to enter the city and much business was transacted here. It is not surprising then that the fragment of the only possible Israelite *stele* ever found was discovered near the Samaria gateway.[25]

A single square masseba was found at the gateway of the once capital city of Tirzah.[26] The excavator, the late Père de Vaux, associates it with a basin installation set directly within the entryway in several phases of the gate. This puzzling position is best explained by the fact that this was the border of the city. It would have been useful for oath rituals in the business and judicial transactions "at the gate" so often mentioned in the Old Testament (Ruth 4:1, Gen. 23:18). Considering its position, squarely in the center of the narrow entry of the city, de Vaux suggests those passing it may have poured a libation to invoke the protection of the deity as they entered this new sphere.

Yohanan Aharoni unearthed a series of Israelite sanctuaries at the Judean border fortress of Arad.[27] Preliminary reports indicate that on the site of a pre-Solomonic open-air sanctuary, Solomon built a citadel fortress which was later rebuilt by several Judean kings. The main room of the sanctuary measured only 5 by 6 feet, yet apparently was the central shrine, the Holy of Holies. The round-with-face masseba was found thrown down but presumably stood in this central position. It may have stood there already in the earliest phase of the sanctuary; for in that stratum a socket, very shallow but suitable for this stone, stood at this central spot.[28]

In this position the masseba surely functioned as a cultic stone, the focus of the worship there, such as the sacrifices offered on the two incense altars. It might also have been a commemorative stone, marking the victories granted by Yahweh to the garrisons here. Considering the patriarchal traditions connected with Arad and the pre-Solomonic sanctuary, one may even wonder if this stone, like the one at Bethel, did not commemorate a theophany to the patriarchs.[29]

Close examination of the holy place reveals what appear to be two flint massebot built into the right and rear walls. One can imagine that these were commemorative or votive stones in an earlier phase, were considered too important or holy to destroy, and so were rebuilt into the walls that they might remain near the holy place.

Kathleen Kenyon has uncovered two slender rectangular or "square" pillars in a room at the base of the slope of Ophel at Jerusalem.[30] She notes that these must be massebot since the area of the compartment is so small that the roof supports are unnecessary. This is an intriguing suggestion, for the Old Testament reports that there are a number of sanctuaries and massebot just outside Jerusalem in this very area which Josiah and Judah were constrained to destroy (II Kings 23).

The context is curious. This compartment continued a narrow doorway opening to the rock scarp behind it, just 10-30 cm. away. One could hardly walk through it, and Miss Kenyon suggests it was intended to supply access to the rock for some ritual such as pouring libations. In that rock scarp below was a shallow cave with a cache of pottery vessels of about 800 B.C. (but not bones), and yet another cache and cave was just to the south. The hollow installation set on the scarp just above the room has been interpreted as an altar, though this is by no means certain. All of this surely suggests a cenotaph, a memorial installation with two massebot memorializing deceased persons, perhaps parents of an important family.

Still, these nearly two-meter-high pillars are unique among massebot. They are the tallest massebot known in Palestine since the Middle Bronze Age. They are the only *pair* yet discovered (perhaps this is only coincidence?). They are of very rare, rough-hewn, almost square form (perhaps they were quarried as posts but later pressed into service as massebot?). They are set peculiarly, with their wider faces in different planes, unlike any other known group of massebot. Could it be that they are after all strengthening structural posts on this precarious slope, like the posts higher up the slope?

Miniature Massebot

Recently the existence of "miniature" massebot has come to light in the small 15-35 cm. (6-14 inches) high stones from cultic contexts in Hazor[31] and Tell Ta^{c}annek.[32] Though shaped like their larger counterparts, they were too small to function simply as standing stones, that is, to catch the attention of on-lookers from a distance. These miniature massebot are clearly secondary, derived, and symbolic in function. Their small size rendered them cheaper, portable, and easily reusable. Presumably they were for private or individual worship. Size was important for public cult but not when they were meant only for the eyes of the worshipper and, more importantly, the deity.

Their possible functions are many. A likely guess sees them as cultic stones for private or small cultic installations. One found at Hazor was in a small cultic installation at the gateway. Another was on a smaller offering table just inside the Hazor Area H temple and a third was inside the same temple.[33] They are notable for their very careful shaping into conical or round-with-face shapes. Three roughly cut arched slabs were discovered in the storage room of the cultic structure at Taanach. We may imagine that all these were used to "make" a sanctified spot, to form a focus for worship and prayer, much as a crucifix or a menorah today is set up to form a devotional center. Or they may have been left as "stones of petition," after an urgent petition or vow was made. (Is this the function of the two miniature stones?) The Egyptian stones of petition mentioned above were also noted for their small size. It is possible, too, that these miniature stones were used in imitation of the practice of setting up larger permanent stones at the fulfillment of a vow. Here especially the cost factor may be significant. One can well imagine poorer, lower classes appropriating in simpler, less costly form, the practices of those of a higher economic and social status.

Alignments

Most intriguing of all massebot are those in multiple alignments. Rows of huge rude stones have long been known to exist in Transjordan at Lejun, Ader, and Bab edh-Dhra[c]. Rows of massebot have been excavated at Gezer, Hazor, Byblos, and now near the copper mines at Timna. Why more than one stone? Scholars have not seriously advocated that they represent a "council" of a number of deities. Alignments are understood rather as memorials in a mortuary cult or a series of commemorative votive stones. In an important recent contribution, Eugene Stockton has argued persuasively that such stones were intended to serve as surrogates for individuals who wished to be represented continually before their deity in the sanctuary.[34] W. F. Albright has argued that the massebot of the "high places" denounced in the Old Testament were used in a mortuary cult. While other peoples apparently had such cults, the minimal evidence for (or polemic against!) a cult of the dead in the Old Testament renders this doubtful.[35]

The Gezer stones[36] are the most striking, for several stand over ten feet high! Originally ten in number, they stand in a gentle arc 100 feet long, rising above a pavement just inside the Middle Bronze IIC city wall. Quite happily, after excavating these stones in 1903, Macalister covered them over again "till the remote time when a national pride in monuments of antiquity such as this shall have been developed locally." This enabled their restudy in 1968. A remarkably planned and executed excavation of the remaining bits of stratified material was able to show that the stones had been erected simultaneously, not in series, and dated them to MB IIC, *ca.* 1600 B.C.[37] Furthermore the child burials nearby seem not to be directly associated with the alignment. (Intramural child burial was a common MB practice.)

This grand alignment has received a host of interpretations. Scholars have judged them to be victory monuments, sacred pillars of a "High Place," and memorials of ancestors or other notable persons. The present writer suggests another view. They were legal massebot, erected to mark a treaty or covenant relationship between ten groups, either clans inhabiting Gezer or cities in a wider league in the area.

On this interpretation a whole series of data falls neatly in place. The huge size of the stones and of the precious intramural space devoted to them dictates some public, city-wide function. Since they were intended to function as a unity of ten members, they were erected simultaneously. The Gezer excavators have suggested that the new prosperity evident at Gezer in MB IIC, the period of the founding of the alignment, may reflect the formation of this league.[38] In any case, the alignment remained in use for a relatively long period into the Late Bronze Age, unchanged except for the repaving of the area. (In fact Macalister found most of them still erect, *in situ!*) The curious large, hollowed-out, socket-like block before the alignment may well have served as a blood-altar for covenant sacrifices, just as the altar before the twelve massebot of the Sinai covenant ceremony (Ex. 24:4-9). On the other hand, it may have served as a socket for an emblem of the deity of the covenant and league. The dimensions of the socket fit perfectly an eleventh masseba found by Macalister nearby. This stone was more carefully hewn than any of the other ten which would occasion no surprise if indeed this was the emblem of the deity in the treaty alignment.

This primary legal/treaty significance would of course allow for secondary functions. Each stone might also have memorialized the eponymous ancestor of a clan or even have marked some historical event in which the ten groups participated. The obvious paradigm for such an understanding of the Gezer alignment is the 12-stone group at the Gilgal sanctuary (Joshua 4). These marked the unity of the tribes of the Israelite confederation and commemorated their common historical experience, the crossing of the Jordan.

Finally it should be noted that Macalister's reporting does not supply firm enough evidence to decide just how much sacrificial activity was carried on here or to what extent this sanctuary was much used for individual worship as well as public.

The magnificent obelisk temple at Byblos, dating from the first centuries of the 2nd millennium B.C.[39] features more than forty obeliskoid and slab massebot, ranging in height from one foot to a rather impressive eleven feet, standing in the U-shaped court. It is to be noted that the stones were arranged both singly and in groups. Several groups are symmetrically arranged, indicating some relationship. Quite a few had offering tables before the stones, showing some cultic function. The raised platform or cella in the center presumably housed some emblem of the deity. The excavator suggests that the huge block (square masseba?) in the court was somehow displaced from its original position in the cella.

Only one fine obelisk in the Byblos temple (to the cella's right) bore an inscription, in hieroglyphic Egyptian. This broken text mentions a deceased person as well as a deity possibly to be identified with Canaanite Reshef, an underworld deity. These clues suggest that these are memorial massebot set up before the temple of some deity. Thus the offering tables before the stones were for mortuary offerings. The abundant cultic furniture in the court, the basins for libation and lustration, the *naoi* or shrines, need not all have been used in funerary ritual but surely suit it. Drink offerings for the dead in their dry and dusty underworld are well attested, and *naoi* are known from Egypt. In fact, the strong Egyptian influences here—the *naoi*, the obeliskoid shaping, the hieroglyphic inscription—encourage a memorial interpretation since the funerary cult was so important in Egypt. Of course the Semites in this area also used memorial standing stones. One of the reasons why Dan⁾el in the Ugaritic epic wished a son was precisely that he might perform the filial duty of "setting up the stelae of the ancestral spirits in the holy place."[40]

The stones of this temple probably had additional functions. Worshippers might well offer petitions or vows before the stones memorializing revered ancestors of the clan. The stones at the entryway presumably had a cultic purpose. Finally, the excavator notes that several of the long stones built into the cella appear to be old massebot! This calls to mind the reuse of massebot in the Arad sanctuary.[41]

Hazor ranks second only to Byblos in number of massebot produced and is unrivaled in the variety and signficance of its stones. Altogether forty have been found in at least ten different loci, all from the Late Bronze Age. The most important group is that discovered in Shrine 6136.[42] This is worth consideration in some detail both for its intrinsic interest and as an example of the ambiguities involved in understanding massebot.

The unpretentious shrine of one room, probably unroofed, was built originally in the lower city in Stratum IB (14th century). In its earlier phase the room had benches, two offering slabs, a small niche in the western wall, and a number of massebot. One was found in debris filling the room, and seventeen round-with-face stones were found flung on the nearby slope in destruction debris of the stratum.

Among the ten massebot and the statue found in the niche of the last phase of the shrine when it was rebuilt in the 13th century, the focus of attention is the stele incised with a disk and crescent with tassels, the symbol of the deity, and two upraised arms. These small massebot range in size from 22 to 65 cm. They were probably erected over the course of time and not simultaneously, for there are evident groupings; and one at least is set in front of another. The small basalt seated figure holding a goblet in his right hand has on his breast an inverted crescent symbol reminiscent of the incised stele. This attitude is very common and thus ambiguous. It is used of deities, kings, and deceased persons. Two roughly shaped stones less than 20 cm. high, a small anthropoid statuette, and another enthroned figure must also be noted.

Two basic interpretations have been offered of this shrine. Galling suggested that these stones memorialize *personae nobiles* of the city.[43] The seated statue represents some leader, perhaps the founder of the ruling dynasty, or the ancestor of the group memorialized. The small rude stones and figures memorialize lesser individuals. The present writer takes the less-than-royal dimensions and construction of the shrine to indicate that it came from the middle or lower class of Hazorite society, but this by no means rules out Galling's suggested memorial function. In fact, the parallels to the *Totenkultraum* in Tell Halaf are striking. There is a large statue of a king/deity, a monumental statue of a seated couple, and no less than 16 small rude statues of seated and standing figures.[44]

Yigael Yadin suggests that Shrine 6136 is an early antecedent of the shrines of the cult of Baal Hamon and Tannit known in Carthage and other Mediterranean sites some 800 or so years later.[45] It is surely intriguing that hundreds of these Punic commemorative steles include a disk and crescent as well as hands as symbols of the deities. These Punic stones are clearly commemorative/votive, marking *molk* sacrifices and calling for further blessing. Whether or not the same deities are involved,

Yadin's comparison is suggestive. One can well imagine these Hazor stones being erected at the marking of vows as "stones of petition" and/or later as stones marking the beneficence of the deity and piety of the donor on the occasion of the fulfillment of vows or some other sacrifice. This location would then become a most logical location for further supplication and worship since it contained the reminder of previous happy relationship between deity and suppliant.

Stockton nuances this comparison of the Hazor and Punic stones by emphasizing that these stones were set up in a shrine before the deity in order to enhance a favorable relationship with the deity.[46] Indeed, this cuts across the memorial and votive interpretations. The stones had this purpose whether they memorialized the dead before the deity or commemorated the piety and devotion of the living and prolonged the value of his prayer and sacrifices here. In this connection Stockton draws attention to a disk-shaped slab and suggests that it was a base for some emblem of the deity which the massebot were meant to face. On this view one can see the massebot (of the dead?) and the living worshippers joining, ranged together in "worship" about the emblem of the deity.

Were the massebot of Shrine 6136 intended to memorialize the dead or to commemorate individuals and their pious vows and sacrifices before the deity? The plain fact is that we do not yet possess sufficient knowledge of the beliefs and practices of these Canaanites to enable us to decide confidently. There is no compelling reason either to reject the one interpretation or to embrace the other.

The same ambiguity besets the interpretation of the five identical low square stones found set in a row before the altar of the sanctuary at the Timna mining center.[47] Whether intended as memorial or commemorative stones, it appears that it was desired that these individuals be marked in the holy place.

A final note about alignments: the legal function of marking a relationship is latent in the very idea of an alignment or grouping of stones. This possibility must be most seriously considered when a group is erected simultaneously, as at Gezer, or set in a single symmetrical unit, as with some groups at Byblos, or when the stones are obviously intended to be identical, as at Timna.

Prohibition of Massebot

Finally we consider briefly why the massebot which seemed to be legitimate in earlier Israel were later prohibited in the strongest terms (Deut. 16:22; II Kings 23:14). It should be remembered that the Deuteronomic reformation of Josiah aimed at limiting all sacrifice to the single central sanctuary at Jerusalem and destroying all other cult places. Therefore, as the emblem *par excellence* of the cult place, the masseba would have been unpopular among the reformers even if it had not been considered improper for other reasons.

The development may be hypothesized as follows. In early Israel the legal, memorial, and commemorative functions were apparently more significant, relatively speaking, than in later Israel. (In any case, later writers were more concerned about their cultic use.) The non-committal blankness of the massebot enabled many in Israel to interpret them as commemorative of Yahweh's theophanies and historical acts, while their Canaanite neighbors used them in accord with their religious conceptions. But the waves of foreign cults and influences that swept over Israel had a marked effect. First the cult of the Tyrian Baal under Jezebel, then the Aramean and Assyrian influences as Israel and Judah became vassal states, led Israel to use the massebot "like the nations"—to quote the repeated phrase of the Deuteronomic writers (I Kings 14:23-24; II Kings 17:8-11). Unfortunately we do not understand as clearly as we would wish just what ritual and which cults of foreign deities this phrase "like the nations" involved. The biblical writers often considered them unmentionable. This produced guilt by association, if not also by practice.

In addition, the massebot easily took over the transferred function of image, since they were the focus of ritual. At any rate, later biblical writers consider massebot to be a variety of "image" (Lev. 26:1; Micah 5:13). This probably reflects both a sharpened and more sophisticated religious consciousness as well as an increased popular use of massebot as "images." Thus the massebot fell under the prohibition of the second commandment (Ex. 20:4) which prohibited the "magic" use of images or any such attempt to coerce or control the deity in worship. Thirdly, though massebot were standard furniture in the local sanctuaries or "high places," there is not a single masseba clearly attested in the Jerusalem temple! Therefore, the condemnation of the local sanctuaries and the substitution of the Jerusalem temple simply undercut the use of the cultic massebot.[48]

Notes

[1]W. King, *A History of Sumer and Akkad* (1923), pp. 126-29.

[2]J. Pritchard, *Ancient Near Eastern Texts,* 3rd edition with Supplement, (1969), pp. 659-61.

[3]For a superb comprehensive study of these steles see J. Vandier, *Manuel d'archéologie égyptienne* (1952-1958), Vol. I, 724-74 and Vol. II, 389-534.

[4]C. Jean and J. Hoftijzer, *Dictionnaire des inscriptions sémitiques de l'ouest* (1965), p. 164.

[5]L. Woolley, *Annals of Archaeology and Anthropology* XXVI (1939-1940), Pl. III and p. 14.

[6]*Spaethethitische Bildkunst* (1949), pp. 119-25, 152-53.

[7]W. Andrae, *Die Stelenreihen in Assur* (1913).

[8]E. Ebeling and B. Meissner, *Reallexikon der Assyriologie* (1933), II, 412.

[9]H. Tadmor, *Eretz Israel* VIII (1967), 241-45, 75*.

[10]For convenient secondary sources see R. de Vaux, *Ancient Israel* (1961), pp. 444-46 and D. Harden, *The Phoenicians* (1963), pp. 94-104.

[11]H. Donner and W. Röllig, *Kanaanäische und Aramäische Inschriften* (1962-1964), pp. 203-04.

[12]G. A. Cooke, *A Textbook of North Semitic Inscriptions* (1903) and H. Donner and W. Röllig, *Kanaanäische und Aramäische Inschriften* (1962-1964).

[13]W. M. F. Petrie, *Memphis I* (1909), pp. 7 and 19, and Pls. IX-XIII.

[14]H. R. Hall, *Babylonian and Assyrian Sculpture in the British Museum* (1928), Pl. XIII and p. 14.

[15]G. F. Moore, *American Journal of Archaeology* VII (1903), 198-208.

[16]Pritchard, *Ancient Near Eastern Texts,* p. 660, (Sefire II C).

[17]H. Cazelles and A. Feuillet, *Dictionnaire de la Bible, Supplément* (1966), VII, Fig. 701, 3 and 5, p. 954 and S. Moscati, *The World of the Phoenicians* (1965), Pls. 14, 24, 26, 28.

[18]H. Seyrig, *Syria* XL (1963), 17-19 and Pl. I.

[19]P. Lapp, *BASOR* No. 173 (Feb. 1964), p. 36.

[20]F. J. Bliss, *Palestine Exploration Fund Quarterly Statement* XXXI (1899), 322-23 and E. Sellin, *Denkschriften der Kaiserlichen Akademie der Wissenschaften in Wein: Philosophisch-historische Klasse,* Band LII (1905), 18-19, 104-05, and Fig. 10.

[21]M. Burrows, *Journal of the Palestine Oriental Society* XIV (1934), 42-51.

[22]M. Dunand, *Byblos II* (1950), pp. 272-73 and 475.

[23]Y. Yadin, *Israel Exploration Journal* IX (1959), 76 and Yadin *et al.*, *Hazor III-IV* (1961), Pl. IX, 1-4.

[24]G. E. Wright, *Shechem* (1965), pp. 82-87 and Figs. 36-40, 56.

[25]G. E. Wright, *BA* XXII (1959), 77, Fig. 17.

[26]R. de Vaux, *Revue Biblique* LVIII (1951), 428 and Pls. VI-VIII.

[27]Y. Aharoni, *BA* XXXI (1968), 18-32.

[28]See the plan, Y. Aharoni, *BA* XXXI (1968), Fig. 12, p. 18.

[29]B. Mazar, *Journal of Near Eastern Studies* XXIV (1965), 297-303.

[30]K. Kenyon, *Jerusalem* (1967), pp. 64-66.

[31]Yadin, *Hazor III-IV*, Pls. CCXCIV, 12-14 and CCCXXXIII, 2-8.

[32]Lapp, *BASOR* No. 173 (Feb., 1964), pp. 35-36.

[33]Yadin, *Hazor III-IV*, Pls. CXXIX, 1-2 and CXLII, 2.

[34]E. Stockton, *Australian Journal of Biblical Archaeology* I: 3 (1970), 59.

[35]W. F. Albright, *Supplements to Vetus Testamentum* IV, pp. 242-58.

[36]R. A. S. Macalister, *The Excavation of Gezer* (1912), II, 381-406.

[37]W. G. Dever, H. D. Lance, and G. E. Wright, *Gezer I* (1970), p. 3.

[38]William G. Dever, *et al.*, "Further Excavations at Gezer, 1967-1971," *BA* XXXIV (1971), 124. See also the discussion of covenant ceremonies, p. 123, within the detailed treatment of the "High Place."

[39]M. Dunand, *Byblos II* (1950-1958), pp. 643-53, Fig. 767, and Pls. XX-XXXV.

[40]Pritchard, *Ancient Near Eastern Texts*, p. 150, Aqhat, A i 27.

[41]Stockton, *Australian Journal of Biblical Archaeology* I: 3 (1970), 66, 80.

[42]Y. Yadin *et al.*, *Hazor I* (1958), pp. 83-92, and Pls. XXVIII-XXXI; CLXXX-CLXXXI, and *Hazor II* (1960), pp. 97, 105, 111 and Pls. XXXVII, 6, and CCVIII-CCIX.

[43]K. Galling, *Zeitschrift des Deutschen Palästina-Vereins* LXXV (1959), 5.

[44]R. Naumann, *Tell Halaf*, II (1950), pp. 159-61 and 357-60, and B. Hrouda, *Tell Halaf*, IV (1962), pp. 6-7.

[45]Y. Yadin in *Near Eastern Archaeology in the Twentieth Century*, ed. J. A. Sanders (1970), 199-231.

[46]Stockton, *Australian Journal of Biblical Archaeology* I: 3 (1970), 68-69.

[47]B. Rothenberg and A. Lupu, *Zeitschrift des Deutschen Palästina-Vereins* LXXXII (1966) 125-127 and Taf. 11 and 12; and *Museum Haaretz: Bulletin* IX (June, 1967), 53-70.

[48]This development is discussed in greater detail in the writer's unpublished doctoral dissertation, "Studies in *Maṣṣēbôt*," Harvard

University, 1969. This also contains a fuller series of Near Eastern steles and a hopefully complete catalogue of excavated Palestinian and Near Eastern "plain" massebot.

20

THE HORNED ALTAR OF BEER-SHEBA

YOHANAN AHARONI

Until now, the altar of the Arad temple was the only altar for burnt offerings of the First Temple period discovered by archaeologists; it was described in *The Biblical Archaeologist* six years ago (Vol. 31 [1968], 19-21). It was a square structure of five cubits, standing three cubits high (cf. Exod 27:1), built of clay and small undressed stones, in accordance with the biblical law (Exod. 20:25, etc.). On its surface was a large flint slab surrounded by two plastered runnels, and there were no traces of horns at its corners. However, the Arad altar was covered by a white plaster which was not preserved at the corners. It is possible, therefore, that the altar originally had horns made of clay and plaster, which were broken off with its destruction and burial.

This theory now becomes plausible with the discovery of the stones of a large horned altar in the 1973 season at Tel Beer-sheba. Unlike the Arad altar, this one was not preserved *in situ* but its stones were found re-used as part of a repaired wall of the storehouse complex of Stratum II, belonging to the 8th century. This section of the wall was rebuilt with well-smoothed ashlar blocks of calcareous sandstone, a harder substance than the common limestone used in the Beer-sheba buildings.

The four altar horns were found arranged one beside the other in the wall, three intact and the fourth with its top knocked off. Their interpretation as altar horns is assured by their similarity to the horns of the small incense altars found in Megiddo. Other similarly worked ashlar blocks were found above these horns in the same wall, as well as in the area nearby, one of them on the slope outside the gate.

After the stones were reassembled, it was apparent that, except for all four horns, only about half of the altar stones had been discovered. Their arrangement is unlikely to be the original one, but we were able to reconstruct its height with certainty. There are stones of two different sizes, indicating that the altar was constructed of three layers; from this we may conclude that its height was about 157 cm. (*ca.* 63 inches), measuring to the top of the horns. This is the measurement of exactly three large (royal) cubits, similar to the height of the altars at Arad, the Tabernacle (Exod. 27:1) and probably the original altar of the Solomonic temple (2 Chron. 6:13).

Unfortunately, the width of the altar cannot be reconstructed with certainty. The combination of two horns constitutes approximately the same measurement as its height, i.e. a square of three cubits. This is the minimum size, however, because additional stones may have been between the horns. It is therefore possible that its size was a square of five cubits, like the altars at Arad and those described in the biblical references just mentioned.

All stones are well-smoothed ashlar masonry, which seems to stand in contradiction to the biblical law that the altar should be built "of unhewn stones, upon which no man has lifted an iron tool" (Josh. 8:31, etc.). This ancient tradition evidently was disregarded at Beer-sheba; alternatively, we could suppose that the law was taken literally and the dressing was done with tools of bronze or stone instead of the common iron. One stone has a deeply engraved decoration of a twisting snake, an ancient symbol of fertility widely dispersed throughout the Near East. The symbol of a snake was venerated in Israel from Moses' times (Num. 21:8-9) and the bronze serpent was worshipped in the Jerusalem temple until the days of Hezekiah (2 Kings 18:4).

The horned altar is frequently mentioned in the Bible. Though the meaning of the horns is nowhere explained (some scholars believe that they were substituted for original *maṣṣebot* standing on the corners of the altar), they were considered to be the holiest part of the altar. They are mentioned as the first item in its construction (Exod. 27:2; 38:2); on them the blood of the sacrifice was sprinkled (Exod. 29:12; Num. 9:9; etc.); to cut them off desecrated the altar (Amos 3:14). Twice we hear that when a refugee "caught hold of the horns of the altar" he obtained the right to asylum (1 Kings 1:50; 2:28).

Sometimes, incense altars were equipped with horns (Exod. 30:2), the best examples having been found at Megiddo. It is now clear that the shape of their horns is an imitation of those of the larger altar for burnt offerings, which was the central edifice in the courtyard of a temple.

Discovering the altar at Beer-sheba was a highlight of the excavation, but no great surprise for us. In my essay on the Arad temple, I developed the hypothesis that there was an institution of royal border sanctuaries, and, consequently, that the most promising site for the discovery of another Israelite temple would be the tell of biblical Beer-sheba (*BA* 31 [1968], 32). It took us five years to find it, but now with the discovery of the altar we have confirmation of a temple's existence. The goal of the coming season will be to locate the temple's place in the city plan. The beautiful altar indicates that the temple must have been a far more elaborate structure than the simple shrine at Arad.

One other factor, the demolition of the altar, is of much interest. The storehouse in which the altar stones had been re-used was destroyed at the end of the 8th century B.C.E. (Stratum II), probably during Sennacherib's campaign in 701. It appears that the repair of the building and the concomitant dismantling of the altar took place in the reign of Hezekiah. This is a most dramatic corroboration of the religious reform carried out by him, as expressed in the harsh accusations of Rabshakeh in 2 Kings 18:22: "But if you say to me, 'We rely on the Lord our God,' is it not he whose high places and altars Hezekiah has removed, saying to Judah and to Jerusalem, 'You shall worship before this altar in Jerusalem'?"

21

AN ISRAELITE HORNED ALTAR AT DAN

AVRAM BIRAN

(In its first issue of 1974, the BA reported the finding of Dr. Aharoni of a horned altar at Beer-sheba in the summer of 1973. Here, Dr. Biran reports on finding one at Dan. The common geographical description of ancient Israel as extending from Dan to Beer-sheba takes on added meaning when one compares such significant artifacts from the two extremes of the land.—Ed.)

Altars and horned altars figure prominently in the Old Testament, but archaeological excavations have uncovered singularly few. Until the relatively large number found at Megiddo about fifty years ago and fully published by H. G. May in *Material Remains of the Megiddo Cult* (1935), only four altars were known—one from Gezer, two from Shechem, and one at Tell Beit Mirsim. In the last few years, additional ones have been found at Arad, Lachish and Beer-sheba, as well as another one at Megiddo. The altars differ from one another—the Beer-sheba one is not all of one block and is much larger, for example—and not all of them are horned. Now, during the 1974 season of excavations at Dan (for a report on earlier seasons see *BA* 37.2), in the area of the high place and south of the steps, another horned altar has come to light. One of the horns is completely broken away, two others are damaged, but one seems to be in its original state. The altar is almost square (40 by 40 cms., or about 16 inches each way), and stands 35 cms. or about 14 inches high to the tip of the horn. It is made of travertine limestone, and it must have been in use for a relatively long time, because the top surface is calcined to a depth of several inches.

The date of the altar cannot be established with certainty. It was found on the earthen floor of the courtyard which surrounded the 9th century B.C. high place. However, since it may have been used originally at some other location before it was brought to the courtyard, an earlier date is possible. And we cannot be sure that it was in place when the courtyard floor was first laid, so that it may conceivably be later. The closest comparison to our altar seems to be the one from Gezer, but since that one was found in secondary use it is not a safe guide to fix a date. The altar found at Tell Beit Mirsim is dated by Albright to the 11th-10th centuries B.C. Though considerably smaller than the Dan one, it is similar in shape. We are inclined to date our altar to the 9th century or earlier and await additional comparative material from closely datable stratified deposits to fix its dates more accurately.

Part IV

ARCHAEOLOGY AND
NEW TESTAMENT BACKGROUNDS

22

ANCIENT GREEK SYNAGOGUE INSCRIPTIONS

FLOYD V. FILSON

Some of us will admit that we have not given the attention deserved to inscriptions of the period just prior to and contemporary with the emergence of rabbinical Judaism and the Christian Church. There are practical reasons for this neglect. The facts about the finding and wording of such inscriptions are usually found in excavation reports or technical journals not easily accessible to many students. The grasp of the meaning of the data calls for competence in a wide range of linguistic and historical material that gives the interpreting setting for such study. Moreover, the inscriptions are often—or, rather, usually— fragmentary, and so require extensive background information to perceive fully their reference and meaning. The date of the inscription often cannot be determined with certainty.

Nevertheless, inscriptions offer a highly instructive source of historical information. They give specific data for the study of the period in which the inscription dates. They are almost always contemporary with the people and events mentioned. They give not only historical data but also linguistic information about spelling and word forms in the place and time to which the inscriptions point. They give insights into the life of individuals and groups who never come alive or even appear in the written history of the period covered. The cumulative effect of the information which inscriptions yield is great.

A good example of the light which the study of inscriptions can throw on ancient history is the publication by B. Lifshitz entitled *Donateurs et Fondateurs dans les Synagogues Juives*. Its full title may be translated thus: "Donors and Builders in Jewish Synagogues: A Collection of Greek Dedications Relating to the Building and Repair of Synagogues." It appears as No. 7 in *Cahiers de la Revue Biblique* (Paris: J. Gabalda & Cie., 1967) and runs to ninety-four pages.

The scope of this study is limited. It deals with relatively few of the numerous inscriptions by and about Jews of the ancient period. It selects and studies 106 inscriptions which record in Greek the contribution in work and especially in money of Jews who either built or more often repaired, adorned, or enlarged the synagogue where the inscription was found. In a few inscriptions, by the way, it is not certain that the benefactor was a Jew.

The geographical range of these inscriptions is great. It extends from Egypt, Palestine, Asia Minor and the Black Sea on the east to Sicily and Spain in the west. Palestine, Syria and Asia Minor are most frequently represented. Rome and Italy, it is noteworthy, are not included.

The date of the inscriptions included is doubtful in some cases. In general, they cover the period from the 3rd century B.C. to the 6th century A.D. This warns us not to treat these inscriptions as though they all applied fully to any one period. It suggests that recurrent features may have special importance.

In a large number of the inscriptions, the individual or group who has built or repaired or adorned the synagogue is said thereby to carry out (*teleō*) or to fulfill (*plēroō*) a vow (*euchē*); a good example is the inscription No. 19 (hereafter, reference will be made to inscriptions by number in this manner).

Often it is a prominent leader in the local synagogue who has made and fulfilled such a vow. It also occurs that a leader of a strong synagogue in a neighboring city steps in with help that includes financial assistance (No. 38). But perhaps most often it is an individual, or a family group (No. 63), who steps in with the resources needed, and at times such people do it as a kind of memorial. Sometimes a group of donors is listed, with the amount each has given carefully stated (No. 100). If an individual or family or other group has provided the funds for the project, it often is explicitly noted that the expenses were covered without touching at all the funds in the synagogue treasury (but see No. 2, a mosaic financed "from revenues of the synagogues").

The inscriptions use the word synagogue in two senses. It refers occasionally as in No. 10 to the synagogue as a community of God's people whose life centers in this building (e.g. *laos* and *plēthos*), but more often it refers to the building itself. Words are used of the building which recall for us the temple of Jerusalem; these synagogue groups have taken over such words to express their life as centered in the synagogue with no thought of the old temple; they call their synagogue a house, a sanctuary (*naos*), a holy place, most holy, and a house or place of prayer (*proseuchē*).

This last word, found in about ten inscriptions, deserves attention in connection with Acts 16:13, 16. Paul and his companions, on the first sabbath day after reaching Philippi, "went outside the gate to the riverside, where we supposed there was a place of prayer" (*proseuchē*). There they found some "women who had come together." This is widely taken to mean that Paul and his companions attended a synagogue service by the riverside. This can hardly be the meaning of this puzzling verse, for a synagogue consisted of ten or more Jewish men banded together for worship and study and community life. A group of women thus could not constitute a synagogue. Luke seems to know this, for he says, according to the most likely Greek text, that "we *supposed* there was a place of prayer" by the riverside; whenever in Luke-Acts he uses "suppose" (*nomizō*), he refers to a view falsely held. So it seems that Paul and his companions set out to find by the riverside a place of prayer, a synagogue, but on their first try they found there only some Jewish women and a God-fearing Gentile woman named Lydia. Later Paul and his companions found where the synagogue, the place of prayer (*proseuchē*), actually was (Acts 16:13-16). In any case, we find *proseuchē* (literally, a house or place of prayer) as a name attested for a synagogue in Acts and in about ten of the inscriptions which Lifshitz presents. In these inscriptions, the word *proseuchē* occurs almost as often as the word synagogue.

Several titles of synagogue officials are found. "Elder" (*presbyteros*) occurs eight times, "ruler" (*archōn*) half a dozen times, "synagogue ruler" (*archisynagogos*) in twelve inscriptions, and "ruler of the council of elders" (*gerousiarchos*) in one. A man whose name is now lost, with his wife and children, paved the portico of a sanctuary in Syria in the time of a certain Nehemiah, who is called *hazzana* and *diakōn* (No. 40).

The dedications of synagogues are sometimes surprising. Rather unexpected is the dedication of certain synagogues in Egypt to rulers of the Ptolemy line; in No. 93 and No. 94 the dedication is to the reigning Ptolemy and Queen Cleopatra his sister and Queen Cleopatra his spouse. The dedication to the reigning ruler was not intended to compromise the monotheistic faith of the Jews involved. This dedication to a pagan ruler is found in Egypt but is not a general practice. Quite different, for example, is No. 35, the dedication "to the invincible God and to the honorable place of prayer" (*tē kyria proseuchē*). Striking also is the dedication in No. 34 "to the entire fatherland/homeland" (*patris*); Lifshitz explains the *patris* as the Jewish community.

It is not possible here to discuss in detail the personal names that occur in these inscriptions. They are listed alphabetically in an index to the publication. One may note in passing the occurrence of the names Lazarus and Isouos; the latter name seems to represent the name Jesus. Of the names of the twelve Apostles found in the Gospels, only Jacob (that is James) and Judas (Jutas) are found. Among the infrequent names found both in these inscriptions and in the New Testament are Zacharias, Cornelius, Saul, and Silas. More important is the noteworthy number of Greek (and Latin) names. Sometimes it is not clear whether the Greek name really refers to a Gentile donor to synagogue building or repairs, or whether— as it seems to be the case in at least a good many of the donors—we have to do with Jews who have Greek names. The ancient synagogue found at Tiberias on the Sea of Galilee has a mosaic pavement with the signs of the Zodiac and representations of the four seasons; of the seven names now preserved only one is Semitic (No. 76).

Among the inscriptions found at the synagogue on the island of Delos the fragmentary No. 8 has a special interest. It may date from the early part of the first century B.C. It does not now preserve the name of the Jew who put it up. But when we remember the role of ancient Delos as the outstanding slave mart of the ancient world, it stirs the imagination to read the two Greek words that remain of this inscription; they say simply "having become free" (No. 8).

While the most common elements in these inscriptions are the donors' names and the fact that to fulfill a vow they paid for the building or the repair or the adornment of the synagogue or its setting, other concerns find expression. Brief prayers are often included: "Blessing" (No. 30), "Blessing on All" (No. 38), "Blessing on him. Amen" (No. 76), "Blessing on the people" (*laos*, No. 81), "Help, O God" (No. 90), "May he live" (No. 76), "May he be saved" (No. 76), "Save, O Lord. Amen" (No. 84), "Peace and mercy on all of our holy community" (*plēthos*, No. 39), "Peace to the synagogue" (No. 78), "Sela" (No. 78), and the Hebrew formula "*shalom*" (No. 90).

It is important to note that the verb "save" (*sōzō*) occurs twice and the noun "salvation" (*sōtēria*) sixteen times. The meaning here evidently is not—or is not mainly—an otherworldly saving of a soul from eternal punishment and his admission to final and eternal blessing. It centers rather on the divine gift of wholeness, health, and welfare in the entire range of life. This rich meaning is not fully paralleled in the New Testament, where we often sense more of an eschatological outlook than these inscriptions reflect. But the meaning of healing, health, and wholeness is present in the New Testament uses of these words more than is sometimes realized.

Two important inscriptions show that sometimes rooms to provide lodging for traveling Jews were a part of the total synagogue structure. Widely known and very instructive is the Theodotus inscription concerning the synagogue built at Jerusalem in the first century, before the destruction of Jerusalem in A.D. 70 (No. 79); it reads: "Theodotus, son of Vettenus, priest and synagogue ruler, son of a synagogue ruler, grandson of a synagogue ruler, has built the synagogue for the reading of the Law and the teaching of the commandments, and (has built also) the quarters for strangers, both the rooms and the water provision, for the lodging of strangers who need it. The foundation (of the synagogue) had been laid by his fathers and the elders and Simonides." This Greek inscription was set up for the attention of Greek-speaking Jews resident in Jerusalem or—especially—visiting in Jerusalem, particularly at special religious celebrations of the Jewish religious calendar. It is a reminder that at that time Greek would be widely spoken in Jerusalem both by residents and pilgrims, and that ceremonially acceptable accommodations would be a matter of importance, especially to Jews on pilgrimage.

That this provision for suitable lodging for traveling Jews was not a rare feature of ancient synagogues is indicated by a 3rd century inscription found at Stobi (No. 10). It is instructive to translate this inscription: "(Cl.) Tiberius Polycharmos, also named Achyrios, father of the synagogue (that is, the Jewish community centered in the synagogue) at Stobi, who has lived in every respect according to the prescriptions of Judaism, has built out of his own resources in fulfillment of a vow the rooms annexed to the holy place (that is, annexed to the synagogue building proper) and the dining hall with the quadriportico, without drawing at all on the funds of the synagogue." Tiberius Polycharmos adds that he reserves for himself and his heirs during their lifetime the use of the upper rooms, and he and his heirs will be responsible for the repair of the roof of the upper story. Any change in this arrangement, it is added, can only be made by paying to the patriarch 250,000 denarii. This evidently is intended to protect the life tenure of the heirs of the donor.

It is hoped that the items noted will show how instructive for the study of ancient Greek-speaking Judaism the inscriptions Lifshitz has examined can be. It may be of value to make in conclusion three general observations.

1. These inscriptions, dating from days of the early Ptolemies to the close of the ancient period, warn us not to think that the fall of Jerusalem in A.D. 70 and the crushing of the Bar-Cochba revolt in A.D. 135 ended the ties of ancient Judaism with Hellenistic culture. It is true that the future of Judaism lay with its rabbis in Palestine and Mesopotamia and its linguistic setting of Hebrew and Aramaic, but it also is clear from these inscriptions that for centuries there was a widespread continuation of a Hellenistic Judaism that had cultural relations with the Greco-Roman world.

2. As one considers the many parts of the Roman empire from which such Greek inscriptions come, it is clear that while Palestine, Syria, and Asia Minor are prominent in the list, no one place stands out as the center of Hellenistic Jewish culture. The Jews were scattered over the Greco-Roman world, and wherever they were they built synagogues and left their mark in such inscriptions as Lifshitz has presented.

3. To one accustomed to think of Hellenistic Judaism and Jewish Christianity as centered in Jerusalem—as was the tendency in the light of the Old Testament history in the days of the lives of Jesus and Paul—it comes almost as a shock, after reading these

inscriptions, to realize that apart from the Theodotus inscription which antedates A.D. 70, Jerusalem and pilgrimage to Jerusalem play no role in this material. I do not doubt that this observation can be over-emphasized, and we must remember that after A.D. 70 Jerusalem and its temple were not available as places of pilgrimage and focuses of Jewish life. Nevertheless, there are no references to the past temple or a future temple. The focus of attention is on the synagogue, and the titles that might have recalled the former temple—for example, "the most holy place"—are used of the synagogue. It has become the focus of Jewish life and piety, and no aspiration for a rebuilt temple appears and competes with this centering of worship and life in the synagogue.

23

COLOSSUS, COLOSSAE, COLOSSI:
CONFUSIO COLOSSAEA

OTTO F. A. MEINARDUS

The practice of innovating religious stories, by future generations known and revered as traditions, is intimately associated with the history and spread of the Christian Church. We can distinguish various motives that have led to the fabrication of religious stories. In some instances they are told to increase the glory, power, and majesty of God and his saints. In other cases non-theological factors, purely political and economic considerations, have led to the emergence of such stories. The majority of these stories or traditions deal with the objects of God's revelation and consequently center around the lives of the Apostles, saints, martyrs, and confessors of the church as well as their respective writings. We are accustomed to assign the period of their formation either to "the Early Period" or to "the Middle Ages." It should be of interest to the student of Christian history and tradition to learn, therefore, that also in these days of critical scholarship and enlightened biblical studies, New Testament stories are being transmitted which originated in the latter part of the 20th century.

One of those stories which is presently circulated by touristguides and in inexpensive and locally published guide-books on the Island of Rhodes pertains to the Apostle Paul's ministry to the inhabitants of the island. The following account is in the process of becoming a local tradition.

"On his last missionary journey St. Paul stopped over in Rhodes where he preached the Gospel with much success so that many islanders accepted the new faith. Prior to his departure, he appointed Prochorus as bishop of the island. Some time later, he addressed a letter to the islanders, namely the Epistle to the Colossians, since the Rhodians were referred to as the Colossians on account of the Colossus of Rhodes. The church on the island was known as the Colossian church which was later also administered by an archbishop of Colossae."

According to the Acts of the Apostles St. Paul may have stopped in Rhodes on his return from his third missionary journey (21: 1). After his touching farewell message to the elders of Ephesus (20:17-35), the ship continued the journey to Cos and on the following day he passed Cape Triopium and the peninsula of Cnidus before he reached Rhodes.

It is very likely that St. Paul would have seen the remains of the Helios-Colossus, one of the Seven Wonders of the ancient world. Built between 304 and 284 B.C., the colossus had collapsed in 225 B.C. due to an earthquake. Strabo informs us that the colossus was broken at the knees, and because of a certain oracle the people of Rhodes refused to raise it again. Its remains were sold in A.D. 656 by Muawīyah the ᶜUmayyad to a Jewish merchant of Emesa in Syria who employed 900 camels to carry away the bronze pieces of the fallen colossus. There is no archaeological certainty as to the former location of the colossus. A recent local Rhodian tradition places the site near the present Gate of St. Paul, while the Knights had consecrated a Church of St. John the Colossus on the site believed to have been occupied by the Helios-Colossus.[1]

With respect to the story of the Apostle's missionary success on the island, we must place its origin in the 18th or 19th century. A small barrel-vaulted chapel of St. Paul is situated on the beach of the cove of St. Paul in Lindos, where the inhabitants of Lindos celebrate a panegyris on the Feast of SS. Peter and Paul (June 29) in commemoration of the Apostle's arrival on the island.[2] The Greek Orthodox Synaxarium assigns Prochorus, one of the "seven men of good repute, full of Spirit and of wisdom" (Acts 6:2), to the diocese of Nicomedia.[3]

The most remarkable part of the "Rhodes tradition" is the transference of the recipients of the Epistle to the Colossians from Colossae in Phrygia to the Dodecanese Island. Without going into the thorny issue of the authorship of the Epistle to the Colossians, there is nevertheless general unanimity about its destination, namely, the Christians of the town of Colossae on the southern bank of the Lycus River, 15 km. due east of Laodicea. By the 8th century, the Phrygian Colossae was supplanted by Khonai

(Honaz), 5 km. south and 300 m. up the slope of Mt. Kadmos. A local tradition states that St. Michael had saved the people of the Lycus Valley from inundation by clearing the gorge outside Colossae.[4] Over the whole site the scarcity of ancient remains testifies to its having been used as a quarry for at least a thousand years.

At the same time, it is true that during the Middle Ages the name "Colossus" was sometimes given to the island of Rhodes. We are told that the reason for this association was to conserve the memory of the Helios-Colossus.[5] Thus, for example, Denis Possot and Charles Philippe (1532) wrote: "In ancient times it was the home of the golden fleece; and there too, stood the statue of the sun-god which was named the Colossus, from which the Rhodians were called Colossenses."[6]

Moreover, during the time of the occupation of the island by the Knights of the Order of the Hospital of St. John of Jerusalem from 1309-1522, the Latin archbishop was indeed called "Archiepiscopus Colossensis" to distinguish him from the Greek Orthodox metropolitan who was called "Rhodiensis." In 1328, the Latin archdiocese of Colossi on Rhodes was established, and the most important Latin prelate bearing the name of "Archiepiscopus Colossensis" was Andreas Chrysoberges who signed for the See of Rome the Decree of Union at the Council of Florence in 1439.

The confusion is increased by the mistaken assumption that the Latin archbishops of Rhodes were known as "Colossensis" on account of the ancient Helios-Colossus. In fact, it seems much more logical to suggest that the Latin archbishops, who in the first half of the 14th century arrived in Rhodes, acquired their title "Colossensis" from the state of Colossi in Cyprus. Soon after the Latin occupation of Cyprus, the Hospitallers or Knights of St. John of Jerusalem came to the island, and in 1210 they were given the state of Colossi west of Limassol by King Hugh I. In 1291, after the fall of Acre, Cyprus became the headquarter of the Order, and they, together with the Templars, were placed by Henry II of Cyprus in joint occupation of Limassol.[7] When the Hospitallers moved to Rhodes, they named their prelate after the Grand Commanderie of the Order which was at Colossi on the south coast of Cyprus.

There is little doubt that non-theological factors have led to the emergence of the above-mentioned story, especially as it is not transmitted by the members of the clergy but by the agents of the tourist industry. The Greek Orthodox Church on Rhodes considers St. Silas as her patron, just as the Greek Orthodox Church in Crete venerates St. Titus, that in Cyprus St. Barnabas, and that in Athens St. Dionysius Areopagites. Since many Western tourists are largely ignorant about St. Silas, the stories of St. Paul fill a vacuum which, if related with conviction, are readily accepted by the biblically uninformed.

Colossus, Colossae, Colossi: Confusio colossaea!

Notes

[1] S. G. Zervos, *Rhodes: Capitale du Dodecanèse* (1920), p. 234.

[2] Cecil Torr, *Rhodes in Ancient Times* (1885), p. 92.

[3] S. Eustratiados, *Hagiologion of the Orthodox Church* (n.d.), p. 406 (in Greek).

[4] Cf. W. H. Buckler and W. M. Calder, *Monumenta Asiae Minoris Antiqua* (1939), Vol. VI.

[5] Michael G. Mavrides, *Rhodes* (1967), p. 11.

[6] D. Possot and Ch. Philippe, *Le Voyage de la Terre Sainte* (1890), p. 190.

[7] Seven miles west of Limassol stands the 15th century square tower of Colossi built by the Hospitallers. Cf. Rupert Gunnis, *Historic Cyprus* (1936), pp. 276-80.

24

THE CHRISTIAN REMAINS OF THE SEVEN CHURCHES OF THE APOCALYPSE

OTTO F. A. MEINARDUS

Some months ago, I revisited the island of Patmos and the sites of the seven churches to which letters are addressed in the second and third chapters of the book of Revelation. What follows is a report on such Christian remains as have survived and an indication of the various traditions which have grown up at the eight locations, where, as at so many other places in the Orthodox and Latin world, piety has sought tangible localization.

I set out from Piraeus and sailed to the island of Patmos, off the Turkish coast, which had gained its significance because of the enforced exile of God's servant John (Rev. 1:1, 9) and from the acceptance of the Revelation in the NT canon. From the tiny port of Skala, financial and tourist center of Patmos, the road ascends to the 11th century Greek Orthodox monastery of St. John the Theologian. Half way to this mighty fortress monastery, I stopped at the Monastery of the Apocalypse, which enshrines the "Grotto of the Revelation." Throughout the centuries pilgrims have come to this site to receive blessings. When Pitton de Tournefort visited Patmos in 1702, the grotto was a poor hermitage administered by the bishop of Samos. The abbot presented de Tournefort with pieces of rock from the grotto, assuring him that they could expel evil spirits and cure diseases. Nowadays, hundreds of Western tourists visit the grotto daily, especially during the summer, and are shown those traditional features which are related in one way or another with the vision of John. Chiseled out of the rock is a small couch where John is said to have rested his head, and to the right is a hand-hold cut in the rock which supported the seer as he knelt for prayer. On the rocky bookstand to the right of the hand-hold, tradition has it that Prochorus, John's disciple and amanuensis and one of the deacons of the Jerusalem church (Acts 6:5), wrote down the Revelation (as well as the Fourth Gospel), at his

Illus. 35-7

teacher's dictation. The grotto's ceiling is cleft from north to south; local tradition says the split occurred when John heard God's voice saying "I am the Alpha and the Omega" (Rev. 1:8).

Another climb of fifteen minutes brought me to the village of Chora, built around the Monastery of St. John the Theologian, which claims one of the largest collections of relics of the apostolic church. Included are fragments of the skulls of the apostle Thomas and Antipas of Pergamum (Rev. 2:13), as well as parts from Titus, Timothy and Philip. In the new museum, the monks have on exhibit the sad remains of their 6th-century purple parchment Codex 67 of the Gospel of Mark, of which other parts are in the libraries of Vienna, Leningrad, London, the Vatican and Athens. Scenes from the apocryphal *Acts of John and His Travels and Miracles* adorn the walls of the exonarthex of the monastery's catholicon. As an example, one depicts the contest of faith between John and the Patmian magician Kynops. Before a great multitude of Patmians, Kynops challenged John with a display of his magical powers. Finally, he cast himself into the sea, expecting to reappear. John, however, extending his arms in the form of a cross, exclaimed "O Thou, who didst grant to Moses by this similitude to overthrow Amalek [Exod. 17:8-13], O Lord Jesus Christ, bring down Kynops to the deep of the sea; let him never behold the sun, nor converse with living men." As John spoke, the sea roared and the water formed a whirlpool where Kynops went down. In the port of Skala, the fishermen pointed out to me a submerged rock some 900 feet from the dock, marked by a white buoy, which they believe to be petrified Kynops. Also in Skala, just beyond the Patmias Hotel, is a sizeable rock, surrounded by a fence, marked as "the relic of the baptismal font of St. John, 96 A.D."

The panoramic view from the roof of the Monastery of St. John is overwhelming. In the northwest appears the level line of the island of Icaria; further north are the peaks of Samos and the promontory of Mycale; to the southeast is the island of Leros beyond which rise the five summits of Kalymnos. To the southwest lies the island of Amorgos and the distant volcanic island of Santorini, or Thera. This was the view which, with frequent alterations during sunshine and storm, must have impressed John. I found myself wondering whether this scene might not be reflected in the imagery of such visions as "the sky vanished like a scroll that is rolled up, and every mountain and island was removed from its place" (Rev. 6:14) or "every island fled away, and no mountains were to be found" (Rev. 16:20).

Ephesus

Whereas in the first century ships sailed regularly from Port Coressos in Ephesus to the Aegean islands, today it is more difficult to combine a journey to Patmos with a visit to the sites of the seven churches, because the Turkish mainland can only be reached via the Greek islands of Cos and Rhodes in the south and Samos and Chios to the north. I sailed to Pythagoreion on Samos, from where skiffs shuttle back and forth to Kushadasi, the former Scala Nuova, ten miles west of the ruins of ancient Ephesus.

Ephesus is famous for a number of reasons. It is important to the classicists and historians as one of the ancient cities of Ionia and as the capital of the Roman province of Asia. New Testament students associate the city with Paul, John and Timothy, and some claim that Mary, Jesus' mother, and Mary Magdalene spent their last days there. Ephesus, where the first of the seven churches addressed by John was located, remains the most impressive of all sites in Asia Minor. By the 2nd century B.C., its fame had increased so much that Antipater of Sidon counted the Ephesian Artemision as one of the Seven Wonders of the World, together with the Pyramids in Egypt, the Hanging Gardens of Semiramis in Babylon, the Statue of Zeus in Olympia, the Mausoleum at Halicarnassus, the Colossus of Rhodes and the Pharos of Alexandria.

The beginnings of Christianity in this city are shrouded in mystery. Whether we accept Ireneus' statement that Paul founded the church there or the tradition that John the Evangelist settled here with Mary, the mother of Jesus, certainly Christianity had reached the city of Diana-Artemis by the middle of the first century. During his first brief visit to Ephesus, Paul "argued with the Jews" in the local synagogue (Acts 18:19-21). Although the existence of a synagogue is mentioned by Josephus and by Luke, we lack archaeological indication of its location. Probably it was on the northern outskirts of the city near the harbor, because of the need for water for ritual purposes. Josephus informs us of the decision of the people of Halicarnassus to "suffer the Jews to observe their laws and sabbaths and build synagogues, as was their custom, by the sea." Indeed, many of the synagogues which have been excavated, those of Delos, Aegina, Priene and Miletus, were either close to the sea or near a river. One archaeological clue is a *menorah* carved into the steps leading to the 2nd-century Library of Celsus; the only other artifacts pointing toward a Jewish community during the Roman period are several terra-cotta lamps displaying the menorah, and a unique glass showing the menorah flanked by the *shofar* and *lulab*. The lamps and the glass were found in the "Cemetery of the Seven Sleepers."

Three years after his first visit, Paul returned to preach at the Ephesian synagogue (Acts 19:8-9); after three months, however, he was evicted, though he was later able to use the hall of Tyrannus, possibly himself a rhetorician. The Western family of New Testament texts has a plus at the end of verse 9 to the effect that Paul taught from the 5th to the 10th hours, that is, from 11 a.m. to 4 p.m., during the heat of the day—which might suggest that Paul had the use of the hall during the time when Tyrannus rested. Paul's teaching led to the founding of congregations throughout the Roman province of Asia, since "all the residents of Asia heard the word of the Lord, both Jews and Greeks" (Acts 19:10), who were attracted to the famous Temple of Artemis, "she whom all Asia and the world worship" (Acts 19:27).

Luke makes no mention of Paul's being imprisoned in Ephesus, but Paul repeatedly refers to his sufferings—see especially I Cor. 15:32 and II Cor. 1:8,9. The apocryphal *Acts of Paul* elaborates upon his imprisonment in Ephesus, reporting that Eubola and Artemilla, wives of notable Ephesians, visited him in prison by night, requesting to be baptized by him. A local Ephesian tradition identifies the large square tower near the ancient Port Coressos as the prison of Paul. The tower is on the western end of Mt. Coressos and was part of the defense wall built by Lysimachus in the 3rd century B.C. We do not know when the tradition began, but the Western travelers of the 17th century, Thomas Smith, George Wheler, Jacques Spon and Cornelis van Bruyn, all refer to this building as "the Prison of the Apostle Paul."

I strolled along Marble Street, passing the large theater which silently commemorates the silversmiths' riots of Acts 19:23-20:1. At the end of Marble Street, I turned into Curetes Street; here, just thirty paces below the small Temple of Hadrian, lying flat behind the upright row of columns, is a statue base erected by the guild of silversmiths, to which Demetrius apparently belonged.

In Seljuk, three miles from Ephesus, I visited the ruins of the Basilica of St. John situated on a hilltop overlooking the few ruins of the Artemis Temple. Already in the 2nd century, a small church enclosed the traditional tomb of John—but it remains an open question *which* John is supposed to be buried there. Papias, the 2nd century bishop of Hierapolis, according to Eusebius in his *Ecclesiastical History* III.39, "asserts there were two of the same name in Asia, that there were also two tombs in Ephesus, and that both are called John's even to this day; which is particularly necessary to observe." In the 4th century this tomb was enlarged into the so-called Theodosian basilica. By the 6th century, the two Johns had clearly merged into one person, when Justinian demolished the former building and built in its stead "the greatest and most magnificent church of early Christendom." It was 300 feet long and 130 feet wide, with six large domes covering the center aisle and five small domes covering the narthex. In 1106, the Russian abbot Daniel visited the tomb of John and related that a holy dust, which was gathered by believers as a cure for diseases, arose from the tomb on the anniversary of John's death. When the crypt was excavated in 1928, no relics of John were found. On the capitals of the columns one can still see the monograms of Justinian and his wife Theodora.

In the beginning of the 14th century, when Ephesus was occupied by the Turks, most of the valuable vessels of this church were pillaged. The basilica was probably destroyed in 1402 by Tamerlane, since graffiti of 1341 and 1387 inscribed by pilgrims testify to its existence at least that late.

The following day I returned to ancient Ephesus to visit the ruins of the Church of the Holy Virgin, once a 2nd century Roman grain or money exchange. During the 4th century the building was converted into a church, making it probably the first cathedral dedicated to the Holy Virgin. Here on June 22, 431, the Third

Ecumenical Council brought together 159 bishops; among other acts, they bestowed upon Mary the title of "Godbearer" (Theotokos).

Today few visitors go out of their way to walk along the wide aisles of this imposing early church. The octagonal baptistry, north of the atrium, is one of the best preserved from the early Christian period. In 1930, a plaque was discovered in the narthex on which the 6th-century bishop Hypatius had confirmed this church as the site of the Council. On June 26, 1967, Pope Paul VI offered prayer in the ruins of this sanctuary.

Later in the day, I drove to the summit of Bulbul Dagh near Ephesus to visit the traditional "house of the Virgin." The tradition of the sojourn of Mary in Ephesus is based on the assumption that John—assumed to be the "disciple whom Jesus loved" (John 19:26-27)—took Mary to his own home, which some believe to have been at Ephesus. Already in the 4th century, tradition prevailed that Mary spent her last days in Ephesus; this follows from the observation by Epiphanius of Salamis (315-402) that the scriptures are silent about her sojourn in Asia (implying that some claimed she *was* there). Several Syrian Jacobite theologians from the 9th through the 13th centuries accepted the tradition, which, until the 19th century, local Christians of Kirkindje near Ephesus affirmed by their annual pilgrimage to her "house"—now called the house of the All-Holy—on August 15, the Feast of the Assumption. In 1821 and 1822, Catherine Emmerich, a German Augustinian nun who had never visited Ephesus, experienced visions in which she described Mary's sojourn and her home in Ephesus. These accounts, transcribed by Clemens M. Brentano, referred to "her dwelling on a hill to the left of the road from Jerusalem some three and a half hours from Ephesus. . . Mary's house was the only one built of stone. . ." Seventy years later, Eugene Poulin of the Lazarist College in Smyrna went to Bulbul Dagh to verify the visionary account. He found the ruins of an ancient house which had been transformed into a chapel. Some of the ruins of the house can, indeed, be assigned to the early Christian era. Where once pilgrims from all over the world assembed to offer their devotion to Diana-Artemis, the cult of the goddess was replaced by the veneration of Mary the Godbearer.

Smyrna

About an hour and a half by bus separates Ephesus from Izmir, biblical Smyrna. According to the Greek *Menologion* (the document developed by the Church which contains the lives of the various saints, arranged in calendrical order to be read on their respective feast days), Apelles "who is approved in Christ" (Romans 16:10) served as the first bishop of the Smyrnean church; others accord this honor to Ariston, who was succeeded by Strateas, a son of Lois (II Tim. 1:5) and an uncle of Timothy. Strateas was followed by Boucolus, who, so tradition tells us, had accepted the faith from John. The apocryphal *Acts of John* refer to John's return to Smyrna following his exile to Patmos. His letter to the Smyrneans is the most laudatory, as he is in full sympathy with this church (Rev. 2:8-11).

Despite the tragic catastrophe of 1922 at the end of the Hellenic-Turkish war, when the city was set afire and the Orthodox Christian population was either massacred or expelled, John is still remembered in modern Izmir in the 19th century Roman Catholic Cathedral of St. John, where foreign Catholics and Protestants worship every Sunday. This church, adorned with many 19th century paintings of the three great Smyrnean fathers, Polycarp, Ireneus and Ignatius, was granted by Pope Pius IX the honor of being a Minor Basilica, enriched with the same indulgences as those of St. John Lateran in Rome. Moreover, the Anglican Church of St. John at Alsancak, built in 1898 on the site of the former chapel of the Levant Company, provides regular Sunday services.

I spent the larger part of a morning in the Hellenistic-Roman agora of ancient Smyrna searching for Christian ruins. The results were disappointing; except for a few small remnants of a Byzantine church, no substantial archaeological remains testify to the church which was to receive the crown of life (Rev. 2:10). Throughout the Middle Ages, pilgrims came to the site of Polycarp's martyrdom and of his tomb. At the tomb, venerated by Christians and Muslims alike, an ecumenical service was still conducted as late as 1952; today, its location is no longer known.

Pergamum

Izmir possesses the most formidable "Otobüs Garaji" in western Turkey. Here I purchased a six lira (40 cents) ticket for Bergama, the town at the foot of the ancient Attalid capital of Pergamum. In the first century, Pergamum, with its famous temples of Zeus, Dionysus and Athena, was the principal center of the imperial cult in Asia. Here were the temples of Augustus and the goddess Roma with their cult statues to which everyone had to pay homage. Confrontation between the young Christian church and the state was inevitable. We do not know when Christianity found its way to Pergamum. According to the *Apostolic Constitutions*—the 4th century collection of legislative and liturgical traditions compiled by "Pseudo-Clement"—the "beloved Gaius," whom John the Elder addressed in his third letter (III John), was the first bishop of Pergamum. Gaius was followed by Antipas, who died a martyr.

Prior to 1922, the Christians maintained four churches in Pergamum, those of Theodore, John the Theologian, Antipas and Paraskeve, but today the only evidence of its apostolic significance is found among the scattered remains from the Byzantine period. Archaeological work began in the 19th century with Carl Humann's discovery of the high reliefs of the altar of Zeus incorporated into the Byzantine walls. Altogether, four churches were excavated. The best-known, the so-called Red Basilica, was built on the ruins of the large Serapis Temple. Tradition has connected this church with John. Destroyed by the Arabs in 716-717, it was later rebuilt. Another church with two aisles was excavated by W. Dörpfeld in the courtyard of the lower agora, but no remains of this church are visible today. Still another, about forty-five feet long and sixteen feet wide, was built during the 6th century on the site of the Temple of Athena on the acropolis. A few marble fragments of this church may still be seen in place. Ruins of the fourth church were found on the terrace of the Pergamene theater, but no traces now remain.

Thyatira

In Bergama I inquired about a bus to Akhisar, the Ottoman name for biblical Thyatira. Blank stares! Eventually I learned the word "Axari," as the Greeks called Akhisar. A few minutes later, the overcrowded minibus set out, crossing the Caicus River—now Bakir—and reaching Soma, the classical Germa with its Byzantine fortress. A bus change, again "Axari," and into an even more crowded vehicle. I sat next to a well-dressed gentleman who turned out to be a religious dignitary of Akhisar, and he became my guide.

The first Thyatiran Christian, though she was a resident of Philippi in Macedonia, "was a woman named Lydia. . .a seller of purple goods, who was a worshiper of God" (Acts 16:14). Lydia was not the only representative of her trade in Philippi; in 1872, Professor Mertzides found there a text on a fragment of white marble: "The city honors from among the purple-dyers an outstanding citizen, Antiochus, son of Lykus, a native of Thyatira, as a benefactor." About the foundation of the church at Thyatira we know almost nothing. We must assume that by the second half of the first century a Christian community existed, for the threat of internal dissension and schism mentioned in John's letter (Rev. 2:20-23) presupposes some formal organization and some history.

Today Akhisar is a thriving Turkish town of 48,000 inhabitants. Only a few traces of its vanished Christian community can be seen. The 19th century Greek Orthodox Cathedral of St. Nicholas has been made into a movie theater. In the inner court of the Grand Mosque, just to the east of the building, I saw the foundations of a large apse of an early Byzantine church; my guide assured me it was the Church of St. Basil the Great. After removing my shoes, I stepped into the mosque and noticed several Byzantine alabaster columns which may belong to the 10th century. According to another local tradition, the Sheikh Issa Mosque was built on the site of a Church of St. John. In the outer court of this mosque are two Corinthian capitals which may have belonged to the church.

Before the First World War, remains of churches, primarily consisting of slabs of marble with cross designs, were stored in the courtyard of the cathedral. Today, a few marble fragments from early Byzantine churches of Thyatira are exhibited in the archaeological museum in Manisa. Recent excavations at Tepe Mezari in the center of Akhisar, which have unearthed a section of 2nd century A.D. Roman road and a part of a stoa, as well as a 6th century administrative (?) building may throw additional light on the early Christian heritage of the city.

There has been no Christian community in Akhisar since 1922. The abandoned apostolic sees in Asia Minor are occasionally bestowed as titular sees upon the members of the Holy Synod of the Ecumenical Patriarchate of Constantinople. However, it is the Greek Orthodox Archbishop of Great Britain who carries the title of Metropolitan of Thyatira.

Sardis

Since there were no direct buses from Akhisar to the ruins of Sardis, I took the opportunity to stop at Manisa, ancient Magnesia-ad-Sipylum, to visit the exceptionally fine archaeological and ethnological collections. The modern village of Sartmustafa, a sad survival of the former capital of the Lydian kingdom, is situated on the main highway from Manisa to Ankara.

The church in Sardis must have been established in the middle of the first century or toward the latter part of that century. According to the *Menologion*, Clement, one of the Seventy and a disciple of Paul (Philippians 4:3), was the first bishop of Sardis. In many ways, the story of the young fellowship proved to be parallel to the life of the city; as Sardis under Croesus had flourished and then decayed, so the church there flourished and then decayed. John admonishes the Sardian Christians that they are alive and yet dead. In this respect, Sardis was the opposite of Smyrna, which was dead and yet thrived!

Although some of Sardis' ruins had been studied in the 19th century, no systematic investigation had been undertaken before the arrival of the Princeton University expedition in 1910. In 1912 excavations near the north-eastern corner of the Temple of Artemis brought to light a small church, "Church M," built when the ground level around the temple had risen some five feet above the temple platform. The church is nearly square with a narrow projecting apse. A hoard of coins discovered just outside the north doorway indicates that the church was in use in the beginning of the 5th century. Immediately behind the apse is a second apse whose width almost equals that of the church. A primitive altar, found in place, is one of the earliest Christian altars known; it stands in the center of the first apse.

About 300 feet south of the village of Sartmustafa, near the road leading to the Temple of Artemis, George Hanfmann and the Harvard-Cornell-ASOR expedition have recently discovered a 4th century three-aisled basilica, designated "Church E." This church has a second apse built east of the principal one. Returning to the Manisa-Ankara highway, some 700 feet east of Sartmustafa, I saw the restored entrance hall and adjacent buildings of the famous Sardis gymnasium, and almost next to it the Sardis synagogue with its enormous rectangular hall oriented east-west and ending in a broad apse. (Readers of the *BA* should consult D. G. Mitten's article about Sardis in volume 29 [1966], pp. 38-68.) Built in the 2nd century, the synagogue was destroyed by the Persian raid under Chosroes II in 615. I wondered whether this splendid synagogue was built on the site of an older one in which the early Christians of Sardis might have met.

Philadelphia

From Sartmustafa, I hitch-hiked to Salihli and on to Alashehir, the Philadelphia of Attalus II of Pergamum, situated at the foot of the Tmolous mountains. Again, we know almost nothing about the beginnings of the Christian church in Philadelphia. One tradition maintains that Paul appointed Lucius his kinsman (Romans 16:21) as bishop of Philadelphia, but, according to the *Apostolic Constitutions*, the city's first bishop was a man named Demetrius, who had been appointed by John. Two churches are singled out by John for their faithfulness, Smyrna and Philadelphia. Both were poor and weak, both had suffered tribulation, and yet both were full of life and vigor.

Walking through the narrow lanes of Alashehir I was reminded that this city was the last Byzantine outpost in Asia Minor, before it fell to Bayazid in 1390. In the middle of the 14th century the metropolitan of Philadelphia could still sign the synodal decrees with the impressive title "Metropolitan of Philadelphia, Hypertimus and Exarch of all Lydia and Universal Judge of the Romans."

Prior to the events of 1922, the Greek community in Alashehir maintained no fewer than five churches. Today there are no Christians there, although the Turkish population is aware of the biblical and historical role of the city. Almost in the center of the city are the ruins of the Christian basilica, built of red brick. Here and there one can identify the remains of wall-paintings, perhaps of the 11th century, which once adorned the whole sanctuary. The citizens refer to these ruins, opposite the Bayazid I Mosque, as the Church of St. John.

Laodicea

Aware that there is no public transportation connecting Alashehir with Laodicea, the last of John's seven churches, I took a bus as far as Sarigol and was fortunate enough to get a ride across the high mountain range of Boz Dagh to Saraykoy and on to Denizli. From Denizli I took the bus to Pamukkale ("Cotton Tower"), the site of ancient Hierapolis with its tepid waters, which offers a magnificent view over Lykus valley with its ruins of Laodicea. As I swam in the crystal clear, lukewarm waters of the Hierapolis springs, I thought of John's characterization of the church at Laodicea as lukewarm, neither hot nor cold (Rev. 3:15-16).

The church in Laodicea was founded by Epaphras of nearby Colossae, who shared the care of the young community with Nympha, in whose house the congregation assembled (Col. 4:12-13, 15). Goodspeed suggested that Paul addressed Philemon to the church in Laodicea; note the appearance of Archippus in Philemon, verse 2, perhaps the same Archippus whom Paul advised "see that you fulfill the ministry which you have received in the Lord" (Col. 4:17). Presumably, he was no longer head of the community at Laodicea when John addressed his letter to this church. According to the *Apostolic Constitutions*, Archippus was succeeded by a certain Nymphas as bishop of Laodicea.

The present site of Laodicea was inhabited until the latter part of the 12th century, when the citizens relocated at modern Denizli. The ancient site was repeatedly visited from the 17th century onwards. When Thomas Smith (1671) passed through the ruins, he described it as "inhabited by wolves, jackals and foxes." A century later, Richard Chandler (1764) was almost killed by robbers between Denizli and the ruins of Laodicea. Travelers in the 19th century report "no wretched outcast dwells in the midst of it, it has long been abandoned to the owl and the fox"; indeed, "nothing can exceed the desolation and melancholy appearance of the site of Laodicea."

The ruins lie on a flat-topped hill between the villages of Eskihisar and Goncale. Some traces of the old city wall remain. At the south end of the plateau is the amphitheater or stadium, dedicated by a wealthy citizen to the emperor Vespasian. The large building east of the staduim is a gymnasium dedicated to Hadrian. In the center of the city was a monumental fountain, built in the 3rd century during the reign of Caracalla. Sites have been proposed for the locations of two early churches, one near the so-called Syrian Gate, the other north of the fountain. During the 1961-63 excavations of the fountain by archaeologists of Laval University, Canada, several marble slabs with cross designs, so characteristic of the Byzantine era, were found.

* * * * *

The traveler to Patmos and to the cities of the seven churches of Revelation 2-3 can catch many a glimpse of early Christianity enshrined in the ruins and fragments, but enshrined also in the persistent traditions. Several impressions stand out. For one thing, there is much yet to be found out archaeologically which will illumine the early church in Asia Minor. Under prevailing conditions, some traditions are fading, even about old locations of traditional sites. Even at Ephesus and Sardis, the most thoroughly explored and excavated of the sites, only a fraction of what can be learned has come to light. For another thing, tradition about John of the Revelation has become quite mixed with tradition about John of the Fourth Gospel; but the mixture is not complete, if we take into account Eusebius' report about Papias, which I noted in the section on Seljuk near Ephesus. Finally, I can only say that to this traveler, anyway, exploration of the sites and their settings sharpens the language of Revelation, as we seek to envision these struggling congregations standing amidst alien culture and alien ways of life, and to make John's letters relevant to our own day.

Suggestions for Further Reading

William Barclay, *Letters to the Seven Churches* (1957), S. W. H. Bird, *And Unto Smyrna: The Story of a Church in Asia Minor* (1956), E. le Camus, *Voyage aux Sept Eglises de l'Apocalypse* (1896), Richard Chandler, *Travels in Asia Minor or an Account of a Tour Made at the Expense of the Society of Dilettanti* (1775), Vernon P. Flynn, *The Seven Churches Today* (1963), John Fuller, *A Narrative of a Tour through Some Parts of the Turkish Empire* (1830), A. H. M. Jones, *The Cities of the Eastern Roman Provinces* (1937), P. Lucas, *Voyage Fait par l'Ordre du Roi* (1714), Lysimachos Oeconomos, *The Tragedy of the Christian Near East* (1923), Richard Pococke, *A Description of the East* (1743-45), Earl of Sandwich, *A Voyage Performed by the Late Earl of Sandwich in the Years 1738 and 1739* (1799), Gotthilf von Schubert, *Reise in das Morgenland in den Jahren 1836 und 1837* (1840), M. Tournefort, *A Voyage into the Levant* (1718), John Turner, *Journal of a Tour in the Levant* (1820), J. Aegidius Van Egmont and John Heyman, *Travels through Part of Europe, Asia Minor, Etc.* (1759).

25

THE CAESAREA MITHRAEUM:
A PRELIMINARY ANNOUNCEMENT

LEWIS MOORE HOPFE AND GARY LEASE

In the first few centuries of its existence, Christianity's strongest religious competitor was Mithraism, a mystery cult of Persian origin which had spread over the entire Roman Empire.[1] Hundreds of Mithraea (as the sanctuaries of Mithra were called) have been found, but oddly not a single one had been discovered within the boundaries of Roman Palestine. This gap has apparently now been filled as the result of new excavations at Caesarea.

Caesarea Maritima or Caesarea Palestina is a site which has long been of interest to New Testament scholars, church historians, and students of the classical world. Located on the Mediterranean coast, at the site of Strato's tower, built by Herod the Great between 22-10 B.C. and named in honor of his patron, Caesar Augustus, Caesarea served as political capital of the Roman and Byzantine province until A.D. 640 when it was conquered by the Muslims. It was the site of many events recorded in the book of Acts and was the home of many of the leading figures in the early history of the Christian church, including Eusebius who served as bishop of the church of Caesarea.

Since it covers as much as 8000 acres and is dotted with the visible remains of an aqueduct system, a hippodrome, a theater, an amphitheater and a Crusader fortress, the location of Caesarea has never been in doubt. Excavations at Caesarea began in 1945 and continued in sporadic fashion until 1971. A synagogue discovered in 1932 was excavated in 1945, 1956, and 1962 by the Hebrew University; a Byzantine plaza was excavated in 1951 by S. Yeivin of the Department of Antiquities; a Byzantine church was excavated in 1957; the Roman theater and the aqueducts of the city were excavated and restored by Italian archaeologists in 1959 and

1960; and, also in 1960, the Link Expedition explored the underwater remains of the harbor.[2]

In 1971 Professor Robert J. Bull of Drew University and then director of the Albright Institute of Archaeological Research in Jerusalem was issued an emergency license by the Israeli Department of Antiquities for the purpose of establishing that Caesarea was indeed a site of antiquities throughout its full extent. Working four weeks with a small team of volunteers, Dr. Bull opened areas to the north and south of the Byzantine plaza. As a result of his work that season, he was granted a license to continue excavations at Caesarea in succeeding years. A consortium of American schools was established to support the excavation of Caesarea under the auspices of the American Schools of Oriental Research and under the direction of Dr. Bull. Plans were made for major excavations in the years 1972, 1974, and 1976 with smaller groups working in brief sessions in 1973 and 1975. The goals of this excavation are to recover as far as is possible the plan and structure of the city and to illuminate its genetic development.

During the brief 1973 season work was concentrated in the area designated as the "C" field. This area is located immediately to the south of the Crusader fortress and to the east of the Mediterranean beach. In this area there lie three mounds of sand dunes rising some 35 to 50 feet above mean sea level. Teams working in the northernmost of these dunes began to uncover architectural remains almost immediately beneath the surface. In the areas designated as C-7, C-8, and C-9 large vaulted structures were found beneath the floors of the upper buildings. These vaults were constructed on an east/west axis with their entrances facing the Mediterranean harbor. These vaults, along with those which are visible in the Crusader fortress, may have originally been built as warehouses for the harbor area. This is implied by a rather obscure passage in Josephus, in *Antiquities* Book XV.ix.6:

> The city itself was called Cesarea (*sic*), which was also itself built of fine materials, and was of a fine structure; nay, the very subterranean vaults and cellars had no less of architecture bestowed on them than had the buildings above ground.

What has now been uncovered may be the remains of the harbor facilities to which Josephus alludes.

In area C-8 the largest single vault was excavated. Though its westernmost roofing stones had apparently been removed by the persistent stone-robbers of Caesarea in the years following the Muslim conquest, there remains intact a vault measuring approximately 65 feet in length (east/west), 17 feet wide (north/south), and 13 feet from the latest flooring to the peak of the arched ceiling. Within the south wall of the vault, located eight feet west of the east wall, there is a small archway 1.12 meters (about 44 inches) wide and .86 meters (about 35 inches) high. Further excavations during the 1974 season revealed that this archway was an entrance into another east/west vault constructed immediately to the south of the C-8 vault. Excavation within this second vault has been delayed until proper shoring can be erected to protect the workmen from a possible collapse.

The excavations in 1973 in area C-7, located immediately to the east of C-8, revealed that the roof of the C-8 vault had been covered with an elaborately constructed drainage system. To the immediate west of the western entrance of the C-8 vault, the 1974 excavations uncovered a bath which was decorated with a large mosaic on its floor and with frescoes on its walls.

The western entrance of the C-8 vault had been blocked by an accumulation of debris. On top of the debris lay the remains of many human skeletons which indicated that the latest usage of the vault was as a charnel house. No artifacts or coins were found to date the period of the charnel house, but it is believed to have been used during the Turkish period, beginning in the early 16th century A.D. The first probe within the latest flooring of the vault produced coinage which could be dated in the Mamelukan era in Palestine (13th to 15th centuries A.D.).

The second stratum within the flooring of the C-8 vault revealed several features which have come to be identified with a Mithraic use of this structure. In the stratum just beneath the latest floor of the vault a plastered surface was found, apparently a flooring; the plaster also covered benches and what came to be identified as an altar stone. The benches were 51 centimeters wide (about 20 inches) and 35 centimeters (some 14 inches) above the plaster floor and apparently originally ran the east/west length of the vault. But they are not flush against the vault walls; the aisle between the benches as preserved is only about five feet wide. The benches ran up to the

east wall of the vault, connecting to another bench structure, a
meter (*ca.* 39 inches) wide, which ran across the eastern end of the
vault. On the center of this eastern bench was a divider 27
centimeters (ten inches) wide, 35 centimeters (about fourteen
inches) high, projecting out of the eastern wall the full depth of the
bench. Between the side benches, approximately four feet west of
the east wall of the vault, is located the stone which has been
tentatively identified as an altar base. It is 61 by 61 centimeters
(roughly two feet square) in size.[3]

In the excavation of the material beside the altar stone several
artifacts were found which may have been connected to the
Mithraic cult. Three whole lamps and many fragments of lamps
were found at the base of the altar stone. These lamps are late
Roman in style (late 3rd-early 4th cents. A.D.). But most important
was the recovery from beside the altar stone of a marble medallion
about 3-1/8 inches in diameter, roughly 3/8 inches thick. Carved
on this medallion in bas relief is the Mithraic tauroctone, the
elaborate bull-slaying scene so characteristic of Mithraism.
Though the sculpting is coarse, the figures of the tauroctone are
easily identifiable. Mithra wears the familiar Phrygian cap, cape,
and short skirt. He sits astride the sacrificial bull with a dagger in
his right hand poised above the neck of the bull. He is looking
upward over his right shoulder. On either side of him stand his
companions, the torchbearers Cautes on the right with his torch
lifted and Cautopates on the left with his torch pointed down.
Beneath the bull one can barely see the figure of the serpent, but his
head is clearly visible reaching up toward the wound Mithra has
inflicted with his sword. From between the legs of Cautes, the dog
who usually appears in the scenes leaps toward the right shoulder
of the bull. Though they are not clear in this medallion, there may
be representations of the sun and the moon above Mithra. The
lower third of the medallion is divided into three panels. Although
these are not clearly identifiable in the medallion, other
tauroctones indicate that these may be three scenes from the life of
Mithra. In the left panel, there is a scene in which two figures
appear to be eating a meal together. In the right panel is a scene
with two figures behind an animal, perhaps in a chariot drawn by
the animal.[4]

During the 1974 excavation, a circular indentation was found on the stone which divides the bench running north/south along the east wall of the vault. Its size would indicate that the medallion was originally imbedded in it during the period of Mithraic use.

On the south wall of the C-8 vault near its east end is located a series of frescoes. These frescoes have been badly damaged by the salt air and are only faintly visible. They appear to have been arranged in a series of panels. The most visible of the frescoes seems to show a figure kneeling before another figure, in a manner similar to that depicted in Vermaseren, *Corpus*, I, Fig. 59, Monument 191. It is speculated that these frescoes depict various scenes from the Mithraic myth, or more likely represent steps in the initiation rites as found in other Mithraea,[5] but positive identification is impossible at this time.

The Mithraic material in the C-8 vault is currently dated as late third and early fourth centuries A.D. But there is speculation that the materials discovered represent the last in a series of Mithraea in this vault. The lamps which were found at the altar stone were clearly late Roman. Beneath the stratum which contained the Mithraic material were strata which contained large quantities of late Roman sherds. These sherds were from large amphorae and other storage vessels, which gives support to the theory that the original use of the vault was as a warehouse for the harbor area. The fill material which surrounded the benches and altar stone contained sherds which were identified as middle Byzantine, indicating that the vault may have lain unused for a lengthy period after its Mithraic use.

The discovery of the Caesarea Mithraeum is of considerable signficance both for the history of the city of Caesarea and for the study of Mithraism. Of the more than 400 Mithraea identified by Vermaseren and located throughout the Roman Empire world, there was none known between Sidon on the Lebanese coast and Alexandria in Egypt prior to 1973. Thus as noted at the beginning the Caesarea Mithraeum is the first to be identified in the Roman province of Judea.

Of greater interest is the relatively late dating for this Mithraeum. Christianity had become by the end of the 3rd century a major force at Caesarea and played an increasingly greater role in

Christian political developments during the turbulent 4th century. Of course, Mithraism and Christianity coexisted for long periods of time at other locations throughout the Roman Empire, but until now we had no record of such religious pluralism in Caesarea, that is, of Roman and oriental religions. Of course a strong Jewish community persisted at Caesarea throughout its history.[6]

In addition, the dating of the stratum overlying the Caesarea Mithraeum as middle Byzantine suggests that it played a major role in the Julian revival of A.D. 361-363 in which Mithraism occupied a prominent position. The rigorous ethical content found in Mithraism not only aided in reforming Roman religious practices, but also appealed directly to Julian in the setting of his own policies.[7] Indeed, the last periods of Mithraic vitality fall between 284 and 313 and then again during the late 4th century religious revivals exemplified by Julian's reform; these periods correspond to the preliminary dating given the Caesarea Mithraeum.[8] Caesarea's status as a provincial capital and its proximity to Julian's final fields of action make such speculation possible and invite further investigation at the site.

Finally, one must reflect on the status of the famous port at Caesarea, if at the beginning of the 4th century a large public vault located at the harbor's edge was also the site of a cultic center. Of course it comes as no surprise that a Mithraic community would choose such a setting; in remembrance of Mithra's birth in a grotto, most Mithraea were located in cave-like structures, and a vaulted ceiling was highly favored (cf. Vermaseren, *Mithras*, p. 29). Yet we have no record of a Mithraeum built through government support; its places of worship remained in private ownership. Thus municipal officials are not usually associated with Mithraism; on the other hand, soldiers, seamen, and members of the Imperial financial service are linked closely to it.[9] That a Mithraeum be found at Caesarea, a Roman provincial capital and a major port of entry to Palestine, is to be expected; that it is found, however, in a structure which may have been owned and administered by the municipality and during a period of strong Christianization in the city must come as a surprise. Whatever the reasons, the circumstances surrounding the location and date of the Caesarea Mithraeum hold important consequences not only for the history of Mithraism in the late Roman Empire, but also for the reconstruction of Caesarea's civic development.

Notes

[1]For a full description of Mithraism, see S. Laeuchli, *BA* 31 (1968), 73-99.

[2]For a good introduction to the present physical state, see A. Reifenberg, "Caesarea Maritima: A Study in the Decline of a Town," *Israel Exploration Journal* 1 (1950), 20-32. Among archaeological reports and studies, the following will be of interest to *BA* readers: S. Yeivin, "Excavations at Caesarea Maritima," *Archaeology* 8 (1955), 122-29; M. Avi-Yonah, "The Synagogue of Caesarea (Preliminary Report)," *Bulletin Rabinowitz* 3 (1960), 44-48; D. Barag, "An Inscription from the High Level Aqueduct at Caesarea, Reconsidered," *Israel Exploration Journal* 14 (1964), 250-52; H. Hamburger, "A New Inscription from the Caesarea Aqueduct," *ibid.*, 9 (1959), 188-90; C. T. Fritsch and I. Ben-Dor, "The Link Expedition to Israel, 1960," *BA* 24 (1961), 50-59; and, especially for the photographs and plans, the monumental preliminary report of the Italian expedition by A. Frova, *Caesarea Maritima: Rapporto preliminaire* (1959).

[3]M. J. Vermaseren, *Mithras: Geschichte eines Kultes* (1965), p. 31, indicates the presence of altars in other Mithraea and describes their use for sacrificial re-enactment of the Mithra myth. Note by the way, that the altar stone was mistakenly reported to be 1.6 meters square in the *ASOR Newsletter*, No. 3, November, 1973, p. 3.

[4]Of all the Mithraic material identified by Vermaseren, the Caesarea medallion seems to be closest to those pictured in his *Corpus Inscriptionum et Monumentorum Religionis Mithraicae*, II (1960), Fig. 622, Monument 2246 and Fig. 362, Monument 1415. Cf. his *Mithras*, p. 31, where he indicates that the reliefs at the back of Mithraea were most often of plaster or marble.

[5]For example at the Mithraeum in Capua where kneeling figures are prominently portrayed as part of the initiation rites. Cf. Vermaseren, *Mithras*, pp. 107-10, and J. R. Hinnells, *Acta Iranica* 1 (1974).

[6]For a striking example of Mithraism and Christianity existing side by side cf. Vermaseren, *Mithras*, p. 36.

[7]Julian (*ca.* A.D. 331-363), who ruled the Roman empire A.D. 361-363, was the nephew of Constantine the Great. Although Julian was trained in the Christian religion as a child, he later became a devotee of an idealized combination of Hellenic religions and philosophy which included Mithraism. When he became emperor he sought to restore the empire to his

version of paganism. While Julian supported no overt form of persecution
of Christians, he required that paganism be taught in all schools and gave
preference to non-Christians in state office. His reign was too brief to cause
any lasting changes in the religious patterns of the empire.

Also cf. F. Cumont, *Oriental Religions in Roman Paganism* (1911), pp.
154-5, 199-200, 285-6; and above all, Julian, *Caesares* 336 C; see also Julian,
Discourses IV and V; and C. Lacombrade, *Annales de la faculté des lettres
de Toulouse* 9 (1960), 158.

[8]A. D. Nock, *Conversion* (1933), p. 132. Cf. L. Leadbeter, *Classical
Bulletin*, 47 (1971), 89-92, esp. p. 89 where the resurgent Mithraism of the
late 4th cent. is discussed.

[9]Nock, *Conversion*, pp. 75 and 132.

26

THE WAY FROM JERUSALEM TO JERICHO

JOHN WILKINSON

When Absalom proclaimed himself king, his father David decided to escape from Jerusalem to Jericho. Crossing "the gorge of the Kidron" (II Sam. 15:23) he "went up to the slope of the Mount of Olives" (v. 30), and met Hushai as he was "approaching the top of the ridge" (v. 32) and Ziba a little beyond the top (16:1). As David approached Bahurim (v. 5), Shimei came out and began cursing him and showering him with stones: "David and his men continued on their way, and Shimei went along the ridge of the hill parallel to the path, cursing as he went" (v. 13). The king and his people were worn out by the time they reached the Jordan (v. 14).

This is the most circumstantial account we have of the road from Jerusalem to Jericho, but it is mentioned elsewhere in less detail. Down it in 587 B.C. Zedekiah, king of Judah, tried to escape from the Chaldeans (II Ki. 25:4f.), and up it, six hundred years later, Jesus made his final journey to Jerusalem (Mark 10:46-11:1). Then, late in 69 A.D. the Tenth Legion was ordered to come up "by way of Jericho" and camp on the Mount of Olives to begin the siege of the city (Josephus, *History of the Jewish War against Rome*, 5.42, 69f.).

There is evidence that the Ottoman authorities improved the road, and the British authorities altered it so that it would be suitable for automobiles. The major scholarly study of the road was made by Robert Beauvéry, fortunately before the most recent and most radical improvements to the road, which were made in 1961-63 (*Revue biblique* 64 [1957], 72-101). Beauvéry saw and recorded a number of remains which have since disappeared, either through road-building or in subsequent military activity.

The Geographical Setting

The site of New Testament Jericho is about 250 meters below sea level, and Jerusalem 750 meters above. Any road which joins them has to climb one kilometer vertically (one kilometer is 0.62 of a mile) in a direct horizontal distance of about twenty kilometers. The steep slope forms a rain-shadow with important consequences for the landscape through which our road passes. Thus Jerusalem, receiving each year about 500 mm. (or 20 in.) of rain belongs to the Mediterranean environment characteristic of the western-facing slopes which go down to the sea coast. But Jericho, receiving an annual average of less than 200 mm. (8 in.) of rain is an oasis in a desert and would itself be desert were it not for Elisha's Spring; all its affinities are with not the Mediterranean, but Africa.

The abruptness of this reduction in rainfall can be appreciated by a comparison. It is twenty kilometers (about 12-1/2 miles) on an east-west axis from Jerusalem to Jericho. But if we look for the same reduction in rainfall on the north-south axis, we find that it occurs, for example, between Beer-sheba and Ramla, which are about 75 km. apart (46-1/2 miles), or between Jericho and Tiberias, about 100 km. distant (62 miles). The reduction seems to have remained constant throughout history since the "Mediterranean brown" soil found near Jerusalem could not have been formed without humus from the forests which once grew there, whereas the shallow covering of "skeletal desert soil" surrounding the lower half of our road was formed almost entirely from chalky limestone of the type over which it lies.

The rainfall chart thus has important implications which seem to hold good for all periods. There will be hardly any trees east of the 400 mm. line, the cover of steppe shrubs will end at about the 300 mm. line, and wheat and barley will be impossible to grow without irrigation beyond some point between the 300 and 200 mm. lines. Without irrigation only desert plants can survive anywhere east of the 200 mm. line.

The Remains of the Road

It is only twenty years since Beauvéry wrote his article. If in that period several changes have taken place, then much more will have happened in seventeen hundred years, which is the probable age of our road. Yet, perhaps surprisingly, it is still possible to locate the road exactly over most of its length, mainly for three reasons. The most important of these is the massiveness of the engineering, especially in the cuttings and embankments. Secondly, the roads when they were still in use were protected by heavy paving stones. Nowadays it is hard to imagine their existence since not one remains in place, but in many places the cut rock steps which served as their foundations are still clearly visible. Thirdly, when the paving stones were removed, travelers avoided wherever they could the discomfort of walking over the exposed foundation stones and walked beside the remains of the road rather than on them. At one place, however, they were unable to avoid the foundations and wore a pathway through them into the virgin rock.

Over a period of several years I have had opportunities to explore the ancient road, most recently in the company of a group of clergy and seminarians spending an Epiphany Term at Saint George's College in Jerusalem. Many of their ideas are incorporated in this article, and I would like especially to thank David Mathus, who is responsible for most of the mapping, and Robert Adams, who spent a strenuous day with David and me walking up the road. Since we started at the lower end of the road at Jericho, our steps took us in the direction opposite to the path followed by David down from Jerusalem in the Samuel passage mentioned at the beginning.

We began at the part of the road which leads into the hills near Jericho. The summit ahead and to the left is Aqabat Jabr, "Jabr" being a word probably deriving from "Cypros," the name of the mother of Herod the Great. On the summit a recent emergency excavation has revealed the ruins of the Herodian castle (Josephus, *War* 1.417) and remains from some earlier period as well. This castle towered over Herodian (and New Testament) Jericho from the south, since the city occupied what is now a flattish plain north of Tulul el Alayiq. A second castle, the Docus of I Macc. 16:15, which occupied the top of the so-called "Mount of Temptation," dominated the site of Jericho from the north.

The precipitous valley, Wadi Qilt, derives its name from the Latin *cultus*, "cultivated." Certainly the only cultivation to be seen in any direction from the first half of our road is in the bed of this valley. The road can be seen climbing up the south side of the valley and stays on the edge of it for the next three miles. This is because the long crest between the Wadi Qilt and Wadi Tala‘at ed Damm leads straight towards Jerusalem. As we climbed the side of the Wadi Qilt, we found that we could see no signs of the road marked by Beauvéry and believe that the ancient road from Jericho will be found to be the same as the modern one, at least as far as the point northwest of the summit of Cypros where it begins to level off. From the castle a new road (perhaps on the line of an ancient one) joins our main route. Not far to the west of this junction it seems that the ancient road ran along the platform. Like several other parts of the lower half of our road, this part is based on soft flaky limestone, which can erode rapidly. While the modern road carries on around the right of a low hill, there seem to be remains of an embankment which carries a modern path around the left side of the hill. This was perhaps the ancient road, which rejoined the line of the modern road in front of Menzil Jabr, the large barrel-vaulted cistern. The form of this cistern suggests that it may have been constructed by Herod the Great to form part of the water-supply for Cypros, and we may judge the amount of erosion which has taken place since his time when we envisage the cistern as having been originally all underground.

Beauvéry's plan shows the road running straight over the hill behind Menzil Jabr. But, there is no embankment under the path there. We believe that the road went the same way as the modern one and notice traces in the next kilometer of a platform beside the modern road and to its right which may well represent the line of an earlier road. We note also the remains of water-channeling higher up which leads to Menzil Jabr.

On the other side of the hill by the road at this point the Wadi Qilt has cliffs on both sides, and into the north cliff is built the great monastery of Choziba. Only later in our journey up to Jerusalem did we begin to appreciate the sanctity of the sixth-century monk of Choziba "who carried people's loads up to the Mount of Olives."[1] Just before reaching the path which leads down to the bed of Wadi Qilt we saw a large fragment of wall carrying a water-channel which looked like part of a Roman aqueduct, and beyond it on the eroded rock the remains of a line of plaster which had once been a feed-channel or pipe. Indeed, the path begins on part of a piped channel on the other side of the road. Just beyond this point where the road continues to run through yellow chalky limestone, we found the floor of an eroded plaster cistern on the left of the road. The level of the bottom of the cistern and its height above the present road-level may well suggest the degree of erosion and wear at this point, and the road may now be between ten and fifteen feet lower than its original level.

When the road emerges from this cutting, which, as we believe, it has worn for itself, the Wadi Tala‿at ed Damm again comes into sight on the left. An embanked ramp rises to the right which evidently carried the ancient road up to a line independent of the Turkish road for a distance of just over two kilometers. The ancient road winds from one side to the other of a succession of hillocks which form a long crest at the edge of Wadi Qilt. Where this takes it along the south of the crest, overlooking Wadi Tala‿at ed Damm, the embankment is preserved, but on the north side, on the steep slopes above Wadi Qilt no ancient remains are identifiable.

Most of the hillocks above this stretch of the road are crowned by foxholes made by the soldiers of various twentieth-century armies. Beauvéry identified the foundations of small buildings on them (mostly gone now) with Roman and Byzantine pottery nearby and is surely right to interpret them as sentry-posts (see *Revue biblique* 64 [1957], 96-100).

From Khan Saliba with its fine Byzantine mosaics as far as the castle at Tala‿at ed Damm it seems likely that the ancient road ran along the same line as the present Turkish/British road. We have no evidence to support this assumption apart from the absence of evidence suggesting another line, and the presence at a certain point of a line of foundation stones in the bank of the north side of the road. The road now runs south of the small castle at Wadi Tala‿at ed Damm, Arabic for "The Ascent of Blood." The biblical Hebrew name Ma‿ale Adummim (Josh. 15:7, 18:17) probably meant "The Ascent of the Red Places," since there are several outcrops of red sandstone in this area. But Saint Jerome chose a more dramatic interpretation, "because of the blood which is often shed there by robbers . . . it is on the way down from Aelia (i.e. Jerusalem) to Jericho, and there is also a soldiers' castle located there to provide help for travellers." Jerome's preference for this interpretation becomes obvious when he says "the Lord also reminds us of this bloody, bloodthirsty place in the parable of the man who went down from Jerusalem to Jericho."[2]

At this point the line of our road is interrupted (since 1961) by the modern main road, but after passing the castle it used to run beside the door of a police post which, as we might judge from its name Khan Hatruri, had once been an inn. Mosaic cubes found in its courtyard suggest that there was already a building there in Byzantine times, but it is hardly likely that Jerome was correct in suggesting that this was the Inn of the Good Samaritan, since Eusebius, who wrote his *Onomasticon* fifty years before Jerome, mentions no such identification; the text of the Gospel would even be consistent with an inn down in Jericho. In the stretch of road to the west of the inn three lines of road can be seen, the oldest at the top, the asphalted Turkish/British road just below, and the present road at the bottom. As usual the lowest of the roads is the newest.

The view westwards from this point promises very different conditions ahead. Cultivation, though not yet visible, begins in the valleys only two kilometers away, and along the Mount of Olives which forms the skyline ten kilometers ahead there are a number of trees. The hills ahead are made of harder, whiter limestone than those behind and carry thicker steppe vegetation. The position of the road in the immediate foreground is hard to identify except at a certain point where Beauvéry identified a line of foundation stones (see his p. 82) and perhaps where another line of stones appears fifty meters further west where the stream has cut itself a bed. The surface of the whole area has been much disturbed by earthmoving equipment and camps. But beyond the small cutting the ancient road becomes clearly visible again as an embanked path above the British road, and this descends into the next valley (Wadi Abu en Nujūm) by a steep and carefully engineered ramp which includes some rock-cut steps for supporting paving stones. This ramp leads naturally to an embanked path beside a stream bed, and its line runs north of Ras Makabb es Samm. We thus agree with Beauvéry on the line of the road, though we can probably see less evidence than he could and often found that modern cultivation has made the road impossible to follow along this stretch.

By following the modern path we were brought to a track coming in from the northwest which we joined and turned south. In a moment we were crossing the line of foundations which belonged to a second ancient road running down the crest from Ras Masaid toward Ras Makabb es Samm, described by Beauvéry (his p. 81). At the crossing-point and just below it the rock is soft and crumbling, and we found that the modern track had cut its way through the ancient foundation stones, which we supposed to be lying roughly at their original level on either side of the pathway. Further down the valley, where the rock is harder, the road runs on a well-defined embankment. Then it crosses the valley and curves around to the west, reaching some ruins after six hundred meters. Beauvéry identified them as a small Roman military post and stables (his pp. 86-94) where official couriers could change horses on their way up to Jerusalem. Here, as earlier, we found the remains of more recent military occupation amongst those of the Roman army and noticed how modern cultivators were damaging the ruins.

From this post the ancient road runs west on its embankment for 100 yards or so, and then merges with a modern minor road leading along Wadi es Sidr. After one-and-a-half kilometers this modern road climbs to the north, whilst the ancient one led on across the stream bed. A distinct line of foundation stones marks its line as it leaves the stream bed and mounts the small valley by which it reaches the top of Iraq Saida. At the top, where the road turned round to go northwards, the rock is too soft to retain its line, but on the short stretch going north occasional cuttings in the violently eroded rock and a short stretch of foundation stones show where it went. The road keeps to the southern flank of Iraq Saida till it has passed the spot-height (and not as marked on Beauvéry's plan), and then after crossing the crest, it makes in an almost straight line for Qasr Ali. Here the line is defined at frequent intervals by foundation stones, remains of embankment walls, and rock-cut steps. The road passes along the south edge of the ruins at Qasr Ali (again, not as in Beauvéry's plan).

Qasr Ali (which has never been described in detail) is probably the village "at the fourth mile" which the eighth-century Georgian Lectionary of Jerusalem calls Entidibara or Embetoara.[3] The saints who were commemorated there included St. Stephen, which could indicate a connection with Empress Eudokia in the fifth century. From this ruin the road now turns towards Jerusalem again and runs straight along the precipitous side of the valley called Wadi Umm esh Shid. Its cutting makes an easily identifiable line along the hillside, and in places two levels of cutting can be seen, both of them containing rock-cut steps. Possibly there were two narrow roads at this point, both of them in simultaneous use; the modern path usually runs just below the ancient cuttings.

Two kilometers west of Qasr Ali and beside the modern path a little down the slope are the remains of four milestones. Their position marks the third mile from Jerusalem, and they were erected to commemorate successive repairs or improvements to the road. The ancient line continues for about 500 meters on the south of the valley and then crosses to pass somewhere beneath the modern tomb of Sheikh Anbar and beside the lower slopes of Ras et Tmim till it reaches a crossroads. The path straight ahead leads to the lowest point on the ridge joining the Mount of Olives and Mount Scopus, and the one to the left goes to Bethany. Thus Ras et Tmim seems to correspond with the place which a sixth-century pilgrim identified as Bahurim. He tells us that after coming from Jericho, "as we went up the mountain road to Jerusalem, not far from Jerusalem we came to Bahurim, and then turned off left to the towns on the Mount of Olives, Bethany and Lazarus' Tomb."[4] At this point Jesus would also have taken the road to the left in the journey described in Mark 11:1.

The line of the road which went straight up over the Mount of Olives can be followed in a general way by a continuous scatter of flinty foundation stones, but it is hard to locate it precisely on the final eastward-facing slope. The last definite trace of the road to be identified so far is a line of foundation stones on the western slope in the bank south of the road, and it is not known how the road reached Jerusalem or to which gate it was leading.

The Date and Purpose of the Road

The engineers of the Roman legions were ready to undertake works on a vast scale if they offered tactical advantages, as we can see from the wall and ramp at Masada or the siege road with its hairpin bends at Nahal Arugot. It is therefore possible that the road engineers (*viarum stratores*) of the Tenth Legion carried out works of considerable size to help the unit and its siege engines climb to Jerusalem. But Josephus does not say that they built a complete road, and in *War* 3.118 he does in fact describe the tasks of *viarum stratores*. They were responsible for "straightening out crooked places on the road, levelling the rough places, and cutting down any plants which might cause obstruction, so that the army would not suffer from any difficulties on the march." All this seems to be on a more modest scale than the construction of a road, and would hardly cover the construction of the many embankments which remain along the line of our road.

We know that the remains we can see are the result of at least the four stages of construction or repair which are commemorated by the milestones. We know that the pottery associated with the road and its ancillary buildings is of the Roman and Byzantine periods. But we know nothing which enables us to date the road as early as 70 A.D. All we can say is that, like most of the other roads in Roman Palestine, it probably belongs to the time of Hadrian or a little later. Its purpose would therefore be to provide a well protected and rapid means of transit for the imperial couriers.

In the present dilapidated state of the road it serves more as a reminder of the civilian users of the road, the Roman and Byzantine riders of donkeys and camels whose successors are still to be seen on it. It teaches also something of the demands which travel used to make in terms of time, for it took us seven hours and forty-nine minutes to walk from Jericho to Jerusalem, and even the journey down would probably occupy about six hours. Either is a long time for a journey of twelve-and-a half miles.

Are our remains those of the road used by King David or by Jesus? We can be sure from the lie of the land and the direction of the valleys that the road they knew cannot be far from the remains we have described. But we can also be sure from the degree of erosion we have noticed that it is unlikely that we shall ever find any trace of the earlier road. At least the travelers of biblical times went among the same hills and valleys and witnessed the same transformation in the landscape as they made their journey from Jericho up to Jerusalem.

Notes

[1]John Moschus, *The Meadow* 24, in J. P. Migne, ed., *Patrologia Graeca* (1857-66), Vol. 87, p. 2869.

[2] Jerome, *Liber Locorum* in *Eusebius: Das Onomastikon der biblischen Ortsnamen,* ed. by E. Klostermann (1904), p. 25, lines 11-16; see also Luke 10:30.

[3] M. Tarchnischvili, *Le grand lectionnaire de l'Eglise de Jérusalem (Ve-VIIIe siècle),* Tome 2 (1959), No. 1067, p. 19.

[4] Antoninus Placentinus, *Itinerarium* 16, *Corpus Christianorum (Series Latina),* Vol. 175, p. 137.

27

AN ARCHAEOLOGICAL CONTEXT FOR
UNDERSTANDING JOHN 4:20

ROBERT J. BULL

While at Jacob's Well and during the course of an argument with Jesus about the proper place to worship God, a Samaritan woman exclaimed "Our fathers worshiped on this mountain," and thereby directed attention to Mt. Gerizim. It has been assumed that she was referring to the mountain in general as the location of Samaritan worship. Recent archaeological discoveries, given preliminary description in *BA* 31 (1968), 58-72, and *BASOR* No. 190 (April 1968), pp. 4-19, suggest instead that she was directing attention to a particular place on Mt. Gerizim and that her reference to the termination of Samaritan worship in the past may have been attached to the ruins visible to Jesus and herself as they talked at the well.

The eastern slopes of two of the five major peaks of the sprawling mountain rise from beside the current traditional site of Jacob's Well and a little to the south of nearby Tell Balatah where lie the remains of the city of Shechem, the erstwhile chief city of the Samaritans. From both well and tell, the higher (elevation 2858 ft.) and more distant of the two peaks can be seen, its rocky slopes devoid of trees. At its summit, the tomb or *weli* of Sheikh Ghanim, built on the northeast corner of a fortification the Emperor Justinian (A.D. 527-65) had constructed to protect the 5th century octagonal Theotokos church from Samaritan attack, is the one building visible. (It is Procopius of Caesarea who reports on the work of Justinian, in his *De Aedificiis* V. 7.)

A hundred yards south of the *weli* on the same summit is a flat rock which the Samaritan community has designated as the place where their temple once stood. The nearer and lower of the two peaks (elevation 2727 ft.), however, is the one which looms immediately above anyone viewing the mountain from Jacob's Well or from the nearby remains of the destroyed city. This peak, representing the northernmost extension of Mt. Gerizim, is now partly covered by a stand of pine trees planted in regular terraces over fifty years ago under British Mandate rule. Close inspection of the saddle which joins the northern promontory with the higher peak to the south discloses that a transverse fosse or ditch some 250 feet across and thirty feet deep was hewn from the solid rock of the ridge in an ancient effort to separate the northern peak more noticeably from the rest of the mountain. At the summit of this northern, lower peak is a small bare mound called Tell er-Ras, and the mound is visible through the pines on the slope from Jacob's Well in the valley below.

The prospect before Jesus and the Samaritan woman when she called attention to Mt. Gerizim would have been the mountain profile described above, minus the more recent additions of the *weli* and the terraced stand of trees. But the prospect would have included a large ruined structure on the near promontory.

In the summers of 1964, 1966, and 1968,[1] there was discovered and excavated on Tell er-Ras a temple of Zeus Hypsistos built under the aegis of the Emperor Hadrian (A.D. 117-38)—about which regular readers of *BA* will have read in 1968. Beneath the Zeus temple was discovered a second structure which we first called Building B. Building B was founded on the bed rock of the mountain top and was set in the midst of a surrounding rectangle of walls which were also for the most part founded on bed rock. The remains of Building B constituted a half cube, sixty-five feet on a side and standing thirty-two feet high. It was constructed of unhewn stone laid in without cement and without any kind of internal structuring. The surrounding rectangle of walls, four and a half feet thick, rises to a height of about sixteen feet; together they formed a courtyard 135 feet wide with the half cube in the center. Pottery taken from a foundation trench into which part of one of the walls was set belonged to the 3rd century B.C.

The existence of a monumental structure from the Hellenistic period, built immediately above ancient Shechem, the former chief city of the Samaritans, combined with such literary evidence as Josephus in his *Antiquities* 13.254-7, that the Samaritan temple on Mt. Gerizim continued its life until John Hyrcanus destroyed it in 127 B.C., led us to conclude that Building B and its related walls were part of the Samaritan temple complex and that the half cube of unhewn stones was probably the remains of the Samaritan altar of sacrifice. From the top of the existing remains of the altar (elevation 2691 feet), one can see through the trees on the slope of the mountain the location of the Well of Jacob.

The well had a church built over it by A.D. 380, but the church was probably destroyed by the Samaritans in A.D. 529. Its cruciform shape, however, could be sketched by Arculf in A.D. 670. The Crusaders found it in ruins, and in the 12th century built a church with a nave and two aisles above a crypt which contained the well. The Greek Orthodox Church bought the land in 1885 and began to build the present unfinished church in 1903. Construction was stopped during World War I and has not been resumed.[2]

The mouth of Jacob's Well (elevation 1641 feet, just 1050 feet below the top of the altar on Tell er-Ras) is found in the crypt mentioned above, some ten feet beneath the floor of the unfinished Greek Church. It required a theodolite and some trigonometric calculation to determine it, but it is clear that the remains on the top of Tell er-Ras could have been seen from the well mouth. And this well mouth, by the way, is one of those traditional locations of places in Palestine which scholar and pilgrim alike can take as extremely likely to be genuine. That the existing top of the ruined altar and the present height of its surrounding courtyard walls were standing in the first century A.D. at least as high as they are now is assured by the fact that the Roman engineers of the 2nd century A.D., when charged by Hadrian with building a Zeus temple on an elevated platform, did their job by covering all of the existing remains within the perimeter walls of the Samaritan platform with rubble and cement to a depth of thirty-two feet.

When the Samaritan woman called to the attention of Jesus that her forebears had worshiped on Mt. Gerizim, there was visible to both, immediately above them, on the nearest peak of that mountain, the ruin of the Samaritan temple. And when the woman referred to the termination of Samaritan worship in the past, the poignancy of her remark would have been appreciated by her hearer, since near them both lay the ruins of Shechem, capital of her people, destroyed by the "Jerusalem" Jew John Hyrcanus some 150 years before, while above them could be seen, as the most evident ruin in the destroyed Samaritan temple complex, the great altar of daily sacrifice, disused since its destruction by that same John Hyrcanus.

Notes

[1] The excavations on Tell er-Ras were under the direction of Robert J. Bull of Drew University and were sponsored by ASOR. The late G. Ernest Wright, director of the Joint Expedition to Tell Balatah-Shechem, provided men and material, and the Smithsonian Institution made a generous grant toward the 1968 campaign. In 1964 and 1966, Tell er-Ras was excavated under a license issued by the Department of Antiquities of the Hashemite Kingdom of Jordan. In the summer of 1968, the excavation operated under joint license of the Hashemite Kingdom of Jordan, the Department of Antiquities of the State of Israel, the Military Governor of Nablus, and the endorsement of UNESCO.

[2] For a history of the churches at Jacob's Well see the French article by F. M. Abel in *Revue biblique* 42 (1933), 384-402.

28

EARLY CHRISTIANS AND THE ANCHOR

CHARLES A. KENNEDY

In addition to the twenty-six letters of the alphabet and the usual array of punctuation marks, there is a symbol called the ampersand (&) used in printing. The symbol is purely functional, signifying the word "and," although probably most people have little idea of how or why the sign means what it does. Even the word ampersand is not readily intelligible, adding to the basic obscurity of the symbol. With a little research one may learn that the "ampersand" stands for "and *per se* and" ("and-by-itself-and"), indicating that the symbol was a ligature used in Latin writing to designate the word *et* ("and"). Older forms of ampersand still show the original pair of letters (&) but in many of the graphic forms of the sign devised over the years, the original has for all intents and purposes disappeared. The sign itself will not give the reader any clue as to its pronunciation or meaning.

A much more direct example of the same phenomenon is the exclamation point (!) which started its typographical life as the Latin word *io*, an interjection of exclamation. The two letters were then written vertically and finally the circle of the "o" was filled in, making it look like a period. Once this happened, it was hard to see the original forms and thus the source of the mark became obscure.

In both instances a given symbol has moved from one language to another. The original force of the symbol has been retained, but the descriptive word to convey the meaning of the symbol has been recreated in the new language. Among religious symbols this transformation can best be seen in the Christian monogram IHS. For the Greek church the letters are the first three in the name of Jesus (IHSOUS). The monogram was Latinized in accordance with the vision of the Emperor Constantine at the Milvian Bridge as *in hoc signo* ("in this sign [conquer]"), or in the 15th century as *Iesus Hominum Salvator* ("Jesus Savior of Mankind"). As church

Illus. 41-2

Latin ceased to be used, popular English interpretations, such as "In His Service," have been invented.

This durability of the symbol itself, even surviving transpositions from one language and culture to another, confirms the observations that "symbols are not made, but they are there; they are not invented, but only discovered." This article is concerned with just such a phenomenon involving the anchor which has a long history in Christian symbolism, but a history that is strangely interrupted between the end of the 3rd century and the Renaissance. The later history of the anchor symbol is quite straightforward and open; but the earlier phase, during the first centuries of the Christian era, poses an iconographic riddle.

The anchor, we are told, is the sign of hope (Heb. 6:19 is the prooftext) and its appearance on epitaphs verifies that the dead were interred "in the sure and certain hope of the Resurrection." But if this in fact is the case, why does hope, as expressed by the anchor, begin to wane in the 3rd century A.D., at the moment when Christianity is becoming the religion of the Empire?

Another part of the puzzle is the silence of the Church Fathers in speaking of the anchor as the sign of resurrection hope. Unlike the fish symbol (ichthus) which is explained as a confessional acrostic, the anchor as *symbol*, not metaphor, is never mentioned. While an argument from silence is hardly ever convincing, we are left with some possibilities. One simple solution is that there is no need to explain the obvious. If the anchor is a nautical device for making fast and gaining security, it seems only natural that it should be used symbolically to express reaching the safe harbor of the blessed shores. Non-Christians, however, used the ship imagery for the afterlife in their literature but did not employ the anchor on their epitaphs. Another solution suggests itself: that the anchor is in fact pointing to something else, the precise meaning of which gradually faded from common memory until the sign was discontinued or replaced by a new one. To see how this latter state of affairs could develop, it will be necessary to look at the epigraphical and literary evidence.

I

There are no less than thirty-five types of anchor designs recorded from excavations, primarily in Rome.[1] In the Priscilla

Catacombs alone some seventy inscriptions have the anchor, either alone or with fish, palms, or birds. The anchor appears alone most frequently in the earlier section of the cemetery (2nd century A.D.), but by the year 300 the anchor sign is no longer in use. In the Catacombs of Callistus the case is much the same: twenty-five inscriptions from the end of the 2nd century have the anchor. The epitaphs are painted or inscribed with the name of the deceased and an anchor or the formula PAX TECVM with the name and anchor. Kirsch does not hesitate to identify the anchor as being of purely Christian origin and among the oldest of the Christian symbols, but he must interpret the symbol in the language of the Council of Trent, not Scripture or the Church Fathers, and regard the anchor as a sign of hope or an early form of the Cross.

When we examine these various anchors, it becomes obvious that the artists were not sailors. Some of the anchor shapes would be useless at sea. The arms with compound curves may look artistic, but would have functioned rather poorly. The key to success in the type of anchor shown (the so-called Admiralty anchor) is a heavy crossbar or stock made of stone or metal that holds the shaft to the bottom so that the arms, which of course must be perpendicular to the stock, can grab the bottom. At least four types of anchors in the epitaphs have no stocks at all, unless one assumes that the ring drawn at the top of the shaft is really a hole left for the insertion of the stock or is the stock itself shown in section. The physical state of the epitaphs argues against such assumptions. They are rudely painted or inscribed on tiles and walls. Only a few are cut by trained hands.

In the literature the classic text for identifying the anchor as a symbol of hope is Hebrews 6:19, 20:

> We have this as a sure and steadfast anchor of the soul, a hope that enters into the inner shrine behind the curtain, where Jesus has gone as a forerunner on our behalf, having become a high priest forever after the order of Melchizedek.

The interpretation of this verse has generally followed that of John Chrysostom, that the word "hope" is an appositive to the first phrase, making it read, "Which [hope] we have as an anchor of the soul. . . ."

> For just as the anchor when it is dropped from the vessel does not allow it to be carried about, even if ten thousand winds agitate against it, but being fastened and dropped makes it steady, so also does hope (Homilies on Hebrews 11:3).

If, however, one understands the antecedent of "this" in v. 19 to be the promise of God to Abraham in vv. 13, 14: "Surely I will bless you and multiply you," the anchor of the soul is then God's faithfulness to his word which is the Christian's hope. Only by a secondary application would it refer to Christ or to the Cross. In any event, the *metaphorical*, not symbolic, use of the anchor in Hebrews 6:19 is in keeping with what we find in the Church Fathers. Asterius, for example, employs the metaphor in a discussion of the Psalms:

> When the universal shipwreck occurs, when life is drowned in the waves of ungodliness, in order that the Christian may not perish with the ungodly, David has given him—as it were an anchor of safety for a ship buffeted by the winds—the words of a psalm: so that, like a pilot turning his gaze to the sky, he cries out: "Save me, Lord, for there is no righteous man" (*Homilies on the Psalms*, xxi, 17).

In a much more worldly context, Clement of Alexandria could speak of an advantage the aged have over youth:

> Securely moored by the anchors of reason and maturity, [the aged] easily bear the violent storms of passion aroused by drink, and they can even indulge in the merriment of feasts with composure (*Paedogogus*, II, 2, 22).

The most famous, and perhaps most misinterpreted, reference to the anchor in the literature also comes from Clement:

> Let our signets be a dove or a fish or a ship running before a favorable wind or a musical lyre, which Polycrates used, or an anchor, which Seleucus had engraved on his signet, and a fisherman will remember the apostle and the children drawn out of the water. For it is forbidden for us that the image of a god be impressed (on our signets) or the sword or bow for us pursuers of peace or the goblet for us temperate people (*Paedogogus*, III, 11, 59).

The passage is important and so widely quoted in support of the Christian iconographic use of the anchor because it is the only one in which any early Christian author refers to the *design* of an anchor and not merely to a metaphor. But there are several difficulties with this patristic proof text. In the first place, Clement justifies his choice of the anchor with a reference to Seleucus, successor to Alexander the Great and founder of the Syrian dynasty that bears his name. On religious and political grounds alike this seems like a strange endorsement for Clement to make until one realizes that Clement is equally at home in the classical tradition as he is in the Christian. In condemning indecent language, for example, Clement cites Romans 12:9, Matthew 12:36 and Meander's *Thais*: "Evil associations corrupt good manners" (*Paedogogus*, II, 6, 50). Polycrates and Seleucus are both famous in Greek histories for episodes involving their signet rings. Polycrates threw his overboard to appease Fate and forestall a worse calamity, only to have the ring returned unexpectedly in a fish prepared for his dinner a week later.[2] Seleucus, according to Appian, had an iron ring with an anchor engraved on it, a gift from his mother. She had been told that her son would be king at the place where he would lose the ring, which proved to be near the Euphrates.[3] Seleucus adopted the anchor sign as his royal emblem, having it stamped on his coins and other royal imprints.

A second difficulty is the failure of the commentators to emphasize that Clement is talking about *signet* rings, not ornamental jewelry.

> He [Reason] permits women the use of rings made of gold, not as ornaments, but as signet rings to seal their valuables at home worth guarding, in the management of their homes. If all were under the influence of the Educator [Christ], nothing would need to be sealed, for both master and servant would be honest. But since lack of education exposes men to a strong inclination to dishonesty, we always stand in need of these seals . . . But we should not wear any other rings, because, according to the Scriptures, it is only learning that is "an ornament of gold to the prudent"[Ecclesiasticus 21:21] (*Paedogogus*, III, 11, 57, 58).

A good indication of the separation between the theological symbol and the literary metaphor in Clement's thinking is his endorsement of the lyre design as a signet with no reference to any religious meaning, when he has previously (III, 4, 43) interpreted the phrase "Sing to Him with the lyre" (Ps. 32:2) christologically:

"There can be little doubt that the lyre with its ten strings is a figure of Jesus the Word, for that is the significance of the number ten" [*iota* (the initial letter in "Jesus") equals 10 in the Greek notation].

A third difficulty with Clement's so-called endorsement of the anchor symbol is the lack of archaeological evidence from the eastern Mediterranean to confirm its use other than as a signet device. One epitaph from Alexandria has been published which has two anchors under the Latin Text, "He lived 50 years, 6 months, and 18 days."[4] There is nothing else to identify the decedent's religious affiliation except the two anchors.

To summarize, the evidence from Clement shows that he was concerned more about the Christian protecting his property than any theological lesson an anchor, among other emblems, might convey.

This discrepancy between the literary and archaeological records of the first few centuries A.D. brings into focus the iconographic riddle. So far as is apparent the textual evidence is restricted to metaphorical anchors, not symbolic ones. The one instance known referring to an actual image of an anchor, in Clement of Alexandria, on closer examination proves to have a humanistic, secular origin, unrelated to any theological expression. This suggests that when we analyze the archaeological evidence, we are not seeing what we were intended to see, that the signs placed on the early graves had another meaning only tangentially related to Hellenistic mysteries of sailing to the blessed shores.

II

Cullman once remarked that a major crisis was faced by the earliest church as the first post-Easter death of a Christian. Would the dead be raised on the third day? How should the church behave if the dead remained "asleep"? Questions like these underlie the statements in the Epistles about "the dead in Christ" and "those who are asleep":

> We would not have you ignorant, brethern, concerning those who are asleep, that you may not grieve as others do who have no hope. For since we believe that Jesus died and rose again, even so, through

Jesus God will bring with him those who have fallen asleep (II Thess.
4: 13-14).

There is no doubt for Paul that the "dead in Christ will be raised
first" at the Parousia (I Thess. 4:16). But it is equally certain that
for Paul there is an indefinite interval before the eschaton during
which time other Christians will die and be buried to await the Day
of Resurrection. For all Christians the key to participation in the
Resurrection is to "have heard the word of truth, the gospel of your
salvation, and have believed in him." Those who did "were sealed
with the promised Holy Spirit, which is the guarantee of our
inheritance until we acquire possession of it, to the praise of his
glory" (Eph. 1:13, 14). The seal is baptism (II Cor. 1:22), the
sacrament which is not a *symbol* for the earliest Christians, but a
miracle-working rite which was, like the Eucharist in Tertullian's
phrase, "the medicine of immortality." Christian baptism was
more than the baptism of John (cf. Acts 1:15), a washing away of
sins. It was a rite by which one was put under the name of Jesus (cf.
Acts 2:38; and Paul's rebuke in 1 Cor. 1:10-17). The Christian has
life through his name (John 20:31), or "under his sign and seal" in
the legal phrase.

The imagery of being sealed also appears in Revelation 7 and 14.
The angel descends with the seal of God to imprint the foreheads of
the faithful (Rev. 7:3 ff.; cf. Ezek. 9:4, 6). In Revelation 14:1 the seal
is explained as the name of the Lamb and the Father's name, in
contrast to the seal of the beast that will be on the foreheads of the
unrighteous, who thereby assure themselves of the cup of wrath.

In Matthew 27:66 a Roman seal is used to certify the secured
sepulchre of Jesus. This combination of closing a tomb and
sealing it with a sign or epitaph as a protection against grave
robbers is known also from Jewish sources. One of the most
famous instances is the epitaph of Uzziah found on the Mount of
Olives in 1931:

Hither were brought the bones of Uzziah, king of Judah.
Do not open!

Secondary burials in ossuaries in Palestine also show this
custom. Dinkler has shown that a + mark was placed next to the

name of the deceased as the sign of God. The + was the Hebrew letter *taw*, following the example of Ezekiel 9:4 where the angel was to mark the righteous with a mark (MT *taw*; LXX *sēmeion*) to distinguish them from the ungodly in the coming destruction. Dinkler concluded that "the Jews knew and employed the sign of the cross as an expression of confession to be Yahweh's property and as an eschatological protective sign."[5]

The same understanding appears to be operative in Christian burials, with the added knowledge that the one who will bring in the day of triumph, the Messiah of God, is Jesus Christ. The Christian benediction repeated in Revelation 14:13 is "Blessed are the dead who die *in the Lord.*" For the dead in the Lord, as in the case of the Jewish burials, there is a mark that can be placed on the tombs, that will indicate to any *Greek-speaking* person that the deceased "died in Christ." It needs to be remembered that in the Mediterranean world, Jew and Gentile alike spoke Greek. For the first five centuries of the common era Hebrew was not a spoken language of the Jews in the Diaspora. The evidence from Italy shows that most Jewish epitaphs were in Greek (76 percent of those in Rome). Jewish Christians followed the same practice, speaking Greek and using the Septuagint as their Bible.

When the anchor is viewed as a word-symbol instead of a theological or mystical emblem, the reason for its presence on the tombs is evident. *Ankura* is a pun on *en kuriō* ("in the Lord"), a form of wordplay best known in the Gospel example of Peter-petra in Matthew 16:18.[6] In the Greek text of Paul's letters and Revelation the phrase is always written without the article when referring to Jesus, even though the article is regularly used when speaking of "the Lord" or the day "of the Lord." This grammatical peculiarity provides a striking confirmation of the wordplay hypothesis. It also indicates a future problem for Christian theology since the omission of the article before the word "Lord" is also found in the Old Testament phrases referring to *God* (e.g., Acts 5:9, 19) quoted in the New. A Christian epitaph now in the Vatican Pio-Christian Museum shows the conflation that occurred: "Thou shalt live in the Lord God Christ."[7]

In the Greek world a number of city-states issued coins which used as a kind of trademark or "logo" emblems that would identify the minting city by similar wordplays. Trapezos in Turkey employed the table (*trapeza*); the island of Rhodes, the rose (*rhodon*); the Greek city of Aigai, the goat (*aix, aigos*); and the city of Silenus in Sicily the wild celery (*selinon*). The symbol pun is the seal and authentication of the owner and maker. The Christian dead are sealed with the name of the Lord; they are "in the Lord," under his protection and sharing his resurrection glory. "Christ is the first fruits; then at his coming those who belong to Christ" shall be raised (I Cor. 15:23).

The interpretation of the anchor emblem as a play on the Greek phrase *en kuriō* also explains its eventual disappearance from the Roman catacombs. The majority of the epitaphs are in Greek, not Latin, in the earliest sections of the catacombs. Gradually the Latin texts begin to increase, but frequently the Latin is written with Greek letters. By the end of the third century, Latin and the Roman alphabet have replaced the Greek, and with this linguistic shift the wordplay association of *ankura-en kuriō* becomes meaningless. The Latin *ancora* matches the Greek *ankura*, but *in domino* for *en kuriō* breaks the chain. The disappearance of the anchor sign coincides with the triumph of the Cross and the Crucifix as the primary symbols, where the sign of God, Ezekiel's *taw*, has been translated by Tertullian into the Greek *tau*, hence the Roman T, and the Incarnate Crucified replaces the eschatological Son of Man as Lord of the Church.

In the context of the persecutions that underlie the text of Revelation the benediction for any Christian dead becomes a testimonial to martyrdom. The blessing then is interpreted as being reserved *only* for those who suffered and died in the "great tribulation" because of their Christian witness. Jerome's Latin translation, "Blessed [be] the dead who die in the Lord" is made even more limited to circumstances or persecution in Beza's Latin (1642): "Blessed are the dead who died for the sake of the Lord." Such linguistic niceties notwithstanding, liturgical practice has preserved the benediction as being suitable for general use. Both the service for the Burial of the Dead and the Epistle for the Daily Mass for the Departed require the recitation of Revelation 14:13 as applying to all Christians, not just the martyrs, in keeping with Paul's understanding that God "has put his seal on us and given us his Spirit in our hearts as a guarantee" (II Cor. 1:22).[8]

Notes

[1]J. B. Kirsch, "Ancre" in *Dictionnaire d'archéologie chrétienne et de liturgie*.

[2]Herodotus (*Persian Wars*, iii, 39-42) describes the ring as an emerald set in gold. It is not known where Clement learned of the lyre design (see "Lyre" in *Dictionnaire d'archéologie chrétienne et de liturgie*, Vol. 10, Col. 402, Fig. 7342, for a Roman ring with such a design).

[3]Appian, *Syrian Wars*, IX, 56.

[4]G. Botti, *Bessarione* (1900), p. 280, no. 18.

[5]Dinkler, *Theology and Church, I* (1965) 144.

[6]Some commentators have tried to see a pun in Philemon 10 on the name Onesimus ("useful") and Paul's remark that the slave had been profitable (*euchrestos*) to him, but the Greek text shows no pun. There is a potential pun on the name in Philemon 20 *(onaimen en kurio*—"benefit in the Lord"), but Paul chooses to ignore it. See F. Blass and A. Debrunner, *A Greek Grammar of the New Testament*, trans. and ed. by R. W. Funk (1961), Para. 488 (1b). The few discussions of puns in the NT have been generally confined to Aramaic reconstructions to help explain the Greek text: e.g. in Matt. 23:24 *konopa* ("gnat") and *kamelon* ("camel") may represent an assonance between *qamla* and *gamla* (see C. F. D. Moule, *Idiom Book of NT Greek* [1969] p. 186).

[7]Orazio Marucchi, *Christian Epigraphy* (1912), p. 92, no. 36.

[8]Another, admittedly speculative, suggestion concerning the use of the anchor-sign on epitaphs relates to the baptism of the dead (I Cor. 15:19; cf. Rom. 6:4 "buried with him in baptism"). Whatever Paul's personal opinion of the practice was, his line of argument in I Cor. 15 accepts the fact that it was being performed. Theological questions aside, there is the practical problem of how to conduct such a rite. The anchor-sign provides a possible clue—it becomes the "seal" placed with appropriate liturgical accompaniment on the graves of the unbaptized dead.

ILLUSTRATIONS

[1] Jewish ossuary from Jerusalem (18″ long, 10″ wide, 10½″ high). The gabled lid bears the inscription *š°wl* "*Sheol*," and the decoration between the familiar rosettes is reminiscent of the entrances to tombs in the Kidron valley. **ch. 6**

[2] Undisturbed chamber of Tomb A 69 at Bâb edh-Dhrâ. Note the basalt cup at left, the disarticulated bone pile on a mat in the center (skulls separated from long bones), and part of the tomb's pot group at the right. **ch. 6**

[3] Interior of a shaft tomb from cemetery B, Jebel Qa-ᵓaqir, *ca.* 2000 B.C. Note two disarticulated burials, part of a sheep or goat carcass (even the animal burial is secondary!), the single grave offering and small amphoriskos. **ch. 6**

[4] Basket with skulls from Locus 2, Bar-Kokhba cave. **ch. 6**

[5] Room VII of catacomb I at Beth She^carim: arcosolia, kokhim, and pit graves. **ch. 6**

[6] Wooden coffin from Naḥal David in The Judean desert. Note the gabled lid and its resemblance to that of the ossuary in Fig. 1. This wooden example may be the prototype of limestone ossuaries. **ch.6**

[7] Charnel-house at St. Catherine's Monastery in Sinai. **ch.6**

[8] The hoard from Nahal Mishmar as found in the cave, covered with a mat and hidden in a niche.　　　　　　　　　　**ch.16**

[9] A "wand" or "standard" from the hoard of Nahal Mishmar. **ch.16**

[10] A "crown" from the hoard of Nahal Mishmar, decorated with projecting wings and bird figurines.   **ch.16**

[11] Clay figure of a woman bathing in an oval bathtub, probably 8th–7th centuries B.C., from a tomb in the er-Ras cemetery at Achzib on the Mediterranean coast about 12 miles north of the Carmel peninsula. Found in 1942, the figure herself is about 2 1/4" tall as seated.   **ch. 9**

[12] A stone-lined and stone-topped sewer of MB II C (16th century B.C.) Jericho, running under a street adjacent to houses and apparently receiving domestic sewerage.   **ch. 9**

[13] Excellent stone-lined drain from Bethel of the late Bronze age, with flat capping stones and flat stones at base of the trough.   **ch. 9**

[14] A typical Iron age oven from Megiddo, made of packed clay hardened by the oven fire and lined on the outside with broken sherds of discarded vessels. The scale has ten-centimeter divisions, that is, about 4″.

ch. 9

[15] Pot burial from Megiddo, which proved to contain bones of an infant, dated to the 17th century B.C.

ch. 9

[16] Hazor, slab masseba broken in 13th century with offering before it, and two "miniature" tapering massebot beside it.　　　　**ch.19**

[17] Arad, raised holy place of the Israelite sanctuary. The round-with-face masseba is reerected in center. To its right a square masseba was built into the wall. Another square masseba was built into the wall beside the incense altar on the right.　　　　**ch.19**

[18] Hazor, niche of Late Bronze Shrine 6136, with offering table before ten small round-with-face massebot and an enthroned figure. **ch. 19**

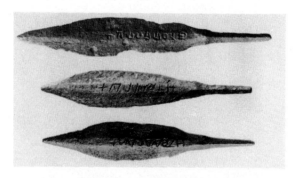

[19] Three arrow or javelin heads found near Bethlehem. Made of copper, each is inscribed with the words "Arrow of ᶜAbd-lebaᵓat." Probably of the 12th century B.C. **ch. 10**

[20] Portion of a fresco from the palace at Mari. Figures at right are dressed in garments made of many small rectangular panels of multi-colored cloth sewn into a strip. **ch. 2**

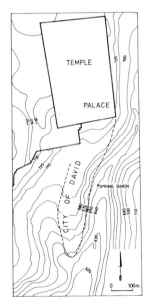

[21] Conjectured plan of Solomonic Jerusalem. The present walls of the Old City and the Haram el-Sherif and included for orientation. **ch. 13**

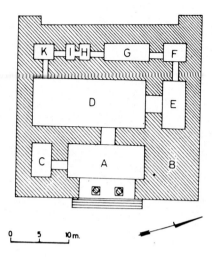

[22] A ground plan of Hilani III at Zinçirli; only the foundations of the building were preserved and thus all the entrances are arbitrarily indicated.   **ch. 13**

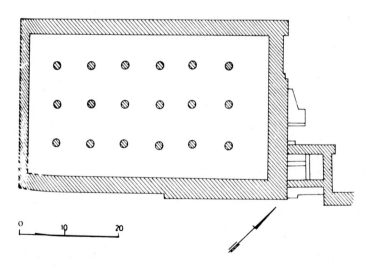

[23] A ground plan of the column building in the Urartian citadel of Altintepe in eastern Anatolia. The scale is in meters.   **ch. 13**

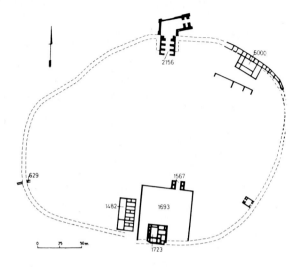

[24] A plan of Megiddo, showing the southern palace compound, the northern palace complex, and the Solomonic city-gate. **ch. 13**

[25] Airview of the foundations of the southern Solomonic palace at Megiddo. The "filled" unit 1728 is on the left-hand side. Note the ashlar masonry incorporated in the foundations. **ch. 13**

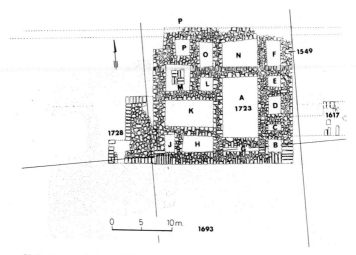

[26] A ground plan of the foundations of the southern palace, (No. 1723) at Megiddo, reproduced from the excavation report, *Megiddo*, Vol. I, Fig. 12. The arrow is pointing south. ch. 13

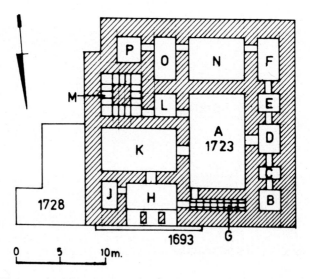

[27] A suggested reconstruction of the ground plan of the southern palace (No. 1723) at Megiddo. ch. 13

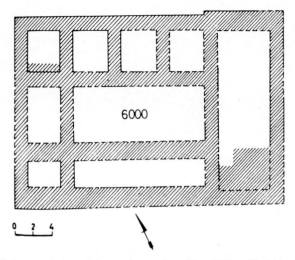

[28] A ground plan of the northern palace (No. 6000) at Megiddo; it is based on Dunayevsky's plan published in BA 33 (1970), 73, Fig. 3, and information in *Israel Exploration Journal* 22 (1972), 163. The sacle is in meters. **ch. 13**

[29] Seals of two witnesses on the left edge of UM 148. **ch. 29**

[30] The inscribed bottle from Tell Siran; lines 7 and 8 are clearly visible.

ch. 15

TELL SIRAN BRONZE BOTTLE

DRAWN BY BERT DEVRIES

JULY 4 1973

SCALE   CM.

0   1   2   3   4   5

[31] The inscription on the Tell Siran bottle, drawn by Bert Devries, July 4, 1973. The figure is 80% of original size.   **ch. 15**

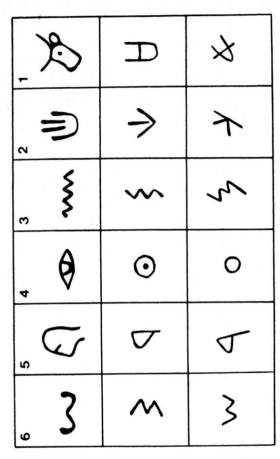

[32] The early development of the alphabet. Top row: Proto-Sinaitic pictographs. Middle row: transitional forms, ca. 1200 B.C. Bottom row: ninth-century Phoenician forms. Letters shown are: (1) *ʾalep* ("ox"); (2) *kap* ("palm"); (3) *mem* ("water"); (4) *ʿayin* ("eye"); (5) *reš* ("head"); (6) *šin* ("composite bow").

ch. 11

[33] Selected Phoenician inscriptions from the Mediterranean: (1) tomb inscription from Cyprus, early ninth century B.C.; (2) the Nora Stone, Sardinia, late ninth century; (3) inscribed bowl from Kition, Cyprus, early eighth century; (4) bronze votive bowl from Cyprus, mid-eighth century; (5) stele from Seville, Spain, mid-eighth century; (6) gold pencant from Carthage, late eighth century; (7) votive stele, Malta, late eighth century.

ch.11

[34] Selected early Greek inscriptions, late eighth or early seventh century B.C. (local script types in parentheses): (1) the Dipylon jug (Attic); (2) skyphos from Pithekoussai (Euboic); (3) inscribed statuette (Boeotian); (4) votive graffiti (Theran); (5) school tablet from Marsiliana (Euboic); (6) cauldron from Thebes (Boeotian); (7) Cumaean aryballos (Euboic); (8) inscribed statue (Eastern Ionic); (9) law code from Dreros (Cretan). The bottom row shows a hypothetical "earliest Greek alphabet."

ch. 11

[35] St. John sends Kynops into the deep. Seventeenth-century wall-painting in the Monastery of St. John on Patmos. **ch. 24**

[36] The first-century theater at Ephesus, site of the silversmiths' riot of Acts 19. **ch. 24**

[37] Ruins of the Church of the Holy Virgin in Ephesus, site of the Third Ecumenical Council in 431 A.D.   ch. 24

[38] Wood paddles and fired clay anvils used in the paddle and anvil
process of hand-building pottery. **ch. 12**

[39] A typical Middle Eastern updraft kiln with fire box into which camel-
thorn and straw can be fed. **ch. 12**

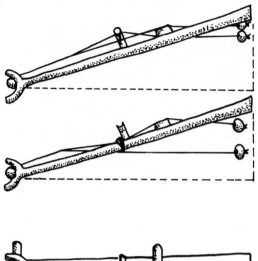

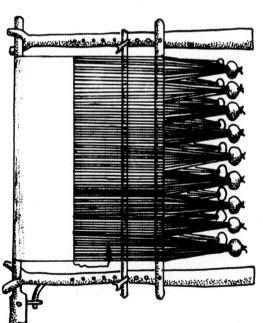

**WARP-WEIGHTED LOOM
USING CLAY LOOM WEIGHTS**

[40] Diagram showing use of clay loom weights on a warp-weighted loom.

[41] Selected anchor signs from the catacombs of Rome.　　ch. 28

[42] Epitaph of Licinia Amiata from the Vatican.　　ch. 28